PATRIARCHY AND
SOCIALIST REVOLUTION
IN CHINA

Judith Stacey

PATRIARCHY AND SOCIALIST REVOLUTION IN CHINA

UNIVERSITY OF CALIFORNIA PRESS · Berkeley
Los Angeles
London

University of California Press
Berkeley and Los Angeles, California
University of California Press, Ltd.
London, England
©1983 by
The Regents of the University of California

Library of Congress Cataloging in Publication Data
Stacey, Judith.
 Patriarchy and socialist revolution in China.
 Bibliography: p.
 Includes index.
 1. Family—China. 2. Patriarchy—China. 3. Women and
socialism—China. 4. Family policy—China. 5. China—
Social conditions—1949-1976. I. Title.
HQ684.S7 1983   306.8′5′0951   82-8482
ISBN 0-520-04825-3 (cloth)
ISBN 0-520-04826-1 (pbk.)

Printed in the United States of America
 2 3 4 5 6 7 8 9

For Herb

CONTENTS

ACKNOWLEDGMENTS

This book about family and revolution in China had its origins in a cultural revolution here in the West. The feminist movement of the late 1960s and early 1970s stirred passions and posed challenges that set me on the lengthy intellectual and personal odyssey represented by this book. I owe that social movement many debts. Not the least is kindling my interest in sociology and my commitment to family studies and family renovation.

My debts to numerous individuals are equally profound, and more specific. Like quite a few first scholarly books, this one began as a dissertation. I thank George Ross, Theda Skocpol, and Charlotte Weissberg, the members of my dissertation committee, for the intellectual guidance and personal encouragement that they gave to my maverick project. George and Theda fostered my interest in historical sociology while establishing rigorous standards for its practice. Charlotte prodded me to keep my attention on the human motivations that underlie macrohistorical events. My years as a graduate student at Brandeis University were enriched by the friendship and intellectual community provided by Wini Breines, Margaret Cerullo, Jeffrey Herf, Elizabeth Long, and Ann Popkin. Ellen Kay Trimberger befriended me and my project when, just at the thesis-writing stage, we moved to California. She read drafts of the dissertation, directed me to theoretical literature, engaged in endless discussions of patriarchy and revolution, and in all possible ways helped me to complete it. Then Kay, more than anyone, encouraged me to turn the dissertation into a book, and as stalwart friend, critic, and housemate, she has lived with this work ever since.

Transforming the dissertation into this book made me dependent upon the wisdom and generosity of many other friends and colleagues. Two made contributions too extensive to recount adequately. David Plotke, a dazzling critic and superb editor, guided me through the process of revision. Whatever refinements of analysis and lucidity this book contains owe much to David's good judgment and encouragement; most of the book's rougher qualities reflect my inability to solve the problems he uncovered. Randall Dodgen, my research assistant, quickly became one of the best colleagues imaginable. His enthusiasm for Chinese history was infectious, and he greatly enhanced my understanding of Confucian culture and society. I have also relied heavily upon extensive comments on the dissertation received from Rose Coser, Kwang-Ching Liu, Richard Madsen, Margery Wolf, and Marilyn Young. Their challenging, but supportive criticism forced me to deepen my research and refine my analysis. Others who carefully read portions of the book at various stages have strengthened it through their invaluable criticism. I particularly wish to thank Tani Barlow, Wini Breines, Yung-fa Chen, Barbara Epstein, Gary Hamilton, Kay Johnson, Susan Mann, G. William Skinner, Louise Tilly, Frederic Wakeman, Jr., and John Walton. Presenting the work-in-progress to seminars and conferences elicited additional helpful criticism. Phyllis Andors, Nancy Chodorow, Suad Joseph, Temma Kaplan, Mary Ryan, Batya Weinbaum, and the members of the Bay Area Faculty Women's Research Forum deserve specific appreciation. I have not solved all the problems, nor followed all the advice my friendly critics presented, but this book is far stronger than it would have been without their efforts.

Studying China as a nonarea specialist, I incurred a special kind of debt. This work would not have been possible without the unusual generosity and encouragement of sinologists, who shared with me their knowledge, ideas, personal libraries, and even primary data. Equally important, they made me welcome in an alien field, often by displaying more confidence in the legitimacy of my intrusions than I myself sustained. For this I am especially grateful to Tani Barlow, Deborah Davis-Friedmann, Randall Dodgen, Kay Johnson, Susan Mann, Kwang-Ching Liu, Richard Madsen, Roxanne Prazniak, Frederic Wakeman, Jr., and Margery Wolf. The staff of the library of the Center for Chinese Studies at the University of California, Berkeley, offered much practical assistance of this kind.

The calligraphy that appears on the first page of each chapter and on the book jacket is attributed to Wang Hsi-chih (A.D. 321–379) and is reproduced in *Tzu Yüan* [Etymologia], p. 366 (Taichung: I-shih Chu-pan-she, 1972). The Chinese character for the word *fu*, "woman, wife," consists of pictographic representations of a woman and a broom. An ancient Chinese lexicographer associated this word with another word *fu*, written with a different character, which means "to submit, to serve." He may have committed an etymological error, but one that accurately reflected the cultural status of Chinese women. The calligraphy is reproduced here through the courtesy of the East Asiatic Library, University of California, Berkeley.

Several of the basic ideas of this book and a version of one of its chapters were published first as articles in *Social Problems*, *Theory and Society*, and the *Journal of Comparative Family Studies*. Faculty research funds and a Faculty Development Award granted by the University of California, Davis, provided research assistance and release time from teaching for part of the final writing of the book. Then my friend Linda Collins, who joined me in the laborious preparation of footnotes, bibliography, and final typing, still managed to engage with the core ideas of the book. Additional bibliographic assistance came from Judith Lucero and Dawn Nichols. Expert typing of drafts of the manuscript was done by Iris Bavister, Wava Fleming, Nancy Laleau, Dawn Nichols, and Nancee Vandale. At the University of California Press, I was fortunate to benefit from the expertise of two fine editors. I am grateful to Grant Barnes for arranging an exceptionally constructive review process and to Phyllis Killen for an extraordinary amount of assistance with the preparation of the manuscript. My infant son, Jake, deserves thanks here, too, for he discovered laughter just in time to cheer me through the tedious final round of revisions. Finally, this book is dedicated with loving appreciation to Herb Schreier, who has shared his life with me and these Chinese peasant families from the start, and whose never-flagging commitment to our personal efforts at family reform nurtured and sustained me through every stage of this project.

June 1982
Berkeley, California

NOTE ON
TRANSLITERATION

Because the vast majority of the Chinese terms that appear in this book refer to Chinese authors or place names in works published before the pinyin system of transliteration was adopted officially by the government of the People's Republic of China, I follow the Wade-Giles system as the basic method of romanization. However, in a few instances where bibliographic items include proper names in pinyin, I have left these as they appear in the original works.

1 Introduction

China, as symbol and reality, haunts many of the theoretical and political debates of the past decade in the West. Cast in the role of Socialist Redeemer by a mélange of Western visitors, China seemed to offer new answers to problems that had preoccupied social scientists and political activists for much of this century. And so China appeared to me as I began, in the early 1970s, to explore relationships among socialism, family transformation, and the liberation of women.

Interest in the long-dormant question "Does Socialism Liberate Women?" had been revived by the radical political movements of the period: by a New Left, which by the late 1960s and early 1970s was focused on resisting a war against socialist revolution in Vietnam; and by the rapid growth of a vigorous feminist movement determined to unearth and eliminate the social roots of sexual inequality in the West. This setting prompted reconsideration of pessimistic analyses of socialism's capacity to liberate women, which events in the Soviet Union had justified. According to those analyses, socialist revolutions begin as antipatriarchal movements. Partly to honor socialism's historic ideological commitment to the liberation of women, partly as a strategic attack on "the formidable stronghold of all the turpitudes of the old regime,"[1] socialist revolutionaries find it useful to devise a radical

---

1. A Bolshevik revolutionary, quoted in Nicolas S. Timasheff, "The Attempt to Abolish the Family in Russia," p. 55.

assault upon their society's patriarchal family system. Yet this union of socialism and antipatriarchal politics amounts only to a short-lived marriage of convenience. As soon as a revolutionary regime consolidates its power, it seeks to stabilize an increasingly repressive social order in the name of socialist accumulation. There is no further role for family instability or sexual radicalism, and thus occurs the reversal of revolutionary family policy that Trotsky ruefully had termed a Thermidorian reaction. Scholars of the family had come to view the Thermidor as a necessity dictated either by the requirements of modern industrial societies or even by universal functional requisites of family and social structure.[2] Feminists found the Thermidor fit cause for skepticism regarding the liberatory promise of a socialist revolution.

But Maoist China seemed to open new possibilities. Far from seeking the calcifying stability of other postrevolutionary societies, its leaders had launched the Cultural Revolution, which European and Americans of the New Left embraced as the revolutionary antidote to the bureaucratic conservatism of socialist practice elsewhere. Under conditions of "permanent revolution," all varieties of further transformation were imaginable, and sexual equality appeared high on the Chinese agenda. Reports of the progress of women in the People's Republic of China (PRC), now understood as wildly inflated, inspired feminists then to renew their interest in socialist revolution.[3]

This book was born in that optimistic moment, but it has matured under more sobering circumstances. The decline of radicalism in the United States coincided with gradual disenchantment with China among Western socialists, as the Cultural Revolution receded and China's foreign and domestic policies turned increasingly pragmatic and economistic. Likewise, greater access

---

2. For interpretations of the inevitable failure of family revolutions, see Rose and Lewis Coser, "The Principle of Legitimacy"; Kent Geiger, *The Family in Soviet Russia*; Alex Inkeles, *Social Change in Soviet Russia*; Neil J. Smelser, "Classical Theories of Change and the Family Structure"; and Timasheff, "Attempt to Abolish the Family."

3. Among the many optimistic feminist interpretations of women's liberation in the PRC were Claudie Broyelle, *Women's Liberation in China*; Sheila Rowbotham, *Women, Resistance and Revolution*; Linda Gordon, "The Fourth Mountain"; and Ruth Sidel, *Women and Child Care in China*. My first essay on Chinese patriarchy assumed that Chinese women had moved closer to sexual equality than women elsewhere in the world. See Judith Stacey, "When Patriarchy Kowtows."

to and closer scrutiny of China in the 1970s led most feminists to reconsider earlier claims. The Chinese revolution began to appear as one more instance of the failure of a socialist revolution to liberate women.[4] Most Western feminists, therefore, abandoned China to the sinologists, but by then real and symbolic China held me in its grip. The most important and interesting theoretical questions regarding socialist revolution and the patriarchal social system were far from resolved; the "real China," which was at last becoming accessible to scholars, still seemed very much worth decoding.

As my analysis began, it was easy to find surface similarities between the Russian-based model of socialist revolution and family change and the more recent course of revolutionary family transformation in China, but there were striking contrasts as well. Russia and China had each experienced a family revolution— a radical attempt to restructure the gender and generational relationships of a patriarchal family system in the broader context of a revolutionary social transformation.[5] And the outcomes appeared to be similar, for the Chinese family revolution could be read as a mild Thermidor pattern.[6] Antipatriarchal family reforms were, from the outset, interwoven with China's revolutionary process. Then, immediately after assuming state power, one of the important pieces of legislation the Chinese Communists enacted was the Marriage Law of 1 May 1950—an explicit assault on China's patriarchal family system. No mere paper document, the law was the occasion of implementation campaigns of mass mobilization during the debut years of Communist rule. However, this activist approach to family reform largely ended in 1953,

---

4. See, for example, Batya Weinbaum, *The Curious Courtship of Women's Liberation and Socialism;* Suki Colgrave, "Chinese Women"; and the scathing self-critique of her earlier analysis by Claudie Broyelle, in Broyelle et al., *China, A Second Look.*

5. This is a different, and narrower, use of the term from that of most modernization theorists, who employ it to designate the evolutionary cultural, attitudinal, and structural family changes that accompany "modernization." See, for example, Marion J. Levy, *The Family Revolution in China,* and William J. Goode, *World Revolution and Family Patterns.*

6. This, my own initial assumption, was reflected in the title I proposed, then discarded, for my dissertation: "Thermidorian Reaction to Family Revolution." The following sources all interpret the Chinese revolution in this way: Coser and Coser, "Principles of Legitimacy"; Weinbaum, *Curious Courtship;* and Peter Laslett, "The Family and the Collectivity."

after which the Chinese Communists stiffened their divorce policy, never to relax it substantially again. Judged by feminist standards, the family revolution in China, as in Russia, appeared to be a failure. One can readily identify a persistently strong patriarchal basis to family and social life in both postrevolutionary societies. Although Chinese women made significant progress over their prerevolutionary status, twenty (and now thirty) years after the revolution there are few indications that the large remaining social inequalities between women and men will continue to diminish substantially. Chinese women endure educational, economic, political, and cultural inequities that are international features of women's secondary status.[7]

However, closer inspection reveals that the Chinese family revolution diverged notably from the Russian case. The Chinese Communist attack on traditional patriarchy had never been as radical as that of the early Bolsheviks. The Chinese Communist Party (CCP) never advocated the "withering away of the family" or sponsored a free-love ideology. An article in a provincial PRC newspaper, printed in 1959, summarized the historically predominant CCP approach to family life.

> The breaking down of the system of patriarchy will not and cannot lead to "destruction" or "elimination" of the family. . . . The family as a form of joint life of two sexes united in marriage, we may definitely say, will never be eliminated. The existence of this form of joint life is dictated not only by the physiological differences of sexes but also by the perpetuation of the race. Even in the communist society we cannot conceive any objective basis and necessity for the "elimination" of the family.[8]

While CCP attacks on patriarchy were comparatively temperate, its family reform program was more effectively implemented. Thus, unlike the Bolsheviks, the Chinese Communists have not felt the need to repudiate the essence of their early policy. This study will show that, far from attempting to abolish family life, the Chinese Communists consistently sustained it, and despite the 1953 shift in divorce policy, there has been no genuine reversal

7. For data and discussion of sexual inequality in the PRC, see chap. 6, below.
8. "The Breaking Down of the System of Feudal Patriarchy," excerpted in Elisabeth Croll, ed., *The Women's Movement in China*, p. 58.

of family policy in the PRC. A final contrast concerns the differing consequences of Bolshevik and Chinese Communist approaches to family transformation. Whereas Bolshevik family policy exacerbated family crisis conditions and seriously alienated mass support for the revolution,[9] CCP family policy has had opposite effects. In rural China, socialist revolution has had the ironic role of strengthening a reformed version of traditional peasant family life, and this, in turn, has strengthened peasant support for the revolution.

These comparisons between the Soviet and Chinese experience with family revolution raise many questions of interest to sinologists, as well as to sociologists, feminists, and socialists. What is the relationship between family transformation and social change? Does a socialist revolution make any significant difference, or is modernization the relevant process in any political economy? Does a family system play a merely reactive role in social transformation, or can it contribute to the direction and pace of change? And, more broadly, are traditional peasant values and culture primarily barriers to social change, or can they catalyze massive social movements? Why has socialism not liberated women in China? Does this failure provide support for a convergence theory—a theory that all modern nations converge towards similar patterns of sexual inequality? Does the failure reveal anything general about the relationship between family change and female liberation? Answers to these questions would advance and integrate contemporary intellectual discourses in family sociology, feminist theory, and peasant studies.

THE FAMILY AND SOCIAL CHANGE

Resurgent academic interest in family studies continued to flourish in the 1970s, fueled partly by increasing public controversy over the state of contemporary family life. Two decades ago, two major works, *Social Change in the Industrial Revolution* by Neil J. Smelser and *World Revolution and Family Patterns* by William J. Goode, revived sociology's then-dormant interest in the relationship between social and family change. Together these books

---

9. The most dramatic instance of this occurred in Moslem Central Asia; see Gregory Massell, *The Surrogate Proletariat*.

initiated a revisionist modernization perspective, which challenged the orthodox view that industrialization, urbanization, and rationalization in the West had yielded a unidirectional historical trajectory from the patriarchal, extended family to the egalitarian, nuclear family.[10] Smelser and Goode argued that the family patterns of different societies and social classes develop in uneven directions and rates.[11] Moreover, these works initiated the now-popular attempt by family scholars to rescue the family from its prior status as a passive dependent variable by suggesting the family could play an independent, active role in shaping other institutions.

An interdisciplinary dialog on the direction and cause of family transformation ensued. Historians, led by the Cambridge Group for the History of Population and Social Structure, married cliometrics to the concerns of the "new social history" and developed the family reconstitution method of research. Their still-controversial findings claimed that the nuclear family preceded industrialization in the West.[12]

Others conducted studies that argue, in interesting counterpoint to the thesis of the Cambridge school, that extended kin ties survived, even expanded, during capitalist industrialization because families served as informal labor recruiters, housing agents, and unemployment insurance companies.[13] The effort to portray the family as an active causal agent in the shaping of the modern world led to studies centered upon the capacity of families to sustain certain traditional values and practices while resisting

10. Talcott Parsons, the major theorist to generate this model of family change, based it on the gemeinschaft/gesellschaft paradigm of classical thinkers like Ferdinand Tönnies and Emile Durkheim. Examples of Parsons's use of this framework appear in "The Kinship System of the Contemporary United States," and Talcott Parsons and Robert F. Bales, *Family, Socialization and Interaction Process.*

11. Smelser demonstrated that the British working-class family retained partial integrity as a production unit during the early stage of factory organization. For Goode, uneven development refers to the fact that different nations start from different points in the development process. Therefore, different nations can be simultaneously involved in contrasting directions of change in their divorce rates, fertility patterns, and the like.

12. Peter Laslett and Richard Wallis, eds., *Family and Household in Past Time.* E. A. Wrigley draws on this research to make the same argument in "Reflections on the History of the Family." Jean-Louis Flandrin, in the first chapter of his *Families in Former Times,* provides a useful summary of the controversy.

13. For this argument see Michael Anderson, *Family Structure in Nineteenth-Century Lancashire;* and Tamara Hareven, "Family Time and Historical Time."

and adapting to processes of capitalist development.[14] According to the editors of the special 1977 issue of *Daedalus* on the family, such work serves "to lay to rest the canard that the family 'broke down' under the impact of urbanization and industrialization" and to demonstrate instead that "the resilience of the institution was so great . . . that it actually ended up by contributing to both processes."[15]

Joan W. Scott and Louise A. Tilly have elaborated the revisionist perspective into a model of the relationship between traditional peasant family economy and values and massive processes of social structural change.[16] Their study of women, work, and family in modern Europe aims to establish the continuity of traditional family values and behavior amidst dramatically changing circumstances. They argue that as capitalist industrialization proceeded peasant families devised new strategies designed to attain the traditional goals of the family economy in a new situation. Peasant family relationships were affected by the new experiences the members encountered, and these, in turn, gradually modified members' traditional ideas about family relationships. European peasant families, in other words, reached backward toward modernization.

Contemporary revisionist scholarship on the family and modernization has thoroughly undermined unidirectional or deterministic models of family change and has established a healthy appreciation of the resilience of traditional family values and practices. However, the effort to demonstrate the family's role as a causal agent cannot yet be judged a success. The studies fail to show that families were able to do more than adapt to or temporarily resist incorporation into the capitalist reorganization

14. This was the genre of interpretation launched by Neil J. Smelser in *Social Change in the Industrial Revolution*. It has been pursued most vigorously by Tamara Hareven. See Hareven, "Family Time and Industrial Time"; idem, "Modernization and Family History"; and Hareven and John Modell, "Urbanization and the Malleable Household." Another example of this focus on the resilience of preindustrial family work patterns can be found in Virginia Yans McLaughlin, *Family and Community*.

15. Editors' introduction, *Daedalus* 106 (Spring 177):viii.

16. The model is explicated in "Woman's Work and the Family in Nineteenth-Century Europe." The article begins with a critique of Goode's model of family and social change as overly simplistic and unidirectional. For a book-length treatment of family and social change in Europe, see Louise A. Tilly and Joan W. Scott, *Women, Work, and Family*.

of work and social life, which in the end succeeded in changing family structure and values. No one has demonstrated that families actively shaped the direction, or even the overall pace, of the social structural changes that accompanied capitalist development in the West.[17]

This study of China's family revolution will go further by elucidating a dynamic reciprocal relationship between family and social change. Not only will it analyze the changes in family structure and values achieved by the revolution, but it will demonstrate how China's traditional peasant family system played a crucial role in shaping the revolutionary process and patterns of socialist development in the PRC.

FEMINIST THEORY

A feminist political and intellectual renaissance has paralleled and occasionally intersected these developments in family studies. Having identified the family as a major institutional locus for the reproduction of female subordination, feminists generated a critique of the predominant scholarly conceptualization of the family.[18] Most of the new family scholarship, feminists charge, reifies the family by treating it as a natural and undifferentiated unit. Instead, the analytical task of family history should be "to deconstruct the family as a natural unit and reconstruct it as a social one."[19]

Rather than analyzing the relationship between the family and social change, feminist theory has generated a parallel dis-

---

17. For an elaboration of this critique of revisionist family and modernization studies, see Wini Breines, Margaret Cerullo, and Judith Stacey, "Social Biology, Family Studies, and Anti-Feminist Backlash."

18. Ibid. See also Rayna Rapp, Ellen Ross, and Renate Bridenthal, "Examining Family History"; Michelle Barrett, *Women's Oppression Today*, chap. 6; Barrie Thorne, "Feminist Rethinking of the Family"; and Jane Collier, Michelle Z. Rosaldo, and Sylvia Yanagisako, "Is There a Family?"

19. Rayna Rapp, "Household and Family," in Rapp, Ross, and Bridenthal, "Examining Family History," p. 181. Rapp goes so far as to argue that scholars should abandon the term "the family," as well as their search for its role as a causal agent. "The family," she argues, has no material existence; it is simply an ideological concept, which recruits people into households where they engage in the material relationships and activities of production, reproduction, and consumption that vary by gender and class. Thus, there can be no history of "the family," and "the family" cannot act.

course on the causal relationships between the sex-gender system and the mode of production, with attention focused overwhelmingly on the relationship between patriarchy and capitalism. The concept of sex-gender system, defined by Gayle Rubin as "the set of arrangements by which a society transforms biological sexuality into products of human activity, and in which these transformed sexual needs are satisfied,"[20] represents an attempt to establish the relative autonomy of gender relationships from those of production. Intended as an analog to the Marxian concept of mode of production, it was meant to generate research into the varying historical systems of gender stratification.[21] As such the term contributes to controversy among feminists over the proper use of the concept of patriarchy.[22] The sex-gender formulation encourages feminists to historicize the more commonly used concept of patriarchy and to allow, as well, for the theoretical possibility of future transformations in gender relationships.

Recently an internal debate has emerged over the effort to identify an autonomous realm of gender relationships, whether or not they are labeled patriarchal. Several feminists have criticized this "dual systems theory" for employing a conceptual apparatus that segregates analysis of gender from that of the economy. These critics maintain that to reserve Marxism for an analysis of political economy while relegating feminist theory to analyses of the domestic sphere not only mirrors the actual social segregation of the sexes but allows Marxist theory to develop in comfortable immunity to the challenges of feminist inquiry. Iris

20. Gayle Rubin, "The Traffic in Women," p. 159.

21. Many feminists have viewed this theoretical effort as a necessary intellectual defense of the political effort to establish an autonomous women's movement. However, as Barrett argues in *Women's Oppression Today,* such a defense is unnecessary.

22. Several feminists have criticized the prevalent universalistic use of the term "patriarchy" to designate all varieties of male domination. They argue that it is an inappropriate label for the system of sexual inequality that exists in advanced capitalist societies. See, for example, Sheila Rowbotham, "The Trouble with Patriarchy"; Veronica Beechey, "On Patriarchy"; Barbara Ehrenreich and Deirdre English, *For Her Own Good,* pp. 11ff.; and Barrett, *Women's Oppression Today,* p. 19. Others defend its retention by emphasizing the value of the concept in tracing the historical continuity and the relative autonomy of gender oppression in precapitalist and capitalist society. See, for example, Sally Alexander and Barbara Taylor, "In Defense of 'Patriarchy' "; Heidi Hartmann, "The Unhappy Marriage of Marxism and Feminism"; and Zillah Eisenstein, *The Radical Future of Liberal Feminism,* pp. 18–22.

Young calls upon feminists to develop instead a "feminist historical materialism" that integrates the objects and methods of feminist and Marxist analyses.[23]

My study of patriarchy and socialism in China will develop such an approach without discarding the concept of a relatively autonomous sex-gender realm. I will present a feminist, historical materialist analysis of why socialism has not liberated women in China.

PEASANTS AND REVOLUTION

While family scholars and feminist theorists have focused on the history of family and gender in the advanced capitalist societies of the West, there has been a revitalization of scholarly interest in the peasant revolutions of the East. Because peasants rather than proletarians have been the decisive agents in these revolutions, neo-Marxist scholars have been moved to reappraise classical Marxist views of the incapacity of the peasantry for progressive social action. James C. Scott's work on peasant rebellions and the work of sinologists, such as Edward Friedman and Ralph Thaxton, has interpreted the Chinese revolution as impressive evidence of the revolutionary capacity of the peasantry.[24] To address the apparent discrepancy between this historical reality and the canons of Marxist theory, they focus on the traditional political culture and moral economy of the peasants.

James Scott suggests that the peasantry has "progressive advantages" over the proletariat. The paramount advantage, paradoxically, is precisely the precapitalist nature of peasant values and social structure, which Marxists have misunderstood and disparaged:

The relative isolation of the peasantry from the cultural and institutional life of the state and its ruling elites has meant that, as a class, it has been more immune than has the proletariat to the

23. Iris Young, "Socialist-Feminism and the Limits of Dual Systems Theory." See also Beechey, "On Patriarchy," and Barrett, *Women's Oppression Today*.

24. James C. Scott, "Hegemony and the Peasantry"; idem, "Protest and Profanation"; Edward Friedman, *Backward Toward Revolution*; Ralph Thaxton, "Tenants in Revolution"; and idem, "When Peasants Took Power."

social and moral *hegemony* (in the sense in which Gramsci used that word) of the dominant classes.[25]

Scott suggests that in such comparatively autonomous cultural circumstances peasants create and transmit a Little Tradition that furnishes them an invaluable system of shared values and moral cohesion, distinct from and oppositional to that of the corresponding elite tradition. At its center is a moral economy that guarantees to each peasant family its subsistence niche in the local community. Scott claims that a utopian vision is embedded in the peasants' millennial expectations for the earthly fulfillment of these values, one that almost always is "a society of brotherhood in which there will be no rich or poor and in which distinctions of rank and status (save those between believers and nonbelievers) will vanish."[26] When the values of the Little Tradition are violated or threatened severely, peasants can be aroused to pursue restorations of the values with that passionate intensity crucial to revolution.

In the Chinese revolution, according to this line of analysis, modern revolutionaries learned to root the revolutionary movement in the restorationist motives of the peasantry. Edward Friedman identifies twentieth-century China as a village society whose members took up arms to restore traditional values that had been massively undermined.[27] Likewise, Ralph Thaxton attributes a large part of the CCP's success in mobilizing rural tenants in North China to policies that enabled them "to regain the world they had lost." Communist legitimacy among these peasants "may be understood," Thaxton argues, "largely in terms of a return to traditional morality, to the customary principles and practices of subsistence and security among the rural poor."[28]

Analysts employing this perspective tend to portray the PRC as a society that has not betrayed the peasantry but has largely served its interests. They link this novel outcome to the long period of interdependence of the CCP, the Red Army, and the peasantry, during which the party adopted the restorationist motives of the peasantry as a crucial aspect of the revolutionary

25. James C. Scott, "Hegemony and the Peasantry," p. 270.
26. Ibid., p. 285.
27. Friedman, *Backward Toward Revolution*, p. 118.
28. Thaxton, "Tenants in Revolution," pp. 348–49.

project.[29] In other words, Chinese peasants experienced a process analogous to that of the European peasant families analyzed by Scott and Tilly—they reached backward toward socialist revolution.

While contributing fruitful insights into peasant consciousness and activity, this literature tends to romanticize the Little Tradition and its relationship to socialism. One reason for this, I believe, is the isolation of this discourse from the discourse of family scholars and feminist theorists. I address this problem by centering on the role of the patriarchal family in traditional peasant culture. As a result, this book unearths painful contradictions in the relationship between traditional cultures and progressive social action.

This book presents a feminist historical materialist analysis of patriarchy and socialist revolution in China. That is to say it offers an historical interpretation of processes of family and social transformation that focus on a patriarchal sex-gender system as it shaped and was shaped by the revolutionary drama.[30] China is an agrarian society that experienced a peasant revolution, and this analysis takes the peasant family economy as the major unit of investigation. As a social, not a natural, entity, the family unit will always be situated in the broader social, economic, and political context of its period. The format of the book includes chronological elements, but it is not a narrative chronological history. Instead, I offer an interpretive analysis of themes that have dominated Chinese history from the late imperial era to the present day. I attempt to explain the distinctive aspects of revolutionary family and social policies and their outcomes in

---

29. Thus Scott observes: "The extent to which both the Vietnamese and Chinese revolutions have served peasant interests is in no small degree a consequence of the long-time dependence of the very survival of the revolutionary cadres upon an active identification with concrete, day-to-day peasant claims. Learning, like most everything else, follows power, and the program of Vietnamese and Chinese communism reflects the obligation of the party in each case to learn from its peasantry or perish." James C. Scott, "Hegemony and the Peasantry," p. 296.

30. For the purposes of this study, I have adopted a restrictive use of the term "patriarchy." I employ it to indicate a family and social system in which male power over women and children derives from the social role of fatherhood, and is supported by a political economy in which the family unit retains a significant productive role.

China through a close analysis of distinctive features in the pre-revolutionary family and social system and in the nature of the revolutionary process. Chapter 2 analyzes the structural features of the Confucian patriarchal family and social system in late imperial China. I describe the mode of production as a patriarchal family economy in which the individual family served as the basic social and economic unit of a social formation characterized by an unusually explicit system of patriarchal authority. Chapter 3 identifies and interprets the significance of the emergence of a crisis in the family system during the prerevolutionary period. I suggest the contradictory nature of elite and peasant experiences with family crisis and explore the challenges and opportunities these provided Chinese revolutionaries. Chapters 4 and 5 analyze the revolutionary reconstruction of rural Chinese family and social life. I argue that a family revolution with great significance for socialist victory took place in rural China, but it was not quite the family revolution that socialists tend to advertise or feminists tend to envision. The result of this family revolution was a new rural family system, best identified as a new democratic patriarchy. The development and limitations of patriarchal-socialism, the next stage of peasant family and social transformation in the PRC, are the subjects of chapter 6. The conclusion, chapter 7, returns to a discussion of the basic theoretical concerns raised in this introductory chapter. The epilog briefly extends my analysis of the relationship between patriarchy and socialism in China to the post-Mao period of the "Four Modernizations."

NOTE ON DATA AND SOURCES

Nonarea specialists, such as myself, who undertake an historical sociological case study work with a serious methodological handicap. Almost all of the empirical evidence available comes at second or third hand. This makes the historical sociologist vulnerable to the efforts and errors of others, as well as heavily in their debt. All of the source material consulted for this book presented selection biases that complicated my task. The dominant category is properly regarded as secondary information—the published and unpublished works of those who have had direct access to primary data. Monographs and ethnographies of sin-ologists, as well as narrative and analytic accounts of journalists and visitors—invited or not—form the basic empirical resource upon which my historical interpretations have been shaped.[31] My appreciation of these secondary works has been supplemented and, to some extent, influenced by a second category of literature —synthetic, comparative-historical, and theoretical works, which, like the present book, are one step further removed from direct cultural and/or archival experience.

Certain limited varieties of primary materials—translations of emigré interviews conducted by Western scholars, periodicals, political and legal documents, autobiographies, short stories, and so forth—have helped me to part the curtains to better view the secondary literature. In addition, I conducted interviews with a small number of Chinese emigrants and travelers, and I visited China as a participant in a "women's rights" tour to enjoy one direct encounter with the people and society who are the heirs to the family revolution I have studied from afar. The primary material provided a rich, but inadequate, check upon judgments based on secondary and tertiary literature. But here, too, preselection processes determined, via criteria rarely self-evident, exactly which documents, artifacts, and people became accessible. How representative each was of a given period, genre, or population was not always possible to determine.

With obstacles so formidable, why dare a secondary synthetic work on the Chinese revolution, a subject complex and beset with methodological difficulties for even the most experienced specialist? My defense is modest. By reinterpreting the best of relevant works by China specialists, I hope to suggest new questions and issues for them to pursue and, at the same time, to distill the theoretical implications of their work for the concerns of sociologists and feminists.

---

31. This book then is a work of secondary, or tertiary, sinology. Rather than competing with works by sinologists on women and family in China, it builds upon these as the crucial base for synthesis and interpretation. Among the major, book-length studies I have drawn upon in this way are Delia Davin, *Woman-Work*; Elisabeth Croll, *Feminism and Socialism in China*; idem, *The Politics of Marriage in Contemporary China*; Kay Johnson, "Feminism and Socialist Revolution in China"; and William L. Parish and Martin King Whyte, *Village and Family in Contemporary China*.

婦

2 Principles and Contradictions of the Confucian Patriarchal Order

Because the Chinese revolution was a peasant revolution, most discussions of its origins include an analysis of what has come to be called the agrarian crisis of late Ch'ing and early Republican China. So far as I am aware, these discussions have neglected to make explicit a simple, but telling point. The Chinese agrarian crisis was in essential ways a family crisis.[1] In this chapter and the next, I wish to argue that a crisis in the Confucian family system contributed to and shaped important contours of the revolutionary situation in twentieth-century China. Here lie many historical roots of the distinctive aspects of Maoist family and feminist policy and of the postrevolutionary course of the Chinese family revolution. Here, too, we can discover factors that helped to shape the character of that revolutionary process and the postrevolutionary development strategy popularly known as the Yenan Way. To understand the nature of the family crisis and

---

1. Two works that do not discuss the agrarian crisis in detail but do identify a family crisis in prerevolutionary China are Edward Friedman, *Backward Toward Revolution*, and Kay Johnson, "Feminism and Socialist Revolution in China." Embedded in the concept of "crisis" is an unfortunate normative connotation which, if left unchallenged, can distort one's understanding of historical process. "Crisis" implies an abnormal set of circumstances, the failure of the "normal" functioning of the system in question. Yet even the most superficial glance at the historical record should give pause to such notions. Periods of social crisis are at least as "normal" as those of social stability. A full understanding of a social system requires an analysis of its operations under both sorts of conditions, and, most important, of how both sorts of periods interrelate.

its historical legacy, it is necessary to begin with an awareness of the basic principles of traditional Confucian social and family structure.

The essential starting point for an appreciation of the nature of the old regime in China is the recognition that it is impossible to fully separate discussions of social and family structure. This is true for two major reasons. First, in profound ways the economic order that supported the Celestial Empire was a family economy. Second, Confucianism, the "state religion"[2]—a set of social structural principles, ethical precepts, and behavioral norms— was at once an exceptionally well-articulated ideology for ruling-class hegemony and for family relationships and organization. Thus, traditional China offers an unusual opportunity to perceive the causal contribution a family system—and the principles of sexual and generational relationships that underlie it—can make to the construction of seemingly broader arenas of political and economic order.

For analytical purposes, I will attempt to separate discussion of social and family structure. The difficulty this entails serves as a measure of the inextricable nature of Confucian family and society and as important evidence for the assertion with which this chapter begins—that in China, a social crisis was in important ways a family crisis.

CONFUCIAN SOCIAL STRUCTURE: A PEASANT ECONOMY, A FAMILY ECONOMY

Imperial China commanded a social order of exceptional size, population, and longevity. The history of the Chinese empire was dominated by a cyclical rise and fall of dynasties that changed the personnel (even, at times, the racial and national origins) of imperial officialdom, but not (at least during its last 1,000 years)

---

2. I am using this term in an evocative, but imprecise manner to suggest the extraordinary integration and coherence of Confucian spiritual and political doctrine. However, Charlotte Furth suggests that Confucianism was not considered a religion at all before the concept of "religion" as an autonomous realm was introduced by Western missionaries in the nineteenth century. Then, in 1895 during the twilight years of dynastic rule, K'ang Yu-wei initiated a campaign to make Confucianism an actual state religion. By that time, however, Confucian society and ideology were in the midst of irrevocable decline. Charlotte Furth, "The Transformations of Time," pp. 82–83.

the basic nature of its social order. From the decline of feudalism during the T'ang dynasty (A.D. 618–906) until the fall of the Ch'ing dynasty (in 1911), China was an agrarian civilization governed by an imperial bureaucracy. Each royal lineage, in turn, maintained dynastic control until economic decline, peasant rebellion, and earthly military defeat gave evidence that the dynasty had lost the Mandate of Heaven. The state administrative apparatus was manned by the literati, Confucian scholars stratified into ranks via a complex, hierarchical examination system. Access to this system was dependent upon a classical education, the acquisition of which necessitated leisure and wealth, which in the agrarian economy were two facets of the same phenomenon. So scarcely distributed was such privilege, and so rigorous were the examinations that controlled the gateway to further privilege, that less than 2 percent of the Chinese population belonged to families of Confucian degree holders.[3]

Three major social statuses—officials, commoners, and the "mean people"—were differentiated explicitly by traditional Chinese law and society. The first, drawn primarily from the literati, were entitled to legal and political privileges, a distinctive style of life specified down to details of attire, diet, even the means of physical transport, and multiple opportunities for monetary gain. Officials invested a goodly portion of the money they acquired in land, the material basis of social status and local hegemony. Thus they, as the prestigious stratum of the scholar-gentry class, linked the state apparatus to the local landed gentry. These mutually dependent entities cooperated in appropriating wealth from the peasantry, the numerically dominant and economically pivotal class among the commoners. Commercial wealth was disparaged, and officially merchants were the social inferiors of the peasants. But successful merchants provided their families an effective means of entrée into scholar-gentry ranks: "money went into land and sons into the exams."[4] Whereas mobility of class and status was possible among people of official or common rank, "mean person" was virtually a hereditary caste identity affixed to slaves, members of morally tainted occupations such

---

3. Chung-li Chang, *The Chinese Gentry,* p. 139; Ramon H. Myers, *The Chinese Economy,* p. 32.
4. Maurice Freedman, *Lineage Organization in Southeastern China,* p. 58.

as entertainment and prostitution, and regional pariah groups like the boat people of Kwangtung and the beggars of Kiangsu. In addition to suffering social and legal discrimination, "mean people" were forbidden to intermarry with members of the superior classes.[5]

The labor of the peasantry was the productive base of this social order. Peasants traditionally comprised approximately 80 percent of the Chinese population and farming absorbed 75 percent of Chinese labor.[6] This, in itself, makes it useful to characterize the traditional economy as a peasant economy. But here I am using the term "peasant economy" in a more precise way in order, first, to distinguish the presocialist [7] political economy of China from lingering misconceptions that it was feudal and, second, to provide a conceptual framework that will allow us to perceive the centrality of the family system within that political economy.

Across several social science disciplines there is a literature that argues persuasively that "peasant economy" should be understood as a particular form of economic organization.[8] It is a term that describes not only the economic relationships and attributes of the cultivator class but also the dominant mode of production in the societies to which it pertains. Peasant economy, as I use the term, denotes an agrarian society in which the four following features are present. (1) Agriculture dominates both the total product and the working population. (2) The family farm is the basic unit of society and economy. The peasant family household operates as a multifunctional unit of production. Ideal-typically, peasants control their own labor and their own means of production. Their production has a dual orientation—towards

---

5. For details and a discussion of restrictions on "mean people," see T'ung-tsu Ch'ü, *Law and Society in Traditional China*, pp. 129–32.

6. These approximate figures are derived from studies conducted during the 1910s and 1920s, reported in R. H. Tawney, *Land and Labour in China*, p. 26.

7. Just as feudalism has been appropriately criticized for its ethnocentric European bias, so too should the standard Marxist categorization of "precapitalist" modes of production be subject to critical reflection. The history of the transformation of the political economy of China is a story of a bureaucratic imperial peasant economy becoming a state socialist one.

8. The originator of this position was the Russian economist, Alexander Chayanov. His work is discussed favorably by Daniel Thorner, "Peasant Economy as a Category in Economic History," pp. 202–18. Teodor Shanin, "Peasantry as a Political Factor," also follows this interpretation. See also idem, "The Nature and Logic of the Peasant Economy 1."

familial sustenance and towards the world beyond the village to which it is linked through market relationships. (3) Peasants produce a surplus that is extracted and transferred to dominant classes. (4) A territorial state exists that plays a crucial role supporting the extraction of surplus.[9]

From the period of the T'ang dynasty forward, the peasant economy of imperial China fulfilled these general criteria. The peasant economy decidedly was not feudal if by feudal we mean a paternalistic social system based on fixed social status and landed estates. The nonhereditary nature of the Chinese aristocracy was one of its distinctive features. Old-regime China had an open class system in which upward mobility from peasant to gentry ranks was structurally possible, although infrequent, and downward mobility was widespread. Men other than the "mean people" were eligible to compete in the imperial civil service examinations, whose successful candidates filled from one-third to one-half of the positions of officialdom, and almost all the important ones. The examinations tested contestants on their mastery of the Confucian classics, central to which, as we shall see, was a patriarchal, family-centered philosophy of government. While scholar-gentry background provided the leisure, schooling, and ideological influences that facilitated success in the examinations, no more than 60 percent of the top-scoring candidates were reared in official families.[10]

The existence of a system of small-scale private landholding, access to which was contractual and significantly monetized at an early date, is the second important feature that distinguished the Chinese peasant economy from a feudal one. Scholars continue to debate the extent to which paternalistic relations were embedded within the outwardly contractual order.[11] One can identify a

9. I have based this selection of characteristics on models presented in Shanin, "Peasant Economy"; idem, "Peasantry as a Political Factor"; Thorner, "Peasant Economy"; and Eric Wolf, *Peasants*.

10. E. A. Kracke, Jr., "Family vs. Merit in Chinese Civil Service Examinations Under the Empire," p. 116.

11. For an argument that customary rights were important in prerevolutionary China, see Ralph Thaxton, "Tenants in Revolution," and idem, "Some Critical Comments on Peasant Revolts and Revolutionary Politics in China." Ramon H. Myers argues against the significance of paternalistic relationships in "Socio-economic Relations in Northern Chinese Villages During the Republican Period." An intermediate account that still supports the significance of paternalism is offered by Frederic Wakeman, Jr., "Rebellion and Revolution."

variety of paternalistic practices in Confucian China. Seasonal feasts were provided by landlords for their tenants and laborers. Public granaries were maintained by village elites to defend the local community against famine. We will see that the erosion of customary rights played a meaningful role in peasant revolutionary history. But one must acknowledge that, compared with feudal Europe, agrarian China's tradition of economic paternalism was weak. Competition fostered by the structurally open mobility system combined with the predatory nature of the tax system to limit such a development. The major exception to this generalization, and an important one for our case, involved the Confucian family system.

Characterizing China's presocialist mode of production as a peasant economy also underscores its identity as a family economy. As the Russian economist Alexander Chayanov was the first to point out, this is the fundamental feature of a peasant economy.[12] In such an economy the social, political, and productive activities of peasants cannot be distinguished: "The individual, the family, and the farm appear as an indivisible whole."[13] Moreover, family processes are central to the working of peasant economies. The size and composition of the peasant family is the proper unit, Chayanov argued, from which to understand labor supply and deployment as well as demands for consumption. Hence, the working of a peasant economy's class system can only be understood through an approach which incorporates an analysis of the natural history of the family. In the course of the peasant family life cycle, the expansion and contraction of the labor resources and consumption demands of its members inform the logic and behavior of the family's economic activity: the buying, selling, and renting of land; the participation in wage labor; the degree of involvement in market relations; and so forth. Such activities are integral to processes of social mobility and, therefore, to understanding class relations themselves. Later I shall discuss the ways in which the Chinese peasant family economy affected

---

12. Eric Wolf, *Peasants*, p. 14. Chayanov's theory of peasant economics led ultimately to his repudiation and imprisonment as a kulak-sympathizer, in part because his theory began to challenge classic Marxist concepts of class formation. See Basile Kerblay, "Chayanov and the Theory of Peasantry as a Specific Type of Economy," pp. 150–60.

13. Shanin, "Peasantry as a Political Factor," p. 241.

presocialist class relationships. Now, I wish to show the ways in which it is appropriate to consider China's presocialist agrarian economy to be a family economy. This requires a look at the prevailing system of land tenure and the characteristic organization and distribution of productive activities.

Traditional Family Farming • Independent family farming, a universal peasant ideal, was more realizable in traditional China than in most other agrarian civilizations. This was both cause and consequence of the most striking feature of traditional Chinese agriculture—the division of cultivated land into minuscule, fragmented plots. Peasants worked this land as owners, tenants, and hired laborers, and, frequently, in some combination of these three tenure relationships. There were significant inter- and intraregional variations in the prevalence of each form. Most important was the contrast between the Northern and Southern agricultural regions, corresponding roughly to the division between dry-land grains of wheat and millet and the irrigated multiple-cropping areas of the Southern rice bowl. Tenancy rates were much higher in the Southern rice regions, where the land was more fertile and productive, and where, as a result, families could support themselves on holdings even smaller than in the North. However, Southern tenant farmers frequently secured long-term leases and quasi-ownership of their plots in the form of a system that allowed them to purchase surface rights to land.[14]

Individual family owner-cultivation was more prevalent in the North, where population was less dense, land less fertile, and water resources dramatically less reliable. Because Northern crop yields were so much lower, individual farms tended to be larger in the North than in the South.[15] Corporate landholding, especially of cultivated land, was present, but quite secondary. The dominant form of corporate land ownership was clan property, which was most prevalent in the Southeast where lineage structure was

---

14. Data on tenancy rates are available in Tawney, *Land and Labour*, pp. 64–66; Chen Han-seng, *Landlord and Peasant in China*, pp. viii–ix, 3–4; and Myers, *Chinese Economy*, pp. 166–67. Surface and subsurface rights and other leasing arrangements are discussed in Myers, *Chinese Economy*, pp. 103–107.

15. Data on farm size are available in John Lossing Buck, *Land Utilization in China*, and Tawney, *Land and Labour*.

strongest.[16] Even corporate lands were characteristically leased in small, fragmented plots to individual peasant family heads.

Peasant families cultivated as many of the small, scattered plots as their family labor and economic resources would permit. In turn, their chief resource, family membership, was closely keyed to the availability and affordability of land to cultivate. That is why investigators of land utilization in traditional China have all noted the strong correlation between the size of the farm and the size of the household.[17] Peasant families in China, as elsewhere, struggled to maintain a delicate balance between the number of hands they could set to labor and the number of mouths the rewards of such labor had to feed. Basic events of family composition—birth, marriage, death, adoption (and certain less-ordinary ones, such as the purchase and sale of members or partition of the household, whose significance will concern us shortly)—shaped and were shaped by local economic opportunity. Even the best of circumstances could not provide a perfect fit. During periods of peak agricultural activity—planting, transplanting, harvesting—most families lacked adequate labor resources. Families who could afford it hired laborers for such periods. Others devised traditional peasant forms of labor exchange that provided models upon which reformers and revolutionaries alike would later attempt to draw.[18] During the slack period before the harvest, on the other hand, labor was abundant but food was often scarce. Hence an extensive, rather complex system of credit was integral to the agrarian economy. This was an important mechanism for tying seemingly independent owner-cultivators to the dominant classes in a dependent relationship.

---

16. For discussions of the relationship between lineage strength and property conditions, see Maurice Freedman, *Chinese Lineage and Society*; idem, *Lineage Organization*; and Jack Potter, "Land and Lineage in Traditional China."

17. See, for example, John L. Buck, *Land Utilization*, p. 276; Sidney D. Gamble, *Ting Hsien*, p. 66; and C. K. Yang, *A Chinese Village in Early Communist Transition*, p. 37. Data on correlation of farm and household size understate the relationship because smaller farms on fertile land sustained larger families than similar farms on less-fertile land, and the variable labor demands of different crops affected the economy of family production in ways not reflected in the aggregate data. See Myron Cohen, *House United, House Divided*, for a good ethnographic description of the relationship between tobacco farming and large joint-household economy.

18. For discussions of the forms of traditional peasant labor exchange, see Morton H. Fried, *Fabric of Chinese Society*, p. 116, and Thaxton, "Some Critical Comments," p. 287.

Not only did farm and family size correlate closely, but the specific nature of a family's economic activity was significantly shaped by the size and structure of its membership. Sex, age, and family status structured the division of labor within the family unit. The patriarchal head of the household was its production chief as well. He determined the economic activities of all members and directly supervised the work of the men, who dominated the agricultural landscape and performed approximately 80 percent of farm labor nationwide.[19] Women played crucial, but secondary, roles cultivating the land. Regional differences were significant in the distribution of female labor on the land. In the North, women played a minor role; they participated primarily during periods of peak labor demand. In the multiple-cropping rice regions of the South, however, female participation in weeding, transplanting, and harvesting the crops was more constant. In a few atypical areas, women carried almost exclusive responsibility for farm work. In all regions peasant women worked continually. They had full responsibility for the arduous sphere of peasant domestic labor—pounding rice; tending livestock; making, laundering, and repairing clothing and shoes; preparing meals; and rearing children. They also participated substantially in domestic handicraft industries like spinning and weaving. But the extent and value of female labor was obscured, as it is generally, by its less public character.

The fractured, tiny farms were cultivated with an intensity of human labor that has properly earned Chinese agriculture the reputation of gardening. Primitive machinery and the relative absence of work animals, factors which were themselves partly the product of a familial pattern of land utilization, placed an enormous burden on human toil. The small size of family holdings made the greatest possible yields essential. Flexibility of pooled resources of family labor made them possible.

Despite the extraordinary intensity of agricultural labor, the smallness of the holdings and the extraction of surplus from even these small farms by the dominant classes had the consequence that farming was an inadequate means of subsistence for the majority of peasants. Hence, the rural economy, even in pre-Communist China, "walked on two legs." Small farms could

---

19. John L. Buck, *Land Utilization*, p. 292.

productively absorb just so much labor. The seasonal nature of agriculture combined with this factor to make available a labor surplus that could be deployed in whatever subsidiary production and wage labor was locally available. The paucity of the returns this supplementary activity might earn was a poor deterrent, given the gravity of the need.[20]

China's highly developed marketing system meant that self-sufficiency of family production units was neither necessary nor efficient. Still, peasant families practiced a diversified economy, and the smaller ones were badly handicapped by economic pressures that forced them to be more specialized.[21]

Field studies conducted after the demise of imperial China are the richest source available for an appreciation of the familial nature of the peasant economy. During the late 1930s and early 1940s, for example, Hsiao-tung Fei and Chih-i Chang investigated three rural villages in Yunnan whose land tenure arrangements and employment opportunities varied significantly. Yet everywhere a family-based economic strategy was characteristic. In the village of Yuts'un, duck raising was a disparaged, but important, subsidiary economic activity. Fei and Chang found that duck raising was engaged in by the most populous households among those peasants poor enough to disregard the loss of face associated with this occupation—but not too poor to raise the small amount of capital necessary to purchase the ducklings. The most populous of such households raised ducks because they had the necessary spare labor to employ in caring for the flock, and their land was usually inadequate to meet their needs.[22]

The dominance of a familial system of economic organization is striking in the case of the paper industry of Yits'un, Yunnan. The relatively large capital investment required in a factory caused comparatively prosperous families to engage in joint ownership—generally along kinship lines—of the means of production.

---

20. Women weavers in Yuts'un, a Yunnan village studied by Hsiao-tung Fei and Chih-i Chang between 1939 and 1943, for example, earned less in a full day's weaving than was necessary to provide them with one day's food; nevertheless their weaving remained crucial to the household economy (*Earthbound China*, pp. 242ff.).

21. Myers, *Chinese Economy*, pp. 100–101, suggests the greater specialization of smaller families, but does not emphasize the disadvantageous implications for the family economy.

22. Fei and Chang, *Earthbound China*, pp. 236–37.

Nonetheless, individual family households served as separate management units, each taking its turn at operating the factory, hiring and managing its own labor force, reaping its own profits.[23]

The situation Myron Cohen discovered in rural Taiwan in the 1960s was even more dramatic. Contrary to his expectation, he found a high proportion of farmers in Yen-liao maintaining the large, complex, joint-family size and structure prescribed by Confucian doctrine. His study of the community led him to an economic explanation. Tobacco, an important local crop, demanded comparatively steady and high labor input that a large family labor force could most cheaply provide. Moreover, the region offered an unusually diversified structure of employment opportunities, which made the economic flexibility and interdependence of the large, joint-family household an economically sensible pattern.[24]

To understand why Cohen put so much emphasis on the economic rationality underlying large, joint-family structure, one must place his study in the historiographical context of sinological treatments of the Confucian family. For many years this subject had been dominated by attempts to counter the misconception generated by late imperial Confucian literati that extensive, complex households were prevalent in imperial China. Twentieth-century field studies and sociological treatments of the Chinese family emphasized instead the rare appearance of the officially prescribed form. Such families, they have claimed, were realized almost exclusively by members of the gentry because they alone possessed either the material or cultural resources that were demanded by large-scale, extended family existence.[25] Cohen demonstrates, however, that no simple, dichotomous gentry-peasant model will do to explain the distribution of extended family households in traditional China. His Yen-liao farm families with an average membership of 17.1 per household would not

---

23. Ibid., pp. 178ff.
24. Cohen, *House United*.
25. Classic studies with this thesis are Olga Lang, *Chinese Family and Society*, and Marion J. Levy, Jr., *The Family Revolution in Modern China*. Hsiao-tung Fei, *China's Gentry*, also contains this view. See Francis L. K. Hsu, *Under the Ancestors' Shadow*, for a cultural analysis of the presumed peasant-gentry dichotomy in family structure. A useful critical overview of the literature on traditional family structure in China appears in Cohen, *House United*, pp. 227–36.

have qualified for gentry status. The rarity of such families in traditional China should be understood, Cohen believes, by the relative absence of the economic conditions that made this a rational family strategy.

This analysis of the economic underpinnings of joint family life is ingenious and illuminating. But Cohen's attempt to counter cultural explanations for family structure goes too far. Family strategies should not be divided theoretically into their cultural and economic dimensions. They do not so divide in practice. In the case of Yen-liao one could as reasonably claim that it made sense for large, joint families to engage in tobacco farming and diversified economic strategies as to put it the other way round. Indeed, I believe Cohen's sophisticated study may be read most usefully as evidence that Chinese patriarchs from all social classes were predisposed to take advantage of whatever economic conditions facilitated large, extended family life. They even may have attempted to generate such conditions themselves because that was the family structure most conducive to the realization of Confucian patriarchal ideals. The point is the one belabored in this chapter—family and economy are truly indivisible in a peasant economy.

This issue bears on another relevant scholarly discourse—a broad and interdisciplinary debate over whether peasant economic consciousness and behavior generally can be understood better in moral or in political terms. The debate represents an attempt to retrieve respect for peasants as social actors from a scholarly tradition that too readily portrayed them as irrationally cautious, ignorant, and economically shortsighted. Contributors to this discourse view peasant behavior as thoroughly rational, but disagree about the essential framework in which peasant rationality is manifested. The "moral economists" argue that peasants go about their rational calculation of economic risks and benefits within the framework of a subsistence ethic and a norm of reciprocity that attempts to guarantee all community members their survival niche in a traditional social world with customary and unequal standards of living. Behavior that appears irrational from the perspective of profit maximization is often the most rational way to secure survival in a precarious economy. The "political economists," in contrast, do not agree that peasants are motivated primarily by a desire to maintain a customary standard of living. Profit maximization, they argue, is, in fact, a peasant goal. Peasants are willing to take long-term investment risks so long as they possess a surplus adequate to assure short-term survival; they are impeded in this effort by the overwhelming political inequality that defines their access to investment resources.[26]

Serious issues concerning peasant politics are embedded in this controversy. Are class relations in peasant societies experienced primarily in paternalistic or coercive terms? What role does class struggle play in determining the terms and conditions of the traditional standard of living? Are the sources of revolutionary action among the peasantry essentially restorative or initiative—a response to the loss of subsistence rights in order to restore a customary world or a response to a mobility crisis and an attempt to restructure and improve the terms of the social order? What role do outside organizers play in mobilizing peasant action?

While these represent legitimate and weighty disagreements, the debate as it has been formulated rests, I believe, on an overly dichotomous view of moral and political rationality. All economic behavior takes place in social contexts that are at once moral and political. Distinct moral frameworks underlie different modes of production. The predominant moral characteristic of preindustrial, agrarian economies is the framework of reciprocity in which unequal material and power relationships are explicitly legitimated and reinforced structurally. Thus the presence or absence of a peasant's interest in economic gain is not the place to look to determine whether moral or political factors chiefly govern peasant behavior. Most Chinese peasants strove to maintain both short-term security and long-term gain, but generally they did so within the context of the given social structure with its given moral framework. Moreover, the distinctive moral feature of peasant

---

26. James C. Scott is the major theorist of the moral economy perspective. See his *The Moral Economy of the Peasantry*, as well as his "Protest and Profanation." Others with compatible analyses of peasant economy include Shanin, "Peasant Economy"; Eric Wolf, *Peasants*; and John Berger, "Towards Understanding Peasant Experience." Scott's framework has been applied directly to the Chinese peasantry by Thaxton, "Tenants in Revolution." The major work with the political economy perspective is Samuel Popkin, *The Rational Peasant*.

economy is the centrality of the peasant family as the moral unit and idiom. Peasants calculate their interests in familial rather than in individualistic terms, making economic decisions that deploy family resources in order to achieve family security, prosperity, and social respectability. This familial basis is overlooked entirely by the "political economists," who draw a false distinction between political and moral action by projecting an individual calculus onto peasant strategy. The "moral economists," on the other hand, assume, but fail to analyze, the significance of the familial basis of peasant morality. What all parties to the discourse miss is the essential patriarchal nature of the peasant, moral economy.

Identifying the peasant social order as patriarchal rather than paternalistic eliminates the temptation to choose between moral or political analyses or to separate cultural from economic interpretations. Patriarchal systems are based on unambiguously hierarchical principles of unequal rights and obligations. Moreover, to focus on patriarchy allows us to remove the screen that projects the family as an undifferentiated unity. It properly fixes our attention on the systemic principles that structure the relationships of gender, generation, and social integration within a peasant family and society. In the Chinese case, as we shall see, the patriarchal essence of the peasant moral economy attained an extraordinary degree of explicit expression. Its economic basis—independent, nearly self-sufficient farming and subsidiary production—was the goal of most peasant families. Enough of them were successful in this attempt to make it modal in what are generally called normal times.[27]

In normal times this peasant economy seemed to work reasonably well. Although prescientific, the laborious intensity of Chinese cultivation rewarded the society with yields adequate to support an increasingly dense population. Certain scholars have read the historical record of this economy to indicate that, until late in the eighteenth century, the living standards of the Chinese peasantry exceeded those of Europe and Japan.[28] And

27. Data and discussion of private landholding can be found in Tawney, *Land and Labour*, pp. 97–101, and Myers, *Chinese Economy*, chap. 4.

28. Ping-ti Ho, *Studies on the Population of China, 1368–1953*, and Albert Feuerwerker, *The Chinese Economy, 1870–1911*.

there is considerable support for the ironic view that early successes of Chinese agriculture, particularly in the realm of crop improvement, contributed significantly to the ultimate demographic crisis—the extremely adverse human-land ratio, which by the middle of the nineteenth century played a weighty role in that economic stagnation whose familial aspects soon will absorb our attention.[29] Even before the nineteenth century, demographic and political processes were noticeably interrelated. Periods of political stability fostered spurts of agricultural and human reproduction that intensified pressure on the land. When available land and technical resources were exhausted, immiserization fueled endemic peasant rebellions that periodically contributed their share to the cyclical decline and fall of the dynasties. Ralph Thaxton has suggested, aptly, I believe, that loss of the Mandate of Subsistence rather than that of Heaven cost a Chinese emperor legitimacy among his peasant subjects.[30]

There is considerable agreement that, although the traditional Chinese peasant economy was comparatively viable, by the middle of the nineteenth century it had exhausted its capacity to develop adequately within the parameters of the existing social and technical organization of production.[31] In the best of times it was a precarious system that tread a thin line between stability, stagnation, and starvation. The victories of the British in the mid-nineteenth-century Opium Wars rang the decisive curtain on normal dynastic times. Thereafter the internal vulnerabilities of the old regime were aggravated far beyond their limits by incursions of Western and Japanese imperialism. It is time to explore the role the Confucian family system was prepared to play in the ensuing dialectic of dynastic decline and social revolution.

---

29. Ho, *Population of China;* Albert Feuerwerker, *Chinese Economy, 1870–1911;* and Lucien Bianco, *Origins of the Chinese Revolution, 1915–1949.*

30. Thaxton, "Tenants in Revolution," p. 281. Here he follows the suggestion of James C. Scott, *Moral Economy,* that this generally is a characteristic of peasant rebellions.

31. Albert Feuerwerker, *Chinese Economy, 1870–1911,* p. 15; Ho, *Population of China,* pp. 153, 208, 270; Bianco, *Origins of the Chinese Revolution,* p. 92; and Wolfram Eberhard, "Research on the Chinese Family," p. 37. Dwight H. Perkins has called the problem "the high level equilibrium trap" (*Agricultural Development in China, 1368–1968*). For a dissenting view, see Ramon H. Myers, *The Chinese Peasant Economy.*

CONFUCIAN IDEOLOGY

All agrarian civilizations rest on patriarchal familial foundations. Few patriarchal systems approach the degree of explication, elaboration, or hegemony Confucianism achieved in imperial China. For more than 1,000 years it was the dominant cosmology, political philosophy, and doctrine of proper ethics and comportment of the Chinese people; Confucianism is nearly synonymous with traditional Chinese civilization. Over the centuries Confucianists developed an ideology and social system designed to realize their conception of the good society, a harmonious and hierarchical social order in which everyone knew and assumed proper stations.[32] Confucianists expressly took the well-ordered family as both the microcosm and basic unit of sociopolitical order, advising ruling dynasties to "put the family in order and rule the state in peace."[33] Order in family and state alike was to be based on filial piety, which the *Hsiao Ching*, the Confucian classic on that subject, identified as "the foundation of virtue and the root of civilization."[34] Infractions of filial piety were punished with severity related directly to the intimacy and authority of the familial relationship involved.[35]

Confucian scholars identified "five human relationships" as pivotal to the system: sovereign and subject, father and son, husband and wife, elder and younger brother, and friend and friend. The husband-wife relationship was thought to be the first in origin, the first step towards social organization.[36] The relationship between father and son, however, was indisputably the first in importance. Each of the relationships was supposed

---

32. In a fascinating essay comparing Chinese and Western patriarchy, Gary Hamilton suggests that one of the distinctive features of Chinese patriarchy was its emphasis on positional rather than personal power. The power of Chinese patriarchs, Hamilton argues, was not discretionary, but a matter of upholding prescribed moral principles by enforcing obedience to the dictates of roles ("Patriarchy, Patrimonialism, and Structures of Orthodoxy").

33. Quoted in Lin Yu-tang, *My Country and My People*, p. 172.

34. The *Hsiao Ching*, p. 3.

35. See Ch'ü, *Law and Society*, for detailed discussion and graphic illustrations of filial piety and the law.

36. Claude Lévi-Strauss has theorized, in a compatible fashion, that the family constructed via marriage represents the passage from nature to culture ("The Family").

to be governed by a distinct principle of propriety: "Father and son should love each other. Sovereign and subject should be just to each other. Husband and wife should distinguish their separate spheres. Elder and younger brothers should have a sense of precedence. Between friends there should be good faith."[37]

But whatever reciprocity the ancient sages intended these relationships to embody was transformed into an authoritarian doctrine of strict obedience by the neo-Confucianists of the Sung dynasty (A.D. 907–1279), whose teachings were increasingly embraced by rulers of the Ming (A.D. 1368–1644) and Ch'ing (A.D. 1644–1911) dynasties. It is a mistake, however, to view this as an anomalous development.[38] The rigid gender and generational principles at the center of Confucian patriarchy made such a development near irresistible. And according to the *Analects* (one of the primary Confucian classics), Confucius himself had made explicit the salutary political effects wise rulers could achieve by inculcating filial behavior in their subjects:

> Master Yu said, "Those who in private life behave well toward their parents and elder brothers, in public life seldom show a disposition to resist the authority of their superiors. And as for such men starting a revolution, no instance of it has ever occurred."[39]

In essence, Confucianism was a protocol for proper family life. It prescribed a patriarchal, patrilineal, and patrilocal family system. Sex, age, and generation were the coordinates that defined an individual's status, role, privileges, duties, and liabilities within the family order. Men officially dominated women; the old dominated the young. The ideal family structure was an extended joint household, in which all married sons, their wives, and their progeny lived with the unmarried siblings under the guidance of a patriarch who was served and assisted by his wife and whatever concubines and servants he possessed. Ideal-typically the eldest male of the family was the patriarch, head of the

---

37. Mencius, quoted in Yu-lan Fung, "The Philosophy at the Basis of Traditional Chinese Society," p. 25.

38. Fung argues that the authoritarian outcome violated the intentions of Confucius ("Philosophy of Traditional Society," p. 25).

39. Quoted by David Raddock, "Growing Up in New China," p. 202.

household and estate, and hence of the family economy. The unit he headed was known as the *chia*, best defined as all the members of a household, present or absent, with reciprocal obligations who participated in a common budget and had claims to a common estate.[40] The *chia-chang* (household head) had the authority to decide who worked where, when, and at what; who spent what and how; and when and whom *chia* members would marry. What is more, his disciplinary obligations and discretion were so unlimited that he legitimately wielded the power of life and limb over *chia* members.

The patriarch's goal was to maintain an unbroken lineage which would reside together on the ancestral property for all time—past and future. Thus ancestor worship was no mere supernatural cult; it was an expression of and a contribution to the stability and continuity of the lineage. And the *chia-chang* led ceremonial rituals in his capacity as "family priest."[41] The emphasis on lineal continuity intensified the importance of producing male heirs. "There are three things which are unfilial," said Mencius, "and the greatest of them is to have not posterity."[42] Concubinage thus received official sanction as a means of assuring lineal descendants.

Land was the idealized foundation of the Chinese family. Land was the major form of property that passed exclusively to sons through the male lineage and thereby perpetuated the desired goals of family continuity and prosperity. Land was so basic to this system that it has been suggested that the "strong sense of the importance of kinship ties is extended to a symbolic kinship between man and the earth."[43] Peasants in Taitou, Shantung, graphically expressed the centrality of this relationship: "When we say a family is broken, we mean that the family's land is gone."[44]

---

40. For a definition and discussion of the *chia* economy, see Cohen, *House United*, pp. 57ff.

41. Ch'ü, *Law and Society*, p. 20.

42. Quoted in Ch'u Chai and Winberg Chai, *The Changing Society of China*, p. 81, n. 3.

43. Hsiao-tung Fei, *China's Gentry*, p. 130.

44. Quoted in Martin Yang, *Chinese Village*, p. 46.

Primogeniture in the Confucian family was exclusively ceremonial, whereas inheritance was partible. This was the basic
structural factor that underwrote the fragmented landholding
pattern described above. Partible inheritance both reflected and
perpetuated an economy with a paucity of alternative employment
options to farming. Although its origins remain obscure, Eric
Wolf has suggested that the state favored partible inheritance
because it produced more tax units and curbed the growth of
the monopolization of local power implied by the successful
functioning of the lineage system.[45] Partible inheritance was also
a crucial mechanism of the mobility system, facilitating downward
mobility most directly.

Even more than many peasant family systems, Confucianism
subordinated the needs, interests, and desires of the individual
to those of the family group. This was the explicit intent of the
filial code: "Restricting one's personal desires and enjoyment in
order to support one's parents—this is the filiality of the common
people. So it is that from the Son of Heaven to the commoners,
if filial piety is not pursued from beginning to end, disasters are
sure to follow."[46] Individual identity was so effaced that individuals
were properly addressed by kinship designations, such as Elder
Brother, First Daughter, Third Uncle, and the like. In fact, Eberhard
claims that the Chinese language included no words for "individual," "individualism," or "freedom" prior to China's contact
with the West.[47] Family systems which demand such extreme
individual suppression generally develop a significant portion
of ceremonial elaboration. This was likely one of the major reasons
for the highly ritualized and ruinously expensive nature of proper
Confucian weddings, funerals, and ancestor rites.[48]

The Confucian marriage system clearly reveals the dominance
of the interests of the family—particularly the dominance of its

45. Eric Wolf, *Peasants*, pp. 75ff.
46. *Hsiao Ching*, p. 13.
47. Wolfram Eberhard, "The Upper-Class Family in Traditional China," pp.
70, 75.
48. For data and discussion of these traditional ceremonies, see Fei and
Chang, *Earthbound China*, p. 102; Hsiao-tung Fei, *Peasant Life in China*, p. 132;
John L. Buck, *Land Utilization;* Gamble, *Ting Hsien*, p. 18; and Ch'ü, *Law and
Society.*

patriarchal principles—over those of the individual. In all peasant societies marriage is arranged with the concern of the family rather than that of the individual dictating the criteria of mate selection. But, once again, the Confucian case was unusually extreme. Ideally individuals had no role in the choice of their spouses. Courtship was the province of men seeking concubines, mistresses, and victims; it had no place in conventional marriage. Early betrothal and early marriage were preferred. The family of the groom initiated the transaction, which it is fair to label an exchange of women.[49] Because the marriage residence pattern was patrilocal in a culture that ideally practiced clan, surname, and—in general—therefore village exogamy, a woman moved at the time of her marriage to the home of her husband's family. The arrival of the bride's sedan chair so literally marked a commodity exchange that wedding guests in one village were observed to inspect the bride "as if she were an animal just purchased at market."[50] All control of and responsibility for a woman was transferred at this moment from her natal to her marital lineage. She had few opportunities to escape from her new home. She was not allowed to die in the home of her natal family. She could be divorced or repudiated by her in-laws for a flaw such as excessive verbosity, but there was almost no ground for divorce on the woman's part. Restrictions on remarriage of a widow were severe, because widow chastity was idealized as an expression of wifely fidelity, the highest feminine virtue in the Confucian pantheon. In any case, authority over a widow's fate remained the province of her husband's lineage, which retained custody of her children regardless. To cement these marriages that were so often in violation of the desires of the individuals, and especially those of women, an elaborate exchange of gifts

---

49. The concept "exchange of women" comes from the work of Claude Lévi-Strauss. For a concise presentation, see "The Family." The concept has become a subject of considerable discussion among feminist anthropologists and theorists. A particularly lucid interpretation of its relevance to feminist theory appears in Gayle Rubin, "The Traffic in Women."

50. Arthur H. Smith, *Village Life in China*, p. 250. Smith, whose patronizing attitude towards Chinese peasants is evident throughout his episodic account of late-nineteenth-century rural Chinese life, was a Protestant missionary.

between the negotiating families was expected to occur—a system of dowry and bride-price.[51]

Family life and sentiment digressed in China, as elsewhere, from the paradigm of the official ideology, and the most significant of these digressions soon will occupy our attention. However, it would be a serious mistake to dismiss Confucian familism as an idle fashion cultivated by an esoteric fraction of the Confucian literati. Confucianism was, instead, a hegemonic cosmology that received a truly extraordinary degree of codification, as well as direct indoctrination among all classes of the Chinese populace. This is why it is properly regarded as the state religion of imperial China.

Li and law were the major vehicles through which Confucian doctrines were promulgated and transmitted. *Li* were norms and rules of social behavior specified as appropriate for varying social statuses and relationships. Enforced by social sanctions, they were explicated and illustrated in considerable detail through classical and popular educational works. Confucian classics, such as the *Hsiao Ching* and the *Analects,* generally consisted of dialogues between a Confucian master and his disciple and were designed systematically to indoctrinate male children with filial virtues. The classics were the core curriculum in schools that began the preparation of examination aspirants, and they were commonly used for moral instruction in the households of the literate. Thirty to forty percent of Chinese males may have possessed literacy adequate for this function.[52] And these males were widely dis-

---

51. Jack Goody claims that dowry rather than bridewealth is the dominant pattern in Eurasian kinship systems because it facilitates the sharp class-stratification patterns characteristic of those societies. Bridewealth, which circulates wealth, is prevalent, he claims, in more egalitarian societies, such as prevailed in much of Africa. See his *Production and Reproduction* as well as Jack Goody and S. J. Tambiah, *Bridewealth and Dowry.*

China, which had a mixed system of dowry and bride-price, only partially matches Goody's description. Although expenses for gifts incurred by the families of the bride and the groom were similar, a small net gain typically accrued to the dowry, which was used by the bride to launch the fund on which her own conjugal family would ultimately attempt to construct an independent household. See Cohen, *House United,* for a detailed discussion of the private money to which dowry was applied.

52. This rather high estimate comes from a revisionist work on this subject by Evelyn S. Rawski, *Education and Popular Literacy in Ch'ing China,* p. 23.

persed in Chinese families that served as exemplars and authorities to peasants in all parts of the empire.

The presumed inferiority of women and their exclusion from public life made it appear pointless to introduce females to the classics. Instead, separate women's versions were published for the benefit of the rare few who were permitted to attain literacy. It was customary, for example, to give all literate Chinese women a copy of *Biographies of Chinese Women*, which contained models of good and bad female conduct grouped under headings such as "the virtuous and the wise," "the chaste and obedient," and "the pernicious and depraved."[53]

The classics were supplemented by popular works that served to disseminate Confucian education more widely and to modify the contents of Confucian culture through influences from below. One variety was the popular encyclopedia, which was designed as a study guide for the examinations but which came to be used also as simplified educational material for children. Merchants who purchased degrees frequently turned to these encyclopedias to obtain a gloss of Confucian erudition. Confucian morality was thereby disseminated among upwardly mobile sectors of the society. A second type of popular work, which enjoyed particular success during the late Ming dynasty, was the morality book that drew on popular stories to illustrate moral messages. From these grew the *Ledgers of Merit and Demerit*, which set out to calculate the moral worth of human deeds empirically on a point system. Initially points correlated strongly with the material expense of the good deed, but the belief that virtue should be available to all led to the seventeenth-century work, *Meritorious Deeds at No Cost*. Here the central Confucian virtues were interspersed with bits of etiquette and practical advice, all of which were translated into specific behavioral norms addressed to different status groups. Peasants, when plowing, for example, were advised, "Do not infringe on graves or make them hard to find." Local gentry were urged, "Rectify your own conduct and transform the common people." And people in general (which did not include women, who were addressed under a separate and differentiated heading) were exhorted, first of all, "Do not show

---

53. Data on female literacy are available in ibid., p. 6. Translation and discussion of the biographies appear in Albert O'Hara, *The Position of Woman in Early China*.

anger or worry in your parents' sight."[54] Through educational materials like these, the Confucianists made their patriarchal value system accessible and familiar to the vast majority of Chinese.

The Confucianists did not rely for their success in this endeavor exclusively on the force of social sanction. Over time the *li* came to be incorporated into the imperial legal codes. The Confucian family and class system were the fundamental features of traditional Chinese law. The law served to codify and reinforce the basic authority principles of Confucian patriarchy. Patriarchal authority was officially recognized, strengthened, and occasionally implemented by the dynastic legal codes. Parents were granted nearly absolute power over children; a husband's power over his wife was scarcely less extreme; and the authoritarian powers legitimated by the codes became considerably more extensive during the later dynasties. Rights to corporal punishment extending even to death were central to the familial and social penal system. For example, one set of clan rules, the Family Instructions of Yen, advised: "If beating and anger are abandoned in the family, the faults of children will immediately appear; when punishments are not properly administered, the people do not know how to move hand or foot. To rule a family strictly should be the same as to rule a nation."[55] And the Chinese legal codes proceeded to specify the proper principles, causes, and degrees of corporal correction. The status of the parties and the intimacy of the relationship between plaintiff and defendant determined the nature and degree of criminal responsibility and punishment. Crimes other than theft were punished more severely when directed against family members. The more subordinate and intimate the transgressor, the more likely the guilt and the more heinous the crime. So, for example, a child was held responsible for murdering a parent if the parent committed suicide or died accidentally in response to anger caused by the child. A wife was guilty of murder if she accidentally killed her husband, but he could not be held responsible for her accidental death. More pointedly, parents-in-law were not responsible if they un-

---

54. Selections from the *Ledgers of Merit and Demerit* and *Meritorious Deeds at No Cost* are translated in Tadao Sakai, "Confucianism and Popular Educational Works," pp. 352–60.

55. Quoted in Ch'ü, *Law and Society*, p. 21.

intentionally killed their daughter-in-law while beating her, as they should, for disobedience.[56] The very definition of a crime was drawn in Confucian patriarchal terms. And while most classes of Chinese did their best to mediate disputes informally, the imperial legal system served to underscore coercively the patriarchal familism at the center of Confucian society. Fung Yu-lan, a neotraditionalist of the Republican era, exaggerated only slightly when he declared: "The family system *was* the social system of preindustrial China. . . . The state was an organization which might be called 'united families.' "[57] Identifying the Confucian polity as "united patriarchs" is closer to the mark.

CONTRADICTORY REALITIES

The "Inside Person's" Family ▪ It should be evident that the structure and values of the Confucian family were vastly less attractive from a woman's perspective than from a man's. The Confucian emphasis on feminine loyalty was a euphemistic prescription for absolute subordination of women to men. Margery Wolf has pointed to the sharp contrast in the Chinese family structure that the view from the female stance provides.[58] The dominant male perspective conjures up an unbroken lineage with power, property, and esteem passing in orderly and gradual fashion from generation to generation. From the female perspective, family structure appears dramatically opposite. During her lifetime a Chinese woman lived with at least two distinct, unrelated families—in her natal and marital homes. Instead of an unbroken lineage, the woman was not fully a member of any family at any time during her lifetime. She could not inherit lineal property.[59] Her name was not even recorded in her father's genealogy; and when she died, only her family surname was

---

56. Ibid., pp. 107, 115.
57. Fung, "Philosophy of Traditional Society," p. 25.
58. Margery Wolf, *Women and the Family in Rural Taiwan.*
59. Women could inherit movable property through the dowry. However, this and whatever subsidiary earnings a woman accumulated belonged to her present or future conjugal family. See Cohen, *House United,* for discussion of the significance of a woman's "private" money. It was possible for widows to attain de facto control over lineal property, but this arrangement was temporary and tenuous. For an illuminating vignette of a peasant widow who gained and lost such autonomy, see Alan Sweeten, "Women and Law in Rural China."

entered in the genealogical charts of her husband's family. Even then her remains had to await the death of her husband before they could be granted their final resting place. Wolf has described the Chinese woman's family as a "uterine family,"

> a contemporary group that comes into existence out of a woman's need and is held together insofar as she has the strength to do so. . . . The uterine family has no ideology, no formal structure, and no public existence. It is built out of sentiments and loyalties that die with its members, but it is no less real for all that.[60]

In countless additional ways woman's subject status in the Confucian family was made clear. She was officially subject to "the three obediences": to her father in her youth, to her husband in her marriage, to her son in her widowhood. Indeed her social status legally as well as economically depended, in turn, upon the position of each of these masters. Fidelity to the patrilineage was the central virtue demanded of a woman because her chief function in life was to provide her husband's lineage with male heirs. Temptations to transgress that could be controlled were removed from her path. From the middle years of childhood on, the sexes were socially segregated. Sex segregation was carried to such extreme symbolic length that husbands and wives were admonished not to hang their clothes on the same rack.[61] As fully as circumstances would allow, women were secluded and confined to the innermost compartments of the domestic sphere. Thus, *nei jen* (inside person) came to be the common term for woman, and a traditional Chinese character for wife was a figure with a broom.[62] Exclusion of women from public life, implemented structurally by denying them access to education or eligibility for the examinations, was considered essential for the preservation of social stability and civilization itself:

> If women are entrusted with tasks involving contact with the outside, they will cause disorder and confusion in the Empire, harm and bring shame on the Imperial Court, and sully sun and moon. . . . The Book of Documents cautions against the hen an-

---

60. Margery Wolf, *Women and Family*, p. 37.
61. R. H. Gulik, *Sexual Life in Ancient China*, p. 45.
62. Ch'ü, *Law and Society*, p. 103. Ch'ü claims that this character also meant "to serve" or "to submit."

nouncing dawn instead of the cock, the Book of Odes denounces a clever woman overthrowing a state.[63]

Chastity was the crucial expression of female fidelity. The Confucians made a veritable cult of the chaste widow, with patrilineal clans spending more money and effort to erect monumental arches in her honor after death than they spent to support her when alive.[64] For a woman's life was of less value to the lineage than her virtue. When her chastity was threatened, even by a rapist, suicide was not too extreme a measure to adopt in its defense.[65] Within the family, however, virtue was appraised on a different scale. A father-in-law could rape his daughter-in-law with impunity, and a female slave was virtually her master's sexual prey.[66]

Patriarchal brutality was legitimate. Extensive, recurrent wife beating was reflected in popular proverbs, such as: "Women are like wheelbarrows; if not beaten for three days they cannot be used."[67] As prevalent was the beating of the daughter-in-law, most frequently by her mother-in-law, her virtual overseer in the family economy.

Footbinding is the most infamous of the uniquely Confucian variety of brutal patriarchal practices. "Golden lilies" or "lotus petals," as small feet were called, were an upper-class erotic fetish that took hold in the tenth or eleventh century and rapidly percolated down the status hierarchy. Three-inch lilies were achieved via a torturous process that mothers inflicted on their small daughters. When a girl reached the age of six or seven,

---

63. Yang Chen, a Confucianist of the latter Han dynasty (A.D. 25–220), as quoted in Van Gulik, *Sexual Life*, pp. 86–87.

64. Hui-chen Wang Liu, "An Analysis of Chinese Clan Rules," p. 47.

65. Exemplary tales from local histories illustrate this attitude. See Jonathan D. Spence, *The Death of Woman Wang*, p. 100.

66. Ch'ü, *Law and Society*, pp. 198–99; Hui-chen Wang Liu, "Chinese Clan Rules," p. 199; and Cornelius Osgood, *Village Life in Old China*, pp. 135–36.

67. Quoted in Jack Belden, *China Shakes the World*, p. 314. Direct evidence of wife beating is presented in most of the ethnographic and historical studies. See, for example, Smith, *Village Life*, p. 277; Margery Wolf, "Child Training and the Chinese Family," p. 42; and Delia Davin, *Woman-Work*, p. 76. Impressive indirect evidence can be gleaned by reading backwards from accounts of Communist campaigns to curtail wife beating. See, for example, Kathy Walker, "The Party and Peasant Women," p. 23; Belden, *China Shakes*, chap. 42; William Hinton, *Fanshen*, p. 51; and Isabel Crook and David Crook, *Revolution in a Chinese Village*, p. 105.

her toes were forced down toward the soles of her feet, which then were bandaged under pressure designed to bring the heels and soles as near one another as possible. Every few days the bindings were replaced with tighter ones, until the desired shape and size were attained.[68] Footbinding was an extraordinarily painful and crippling process, which many female children resisted bitterly and which none forgot. One result was a woman's inability to take any but the tiny, minced steps that produced the lilting gait so admired by Confucian men. Indeed, this constraint on female movement was one of the benefits of footbinding appreciatively noted by Confucian patriarchs: "Why must the foot be bound? To prevent barbarous running around."[69] One girl out of ten may have died of infectious aftereffects,[70] and all were permanently disabled; Chinese parents felt this to be a necessary price to pay.

It strikes the contemporary viewer as remarkable that this was the opinion of the vast majority of traditional Chinese. Prior to the twentieth century, in most regions of China footbinding was a nearly universal practice that transcended the boundaries of social class. The major exceptions occurred among certain ethnic and social minority groups: the Hakkas, the Manchus, the boat people, and the hill tribes.[71] To be sure, footbinding was less prevalent and less extreme where women did extensive agricultural work, notably in the double-cropping rice regions of the South. But there was no linear relationship between the extent or extremity of footbinding and social class or productive activity. In fact, it has been estimated that 14 percent of the women who did farm work had their feet so tightly bound that they were compelled to work in the fields on their knees.[72]

Footbinding provides one of the more extreme examples in the world's vast historical catalog of patriarchal aesthetic perversions that have been allowed to dominate the interests of class, health, and female welfare. It is legitimate to inquire why mothers—especially peasant mothers—would subject their

---

68. Howard Levy, *Chinese Footbinding*, is the most comprehensive source on this subject.

69. Quoted in ibid., p. 41.

70. Samuel Couling, *The Encyclopaedia Sinica*, p. 187.

71. Ibid., p. 86; and Howard Levy, *Chinese Footbinding*, p. 54.

72. John L. Buck, *Land Utilization*, p. 292.

daughters to such a cruel and crippling procedure? The existence of a structurally open system of class mobility and intermarriage in China is probably a crucial factor in the explanation.[73] Because small feet became a prerequisite attribute of a desirable bride, a mother concerned for her daughter's welfare would wish to provide her with these as potential collateral for a higher status marriage. On the other side of the marriage transaction, a prospective mother-in-law whose own future depended upon the status of her son had an important stake in acquiring for him a bound-foot bride. Moreover, such behavior would have been encouraged by the inherently hypergamous pressure of the patriarchal practice of polygamy. Men of the wealthier classes could afford more women, and they would require all of the women to come equipped with the beloved lotuses. Then, women, who tended to marry up the status hierarchy, put pressure on ever-lower-ranking families to prepare their daughters for such an opportunity.

Evidence for both these points can be found in the record of traditional Chinese marriage restrictions and practices. The "mean people," who were forbidden to intermarry with commoners or officials, were also forbidden to bind the feet of their women.[74] On the other end of the status scale, intermarriage was prohibited between the Manchu and the Chinese. It is striking, therefore, to note that when the conquering Manchu worked out intercultural arrangements with the defeated Han, they agreed to prevent their own women from binding their feet.[75]

As for hypergamy, clan rules contained in some of the Chinese genealogies from the Ch'ing dynasty and later advise members that "a wife should come from a family of slightly lower position and a daughter should be married off to a family of slightly better circumstances."[76] This, the patriarchs reasoned, was a way to enhance household harmony by keeping married women sat-

---

73. Frederic Wakeman, Jr., suggested this explanation to me in a personal discussion. Elisabeth Croll presents a similar analysis in *Feminism and Socialism in China*, pp. 18–19. This view is compatible with an intriguing analysis of the relationship between patriarchal control of female sexuality and hypergamous marriage systems offered by Sherry B. Ortner, "The Virgin and the State."

74. Ch'ü, *Law and Society*, pp. 130–31, n.

75. Van Gulik, *Sexual Life*, p. 335.

76. Quoted in Hui-chen Wang Liu, "Chinese Clan Rules," p. 40.

isfied. For, as all who bothered to think about it could hardly help but see, there was precious little else in the Confucian family system that worked in this direction. The most graphic indices of the extreme cultural devaluation of women in Confucian China can be found in the imperfect, but unequivocal, data on the prevalence of female infanticide, mortality, and suicide. Female suicide was a dominant, cultural motif in the literature and lore of old China. It was almost the single recourse to brutality available to a Chinese woman. Because a married woman's suicide brought her husband's family public disgrace and, at times, retribution by her natal kin, it offered an abused woman both vengeance and escape. Evidence gathered by anthropological fieldwork in twentieth-century Taiwan suggests that suicide was particularly commonplace during a woman's newlywed years, clearly the most traumatic, lonely, and difficult period in a Chinese woman's none-too-carefree life. The young bride (usually between fifteen and seventeen years old) had to confront a sudden sexual adjustment for which she was typically unprepared, a household of strangers almost all of whom commanded her subservience, and inordinate pressure to contribute male progeny to her husband's lineage. Moreover, she was under the immediate authority of her mother-in-law, a woman whose only opportunity in life to exercise dominance was concentrated in this legendary tyrannical relationship.[77]

Disappointment at the birth of a daughter was occasionally reflected in the naming practice. Little Mistake and Little Unpleasantness were among the names Chinese peasant families gave to undesired daughters. More commonly a generic name for girl was used to avoid the superfluous difficulty of selecting an individual personal name for one who would leave the family in the end.[78] Because daughters were fated to leave the natal household, their presence was a luxury many families could not afford. This is the material underpinning to the frequency of female infanticide and the traditional imbalance in the Chinese sex ratio. Material and ideological devaluation of females were inseparable. Arthur Smith, a nineteenth-century missionary who

---

77. Margery Wolf, "Women and Suicide in China," and idem, *Women and Family*.

78. Martin Yang, *Chinese Village*, p. 124.

wrote one of the earliest Chinese village studies, noted this when he observed in an accurate, if patronizing, remark: "Could the birth-rate of girls be determined by ballot of all the men of full age, it is probable that in a few generations the Chinese race would become extinct. The expression 'commodity-on-which-money-has-been-lost' is a common periphrasis for a girl."[79] One should not overstate the case. Chinese society was too vast, complex, and differentiated to sustain totally any such generalization. There were many welcomed daughters and areas where female infanticide was unknown. There were even a few areas that traditionally reported an excess of females.[80] But the practice was frequent enough to be reflected significantly in population statistics.[81]

Females who did survive infancy faced the threat of sale by their fathers or husbands if circumstances were dire or, in some cases, if the moral dissolution of the man was advanced. Such unfortunates were vulnerable to sexual abuse and violence for which there was not even the normally inadequate recourse to the opinion of community or kin available to regular wives.[82]

---

79. Smith, *Village Life*, p. 326. In the village Smith visited in the late-nineteenth century, mothers admitted destroying 158 daughters and no sons. Support for their testimony is found in Smith's census data. One hundred sixty women bore 631 sons and 538 daughters; 366 of the sons (60%) lived past their tenth year, in comparison with 205 of the daughters (38%). Data on the traditional imbalance in the sex ratio are presented in Irene B. Taeuber, "The Families of Chinese Farmers."

80. This was true, for example, in the Shensi village Jan Myrdal visited after the revolution (*Report from a Chinese Village*). Ho, *Population of China*, p. 57, suggests that interregional migrations, particularly those associated with the pioneering of maize cultivation, may have been responsible for uneven sex ratios.

81. Data on age distribution by sex are available in Taeuber, "Families of Farmers." John L. Buck, *Land Utilization*, p. 388, indicates a higher female death rate in the North. Fukien Province was particularly noted for the practice of female infanticide (Freedman, *Lineage Organization*, p. 28). Ho, *Population of China*, p. 58, claims there were many areas in which families refused to allow more than one daughter to survive; G. William Skinner, "Family Structure and Politics in Modern China," presents qualitative material which supports this claim. Marilyn Young suggests appropriately, however, that a discussion of infanticide in imperial China must include an awareness that this was also a familiar means of birth control in feudal Europe (personal communication).

82. Smith, *Village Life*, pp. 135, 259, 295; Tawney, *Land and Labour*, p. 76; C. K. Yang, *Village in Transition*, p. 89; and Osgood, *Village Life in Old China*, p. 135. For a poignant biographical account of a woman sold by her husband, see Ida Pruitt, *A Daughter of Han*. A female slave was legally forbidden to resist sexual advances by her owner if such resistance resulted in injury to him. Thus, her choice was to submit or to commit suicide (Ch'ü, *Law and Society*, p. 199).

Poor families were not the only ones eager to divest themselves of the burden of rearing unnecessary daughters. Cultural devaluation of women was so strong that certain wealthy families adopted out their "excess daughters" to avoid the expense of feeding and dowering them.[83]

There are remarkably few limits to the catalog of the dehumanization of women implicit in the ideology and practice of the Confucian family system. Nor is there a dearth of evidence documenting women's despair. Coercion, as we have seen, was an essential buttress to the maintenance of the system. Yet, in itself, coercion is inadequate as an explanation for a system that survived two millennia, often with the active complicity of women.

There are those who maintain that all was not as bleak as the structure and ideology of Confucian patriarchy might imply. Women in old China, according to this argument, wielded significant power behind the scenes.[84] True, a few women of the largest, wealthiest families were able to wield significant influence through their management of enormous household funds and their control over a large, segregated community of female relatives and servants.[85] However, elite families were also far better equipped to seclude and control their women, and whatever powers the exceptional Chinese women wielded were not theirs by right but were delegated to them by men and circumstance. The imperial legal codes, for example, granted a mother the same authority over her children that their father enjoyed, but she derived this privilege from her capacity as a wife. Were there to be a conflict between them in the exercise of authority, the husband's will would always legally prevail.[86]

Conceding this distinction between power and authority, Margery Wolf has suggested that the perilous structural position of women was the very source of an unexpected degree of female

83. Arthur Wolf, "The Women of Hai-shan."

84. Varieties of this interpretation are presented by Smith, *Village Life;* Margery Wolf, "Chinese Women"; Pearl S. Buck, *Of Men and Women;* and O'Hara, *Position of Women.*

85. Rich illustrations of this wealthy women's sphere are provided in Tsao Hsueh-chin, *The Dream of the Red Chamber,* and Pruitt, *Daughter of Han;* in the first from the point of view of the mistress, in the second from that of the servant. Biographies of Chinese women, translated in O'Hara, *Position of Women,* provide further evidence of considerable domestic authority wielded by elite women. Hsui-chen Wang Liu discusses the topic in "Chinese Clan Rules."

86. Ch'ü, *Law and Society,* p. 30.

power.[87] Rudely thrust into a foreign, hostile environment at marriage and provided with no institutional support, the Chinese woman had recourse only to her own resources in her struggle for survival. Wolf contends these served the Chinese woman admirably. One of the more useful resources available to a woman was her anger (an emotion for whose development she must have needed little encouragement). Angry women were a threat because a quarrel with an unrelated woman was considered a bad omen; semimystical powers were attributed to women, who used them to good advantage, not infrequently achieving domestic dominance. Because the Chinese family was a miniature government, and because a girl's position within it was precarious, girls learned early the skills of diplomacy and politics, particularly through their responsibility for the care of younger siblings. Further, unlike upper-class women who lived in virtual purdah, peasant women were forced to participate actively in outside work and in the neighborhood, where they established a community of women who effectively shaped village opinion on local matters of interest and, most particularly, worked to reform undesirable domestic behavior.

Mainland village studies prior to 1949 provide evidence that supports this view of cultural awareness of female anger and of women's capacity to employ it in their own interests and, occasionally, against men. Osgood's 1938 study of Kao Yao, Yunnan, claims that the men who frequented the tea houses gossiped repeatedly about hen-pecked husbands. More pointedly, the villagers attributed the familiar outbursts of mental disorder in women to anger at their husbands. Behavior Osgood observed during the Torch Festival, one of the few culturally legitimated opportunities for the expression of repressed emotions, is revealing. During the event, a group of young visitors attacked the ethnographer's home with fire sticks, and most of the assailants were young girls. Osgood mused about the significance of that fact: "It was not clear whether that was so because they reacted more strongly when released from restraint, or because adolescent females had naturally more courage. Perhaps they just enjoyed burning men."[88]

---

87. Margery Wolf, "Chinese Women."
88. Osgood, *Village Life in Old China*, pp. 129, 260, 328. James C. Scott offers a sensitive, if sex-blind, cross-cultural analysis of such culturally sanctioned reversals, in his "Protest and Profanation."

There were also certain cultural beliefs, the existence of which is documented in the ethnographic literature in rather casual, even offhand fashion, which can be seen to have worked indirectly to women's advantage. They inspire feminist speculation, therefore, about women's manipulation of cultural symbols. For example, Osgood reported a taboo against women tending their sick husbands because it was feared that men might be endangered by the possibility of sexual arousal. One can only suggest that other interests than those of the ailing husbands were being served by such a taboo.[89] Similarly, Gamble's study of Ting Hsien, conducted from 1926 to 1933, reported a ban on the use of needles by women during the first month of the New Year.[90] Although fertility beliefs were likely the cultural basis for such a ban, it is apparent that it simultaneously provided women with a seasonal respite from the overwhelming burden of domestic tasks.

A more impressive, and explicit example of what Eugene Genovese has aptly termed the "dialectic of resistance and accommodation"[91] can be seen in Old Maids' Houses, an institution unique to the South, and particularly to the silk-producing regions of Kwangtung. In some cases, these were residential halls for formerly married women who had escaped from or been expelled from their husbands' families. A popular cultural explanation of the need for such residences was that the souls of married daughters were not allowed to die in the homes of their natal families. Their soul tablets had to find different altars.[92] In fact, the Old Maids' Houses were an aspect of the most important and intriguing example recorded of organized resistance by women to the Confucian marriage system. For nearly a century women silk weavers in rural Kwangtung joined nonmarrying sisterhoods, societies of Women Who Do Not Go Down to the Family. Their

---

89. This particular prohibition would have the dual effect of saving a wife from an additional burden of service while reserving the pleasures of this nurturant activity for the mother-in-law, who frequently resented competition for her son's affection from her daughter-in-law.

90. Gamble, *Ting Hsien*, p. 303.

91. Eugene Genovese presents an analysis of Afro-American slavery in the United States as a system in which subordinates attempted to transform privileges into rights. See his *Roll, Jordan, Roll*. Natalie Z. Davis suggests that cultural reversals that placed women on top in early modern Europe functioned as more than safety valves; they may also have encouraged revolt. "Women on Top," in *Society and Culture in Early Modern France* (Stanford: Stanford University Press, 1975), pp. 124–51.

92. Freedman, *Chinese Lineage and Society*, p. 57.

members tooks vows never to marry or never to consummate marriages their parents had transacted for them. The women lived together, buying their independence from their natal and marital families with the wages they earned weaving silk. These sisterhoods became infamous for female homosexual practices.[93]

All the forms of resistance, cultural manipulation, and spirit exhibited by Chinese women, who were the objects of severe repression, appropriately appeal to feminist sensibilities. However, there is a harsher reality to confront as well—the complicity of women in their own oppression. Even the most impressive female resistance, the nonmarrying sisterhoods, was escapist rather than oppositional. The sisterhoods provided select women of quite particular historical, geographic, economic, and religious circumstances with what was undoubtedly a deeply appreciated alternative to the worst ravages of Confucian patriarchy. But this was an option available only to the few; more important, even those few exercised it within the accommodationist framework that granted the patriarchy its hegemonic due. Through their wages they bought off natal and marital families alike. So valuable did their wages make them to their natal families that the families were at times willing to support daughters in their resistance to marriage. One may draw a parallel to the position of Afro-American slaves in the antebellum American South who were allowed to purchase manumission as a reward for faithful service. Moreover, with few exceptions, evidence of female power, and almost of female visibility, in old China recedes at the domestic threshold.

> When we discuss the household and the family, therefore, we cannot fail to take account of the importance of women. When we turn our attention to wider kinship units we may conveniently think of these groups as being composed primarily of men.[94]

---

93. I first became aware of these sisterhoods and their reputation for lesbianism when reading Agnes Smedley, *Battle Hymn of China*. A fuller and fascinating discussion is provided by Marjorie Topley, "Marriage Resistance in Rural Kwangtung." A variety of the sisterhoods survives today in Hong Kong. See Andrea Sankar, "Strategies for Aging Among Non-Marrying Domestic Servants in Hong Kong." Van Gulik, in *Sexual Life*, claims there was considerable tolerance of "sapphism" in traditional China, and that Buddhist convents were often identified as sites of loose sexual mores.

94. Freedman, *Lineage Organization*, p. 32.

Maintenance of such an oppressive patriarchy required not only coercion by its beneficiaries but also acquiescence, submission, and even active complicity on the part of subordinates. The literature leaves little doubt that coercion was a major buttress of the traditional social order, and particularly so in the case of female subordination. With her feet mangled expressly to restrain as well as to objectify her person, indoctrinated into subservience while barred from education, required to enter into a marriage arranged without her participation, and, most important, denied access to land or control over economic resources so that she remained in a state of nearly complete economic dependency, a Chinese woman had little objective stake in preserving the traditional order.

What stake she felt subjectively is a far more complicated matter. Margery Wolf's work on Taiwan and data from the village studies of the mainland supply an important corrective to any lingering stereotypes concerning universal passivity and subservience on the part of Chinese women. There are, however, two ways in which even these persuasive studies may overstate the case. In the first place, there is an unavoidable selective bias in the nature of the villages that it has been possible to study. Because fieldwork necessitates both access and a modicum of social security, most of the ethnographic material comes from contemporary Taiwan and New Territories, Hong Kong or the Southern coastal provinces, or the more commercialized areas of interior pre-Communist China. Yet, as we have seen, the status and maneuverability of women was generally greater in such areas.[95] Second, regardless of their validity, it is difficult

---

95. Ironically, the greater strength of lineage structure in the South gave women better recourse to natal lineage support against maltreatment in marriage. Fuller participation in agricultural and outside production work gave women greater opportunities to form female networks. According to Jack Potter, there are Southern legends about the existence of "Amazon armies," bands of female friends from a woman's natal village who would retaliate by descending on the village and household of a husband reputed to be tyrannizing his wife (personal communication).

Taiwan data are a problematic basis for sweeping generalizations about female power. Taiwan was a Southern province. Bound feet were uncommon; women participated widely in production and enjoyed an atypical degree of free movement and influence. This was particularly the case because by the 1950s and 1960s, when most of the studies were conducted, Taiwan had been subjected to significant influence from Japanese and American political and economic intervention. While

for iconoclastic arguments to avoid a portion of overcorrection, and the theme of the power of women within the traditional Chinese family seems no exception. The effort to lay to rest the myth of Chinese female docility is a valid one. Women in China, like women everywhere, have not simply worn their oppression meekly. However, it would be a mistake for feminists to deny the seamier side of the story—that, in the course of at least two thousand years of subjugation, considerable numbers of women probably lacked the ability, motivation, or opportunity to avail themselves of even the limited coping mechanisms the few wielded powerfully. Submission, docility, and even extreme self-denigration were likely far from uncommon female traits.[96]

It is reasonable to assume that Confucian patriarchy succeeded in legitimating itself as a system among most Chinese women as well as men. If impressive numbers of Chinese women resisted footbinding, arranged marriages, and martyred chastity with the limited measures at their disposal, at least equal numbers participated willingly and would have been disgraced and aggrieved if they were denied access to any of the rites of proper Confucian femininity. Instances are recorded in which daughters demanded the binding of their feet against the wishes of recently Christianized parents in order to escape social humiliation by jeering neighborhood women.[97] Many teenage Manchu girls bound their own feet in violation of the ban so they, too, would achieve the aesthetic ideal of Confucian feminine beauty.[98] Local histories include many accounts of extraordinary commitment on the part

---

it is possible that female community networks and adaptations, similar to those Margery Wolf discovered in modern Taiwan, held true across province and time, the burden of proof rests with those who would make this claim. Such hypotheses appear considerably less tenable when applied to the Northwest, which, because it was to become the region of the most important revolutionary bases, deserves at least equal stress. At any rate, it is important to stress the geographical and historical limitations of the evidence at hand. See, for example, Margery Wolf, *Women and Family.*

96. A similar argument about women's response to oppression is made by Sheila Rowbotham, *Women, Resistance and Revolution,* p. 127.

97. Croll, *Feminism and Socialism,* p. 43.

98. Howard Levy, *Chinese Footbinding,* p. 225. On the other hand, Margery Wolf discovered women who claimed to have bound their own feet to protect themselves after they heard that Japanese soldiers did not want women with bound feet because they could not march (personal communication).

of Chinese women to the ideals of wifely fidelity and widow chastity. Among the most extreme was the case of a woman, Liu, who insisted on going ahead with her arranged marriage to a groom she had never seen and who died before the wedding ceremonies were completed, and the case of the thirteen-year-old adopted daughter-in-law who hung herself rather than accept release from her marital obligations to a fiancé who had castrated himself after being slandered for an illicit relationship with a widowed sister-in-law.[99] Tales like these were likely embroidered, but they are too plentiful and too consistent to be entirely fabricated.

Although it strains contemporary feminist imagination to perceive any female benefits in the Confucian view of reciprocity between the sexes, such effort is essential if we are to reconstruct the set of cultural expectations, the sense of a woman's rights, that were embedded in the consciousness of presocialist Chinese women. The one that seems most important to consider is a woman's right to marry. The *Li-chi*, the Confucian book of rites, exalted marriage as the pivotal social institution. Van Gulik's account of the social consequences of this Confucian value is as illuminating as it is sexist:

> Every woman, however poor, stupid or ugly, could claim the right to obtain a husband. On higher social levels every householder was bound in duty to provide husbands for every one of the women employed by him, and among the lower classes and the peasantry the supplying of suitable mates to every single maid or woman in their midst was a communal obligation.[100]

The evidence suggests that traditional Chinese patriarchs and communities achieved a high rate of success in fulfilling this responsibility. During normal times, marital expectations among Chinese women were realized almost universally. The traditional imbalance in the Chinese sex ratio and the practice of polygamy meant that the right to marry was more assured in the case of Chinese women than it was for men. In addition, as we have seen, a Chinese woman reasonably could hope to marry into a

---

99. Spence, *Death of Woman Wang*, pp. 100–101.
100. Van Gulik, *Sexual Life*, p. 58.

family of slightly better circumstances than the one in which she was born.

The Chinese woman's right to marry may appear in retrospect as her right to be enslaved. Yet we must entertain the likelihood that most Chinese women regarded it instead as the necessary passage it provided to the only form of culturally legitimate security, respect, and power available to them—the opportunity to assume the role of mother, and ultimately mother-in-law, through which each could establish a uterine family of her own.[101]

To acknowledge the fact that women often willingly sustained the institutional and cultural forms of their own oppression is not to mitigate the critique of Confucian patriarchy, but to recognize the far less-tangible, but equally problematic, realm of social-psychological domination.

Family Fissures ▪ This discussion of the female view of Confucian patriarchy suggests that the family system was, in fact, replete

---

101. There is a second major right that Chinese women may have gained through marriage—a right to heterosexual satisfaction. This, at least, is the implication of Van Gulik's portrayal of traditional sexual beliefs and norms in China. He claims that popular Chinese sexual beliefs, which were articulated in sex manuals that were included in the dowry, viewed sexual activity as healthy and desirable, portrayed women as highly sexual, and enjoined Chinese men to satisfy the sexual needs of their wives and concubines. Moreover, these manuals instructed men to concentrate their energies on facilitating female orgasm while suppressing ejaculation. Van Gulik supplies the following quotation from the Li-chi to support his claim that sexual neglect of women was regarded as an offense: "Even if a concubine is growing older, as long as she has not yet reached the age of fifty, the husband shall copulate with her once every five days" (Sexual Life, p. 60).

The question of sexuality among the peasantry is a topic shrouded in such restraint that it is impossible for a nonarea specialist to evaluate. Van Gulik, Sexual Life, suggests that the Ch'ing dynasty intensified puritanical restraints and imposed extreme secrecy on this subject. A paucity of available evidence is contradictory. Margery Wolf argues rather persuasively that in rural Taiwan, at least, the sexual adjustment for the new bride was traumatic and that village women regarded sex as an onerous obligation (Women and Family). However, there is also a smattering of evidence of active heterosexual sex lives among widows, sometimes tolerated by their communities. See, for example, Spence, Death of Woman Wang, and Sweeten, "Women and Law."

with internal contradictions. The reality of traditional family life diverged markedly from Confucian ideals even for many of the most privileged members of society, men of the elite classes. The goal of a large, extended joint household that shared its resources, lived in harmony, and performed the ancestor rituals under the benevolent guidance of the patriarch was achieved by few. Generally, the *chia* did not extend beyond the stem family. Most family litigation concerned the division of a joint household,[102] because internal pressures drove it apart even before the patriarch was dead.

The basic contradiction that generally thwarted the success of the family structure prescribed by Confucian patriarchy was, appropriately enough, the one between the sexes. Maurice Freedman stated the problem succinctly:

> Of each Chinese family a full half has had or will have interests largely at variance with those of the other half. Every Chinese wife came by no choice of her own from some other family, being suddenly and irrevocably grafted as a wild stock upon the family tree of her husband.[103]

The Chinese bride had powerful reasons to wish for and to work for the division of the joint patrilineal estate that would establish her conjugal family in a household of its own. Joint households tended to display a particularly authoritarian form of patriarchy. The success of the joint household depended most of all on fraternal solidarity, and this was threatened by intimacy among the marital pairs. Hence, such families did whatever was in their power to encourage the former and discourage the latter. Fraternal strains were frequently displaced by the verbal or physical forms of wife abuse which the family actively encouraged. Joint households also practiced sexual segregation stringently, and their sexual division of labor was severe.[104]

---

102. Derk Bodde and Clarence Morris, *Law in Imperial China*, p. 102.
103. Freedman, *Chinese Lineage and Society*, p. 54.
104. Cohen, *House United*, pp. 198–99.

A Chinese woman had a material resource to assist in her campaign for a separate *k'ang*.[105] Her dowry and whatever private income she could earn or gather belonged to her conjugal family unit rather than the patrilineal estate. Moreover, she had the right to manage this money until the joint family divided. Thus a wife often maneuvered secretly and successfully to divert common family resources into this private fund. Such money served as the basis for the independent patrilineage she hoped to help her husband establish when he received his share of his family's partible estate.[106]

The sexual antagonism at the center of the Chinese joint family was expressed not only in hostility between spouses but also in two legendary conflictual relationships between women. Enmity between mother-in-law and daughter-in-law was so intrinsic to the family system as to be taken for granted. The mother-in-law was patriarchy's female deputy in the Chinese family. She was the immediate, unchallengeable supervisor of her daughter-in-law's work and life. She was the one to whom the new bride owed most of her direct service and obedience. Structurally, women in these family roles were locked in competition for the affection and loyalty of the son/husband. This caused many mothers-in-law to favor "minor marriages" for their sons, the adoption and rearing of a young girl to become a future daughter-in-law. Such marriages, although culturally disparaged, mitigated the threat a new bride could pose to a mother's relationship with her son.[107] But in the usual case, the animosity and competition between the women was intense. Everything a daughter-in-law could hope to gain through *fen-chia* (the division of the household)—status, authority, intimacy, and autonomy—would come

---

105. The *k'ang*, a Chinese oven that serves as cooking center and heated sleeping platform in the Northern provinces, was the symbolic and functional center of the Chinese domestic unit. Building a new *k'ang*, therefore, represented the decision to establish a separate domestic unit.

106. Cohen, *House United*, provides a detailed discussion of the significance and effect of this money. See pp. 177ff.

107. A. Wolf, "Women of Hai-shan," p. 100. A comprehensive treatment of the subject of "minor marriage" appears in Arthur Wolf and Chieh-shan Huang, *Marriage and Adoption in China, 1845–1945*.

at her mother-in-law's expense. Time and structural forces were on the younger woman's side.

Sisters-in-law were the second set of antagonists proverbially indicted for the failure of the joint family. Their legendary inability to get along with one another was attributed to female nature; but, as a sensitive analysis by Myron Cohen shows, structural conditions underlay their enmity. Each woman acted as her uterine family's agent in the competition for resources from the common estate. Although her daily labor served the interests of the compound family, the benefits her uterine family might acquire were affected by such factors as the varying numbers and ages of her children and the relative favor they and her husband enjoyed.[108] Sisters-in-law did their best, therefore, to exacerbate fraternal conflict as the most effective strategy to the one goal they shared— early *fen-chia*. As Margery Wolf observed, "The fact that very few joint families in Peihotein survive the marriage and fatherhood of a second son indicates the success of the sisters-in-law."[109]

In general, Confucian family ideals pitted spontaneous emotion against formal obligation. Indeed it has been observed that betrayal was built into the system. In every case in which emotional intimacy between family members was likely to develop, social obligation dictated conflicting allegiances. Thus, while a son was apt to develop a particularly close relationship with his mother, at an early age the responsibility for his socialization was transferred to his father, whose harsh discipline generally did little to win his son's affection. While a woman's entire emotional security was focused on her children, the children owed their primary allegiance to their father, who might well be her chief antagonist.[110] Even if a husband was emotionally inclined to

---

108. Cohen, *House United*, pp. 196–98.

109. M. Wolf, "Child Training," p. 53.

110. According to Margery Wolf, this situation led Chinese mothers to cultivate their "uterine" relationships: "In the midst of this family of strangers a young wife builds her own small circle of security, binding her children, in particular her sons, to her with the emotional ties that only a mother can weave"(*Women and Family*, p. 168). *The Dream of the Red Chamber* is rife with instances of female/child alliances against male kin. And Mao, himself, facetiously remarked to Edgar Snow: "There were two parties in the family. One was my father, the Ruling Power. The Opposition was made up of myself, my mother, my brother, and sometimes even the laborer" (*Red Star Over China*, p. 132).

favor his wife, filial piety demanded that he honor the wishes of her most frequent tormenters—his own parents. Little wonder then that even among the elite the ideal of the joint extended household was honored far more in the breach than the observance.

Peasant Family Realities · More striking than the digressions from ideal Confucian family life among the elite were the variations in family structure and female status dictated by regional and class differences. The major regional distinction in family practice was between the North and the South. Clans were stronger in the South, where they more frequently had the requisite corporate property base. But joint households and larger families were more typical of the North, a pattern correlated with the prevalence of private landholding described above. Average figures are not very meaningful, but for what they are worth they support this generalization, indicating an average household size of 5.5 persons for the North and 5 persons for the South.[111] The paradoxical relationship, noted above, of lower female status where patrilineage structure was weaker and, not so paradoxically, where women participated less in agricultural production was reflected in stricter seclusion-of-women practices in the North. There too, as we have seen, footbinding was more universally practiced.

Social class differences in family practice were, of course, the most important of all. The rough correlation between land, wealth, and family size has been noted. The structure and size of the family tended to contract as one moved down the class hierarchy. Rich and middle peasants might exhibit joint or, more typically, stem households, but this was rarely within the purview of poor peasants or farm laborers. Extended families with a flexible labor supply and pooled resources have proven themselves adept at adjusting to conditions of crisis and adversity the world over.[112] However, maintenance of an extended household over time re-

---

111. John L. Buck, *Land Utilization*, p. 369.
112. For a rich ethnographic account of the relationship between economic deprivation and domestic kin networks among American urban blacks, see Carol B. Stack, *All Our Kin*. The new social history of working-class immigrant families in the United States suggests a comparable pattern of "malleable" households. See, for example, Tamara Hareven and John Modell, "Urbanization and the Malleable Household."

quires the availability of resources adequate to support and take advantage of the presence of permanent workers in addition to those of the conjugal unit.[113]

In times of adversity—which, as we have seen, were recurrent in old China—some peasants could not marry at all. Economic pressures often delayed the marriage of poor male peasants whose families could afford to find them brides.[114] Rare was the peasant patriarch who could afford a retinue or even a single concubine to assure lineal continuity or to satisfy his romantic, erotic, or status fantasies. Predictably also, the despised, irregular forms of marriage were frequent practices of the poor. Poor men were more apt to have to accept the humiliation of a uxorilocal marriage, marrying into the family of the bride. And poor families, because they lacked the resources to support the expensive ceremonial and gift exchanges required for a proper Confucian marriage, had compelling economic incentives to resort to minor marriages for their offspring.[115]

Widow remarriage, too, was inversely related to social class. For one thing, the family of her dead husband was less likely to be able to support his widow without the contribution of his labor. Perniciously, the Ch'ing legal code inadvertently gave a family a positive pecuniary interest in remarrying a widow, even against her will. A clause designed to encourage widow chastity granted the dead husband's family the right to appropriate a widow's dowry if she violated the restriction on widow remarriage. Local histories dutifully record hoary instances of the predictable result—widows harrassed into undesired marriages and stripped

---

113. For a cross-cultural discussion of this phenomenon, see Eric Wolf, *Peasants*, p. 65, and Joel S. Migdal, *Peasants, Politics, and Revolution*.

114. In his study of Ting Hsien, Gamble found a close relationship between a family's economic status and the age of their sons at marriage (*Ting Hsien*, p. 7).

115. There were also dramatic regional and local variations in the incidence of "minor marriage." G. William Skinner hypothesizes that an unusually long period of economic catastrophe in the Southeastern provinces during the late imperial era may have led to a routinization of the practice there, which ultimately granted regional legitimacy to the cultural deviation. "Custom," Skinner suggests, "made a virtue of necessity." See his "Regional Systems in Late Imperial China," pp. 12–18. The meticulous study of this subject by Wolf and Huang, *Marriage and Adoption*, makes clear, however, that the relationship between poverty and the practice of "minor marriage" was quite complex.

of their property. Some poor families even succeeded in collecting money, a second bride-price, by forcing a widow to remarry.[116]

In general, the miserable circumstances of the poor denied them the luxury of the full realization of Confucian patriarchy. This, we will see, bequeathed a complicated legacy to a revolutionary process that was to have for its mass base the Chinese peasantry. Poorer families brought to the revolutionary situation a history of less discrimination of their members by sex and age. They brought, too, a history of family structure in which the husband/wife relationship was stronger due to less likelihood of joint households, the clear value of the wife's labor, the inconvenience of the proprieties of avoidance (some married couples were so impoverished they were forced to share the use of a single pair of winter trousers), and the bonds created by sharing hardship.[117]

Economic adversity similarly played havoc with Confucian ideals of geographic and generational continuity and stability. There is a long history of massive interregional migrations in China, some of which were actually directed by the state.[118] Most interregional migrations were "voluntary" responses to the exigencies of famine, military conflict, and rampant banditry. Family separations of length and distance were common among the poor in old China. The poor traveled near and far for seasonal and for long-term employment.[119] A grievous form of family separation was the sale of wives and, more frequently, the sale of daughters (at the worst of times, sons were sold too) among the poor. They would sell their children before mortgaging their land, so irrevocable was the decline entailed by loss of land. And, of course, death—through childbirth, high infant mortality, and lower life expectancy—in China, as elsewhere, was the fact

---

116. Spence, *Death of Woman Wang*, p. 72, and Hui-chen Wang Liu, "Chinese Clan Rules," p. 46.

117. On the comparative strength of the husband/wife relationship among the peasantry, see Freedman, *Lineage Organization*, p. 47, and Hsu, *Under the Ancestors' Shadow*, p. 251.

118. A comprehensive, informative source is Ho, *Population of China*.

119. G. William Skinner suggests that in many areas affluent lineages also used migration as a mobility strategy, by developing a lineage career specialty and deploying male kin to propitious locations that were geographically dispersed ("Mobility Strategies in Late Imperial China").

of life that made a mockery of the Confucian ideal of large, multigenerational families among the poor.[120]

IMPLICATIONS OF THE CONFUCIAN FAMILY SYSTEM FOR A REVOLUTIONARY SITUATION

The preceding discussion of the ideology and the customary reality of the Confucian family system provides the necessary context for comprehending the structure of motivations, grievances, ideals, aspirations, and fears which the presocialist crisis situation would intensify, and, therefore, with which the revolutionary process would have to contend. It is the baseline of customary standards against which the crisis would be perceived, and, thus, against which the achievements and transformations of the revolution would later be evaluated. It allows us to appreciate the resources, impediments, and challenges the family system bequeathed to revolutionaries. I conclude this chapter by underscoring important aspects of this legacy and then, to further my point about the centrality of the patriarchal family system, I suggest ways in which the family system itself contributed to the eruption of the agrarian and political crises that became the revolutionary crisis. I will reserve a fuller discussion of the legacy of the pre-Communist family system for chapter 3, following the documentation and discussion of the crisis itself.

We have seen that Confucian patriarchy, an exceptionally authoritarian and explicit variety of patriarchy, was the hegemonic family system of presocialist China. Although Taoism, Buddhism, and the practical requirements of everyday peasant life modified and compromised Confucian doctrine, they did not present a fundamental challenge to the ethics or authority structure of the Confucian family. Perhaps this was because many Confucian virtues were elite elaborations of widespread peasant attitudes.[121]

120. Data on sale of wives and daughters appear in Tawney, *Land and Labour*, p. 76. Illustrations and occasional discussion are found in C. K. Yang, *Village in Transition*, p. 89; Osgood, *Village Life in Old China*; Smith, *Village Life*; Crook and Crook, *Revolution in a Chinese Village*; Chen Han-seng, *Landlord and Peasant*, p. 95; and Bianco, *Origins*, p. 103. Tawney cites a variety of sources providing data on infant mortality (*Land and Labour*, p. 72, n. 1).

121. This is suggested by Hui-chen Wang Liu, "Chinese Clan Rules," p. 48, and implied by Mary Clabaugh Wright, *The Last Stand of Chinese Conservatism*, p. 308.

In part, the Confucian elite dominated by synthesizing elements of lower-class culture. Moreover, the authoritarian nature of Confucian familism deepened rather than eroded during the later dynasties.

We have also seen, however, that even in normal times the Confucian social order handicapped the peasantry severely in their effort to practice the family ideals they shared with the scholar-gentry. Class differences in marriage practices and frequency, in mortality, family stability, and integrity document a reservoir of unrealized cultural expectations among the poor. The precarious nature of traditional Chinese peasant family life and the dramatic gap between the cultural ideal to which peasants aspired and the reality their life circumstances necessitated are important factors to recall when trying to comprehend the nature of consciousness that the experience of Confucian family life emblazoned in the peasantry—the memories, fears, hopes, and desires they would carry with them into the revolutionary situation. It is reasonable to assume that for masses of peasants—particularly for male peasants—the realization of Confucian ideals, including certain of the basic patriarchal principles, would be among their dearest objectives.

However, it is equally appropriate to assume that the ideals and consciousness of the peasantry were by no means identical to those of the elite. The very different reality of their political and economic circumstances generated noteworthy cultural distinctions between the two groups.[122]

For the Confucian family, we can detect ways in which Chinese peasant experience generated familial ideals that diverged from elite ones. The peasant family's eternal attempt to be an inde-

---

122. James C. Scott's essay on agrarian rebellion in Southeast Asia, "Protest and Profanation," characterizes this distinction as a dialectical relationship between the Big and Little Traditions. Scott argues appropriately that elite ideals do not simply "percolate down" the status hierarchy, as many scholars have maintained. Rather there are good social and material reasons for such cultural diffusion when it occurs. Scott depicts a complex process by which the religious and political culture of the elite tradition is received and transformed by the peasantry into a Little Tradition of its own. This general framework is a theoretical advance over cultural-diffusion models. However, in the Chinese case, for the reasons I have discussed, Confucianism provided an exceptionally unified cultural universe. Thus, there was less of a discrete, self-conscious Little Tradition than has been documented elsewhere.

pendent unit of production, for example, implies a contradictory legacy, representing both isolationism and self-reliance: isolationism, a factor revolutionaries would have to overcome; self-reliance, a resource upon which they would rely heavily. Moreover, certain features of traditional peasant family experience implied more egalitarian social relationships than those carried by the elite Confucian tradition. The greater solidarity of the husband/wife relationship is one of these. Needs of peasant families led them to value strong, healthy women rather than the frail, cultivated lotus blossoms of Mandarin literature. Likewise, it is difficult to believe that peasants fully shared the disdain of the elite for manual labor.[123] The peasant family economy depended upon hard work and practical knowledge—clearly invaluable resources for the processes of People's War and economic development that lay ahead. Moreover, peasant families entered the revolutionary period with centuries of experience with informal systems of labor exchange and mutual aid. These, too, were important cultural resources for the cooperative economic forms that would develop under Communist leadership.

Hence the Confucian family, in its elite and peasant expressions, left a complex heritage for future revolutionaries. Revolutionaries could tap rich resources from the family experiences and ideals of the peasantry. These resources were supplemented by experiences shared by elite and poor practitioners of Confucian familism. The reservoir of dissatisfaction which patriarchy opened in the souls of women and youth of both sexes was a potent source of energy for mobilization, but one that could draw blood on both edges of the dagger. Confucian families, like families almost everywhere, also housed the invisibility, undervaluation, and flexibility of female labor that has proven to be an invaluable resource for social processes of capital accumulation, be they conducted under capitalist or socialist auspices.

The Confucian family legacy bequeathed obstacles to revolution as well. The power of the clans occasionally commanded loyalty across class lines. There were antagonistic sets of interests of women and men, young and old, mothers-in-law and daughters-

---

123. Nonetheless, Confucian cultural hegemony had effects here, too. Marilyn Young aptly reminded me that many peasants cultivated a single long fingernail in modified emulation of elite practice (personal communication).

in-law. There were cultural, psychological, and even physical restrictions on women's roles that would have to be overcome if women were to participate in mass struggle. Finally, it is important to take note of the significance of the regional differences in family structure and female status documented above. It is plausible that variations in tenancy patterns, family stability, and the sexual division of labor—to mention those most prominent—would keenly affect the content and success of revolutionary family and social policy as it was to be developed in the base areas.

The preceding concentrates exclusively on the heritage implicit in the Confucian family system—should and when it be claimed by a revolutionary situation. It remains for us to assess the extent to which the family system itself contributed to the development of a revolutionary crisis. Here, I wish to take seriously what I believe have been the, in general, rhetorical claims of students of the family, that the family is more than a dependent variable.[124] The traditional Chinese economy and society were no more or less dependent upon the successful operation of the Confucian family system than vice versa. The family, the economy, and the society were, as we have seen, one system. That system was a patriarchy. Hierarchical relationships of gender and generation structured the traditional familial and socioeconomic order. The patriarchal principles that governed such relationships were unusually hegemonic and explicit. This is the sense in which it seems appropriate to view the family system as making a causal contribution to seemingly broader social processes.

It is possible to push the point even further. I consider it fruitful to consider the possibility that the Confucian family system contributed to the development of the endemic agrarian crises in China, which under the new international circumstances of the twentieth century became a revolutionary crisis. This is a bolder, more difficult case to make, and the present effort is merely intended to be suggestive. I believe this may have operated in at least four ways.

First, the Confucian family system contributed to recurrent demographic crises. Partible inheritance, near-universal marriage

---

124. For example, William Goode, *World Revolution and Family Patterns*; Tamara Hareven, "Modernization and Family History"; and Neil J. Smelser, *Social Change in the Industrial Revolution*.

at an early age, patrilineal ancestor worship with its demand for male heirs—all worked to create ever more patriarchal units predisposed to maximize their reproductive potential. Exceptionally high rates of population growth and attendant pressure on the land were the result.

Second, Confucian family principles themselves generated land pressure and inhibited the development of technical solutions to the problem. Partible inheritance caused the fragmentation and diminution of land parcels into inadequate and inefficient farms. This tendency was aggravated by Confucian burial practices that honored ancestors with grave mounds placed in propitious locations, and therefore Chinese farmers had little incentive to use draft animals or to develop machine power for agricultural production. The scale of production was too limited to draw commensurate benefit from such investments of material or mental resources. It may be worth speculating about the extent to which this aspect of the family system served as a fetter on the development of the forces of production.[125]

Third, Confucian family practices contributed to the nature of class exploitation. The exorbitant expenses for ceremonies and gifts that were demanded by the extreme form of exchange of women and the suppression of the interests of the marrying individuals fed the endemic rural feature of peasant indebtedness. This, in turn, contributed to the growth of usury, which became a more lucrative form of investment than most others in the rural order. Furthermore, partible inheritance interacted with the Chinese peasant economy in a manner that motivated families to strive to increase their holdings of land and wealth so as to be able to pass down to each son an estate equal to the one his father had inherited. Within the Confucian framework, this was an act of family loyalty. Because partibility also generated intense competion over arable land, many rich-peasant and modest-landlord families turned to usury as an attractive form of investment. Evidence is too elusive and the matter too complex

---

125. This suggestion is quite a different point from the (untenable, I believe) notion advanced by certain scholars that the particularistic and diffuse nature of relationships in the traditional family bred forms of nepotism, and the like, that impeded development. See, for example, Marion J. Levy, *Family Revolution*, and C. K. Yang, *The Chinese Family in the Communist Revolution*. The claim is admirably refuted in Perkins, *Agricultural Development*.

to push this point far. However, usury, too, may have operated to fetter the development of the forces of production.

Fourth, the Confucian lineage system contributed to regionalism and recurrent political crises. A delicate balance was generally maintained between the center of government and its local authority, particularly in the South where lineage structure was strongest: "Lineages resisted government and relied on that very government for their ability to resist."[126] Maurice Freedman maintains that interlineage violence, governed by rules, was an important, long-term feature of social life in Southeast China. Ruling a vast nation—which lacked adequate transportation and communication systems—with too thin a ruling stratum, the mandarinate was forced to rely on regional powers:

> State and people were locked together in a system; the State promoted centers of local power to which it looked for support and from which it could expect defiance. For most of the time, lineage organization was in the eyes of the State a good thing. In its best form it was eminently Confucian; it fostered scholarship; it taught obedience. But let it go a shade beyond high utility and the good thing was a very bad thing indeed. Suddenly local power was a menace, virtue became vice.[127]

Whenever the center lost its fragile reins—as it did once again in the nineteenth and twentieth centuries—centrifugal forces were unleashed by the lineage system that had the potential to generate social and political chaos.

None of this is an attempt to claim that the family *caused* the Chinese revolution. Such a position would overcorrect deterministic treatments of the family and would reify the institution as well. However, it does seem convincing to claim that basic to the Confucian family system—which cannot really be separated from the economic, political, or social structure of old-regime China—were patriarchal principles that contributed to the development of those causes of the revolutionary crisis which can be attributed to endemic Chinese processes. Of course, it took that unique combination of endemic and external factors that

---

126. Freedman, *Chinese Lineage and Society,* p. 95.
127. Ibid., p. 96.

intersected in nineteenth-century Chinese society to produce the revolutionary crisis of the twentieth century. Let us turn to a discussion of the familial manifestations and implications of that crisis.

3 The Crisis in the Chinese Family, the Family in the Chinese Crisis

The final half-century of Manchu rule (1860–1911) was by no means normal, from the point of view of either rulers or commoners. In the social, economic, and political disarray some saw familiar signs of dynastic decline; it was the turn of the Manchus to lose the Mandate of Heaven. However, this perspective was challenged by the presence of a new, historic force: incursions of Western and Japanese power, which were to integrate China irrevocably into a world political and economic order and thereby foreclose any possibility of the familiar cyclical dynastic solution. Internal and external developments combined to precipitate a political crisis that led to the fall of the last Chinese dynasty. The same array of domestic and international processes exacerbated conditions of economic adversity, which, given the Chinese peasant economy, developed into an agrarian crisis. Together the collapse of the imperial state and the agrarian crisis signaled the emergence of a revolutionary situation in twentieth-century China.

Discussions of the Chinese revolutionary crisis have centered on its political and economic causes and manifestations, and they have largely ignored the significance of family processes in the revolutionary drama. Students of family transformation in China, on the other hand, have been led by predominantly functionalist methodology to evaluate the effect of the revolutionary (or modernization) process on family structure and values. These analyses, too, have overlooked the significance of family dynamics for more general revolutionary processes. Yet, as I hope to demonstrate, a family system can have structural effects on revolutionary transformations. Moreover, if we are interested in the structure of experience and motivation that mediates social structure and human action, we ignore the dynamics of family systems at great cost. Too frequently analytic efforts in this area interpret social action entirely in terms of public issues or of private (and generally individualistic) economic interests. By shifting the level of analysis to the realm of family and personal life, where it is possible to identify the patriarchal dynamics that helped to shape the structure as well as the human significance of the Chinese revolutionary situation, we can grasp the dialectical relationship between social and family transformation.

This chapter indicates that the social revolutionary crisis in China was also a family crisis. Among American social scientists, "family crisis" is a familiar term—concern over the emergence of a family crisis is said to have inaugurated the subspecialty, sociology of the family.[1] Yet scant care has been taken to clarify the meaning of the concept. Arguments over whether or not the family is in crisis fail to specify criteria that might allow a meaningful discussion of the issues. Such debates generally degenerate, therefore, into disputes over the desirability of the changes in familial structures and behaviors perceptible to analysts.

Here I will use the concept of family crisis more precisely: a family system is in crisis only when its material and ideological foundations have been irreversibly undermined. Not only must family life appear to participants to be in alarming disarray, but, more importantly, there can be no possibility of an authentic restoration of the precrisis family system. In this context of decay, politicized forces are arrayed around competing family ideologies and programs. One (or none) of these forces may succeed eventually in establishing the principles of a new hegemonic family order. Family crises are as readily suppressed or displaced as they are resolved. But the existence of a family crisis is a precondition of family revolution, a radical reconstruction of a family system in terms that alter its relationships of gender, generation, and social integration.

---

1. Christopher Lasch, *Haven in a Heartless World,* chap. 2.

By the dawn of the twentieth century the material and ideological foundations of Confucian patriarchy were damaged beyond repair, and the Confucian family system entered the revolutionary period in the midst of a crisis. As I suggested in chapter 2, Confucian patriarchal processes themselves had helped to generate the agrarian and political crises of late imperial China. These crises, in turn, came to be manifested in signs of family decay that were perceptible and alarming to contemporary observers and participants. Because Confucian society so thoroughly submerged the individual within the family, the Chinese experienced and interpreted the agrarian and political crises through a familial filter. Thus public challenges to Confucian principles of gender and generation soon entered the arena of revolutionary politics.

Confucian patriarchy's loss of cultural hegemony was crucial to the revolutionary situation in twentieth-century China. Disintegration of the Confucian state bifurcated the previously integrated elite and peasant culture; the social classes experienced family crisis in significantly different ways. The more familiar family crisis concerned modern educated youth who launched a sustained attack on Confucian patriarchy during the May Fourth Movement of the 1910s and 1920s. A less familiar but ultimately decisive family crisis occurred among the peasantry. Peasant families experienced a "realization crisis,"[2] an alarming decline in their capacity to realize proper Confucian family life, or any family life at all. This chapter documents and analyzes the dual family crisis and explains its significance for the revolutionary process that lay ahead.

ELITE FAMILY CRISIS

The Confucian social system was gradually undermined during the nineteenth century. Unprecedented domestic and imperialist pressures strained the Ch'ing dynasty beyond its capacity to restore the traditional Confucian order. During the 1860s, Manchu rulers took advantage of their defeat of the massive Taiping rebellion to attempt a Confucian restoration, which Mary Wright

---

2. The term "realization crisis" has been used by Marxists to describe a particular form of economic crisis in capitalist societies; see, for example, Paul M. Sweezy, *The Theory of Capitalist Development*, pp. 156ff.

aptly termed *The Last Stand of Chinese Conservatism.* However, no restoration could succeed. Victory over the rebels had cost the imperial regime dearly, and the British victory in the mid-nineteenth-century Opium Wars was to the historic point, forcibly parting the dynastic curtain to admit foreign traders, industrialists, diplomats, customs officials, militarists, and missionaries. The final half-century of imperial rule brought fundamental social transformation, clearly perceived as such by many elements in the ruling class. When modern military technology defeated China once again in the 1895 Sino-Japanese War, even the imperial house lost faith in the superiority of classical learning and civilization.

Despite delays imposed by court politics, the conservative Empress Dowager soon overcame her opposition to reforms and launched the regime in a frantic, last-ditch effort to modernize China within a Confucian framework. Observers perceived the turn of the century as a period of unprecedented change. New institutions, including modern Westernized schools (a few of which were established to educate women), modern armies, and provincial assemblies, proliferated during the last decade of imperial rule. They accelerated the fragmentation of the formerly homogeneous ruling class by producing new bases for class privilege that were incompatible with Confucianism. The abolition of the Confucian examination system in 1905 signified and sealed Confucianism's modern fate. Mastery of filial classics would no longer provide access to officialdom.[3]

The imperial effort to preserve Chinese integrity—and itself— by grafting Western reforms onto a Confucian stem was hopeless. Confucian social structure was injured irreparably. The reforms quickened the disintegration by producing an antitraditional elite with decreasing ties to the rural or to the imperial order.[4] Final defeat of Confucianism came with the fall of the Manchu dynasty

---

3. For a comprehensive summary of social transformations during the last forty years of dynastic rule in China, see Marianne Bástid-Bruguiere, "Currents of Social Change." Meribeth E. Cameron presents detailed information on the Manchu reform efforts in *The Reform Movement in China, 1898–1912.*

4. Mary Clabaugh Wright, *The Last Stand of Chinese Conservatism,* argues convincingly that an authentic Confucian social system is incompatible with industrial development. See Bástid-Bruguiere, "Currents of Social Change," and Joseph W. Esherick, *Reform and Revolution in China,* for analyses of how reforms weakened urban-rural ties and increased urban privilege at rural expense.

in the 1911 Republican revolution. The year 1911 marked the end of a unified state and society in China. The rapid failure of Chinese republicanism that ensued plunged society into a revolutionary crisis, a period of political, economic, and social chaos in which regional warlords, politicians, revolutionaries, and counterrevolutionaries competed to dominate the decapitated nation. Full success eluded all until the Communists took power in 1949, on a basis that was decidedly non-Confucian.

The decline of the Confucian social system undermined the centrality of the Chinese family to the social order. Confucian patriarchy lost its role as the integrating doctrine of state and family structure. With filiality no longer the prescribed route to state service and social mobility, with Western education—both in China and abroad—exposing elite youth to Western family values, erosion of the status of traditional Confucian family life is not surprising. Contemporaries widely shared the view that traditional family practices were declining as well. It is impossible to ascertain the extent of family changes that occurred, but under the circumstances even modest or conventional behavioral shifts took on new portentous meaning.

Many traditional scholar-gentry families fell from wealth and prominence to poverty and obscurity during the final decades of imperial rule. Although the number may not have been greater than in ordinary times, commensurate numbers did not rise to replace them through traditional Confucian channels. Then administrative reform in the imperial bureaucracy further undermined ancestor worship within the ruling class by abbreviating the leave time for an official to mourn a parent's death. Traditionally the requisite three-year period of Confucian mourning for the death of a parent necessitated an official's return to his family property for an extended residence. This had reinforced the imperial bureaucracy's ties to the rural foundations of society. Curtailment of this practice helped to alienate urban and ruling elites from the countryside and furthered broader processes of social disintegration.[5]

By the early decades of the twentieth century, Chinese leaders and intellectuals perceived signs of family instability everywhere. They believed that lineages were losing strength and growing

---

5. Bástid-Bruguiere, "Currents of Social Change," pp. 567–69.

corrupt, and they worried that this adversely affected social welfare and cohesion.[6] Although periodic decay was an inherent, perennial feature of Chinese lineal structure,[7] many Republican elites shared the view of Chen Han-seng, that "in this general situation, the decline of the clan may be regarded as the outstanding symptom of a social disintegration to which all ancient institutions must in turn succumb."[8] Elites expressed alarm as well over what they perceived to be rising rates of divorce, desertion, wife murder, and suicide. Many attributed marital instability to disparities in outlook between Western-educated young men and the traditional brides their families chose for them. Or they pointed to women's expanding access to economic independence through the growing respectability of female employment. The increased incidence of suicide among the middle aged and, particularly, among older men seemed a consequence of the dislocating pressures the elderly experienced as Confucian patriarchy declined.[9] Those, like Fung Yu-lan, who mourned the family system's passing perceived— correctly, I believe—its incompatibility with the social processes accompanying industrialization: "Modern industrialism is destroying the traditional Chinese family system and thereby the traditional Chinese society." Writing in the 1930s, Fung recorded a widely shared perception among Chinese elites that the demise of the traditional family was irreversible: "Now it ceases to be a question of argument. People realize that they simply cannot keep it, even if they want to."[10]

In short, by the turn of the century the erosion of Confucian patriarchy had reached the stage of family crisis. There had emerged increasing numbers who did not wish to preserve it. The decreasing capacity of elite families to maintain the structures

6. See, for example, Martin Yang, *A Chinese Village*; C. K. Yang, *Chinese Communist Society: The Family and the Village*; Chen Han-seng, *Landlord and Peasant in China*; Sidney D. Gamble, *North China Villages*; idem, *Ting Hsien*; Olga Lang, *Chinese Family and Society*; and Hsiao-tung Fei, *Peasant Life in China*.

7. Maurice Freedman, *Chinese Lineage and Society*, p. 35.

8. Chen Han-seng, *Landlord and Peasant*, p. 39.

9. Discussion and illustration of responses to divorce, suicide, and female employment can be found in Roxanne Heater Witke, "Transformation of Attitudes Towards Women During the May Fourth Era of Modern China," pp. 199–200; Marion J. Levy, Jr., *The Family Revolution in Modern China*; Lang, *Chinese Family*; and Martin Yang, *A Chinese Village*, p. 116.

10. Yu-lan Fung, "The Philosophy at the Basis of Traditional Chinese Society," pp. 18, 19.

and values of Confucian family life facilitated a full-scale ideological attack on its basic principles. A critique of the Confucian family system was initiated in the 1890s by reformist intellectuals, such as K'ang Yu-wei, who sought thereby to preserve Confucian civilization. However, the general intellectual and social climate, fostered by their utopian writings and the incremental reforms they inspired, nourished a generation who subverted these intentions. Modern educated youth of the May Fourth Movement transformed the family critique into a radical indictment of the entire Confucian order. This process produced a distinctive Chinese version of radical feminism that preceded and helped to formulate revolutionary politics in mid-twentieth-century China.

The Radical Critique of Confucianism • May Fourth radicals inherited from late imperial Confucian reformers the conviction that the patriarchal family was both the symbol and the agent of China's weakness in the modern world. The belief that China had been handicapped by its failure to develop all its human resources encouraged efforts to free urban elite women from the worst constraints of Confucian patriarchy. For example, reformers K'ang Yu-wei and Liang Ch'i-ch'ao appealed for an end to footbinding on nationalist grounds. Liang thought the practice made China "the laughing-stock of nations,"[11] and K'ang agreed that "there is nothing which makes us objects of ridicule so much as footbinding."[12] Even worse, mothers with bound feet produced weak progeny: "With posterity so weakened, how can we engage in battle? I look at Europeans and Americans, so strong and vigorous because their mothers do not bind feet and therefore have strong offspring. Now that we must compete with other nations, to transmit weak offspring is perilous."[13] Although earlier antifootbinding efforts by the Manchu or by Christian missionaries had met with little success, the new circumstances weakened xenophobic opposition to the reform. Antifootbinding societies proliferated during the last decade of Manchu rule. Yet these were rarely initiated by Chinese women. Chinese men who joined the societies and swore never to marry bound-foot women played

---

11. Quoted in Witke, "Transformation of Attitudes," p. 28.
12. Quoted in Howard S. Levy, *Chinese Footbinding*, p. 72.
13. Ibid.

the crucial role in eliminating the practice.[14] In 1902 imperial edicts outlawed footbinding. Thereafter the thousand-year-old custom rapidly declined among the families of the urban elite.[15]

A similar nationalist logic facilitated the drive for women's education, which furnished China's first generation of public female leaders. Reformers had argued that ignorant mothers *Women's* reared weak sons and, thereby, a vulnerable nation.[16] The Chinese *Education* women who pioneered entry into the public sphere during the first decade of the twentieth century turned this sentiment to their advantage. Claiming that national salvation depended upon the strength of mothers, the makers of citizens, they built women's schools and a women's press, entered the public labor force, campaigned militantly for political rights, and even formed military units that participated in the 1911 revolution.[17]

The May Fourth generation also inherited from the reformers a critique of the authoritarianism of Confucian patriarchy, and this became the center of their radical political philosophy. K'ang Yu-wei and T'an Ssu-t'ung had assailed the oppressive hierarchy of the filial code, in which "those above . . . control those below," because it precluded personal fulfillment and was the source of social inequality.[18] K'ang composed a utopian tract that abolished the private family, replacing its social functions with public nurseries, schools, old-age homes, and the like.[19] But May Fourth youth attempted to construct their family utopia immediately, and on anti-Confucian foundations. The disillusionment with political solutions that followed the rapid failure of republicanism in China nourished a search for fundamental social transformation that made anarchism the most popular radical ideology among youth of the period. Chinese anarchists extended the reformers'

14. Elisabeth Croll, *Feminism and Socialism in China*, pp. 49–50.

15. Bástid-Bruguiere, "Currents of Social Change," p. 570.

16. Arguments of this sort by Yen Fu and Liang Ch'i-ch'ao are presented in Witke, "Transformation of Attitudes," pp. 28–31.

17. See Delia Davin, *Woman-Work*, p. 15; Helen Foster Snow, *Women in Modern China*; Croll, *Feminism and Socialism*, chap. 3; M. J. Meijer, *Marriage Law and Policy in the Chinese People's Republic*, p. 29; and Witke, "Transformation of Attitudes," chap. 2.

18. Charlotte Furth, "The Transformations of Time," pp. 125–27.

19. According to Witke, K'ang's tract was so avant-garde that it was not published in full until 1935 ("Transformation of Attitudes," p. 33).

critique by identifying the Confucian family as the source of all social problems.[20] One movement activist assailed the five relationships as an oppressive tool that had rendered China "a big factory for the production of obedient citizens."[21] Another excoriated the self-interest hypocritically veiled by the filial code:

> The father wishes his son to be filial and exacts this by fear and force, and the son becomes a slave and beast. So filial devotion is the father's personal gain. . . . The son wishes the father's benevolence only for his own benefit . . . and parents become "ox and horse to posterity." . . . So parental benevolence is the son's personal gain.[22]

Attack on arranged marriages

The primary object of their attack was the system of arranged marriage. Indeed, "free choice marriage" would remain the central plank in all future family reform platforms in revolutionary China. But the May Fourth family critique rapidly progressed in more radical directions. The call for "free marriage" led to demands for "free divorce." Soon the entire structure of Confucian patriarchal privilege was assailed, particularly the cult of chastity and the double standard of sexuality it enshrined. Some proposed an upgraded code of chastity based on the new morality of love. Others advocated free sexuality. Not surprisingly, in China as elsewhere, the sexes differed on this subject: radical men were more libertarian, while Chinese women concentrated their interest in sexual reform on eliminating polygamy and the exploitation of women as sexual "playthings."[23]

The Emergence of Radical Feminism • The anarchist commitment to "family revolution" was a natural breeding ground for radical feminism. Feminist revolutionary martyrs, such as Chiu Ch'in, a woman warrior executed in 1907, were among the anarchists' favorite models. Anarchists founded feminist societies and magazines by the score. Although the May Fourth Movement is known as a rebellion of new youth, also the name of the move-

---

20. Furth, "Transformations of Time," p. 123.
21. Wu Yu, quoted in Meijer, *Marriage Law and Policy*, p. 23.
22. Quoted in Furth, "Transformations of Time," pp. 127–28, n. 91.
23. A full discussion of the radical analysis and dialogue on chastity appears in Witke, "Transformation of Attitudes," pp. 123ff. See also Furth, "Transformations of Time," pp. 129–30.

ment's most prominent journal, more journals and articles were written for or about women than for or about youth. Most of the writing, however, was by men, who comprised the majority of radical feminists in China.[24] The most radical attack possible against the traditional family system was to assail its oppression of women, and therefore a critique of gender served young men in their own challenge to generational subordination. The logic of Confucian patriarchy made family transformation the primary idiom of political discourse and induced Chinese radicalism to assume a feminist cast.

Anarchists tried to implement their egalitarian, antifamilistic principles. Groups like the Conscience Society and the Chinese Socialist Party formulated codes forbidding members to marry, to affiliate with a religion, to hold office, to employ servants, or to ride in rickshaws or sedan chairs. Members pooled their economic resources, experimented with communal forms of living, and called for the establishment of public institutions to liberate women from domestic burdens.[25] In this manner, the May Fourth generation rapidly moved beyond the reformist attempt to catch up with Western marriage practices to the utopian goal of transcending marriage as a social institution. Inspiration for this leap probably derived in part from the radicalism of the contemporary, early-revolutionary period in the Soviet Union. However, the communism of the May Fourth radicals was anarchist rather than Marxist.[26] Family issues radicalized many of the future Chinese Communist leaders *before* their conversion to Marxism-Leninism. Mao Tse-tung himself was radicalized in this way. As a member of an anarchist study group, he took a vow never to marry. And before he learned to make class struggle the center of his politics, he issued a call for a family revolution:

> If we launch a campaign for the reform of the marriage system we must first destroy all superstitions regarding marriage, of which the most important is destruction of belief in "predestined marriage." Once this belief is abolished, all support for the policy of parental arrangement will be undermined, . . . the army of the

---

24. Witke, "Transformation of Attitudes, p. 331.
25. Furth, "Transformations of Time," pp. 144–47.
26. Charlotte Furth claims that before 1920 "communism" was understood in anarchist rather than Marxist terms ("Transformations of Time," p. 150).

family revolution will arise en masse, and a great wave of freedom of marriage and freedom of love will break over China.[27]

Charlotte Furth suggests that the emphasis on family revolution of the utopian anarchists led them to make "an un-Marxist claim for the transformation of personal life as a cause, rather than merely an effect, of other changes defining the revolutionary process."[28] In this respect they foreshadowed a major, and feminist, claim of the present study.

Chinese Anarchism w/ a Feminist Core

Although Chinese anarchism, with its feminist core, was the radicalizing crucible for many of the society's future revolutionary leaders, anarchism was rapidly overtaken by political developments. After the May Fourth era, family revolution never again appeared explicitly at the center of revolutionary politics in China. During the 1920s, ideological responses to the elite family crisis moderated, and feminism was subordinated to what came to be considered more basic and pressing concerns. By the 1920s, political revolution was once again the order of the day. The central government had collapsed entirely, and Chinese society entered the decade of warlord rule and international vulnerability that continues to be regarded as the nation's most humiliating period. Nationalist and revolutionary forces emerged, alternately competing and cooperating to restore national integrity. Many of the May Fourth anarchists converted to Marxism-Leninism and founded the Chinese Communist Party in 1921. Greater numbers, and many feminists among them, joined the Nationalist Party (Kuomintang), the heir to Sun Yat-sen's Revolutionary Alliance, which in the 1920s still claimed social revolution as its objective.

During the period of the first united front (1923–1927) between the Kuomintang (KMT) and the Chinese Communist Party (CCP), the bearers of May Fourth feminism accepted what Elisabeth Croll has termed an uneasy alliance with Chinese socialism. Attempting to translate their radical ideology into mass-based activism, they took advantage of the organizational umbrella provided by the allied parties. They established women's departments and unions, which sought to mobilize, first, proletarian

---

27. Quoted in Witke, "Transformation of Attitudes," p. 311.
28. Furth, "Transformations of Time," pp. 150–51.

women and, then, peasant women to the feminist and revolutionary cause. The price of this alliance was the subordination of feminism to priorities of nationalism and class-based revolution. It was a time of intense feminist activism and militancy, but one in which responses to the Confucian family crisis were moderated. The explosive nature of challenges to traditional familial and social order was apparent. Feminist revolutionary cadres, with bobbed hair and antagonism to marriage, often provoked hostile, even counterrevolutionary reactions among the villagers they attempted to organize. Both revolutionary parties attempted to impose discipline whenever expressions of feminist autonomy or radicalism appeared divisive, and both encouraged a retreat from radical feminism and family revolution.[29]

The united front was short lived. The success of the Northern Expedition of the Nationalists in 1926, which reunified a sufficient number of Chinese provinces to establish the semblance of a national government, was quickly followed by Chiang K'ai-shek's violent purge of his Chinese Communist allies. The reign of anti-Communist terror unleashed by Chiang also encouraged a particularly ugly antifeminist reaction. Bobbed hair alone was enough to provoke mutilation and execution. Communist women were spared none of the brutality of the extermination efforts, while the deeply patriarchal context ensured that the violence also would take a sexual course.[30]

The purge of the Communists divided Chinese nationalists into two warring camps proposing incompatible solutions to the national crisis. Now only one of the parties, the badly decimated Chinese Communists, was committed to social revolution, while the other, the triumphant Kuomintang, was determined to avoid it. Chinese feminism was thereby divided and redefined.

The Kuomintang, now more clearly identified as the party of the urban elite, promoted a set of feminist reforms of benefit to that constituency alone. The Family, Kinship, and Succession Books of the KMT 1931 civil code attempted to legislate a family system that was a compromise between modern Western values

---

29. See Croll, *Feminism and Socialism*, chap. 5, for a full discussion of feminism in the 1920s.

30. Details of the terror against women can be found in Helen Snow, *Women in Modern China*, pp. 136–37, and Croll, *Feminism and Socialism*, pp. 150–51.

and Confucian patriarchal principles. The law established the principle of free-choice marriage and granted women rights more equal to those of men in matters of divorce, inheritance, and property. However, it sustained patriarchal authority in instances of marital conflict and in the management of matrimonial property.[31] Although the law was not implemented vigorously, it ratified the prevailing family practices among the privileged urban sector that provided the feminist constituency of the KMT.

The KMT also sought to recast feminism as the ladies' auxiliary division of the national recovery effort. This revisionist KMT feminism reaffirmed gender as a basic, regulating social principle and directed women to assume their "complementary" and decidedly subordinate positions in the realms of motherhood, voluntary social service, and moral uplift. Finally, in the 1930s the KMT officially articulated its thorough retreat from feminism by introducing its most distinctive, and futile, response to the Confucian crisis—the New Life Movement.[32] This largely voluntarist effort sought to reestablish social and moral order through a restoration of Confucian virtues, now adulterated somewhat with those of Christianity. The major objective was to promulgate clear and correct rules of behavior "to help the people, to train them to take their rightful places in society, and to enable them to become useful citizens in a modern democracy."[33] Sung Meiling, the wife of Chiang K'ai-shek, who directed the women's department of the New Life Movement, made the promotion of successful and hygienic domesticity its most hallowed purpose. In short, as most feminist sinologists have noted, by the 1930s the KMT had transformed feminism into the feminine mystique.[34]

Having granted limited reforms to urban elite women, the KMT then denied the further existence of women's oppression. Moreover, the utter irrelevance to the rural order of either the reformist or reactionary components of KMT feminism doomed

31. Meijer, Marriage Law and Policy, p. 29.

32. Wright, Last Stand, pp. 340ff., presents an analysis of the general futility of the KMT New Life Movement.

33. Sung Mei-ling (Madame Chiang K'ai-shek), quoted in Croll, Feminism and Socialism, p. 159.

34. "The Feminine Mystique" is part of the title Norma Diamond and Elisabeth Croll each give to their respective writings on KMT feminism. See the comment on this coincidence by Croll, Feminism and Socialism, p. 153. Chap. 6 of Croll's book is a comprehensive treatment of the subject.

its attempt to reestablish elite cultural hegemony on a New Life basis. Thus, the KMT response to the crisis of Confucian patriarchy must be judged a reformist effort to limit concern among the elite, and a repressive effort to deny its very existence among the peasantry.

The Chinese Communists, forced into the rural hinterland, also moved to subordinate feminism and family revolution to wider social goals. But material conditions and the Communist ideological heritage assured that they would do so quite differently. Thoroughly repudiating the individualistic "excesses" of their anarchist origins, the Communists sought to eradicate the "deviations" of whatever remnants of bourgeois feminism survived among their urban-educated cadres. Cut off from urban society, there would be no feminine mystique in revolutionary Communist ranks. Now the elite family crisis could be safely ignored. Instead, residence in rural China brought the Communists face to face with the realization crisis in the peasant family. How the CCP and the peasantry forged the family revolution that resolved this crisis is the central story of chapters 4 through 6. The remainder of this chapter examines the nature and significance of the peasant family crisis.

THE REALIZATION CRISIS IN THE CHINESE PEASANT FAMILY ECONOMY

The Agrarian Crisis ▪ There is widespread, but not universal, agreement among China scholars that late Ch'ing China experienced agrarian decline, which became a crisis that profoundly shaped the revolutionary situation during the Republican period. Because most agree with Lucian Bianco that "China's basic social conflict was rural,"[35] those interested in the social origins of the Chinese revolution are compelled to focus on the agrarian crisis. Ironically, Ramon Myers summarized the nature of China's prerevolutionary agrarian problem concisely when he assembled the analyses of people he labeled "distributionists" in order to discredit them. His summary is worth quoting in its entirety:

---

35. Lucien Bianco, *Origins of the Chinese Revolution, 1915–1949*, p. 82.

Three major developments were taking place in the nineteenth century and continued on into the twentieth. There was persistent population expansion, which led to rural overcrowding and an increase in landless peasants. There was increased neglect of the rural economic infrastructure, the transport, irrigation, and flood control systems, through corrupt and inept bureaucratic management. And there was the existence of a landlord class which rack-rented the peasantry and tried to accumulate more land for itself. These developments interacted to produce rather alarming consequences for the rural economy. Land ownership distribution became more intense, and the landless peasants became an almost inexhaustible source of manpower for bandits and warlord armies.

By the end of the nineteenth century three new developments began to take place and slowly impinged on the rural economy. First, the import of manufactured goods ruined many handicraft producers and forced peasants to sell their land. Second, the export of agricultural staples came under the control of powerful native and foreign traders, who through credit and price control were able to exploit smaller traders and peasant producers. Third, the establishment of Western enterprise in the treaty ports through special exemptions made it impossible for Chinese entrepreneurs to compete on an equal footing. In the treaty ports, the Western enclave sector grew at the expense of Chinese enterprises, and in the economy proper, the treaty ports grew at the expense of the hinterland. The economy was gradually being twisted in such a way that the cities, rather than stimulating the growth of the more backward countryside, merely exploited the village economy. Instead of agricultural development, there was decline. Peasant living standards became more depressed, and the prospects for reform and a technological revolution in the countryside became more bleak. The rural economy merely reproduced itself in its own image.[36]

Three developments, in addition to the six outlined by Myers, aggravated the deleterious impact on the peasant economy. First, paternalistic customary relationships eroded. While these had

---

36. Ramon H. Myers, *The Chinese Peasant Economy*, pp. 23–24. Myers's more recent book, *The Chinese Economy, Past and Present*, retreats significantly from the scathing attacks on the arguments of "distributionists" presented in *The Chinese Peasant Economy*. Moreover, it presents considerable evidence that can be used in their support.

never been central, they had provided a margin of security to subsistence farmers. This safety net disappeared during the late-nineteenth and early-twentieth centuries, when landlords increasingly refused to grant tenants permanent or long-term contracts to provide them with seed or tools or to suspend rent collections when the harvest was poor. The new abuses encouraged by the rise of absentee landlordism were even worse. Landlords increased rents by manipulating collections according to currency rates and market conditions. The collapse of the Confucian state, the urbanization of the Chinese elite, and the concomitant rise of the power of local and provincial elites without roots in the traditional scholar-gentry class undermined those constraints on exploitation that had once been provided by the Confucian ethic of social and moral responsibility.[37]

Second, peasant families experienced increasing insecurity as they became dependent upon market conditions. This was the most disastrous effect on the peasant economy of the increasing commercialization of agricultural and handicraft production, to which Myers's summary refers, not the absolute increase in exploitation it may or may not have unleashed. The poorest families were the most specialized, and therefore, the most vulnerable. They were generally forced to sell when prices were low and to buy when they were high.[38] So minimal was their subsistence margin that the slightest price fluctuation could mean the difference between survival and dispossession, or even death. Moreover, the gradual integration of the Chinese agrarian economy into a world economy permitted worldwide market and monetary fluctuations to disrupt the precarious equilibrium of the traditional

37. Data and analysis on rents and landlord abuses are found in Bástid-Bruguiere, "Currents of Social Change," pp. 591–93; Esherick, *Reform and Revolution,* p. 67; and Albert Feuerwerker, *The Chinese Economy, 1870–1911,* pp. 12, 35–36. Analyses of the negative impact that urbanization of the elite had on rural economic and political relationships are found in Bástid-Bruguiere, "Currents of Social Change," pp. 579–600; Esherick, *Reform and Revolution;* and Philip A. Kuhn, "Local Self-Government Under the Republic." On the decline of customary rights, see Ralph Thaxton, "When Peasants Took Power"; Chen Han-seng, *Landlord and Peasant;* and Hsiao-tung Fei and Chih-i Chang, *Earthbound China.*

38. Albert Feuerwerker, *The Chinese Economy, 1911–1949,* p. 39, and Ramon H. Myers, "The Commercialization of Agriculture in Modern China," pp. 183–86.

peasant family economy. During the 1920s and 1930s, the acute crisis period, such fluctuations were extreme.[39]

Third, Myers's summary neglects to mention the natural disasters that wreaked increasing havoc on agricultural production in the late-nineteenth and early-twentieth centuries. Myers's recent book suggests the magnitude of these calamities:

> In 1918 a great drought swept the six northern provinces. It persisted for several years and eventually claimed a half-million lives and severely injured crops in 317 counties. In February of 1918 a great earthquake ripped Shensi and Kansu. In 1921, six provinces suffered great floods. In the following year a typhoon struck Swatow, and in the next year twelve provinces experienced both drought and floods. . . . Yunan suffered a tremendous earthquake and then great floods. Six more provinces were beset by crop pests, and floods churned the Yellow River region. The province of Hunan in 1924 virtually became an armed camp as military troops operated to prevent the smuggling of rice out of the province because grain had become so scarce. Hunan, one of the country's major rice bowls, actually ceased shipping grain to the lower Yangtze because of continual flooding and natural disturbances between 1921 and 1924.[40]

Such disasters were not new. They must, as Ping-ti Ho suggests, "be regarded as a normal rather than exceptional phenomenon in a country as large and as dependent upon the forces of nature as China."[41] What was new, however, was the severity of the toll they exacted. This, as most scholars have observed, was caused by social and political factors. Traditional patterns of famine relief had been badly disrupted, public granaries had fallen into disuse and misuse, and neglect of the rural infrastructure impeded

---

39. Albert Feuerwerker minimizes the significance of the impact of the world market upon the economy of Republican China, but he acknowledges that integration into the world market made Chinese handicrafts and agriculture vulnerable to the slightest mishap (*Chinese Economy, 1911–1949*, p. 66). Myers now stresses the vulnerability of poor families caused by their dependence on markets. He considers this an important contributing factor to the agrarian crisis. See his *Chinese Economy*, p. 179, and "Commercialization of Agriculture," pp. 183–86.

40. Myers, *Chinese Economy*, pp. 178–79.

41. Ping-ti Ho, *Studies on the Population of China, 1368–1953*, p. 230.

emergency grain transport, while banditry and warfare disrupted relief efforts altogether.[42]

Controversies Concerning the Agrarian Crisis • Several challenges to the preceding portrait of the agrarian situation have generated controversies relevant for the analysis of peasant family crisis to be presented here. I will briefly consider the three most important issues: the immiseration of the Chinese peasantry, the role exploitation played in their distress, and the viability of the economy during the Republican period.

Uncertainty lingers among China scholars about the validity of the view that Chinese peasants were increasingly impoverished during the Republican period. Myers's book, *The Chinese Peasant Economy*, claimed that peasant living standards suffered no general decline prior to 1937 and implied that there never was an agrarian crisis. Because this matter bears on so many crucial issues of historical interpretation, considerable debate and a detailed reconsideration of the available data ensued. The challenge was found to rest on a faulty reading of the evidence. Thus, the ironic effect of Myers's iconoclastic claim was to strengthen support for the immiseration thesis. Myers himself now reports the increasing impoverishment of the peasantry as an indication of a situation he, too, now labels as agrarian crisis and dates as early as 1920.[43]

---

42. Myers places emphasis on the role warfare played in disrupting famine relief (*Chinese Economy*, p. 178). Thaxton, "When Peasants Took Power," stresses the decline of paternalism and rising exploitation. Graham Peck, *Two Kinds of Time*, describes the extent of governmental corruption involved in relief efforts.

43. The primary targets of Myers's attack were Chen Han-seng, *Landlord and Peasant*, and R. H. Tawney, *Land and Labour in China*. A more recent staunch defender of the immiseration thesis is Thaxton, "When Peasants Took Power." The most direct and careful challenge to Myers's claim was prepared by Thomas B. Wiens in a review of *The Chinese Peasant Economy*. Albert Feuerwerker reported static income conditions prior to 1911, followed by an uneven, but worsening situation (*Chinese Economy, 1870–1911* and *Chinese Economy, 1912–1949*). Bástid-Bruguiere, "Currents of Social Change," dates the income decline earlier, during the last forty years of Ch'ing rule. Ho, *Population of China*, also reports declining living standards beginning the nineteenth century. Myers has revised his view on this issue (*Chinese Economy*, see especially p. 174). Even Thomas G. Rawski, the most virulent defender of the Republican economy, does not challenge this view. His paper, "China's Republican Economy, An Introduction," ignores the question.

While my analysis of the peasant family realization crisis employs data suggesting that peasant families experienced conditions of absolute immiserization as they confronted the revolutionary situation, it does not depend upon this point. Whether or not there was a steady, linear decline in aggregate income, most peasant families were increasingly vulnerable to political and economic conditions, which were more and more unstable. While certain peasants reaped material benefit from such developments, far more experienced these as life threatening. The salient point has been made by E. P. Thompson in summing up an analogous debate among British historians over the effects of the industrial revolution on the emerging British working class:

> Over the period 1790–1840 there was a slight improvement in average material standards. Over the same period there was intensified exploitation, greater insecurity, and increasing human misery. By 1840 most people were "better off" than their forerunners had been fifty years before, but they had suffered and continued to suffer this slight improvement as a catastrophic experience.[44]

Controversy over the role of exploitation of the peasantry in the Chinese revolutionary drama also has generated vigorous debate among scholars. Sinologists continue to disagree profoundly over how much exploitation peasants suffered during the Republican period, whether or not the rate of exploitation was increasing, and whether domestic or imperialistic agents were primarily to blame for whatever intensification may have occurred. What is at stake in these debates is the relative importance of social-political versus natural-technological factors in explaining the agrarian crisis.[45]

As I have suggested, the social and nonsocial forces that generated peasant distress are inseparable. Land fragmentation, for

---

44. E. P. Thompson, *The Making of the English Working Class*, p. 212.

45. Those who have emphasized rising exploitation include Tawney, *Land and Labour;* Chen Han-seng, *Landlord and Peasant;* Thaxton, "When Peasants Took Power"; Fei, *Peasant Life in China;* and idem, *China's Gentry.* The strongest attack on the exploitation thesis appears in Thomas Rawski, "China's Republican Economy." Intermediate positions, which temper recognition of worsening exploitation with demographic and technical dilemmas, include Ho, *Population of China;* Albert Feuerwerker, *Chinese Economy, 1911–1949;* and Bianco, *Origins.* John L. Buck, *Land Utilization in China,* is the classic proponent of the technical sources of peasant distress.

example, a "technical" factor, was primarily the product of the system of partible inheritance. Population growth, another "natural" factor, likewise had its principal roots in the Confucian family system. Natural disasters imposed more appalling consequences as social relationships deteriorated. More to the point, perhaps, was the way natural and social factors fused in peasant consciousness. Peasants interviewed in the late 1920s, for example, had learned to include "bumper crops" in their list of natural calamities because these reduced produce prices on the market in a manner catastrophic for subsistence farmers.[46]

Peasant consciousness is nearer the heart of the matter than most contributors to the debate have allowed. My reading of the literature leads me to believe that exploitation did indeed worsen in the decades before the rural revolution, but attempts to devise and verify a measure of absolute intensifying exploitation miss the crucial point.[47] The perceptible changes in the nature of social relationships described above altered the structure of exploitation. The social agents of exploitation multiplied as central authority and social responsibility disintegrated. There were more kinds of predators exacting more kinds of tariffs from a peasantry with fewer defenses. And this occurred in the context of ideological and political shifts easily identified by the peasants as alien. By the 1920s and 1930s the Chinese peasantry was experiencing its distress in conditions readily recognizable as exploitative.[48]

Predictably, disagreement about the primary sources of the agrarian crisis accompanies controversy over the possibilities for its resolution. China scholars have reproduced the debate that occurred among Chinese intellectuals and activists during the 1920s and 1930s—reform or revolution? Critics of the Communist revolution have defended the viability of the Republican economy. Were it not for the abnormal intervention of international military and economic pressures, they argue, economic development could

---

46. Sidney D. Gamble, *Ting Hsien*, pp. 3, 451.

47. This is the major conceptual error made by Myers and Thomas Rawski. They attempt to use tax and rent data to determine an objective measure of exploitation. They overlook questions concerning corrupt collection procedures and the proliferation of auxiliary taxes and surcharges.

48. Esherick, *Reform and Revolution*, documents the intermingling of antireform and antiforeign sentiments among the peasantry. Kuhn, "Local Self-Government," describes the new forms of predation. Myers, *Chinese Economy*, indicates that constraints on exploitation lessened, but he attributes this to the military situation.

have proceeded under Kuomintang auspices. Revolution was not a necessary solution to the agrarian crisis.[49]

The answer to the question about the prospects for KMT sponsorship of economic development rests largely on one's definition of development. Certainly the success of the Communist revolution was not determined by the existence of the agrarian crisis. Had the Communists failed, as they nearly did, the KMT would have attempted to sponsor economic development through nonrevolutionary means. Like the CCP, the KMT would have confronted a task of overwhelming difficulty. In the unlikely event of KMT success in achieving economic development by other means, it would have likely done so by greatly intensifying social inequities. This has been the cost of development throughout most of the capitalist third world.[50]

More pertinent to the present study, however, is the impossibility of economic development based on the traditional Confucian peasant economy. No restorationist response to the agrarian crisis had any prospect for success. The realization crisis of the Chinese peasant family was embedded in an agrarian crisis that preceded the Communist turn to a rural route to revolution in China. Thus, the stage was set for the competition between the reformist (KMT) and revolutionary (CCP) responses, whose familial logic and consequences are explored in chapter 4.

Peasant Family Distress ▪ While elite families experienced their crisis of consciousness as they witnessed the erosion of Confucian

49. The view that international military and economic intervention may be regarded as accidental is untenable analytically. These are the normal constraints of the modern political economic system. See Immanuel Wallerstein, *The Modern World System;* Theda Skocpol, *States and Social Revolution;* and Perry Anderson, *Lineages of the Absolutist State*—all of which analyze the international order from varying structuralist perspectives.

Myers summarizes and evaluates the reform-versus-revolution debate that took place among the Chinese (*Chinese Economy,* pp. 180–82). Although he defends possibilities for reform, he is deeply critical of the actual reform efforts of the KMT. Thomas Rawski defends the Republican economy and its prospects with the greatest passion and, I believe, myopia. Most of the "distributionists" cited in fns. 43 and 45 above, of course, argue that reform efforts were futile. Although Albert Feuerwerker does not engage the question directly, he argues that the KMT was incapable of gaining control of the agrarian surplus from landlords and local authorities, a precondition for economic development (*Chinese Economy, 1912–1949*).

50. See, for example, Samir Amin, *Unequal Development;* Ivar Oxaal, Tony Barnett, and David Booth, eds., *Beyond the Sociology of Development;* and Robert I. Rhodes, ed., *Imperialism and Underdevelopment.*

patriarchy and the rise of anti-Confucian ideologies, among the peasantry family crisis was first experienced through the irrevocable undermining of the material foundations of patriarchal family life. As in the past, an agrarian crisis expressed itself in alarming symptoms of peasant family decline. But this time the new context made family decay more serious and gave it the new meaning of a family crisis.

In a peasant economy, economic failure spells the failure of family life for significant numbers. To say that by the 1920s, or earlier, the Chinese economy was unable to feed its population is to say that noticeable numbers of peasant families were unable to maintain their members. The dire corollary is that such families were unable to create new ones. Many of those who could reproduce themselves were forced to do so in irregular and, from the traditional point of view, less than satisfactory ways. It is not possible to generalize such trends for China as a whole, as G. William Skinner's work on regional analysis makes clear.[51] However, enough peasants experienced the familial effects of the agrarian decline, particularly in what were to be the major Communist base areas, to make it an important context for understanding revolutionary mobilization. It is useful to categorize the reappearance of the traditional signs of peasant family distress in terms of physical survival, family creation, household size and complexity, and family legitimacy. My documentation of these crisis symptoms rests on inferential logic supported by the sketchy evidence that is available. Relevant evidence is inadequate for at least two reasons. Under the best of circumstances, data concerning the everyday experiences of a society's lower and illiterate classes are elusive. A nonarea specialist, like myself, who is dependent upon the questions posed by specialists, suffers an additional handicap. Feminist questions have been raised by sinologists only recently, and most of these have concentrated on the areas of explicit women's politics. This study suggests additional feminist questions for area specialists to pursue. Closer attention to historical shifts in family patterns as they affected people of differing sex, age, and status groups is sorely needed. We would benefit, too, from more detailed evidence on how peasant women and men interpreted and responded to the shifts

---

51. The most relevant work for issues discussed in this chapter is G. William Skinner, "Regional Systems in Late Imperial China."

in family patterns.[52] However, at present we must make do with the evidence at hand.

1. *Physical Survival.* Wherever the agrarian crisis struck, sheer survival became the basic achievement for a peasant family. Ping-ti Ho suggests that, by the early-nineteenth century, demographic pressures forced the Chinese masses to lower their material aspirations from maintaining customary standards to securing basic subsistence.[53] Although the massive rebellions of the mid-century provided survivors a demographic "breathing spell," they did so, of course, at the cost of millions of peasant lives. The rebellions did not alter the adverse population-land ratio. During the last quarter of the nineteenth century, population surpassed the peak crisis point of 1850. Thereafter, however, the rate of population growth was brutally checked by the catastrophic economic and military conditions of the twentieth century.[54]

Where landlessness increased, so did family mortality. Landless families were likely to suffer the highest rates of infant mortality. Fei and Chang found this to be the case in Luts'un, one of the Yunnan villages they studied in the late 1930s. At the time of their visit only one child survived of the six or seven born to each landless household. Likewise, Gamble's surveys made during the early 1930s found skewed age distributions in villages near Peking. The five-to-nine-year-old and the ten-to-fourteen-year-old groups were abnormally small, suggesting a decade of reduced fertility or survival rates.[55] And while missionary influences had limited the extent of infanticide by the time Chinese fieldworkers conducted their community studies, many such studies, as well as demographic data, record its persistence.[56] It is plausible that

---

52. Arthur P. Wolf and Chieh-shan Huang make an important beginning in addressing such issues in their detailed and ingenious study of marriage and adoption patterns in Hai-shan, Taiwan (*Marriage and Adoption in China, 1845–1945*).

53. Ho, *Population of China*, p. 273. Prior to that time, Ho maintains that Chinese customary standards compared favorably to those of preindustrial Europe.

54. Ibid., pp. 276–77.

55. Fei and Chang, *Earthbound China*, p. 94, and Gamble, *North China Villages*, p. 27. Further evidence on skewed age and sex distributions can be found in Fei, *Peasant Life*, p. 52.

56. Fei, *Peasant Life*, p. 52; Arthur H. Smith, *Village Life in China*, p. 308; Isabel Crook and David Crook, *Revolution in a Chinese Village*, p. 11; and Irene B. Taeuber, "The Families of Chinese Farmers."

infanticide was a more frequent anguish among the landless and that its incidence grew as landlessness spread.

The most catastrophic conditions yielded the most desperate and dehumanized forms of family mortality. Cannibalism among family members is reported in antiseptic terms in survey data on calamities.[57] The unspeakable horror of this final form of family degradation is captured in the report of White and Jacoby on the Honan famine of 1943. One set of parents murdered their two small children to silence anguished entreaties for food. A woman who boiled her baby was spared by authorities because she claimed the child was dead before she began cooking it. Similarly, a woman who cut off her dead husband's legs for meat was exonerated on the ground that he was already dead.[58]

The patriarchal context ensured that women experienced the greatest privations of economic adversity. Females were the traditional victims of infanticide. Periods of dynastic decline yielded increases in infant mortality, and the death rate for female infants rose more rapidly than that for males.[59] Data on sex and age distribution in twentieth century China indicate that females were the primary victims of the agrarian crisis. The 1953 census, conducted by the PRC, reported a sex ratio of 107.5 men to 100 women among the total population.[60] When one considers the disproportionate percentage of male casualties in the massive military campaigns of this century, or views the casualties in contrast with postrevolutionary demographic data in the Soviet Union, the statistic is remarkable.[61] Further evidence that female

57. John L. Buck, *Land Utilization*, p. 45; Gamble, *Ting Hsien*, p. 446; and Ho, *Population of China*, p. 248.

58. Theodore H. White and Annalee Jacoby, *Thunder Out of China*, pp. 171–72.

59. G. William Skinner, "Family Structure and Politics in Modern China," pp. 25ff. This essay records bald accounts from various provinces of female infanticide during the period of Ch'ing decline in the mid-nineteeth century, such as: "The first female birth may sometimes be salvaged with effort, but subsequent births are usually drowned. There are even those who drown every female baby without keeping any."

60. Ho, *Population of China*, p. 232.

61. Even in prerevolutionary Russia the male-to-female ratio indicated a slight predominance of females. In 1897 the ratio was 98.9. It dropped to 93.5 in 1926, reflecting the casualties of World War I and the civil war, and continued to decline to the devastatingly low post-World War II figure of 74.3 in 1946. As recently as 1975, the male-to-female ratio in the Soviet Union had recovered to only 86.4. For more detailed age-graded data and analysis, see Gail W. Lapidus, *Women in Soviet Society*.

mortality was differentially affected by economic distress can be inferred from a peculiar finding in John Lossing Buck's 1929–1931 farm survey. He found a higher percentage of single women than men in the fifteen-to-nineteen-year-old age bracket. Yet he also reported that a greater percentage of women than men ultimately married. And he recorded higher mortality rates for women than for men in all age brackets until women survived their childbearing years.[62] Data like these lend support to Irene Taeuber's claim that "evidence of induced or assisted mortality among females is rather convincing."[63]

2. *Household Size and Complexity*. The agrarian crisis tended to diminish the size and complexity of the households of peasant families that did survive. Higher mortality was not the only source of shrinkage. In the wealthier core regions, continuing population pressure on the land made it impossible for the family economy to support as many members or to absorb their labor. Thus the pressure of population encouraged wide-scale family separation. The search for employment, which had long sent Chinese on the roads and seas seeking income to send their families, expanded as population pressures intensified in the late-nineteenth century. C.T. Gardner, a British emigration officer at Amoy, reported in 1897:

> Thus many villagers now talk of a 20, 30, or 40 crop, or a nobody crop—meaning the crop is such that 20, 30, or 40 of their clan will have to emigrate, or the crop is so good that all the clan can, if they like, stay at home.[64]

Farm size decreased significantly after 1870. "Nobody crops" became so infrequent in the Northern provinces that when Buck conducted his farm survey in the early 1930s, emigration had cost a net loss of 48 males per 1,000. According to Myers's estimate, by 1940 a family would require approximately 25 *mou* (1 *mou* is approximately ⅙ of an acre) of farm land to support five people on farm income alone, and there simply was not enough land

---

62. John L. Buck, *Land Utilization*, pp. 388ff.
63. Taeuber, "Families of Farmers," p. 71. See also Skinner, "Family Structure," pp. 25–26.
64. Quoted in Maurice Freedman, *Lineage Organization in Southeastern China*, p. 10, n. 2.

for most peasant families to survive in this manner. Household heads were compelled to send members out of the villages and into the cities seeking wages to support themselves and, where possible, to augment the family budget.[65]

Family members were separated and households diminished through other more desperate means. Grass widowhood flourished in impoverished regions as destitute husbands deserted their wives and children.[66] Crisis conditions provoked fathers to sell children, and husbands to sell wives. The Great Northwest Famine of 1928–1929 resulted in the sale into servitude of thousands of women and children in Shensi alone.[67] According to Peck the worst famines found women and children sold by the pound, and "the day the price of a pound of human flesh sank below that of a pound of grain could be taken as the point at which the famine settled into its final stretch."[68]

Peasant patriarchs pawned their daughters more readily than they pawned their land:

> Only as a last stand in their desperate struggle do the owner peasants resort to mortgaging their land. Personal properties can be replaced, more children can be bred, but land is hard to get back once it has been lost.[69]

Although the last-gasp reform efforts of the Manchus included a 1910 edict forbidding the sale and purchase of maidservants or concubines, the overwhelming magnitude of the economic forces that led many peasants to dispose of their daughters in this way forced the imperial reformers into a telling compromise. The edict permitted parents to lease out their children for a period of years. As Cameron explains:

> This proviso was made necessary by the prevalence of famine, a condition which had so often led in the past to the sale of superfluous children in order to save the remainder of the family from starvation.[70]

---

65. Buck, *Land Utilization*, p. 396, and Myers, *Chinese Peasant Economy*, pp. 137–39, 158.
66. Crook and Crook, *Revolution in a Chinese Village*, p. 9.
67. Mark Selden, *The Yenan Way in Revolutionary China*, p. 6.
68. Peck, *Two Kinds of Time*, p. 23.
69. Chen Han-seng, *Landlord and Peasant*, p. 95.
70. Cameron, *Reform Movement in China*, p. 177.

In the patriarchal context, "superfluous children" were nearly always female.

Where the crisis struck, joint households became more difficult to sustain and peasants divided their households earlier. The peasants in Hopei and Shantung, who reported a rise in household divisions during the 1930s to Japanese interviewers, were straightforward in their explanation:

> **Question** Has there been a tendency toward more or less division of households in Cha-ching in recent years?
>
> **Answer** Recently, it has become much greater. This is particularly true when the parents die.
>
> **Question** What is the cause of this new tendency?
>
> **Answer** The reason is that it is best to distribute something for everybody before conditions worsen and nothing remains. When family conditions deteriorate, dividing the household wealth must be done quickly or else soon there is nothing left to divide.[71]

Family conditions deteriorated so rapidly, however, that in some areas the practice of partible inheritance was threatened. Overcrowding on the family plot robbed "extra sons" of their patrimony; many of these swelled the ranks of the semiemployed lumpenproletariat, which furnished the secret societies and rebel bands with their most fertile recruiting grounds.[72]

3. *Family Creation.* Impoverished families were less able to generate new ones. Crisis conditions interfered with the capacity of peasant families to arrange marriages for their children, and, particularly, for their sons. Peasant families could not afford ceremonial expenses or to provide for a new household member precisely when the differential rise in female mortality further diminished the traditionally inadequate supply of prospective brides. Those who could manage their sons' marriages often had

---

71. Quoted in Myers, *Chinese Peasant Economy*, p. 116.

72. Esherick, *Reform and Revolution*, p. 122. Edward Friedman, *Backward Toward Revolution*, describes a "familial-religious crisis" in which homeless sons were recruited to rebel bands. Skinner, "Family Structure," depicts a strong relationship between birth order, filiality, and political behavior, with younger sons more likely than first-born sons to engage in both familial and political rebellion.

to delay the proceedings. In his study of Ting Hsien, Gamble found a close relationship between a family's economic status and the age at marriage of the sons. The age of 41.4 percent of the men in a group of 766 couples studied was less than fifteen years when they married. Class differences concealed by this average are striking. Whereas 80.5 percent of the grooms in wealthier families (defined as those holding 100 *mou* of land, or more) were under age fifteen at marriage, this was the case for only 33 percent of the men from families with holdings of less than 50 *mou*.[73]

During periods of economic crisis, increasing numbers could not marry at all. In Kaihsienkung, a village in the Yangtze valley studied in the 1930s by Fei Hsiao-tung, marriage had been suspended entirely in the years since the worldwide depression.[74] Gamble's study of Ting Hsien found 20 percent of family heads to be unmarried.[75] Marriage prospects of agricultural laborers were particularly bleak. Mao considered them "the most miserable class in the village" because almost none were able to marry.[76] Indeed, Martin Yang reported bachelorhood was the characteristic condition of the agricultural laborers of Taitou, Shantung, in the 1940s, and Taitou was a community notable for its relative prosperity.[77] The CCP peasant organizers who arrived in the Kiangsi base region in the late 1920s found that 70 percent of the poor peasants and 99 percent of the farm laborers were unable to marry.[78]

The plight of individuals doomed to lonely bachelorhood in a society that validated few alternatives to marriage and family life is a recurrent theme in the village studies of the pre-Communist period. Fei and Chang describe Lao Wang, a 30-year-old man whose uncle deprived him of his inheritance when his parents died during his childhood. Unswerving dedication to the attainment of security through conscientious work—hiring himself out for agricultural work when available, collecting firewood the

73. Gamble, *Ting Hsien*, p. 7.
74. Fei, *Peasant Life*, p. 53.
75. Gamble, *Ting Hsien*, p. 28.
76. Quoted in Lynda Bell, "Agricultural Laborers and Rural Revolution," p. 19.
77. Martin Yang, *Chinese Village*, p. 51.
78. Hu Chi-hsi, "The Sexual Revolution in the Kiangsi Soviet," p. 479.

rest of the time—earned him the respect and pity of the field-workers, but little more—least of all marriage.

> We were especially smitten by the pathos of this homeless, un-attached man when we saw him among the guests at the celebration of the harvest moon to which Chang had invited us. Surrounded, as he was, by those who had families and occupied secure, comfortable positions in the community, his lack of stable ties and sense of belonging were most striking. Those around him represented the personification of the goals he strove for, but the expression in his eyes betrayed his feeling of hopelessness. When he presented us with a piece of moon cake, which symbolizes the fullness of family life, and we responded with a toast wishing him the joy of a family before the coming of the next harvest festival, he acknowledged to us his sense of the futility to achieve such a desirable state.[79]

In the crisis period, examples like these likely multiplied.[80]

4. *Family Legitimacy.* Clearly, the agrarian crisis jeopardized the maintenance of revered familial values and rituals. The erosion of Confucian patriarchal traditions we observed among the elite had its more brutally induced counterpart among the peasantry. One can only infer the negative impact this had on family pride. Peasants were forced to curtail the ruinous expenditures they characteristically lavished on familial ceremonies. Despite the legendary frugality of the Chinese peasantry, when they arranged marriages for their sons they traditionally threw fiscal caution to the winds:

> Despite the fact, that, as a consequence of the marriage of his son, he was in debt for several tens of dollars and his store of rice had been sold, the smile on his worn face revealed an inner peace which made us feel that his life's goal had been attained.[81]

An old peasant woman gave fieldworkers the simple explanation: "We don't experience real happiness in our own marriage, we achieve it when we accomplish our son's marriage."[82]

79. Fei and Chang, *Earthbound China,* pp. 58–59.
80. See, for example, Morton Fried, *Fabric of Chinese Society;* C. K. Yang, *Chinese Village;* and Freedman, *Lineage Organization.*
81. Fei and Chang, *Earthbound China,* p. 102.
82. Ibid.

But crisis conditions compelled peasants to resort to irregular, less-than-desirable means toward this end. In creativity born of desperation, some peasant families avoided ceremonial expenses by marrying women to grooms who were away in the army or in cities. And landlessness drove some peasant men to the patriarchal disgrace of uxorilocal marriages.[83] Many of the twentieth-century field studies indicate a rise in the frequency of adopted daughter-in-law marriages. Fei Hsiao-tung, for example, found the number of adopted daughter-in-law brides had increased from 17 percent to 39 percent of traditional brides in the decade preceding his fieldwork in a Yangtze valley village. Yet peasants there despised the system because of its traditional association with poverty.[84] Likewise, Morton Fried reported that the peasants he studied "themselves most frequently characterized it as a technique of convenience, dictated by the exigencies of their declining economic positions."[85] It is unlikely, however, that the agrarian crisis produced a sudden aggregate rise in the incidence of "minor marriages." The most dire circumstances encouraged practices such as selling girls as prostitutes or slaves, which depleted the supply of potential foster daughters-in-law. Moreover, as Wolf and Huang have shown, there was internal logic to the demographic and social effects of this form of marriage, which could even decrease the incidence of it during periods of economic distress.[86] Thus the belief that "minor marriage" had become more frequent represents a cultural perception of family crisis more significant than the extent of the practice itself.

Marriage was the most celebrated of family events, and a decline in its ceremonial observance suggests a wane of proper Confucian ritual activities. And, although evidence is scant, local studies do report that ancestral halls and tablets were allowed to decay and that impoverished families suffered intense distress as they became unable to provide deceased kin with proper funerals, coffins, or any sort of burial at all.[87]

---

83. Ibid., pp. 114, 259–60.
84. Fei, *Peasant Life*, p. 54.
85. Morton H. Fried, *Fabric of Chinese Society*, p. 41.
86. Wolf and Huang, *Marriage and Adoption*. See especially chaps. 20–24.
87. Thaxton, "When Peasants Took Power," emphasizes the decline of ceremonial life. C. K. Yang, *A Chinese Village in Early Communist Transition*, reports ancestral-hall decay, as does Gamble, *Ting Hsien*. Freedman argues that neglected

A threat to patriarchal legitimacy in the context of generally weakening social controls characteristically encourages some of the worst expressions of patriarchal license—sexual abuse of women. The nature of this topic and of the relevant data make it impossible to document the historical transformations in its incidence. Given the pervasiveness of sexual abuse in traditional China, one can only surmise that its frequency rose during the crisis period. Village studies indicate that landlords and their agents in many areas regarded unlimited sexual access to local peasant women as a class privilege. Wang Pan-yen of Ten Mile Inn, for example, earned peasant hatred because "he forced his attention on any peasant woman who took his fancy and openly kept as his mistress the wife of one middle peasant."[88] Power over their tenants' livelihood gave landlords access to the wives and daughters of their tenants. Jack Belden recorded one manipulative example:

> In a village in western Shantung I came across a landlord whose common practice was to make his tenant go out into the fields and work while he took his pleasure of the tenant's wife. When Li protested, the landlord had him kidnaped [sic] by bandits. In order to cover his participation in the kidnaping [sic], the landlord pretended to mediate the affair through puppet troops, preparing a banquet on the tenant's behalf. But observe the cleverness of this plot. The grateful tenant was released and borrowed money from the kindly landlord to pay for the banquet. Of course, a high interest rate was charged, the tenant could not repay his debt, and lost his own small plot of ground. The landlord then consummated the whole affair by taking the peasant's wife as payment of the debt.[89]

Military situations generally elicit flagrant epidemics of violent sexual abuse.[90] The sporadic evidence available gives one no

---

ancestral halls were a permanent feature of the lineage system rather than a symptom of lineage decay (*Chinese Lineage and Society*, p. 35). However, once again the cultural perception is as important as the reality.

88. Crook and Crook, *Revolution in a Chinese Village*, p. 26.

89. Jack Belden, *China Shakes the World*, p. 155.

90. The most extensive cross-cultural, transhistorical illustration of the relationship between rape and militarism appears in Susan Brownmiller, *Against Our Will: Men, Women and Rape* (New York: Simon and Schuster, 1975).

cause to imagine the period of warlordism in China was an exception to the general rule. Warlord and KMT armies appear to have taken full advantage of opportunities to commit such abuse. Rape of local women by KMT soldiers seems to have been commonplace. In some regions KMT officers employed middlemen to procure the most attractive young women for the pleasure of officers.[91] While women were the direct victims of sexual abuse, their fathers, husbands, and families were profoundly humiliated by these events. Their women, and hence their family names, were irreparably compromised by the violations. Then, as discussed in chapter 2, virtuous women might feel compelled to save the family honor by taking their own lives.[92] This would provide future revolutionaries with a most delicate mobilization issue.

In sum, the agrarian crisis posed a severe threat to the physical survival, reproduction, household size and complexity, and the legitimacy of traditional peasant family life. The crisis undermined independent family farming, the traditional material foundation of peasant patriarchy. The domain of a peasant patriarch's authority contracted: he had fewer workers to oversee, less income to manage or invest, fewer marriages to arrange, and fewer ceremonies and rituals over which to officiate. In consequence, there was less deference for him to enjoy or old age security and ancestor worship to anticipate. Moreover, a decreasing proportion of peasant men found themselves eligible to claim their share of patriarchy's shrinking domain. The dispossessed swelled the ranks of the floating, homeless population.

While the appearance of symptoms of family decay confronted millions of Chinese peasant families with personal crises, this

---

91. Crook and Crook, *Revolution in a Chinese Village*, pp. 31–32, and Belden, *China Shakes the World*, chap. 31.

92. Nor is this patriarchal conception of family honor confined to China or to the past. In the summer of 1980, for example, a United Nations human rights panel received a report, submitted to its Working Group on Slavery, claiming that each day hundreds of young Arab women are brutally murdered by their families to protect family honor against allegations of the women's promiscuity. Whether the compromise of a woman's sexual purity is volitional, imposed, or merely suspected is of no significance to the family authorities, who consider their patriarchal respectability to have been undermined by allegations alone ("Hundreds of Arab Girls Slain Daily," *San Francisco Chronicle*, 12 August 1980).

did not, by itself, indicate the existence of a crisis in the peasant family system. The signs were painfully familiar, the characteristic familial evidence of agrarian crisis. Nor can we be certain family decay was worse in absolute terms than it had ever been before. This is as likely as is the case for the absolute immiseration of the peasantry, and as secondary to the crucial issues. Family distress was more serious in the twentieth-century presocialist period, not because it was more severe than in earlier times, but because social structural developments made the family more important to the peasantry just as they made it less potent. Social structural supports that traditionally mediated between a family and society collapsed while social conditions became increasingly brutal.

The collapse of the Confucian patriarchal state had removed the most significant stabilizing structure of the old regime. Although one of its principal functions had been legitimating the processes that extracted from peasant families the agrarian surplus, its fall placed them into far greater jeopardy. The absence of public order made families more vulnerable to the ravages of natural and social enemies. "Local bullies and evil gentry" gained a freer reign. Likewise, the disintegration of stable community life occasioned by the new political and economic forces ruptured the traditional relationship between a family and its community. Landlords and tenants no longer formed part of a vertically integrated society, and in many areas mutual trust was lost.[93]

Processes of family decline contributed to the weakening of community structure. As marriage ceremonies became less frequent and less elaborate, many villages lost a traditional form of communal integration. Fiscal crisis and reformist impulses led governments of the Republican era to curtail, as well, the community festivals, parades, and gatherings that traditionally punctuated the agrarian seasons. In Kaihsienkung, for example, the district government suspended all such gatherings, which it condemned as superstitious. Fei Hsiao-tung commented on the social implications of the action:

---

93. Kuhn, "Local Self-Government"; Esherick, *Reform and Revolution*, p. 67; and Thaxton, "When Peasants Took Power."

How far the suspension of community gatherings has weakened the local ties among the people is difficult to ascertain from my present material. But when I sat among the people and listened to their narrations of the past exciting events of the intervillage parade, their feeling of loss and disappointment at the present situation was very clear to me. I am not going to try to reconstruct the grand occasion and estimate the social value involved in it, but the memory of the past forms an important element in the present attitude towards the existing situation. The suspension of these festivities is a direct indication in the minds of the people, of deterioration of social life. Insofar as they are looking forward for a return of the happy days, they will not reject any possible measure which they are convinced as making for improvement. This psychology has its significance in the lack of strong resistance to social change.[94]

The peasant family system was in crisis at this time because family decay occurred in a context that foreclosed the possibility of its restoration on the traditional basis. New material and ideological conditions irreversibly altered the course of family transformation. Independent family farming, the traditional material foundation of the patriarchal peasant family economy, could not persist as the modal basis for peasant family life nor as the modal production unit of the nation's economy. There could be no Malthusian solution to this agrarian crisis because there was no way to reverse the domestic and international forces that were commercializing agricultural and handicraft production, introducing factory production based on wage labor, and integrating the Chinese economy into a world market and monetary system.

These developments undermined the traditional family economy in ways that disrupted the familial division of labor by sex and age, implicitly questioning its relationships of gender and generation. Drastic dislocations of traditional handicraft production, which began in the nineteenth century, became epidemic

---

94. Fei, *Peasant Life*, pp. 130–31. Also see Thaxton, "When Peasants Took Power," for descriptions of KMT attacks on religion, temple affairs, and the like. There was an imperial precedent for this form of repression, however. According to Kung-chuan Hsiao, fear of seditious activities often led Ch'ing rulers to control religious festivals, particularly ones that inspired interprovincial travel (*Rural China*, pp. 229–31).

early in the twentieth century.[95] Hand spinning was the major casualty of the reorganization of textile production that ensued. Scholars disagree somewhat on the aggregate economic consequences of this because its decline was offset partially by the introduction of new hand-weaving and processing industries.[96] However, there is no question that the family economy of millions of peasant households was drastically and permanently transformed. Local conditions determined the content and direction of the shifts in the division of labor. Because little research has directly addressed this question, it is possible only to suggest the barest outline.

The removal of handicraft production from the private family setting was the major structural effect of the reorganization of textile production in many areas near cities. Peasant families responded by reorganizing labor resources in three different ways. First, in some affected areas, women, who generally bore responsibility for hand spinning, suddenly and temporarily became—in part—an expensive, leisure class. For example, the introduction of silk production in factories ruined the domestic silk industry in Kaihsienkang, where women's traditional responsibility for silk spinning had exempted them from rice cultivation. The sudden unemployment of these women destroyed the local economy and rendered them idle burdens to their families, whose farms were too small to benefit from the contribution of additional labor.[97] A similar, but less severe, effect was felt in Taitou, Shantung, where competition from factory cloth left many families concerned about how to occupy idled daughters during the long springs now that their spinning was of little value.[98] No data speaks to the point directly, but it is plausible that the hard-pressed families resorted to traditional methods to rid themselves of "superfluous" females.[99]

---

95. Myers has data on the dislocation of handspinners and the overall decline in handicraft exports (*Chinese Economy*, pp. 134, 175).

96. Myers emphasizes this point, but agrees that the effects of the reorganization were "painful for many communities" (ibid., p. 134).

97. Fei, *Peasant Life*, p. 171.

98. Martin Yang, *Chinese Village*, p. 27.

99. The fact that families in silk-spinning regions traditionally kept their daughters longer than did families elsewhere provides indirect support for this hypothesis.

A second response was to transfer responsibility for agricultural work to women. In a Yangtze valley area studied by Fei Hsiao-tung, peasants with farms large enough to absorb additional labor were willing to break with tradition by integrating their unemployed women into agricultural activities.[100] Among the landless in Kwangtung, women became a higher proportion of the agricultural hired labor force while wages for such labor fell. As Chen Han-seng explained:

> As the more mobile part of the laboring population, it is the men who first come out from under an intolerable burden either by engaging in some other form of labor, if such can be found, or by migrating. When rural employers increase the proportion of women laborers, this is a sign that male labor has become scarcer or less docile or sufficiently less efficient to make the employment of women preferable.[101]

The third, and most common, response was to send surplus family members out of the villages to seek employment in developing cities and market towns. The dislocation of craft production increased the extent of such rural-to-urban migration and modified the traditional sex and age distribution of the population involved. Women and children formed a high percentage of the new urban factory labor force because they could be exploited most intensively.[102] The wage labor they performed under frightful working conditions was far from liberating, but it removed them from the direct supervision and protection of the patriarchal family. Moreover, because the increasing numbers of young people of both sexes who migrated to the cities and towns to work did not sever their familial ties, they served as transmission belts to their native villages for the modern, reformist ideas and values.[103]

Peasant Patriarchy Challenged ▪ The new messages offered little comfort to the threatened patriarchs of the peasant families the youth had left behind. Rather, they were echoes of the explicit

---

100. Fei, *Peasant Life*, p. 171.
101. Chen Han-seng, *Landlord and Peasant*, p. 103.
102. Feuerwerker, *Chinese Economy, 1911–1949*, p. 18.
103. Bástid-Bruguiere, "Currents of Social Change," p. 586, and Martin Yang, *Chinese Village*, p. 229.

challenges to patriarchal authority occurring among the urban elite, and as such they gave the peasants notice of the new ideological conditions in which this agrarian crisis was wreaking its familial havoc. For with the fall of the Confucian state and its supporting institutions went the systemic legitimation of patriarchal authority. No longer was the governance of Chinese family and state united by a system of methodical filial education. No longer did *li* and law reinforce each other. Instead, elite and peasant culture had bifurcated. The Confucian family system had lost its hegemonic status among the urbanizing elite classes. Among the peasantry, however, the traditional patriarchal family system retained its ideological hold. Peasant family practice had always been less ideologically pure. But now the peasant family system was stripped from its Confucian cultural and social structural moorings. Peasant patriarchy contracted to the level of the simple family unit precisely when that unit was besieged.

During the early decades of the twentieth century, peasant families received glimpses of the emerging alternatives to Confucian family life as well as mild, but portentous, challenges to patriarchal authority. Modern schools were introduced in many rural villages, and the school schedules conflicted with the needs of the peasant families for the labor of their children. For example, in Kaihsienkung, where sheep raising was an important domestic industry, children were responsible for collecting food for the family sheep. The new public school in the village challenged farm families in the traditional province of educating their young, and it interfered with their need for child labor.[104] Missionary and public schools conflicted with agrarian values and drew young people off the land into the cities:

> The school is like a bridge, over which the young men of the rich houses enter the outside world and go into occupations other than farming. By spending a few years in school, even if they get nothing else, they get a strong reaction against farming.[105]

Although direct family reform efforts by governmental or independent organizations during the Republican period were lim-

---

104. Fei, *Peasant Life*, pp. 38–39.
105. Fei and Chang, *Earthbound China*, p. 273.

ited, they were not entirely without visibility or meaning in rural areas. The most significant of these efforts was the campaign to abolish footbinding. Rural exposure to such efforts was quite uneven. Antifootbinding societies organized mass meetings, composed popular songs, and actively spread propaganda in villages located near cities or in model reform counties like Ting Hsien. Field study data indicate these enjoyed some success. An antifootbinding society was established in Ting Hsien in 1913; by 1919 all girls under the age of thirteen had unbound feet.[106] In Kao Yao, Yunan, footbinding was successfully terminated in 1930, when the local government was reorganized.[107]

But many of the more remote rural communities were less exposed and likely more resistant to antifootbinding propaganda. There, footbinding continued until Communist campaigns against it were organized. This appears to have been the case in most of what would become the rural revolutionary base areas. Reading backwards from literature on base areas of the Kiangsi Soviet, the Shen-Kan-Ning, and the Shansi-Hopeh-Shantung-Honan border regions, one finds reference to the survival of footbinding.[108]

Antifootbinding propaganda could be couched in traditionalist terms. One appeal pointed out that a daughter with natural feet could purchase medicine for an ailing parent in half the time that walking on bound feet would require.[109] Peasants were probably less hostile to approaches like these, but it is difficult to believe they were oblivious to the challenge to traditional patriarchal relationships the antifootbinding reform implied. In Ting Hsien, for example, the Customs Improvement Society, organized in 1915, coordinated antifootbinding work with attempts to curtail early marriages and expensive funerals.[110] As small feet gradually lost a traditional functional value as collateral for a hypergamous marriage, preservation of the practice of footbinding among the

---

106. Gamble, *Ting Hsien,* pp. 47–48, 140.

107. Cornelius Osgood, *Village Life in Old China,* p. 209.

108. For Kiangsi, see Kathy Walker, "The Party and Peasant Women," p. 28; for Shen-Kan-Ning, see Davin, *Woman-Work,* pp. 33–34; for Shansi, see Crook and Crook, *Revolution in a Chinese Village,* pp. 45–46. Village studies of regions not part of the future base areas also indicate the comparatively late persistence of rural footbinding; compare Fei and Chang, *Earthbound China,* and Martin Yang, *Chinese Village.*

109. Witke, "Transformation of Attitudes," p. 27.

110. Gamble, *Ting Hsien,* p. 140.

peasantry may have become a measure of the strength of rural patriarchal sentiment. Big feet likely retained a symbolic association with the imagined licentiousness of foreign, Christian women,[111] and thus the popularity of footbinding among the new Chinese elite was yet another indication to the peasantry of the bifurcation of Chinese culture.

Scattered throughout the Chinese field studies one finds evidence that ripples of urban family reform washed the rural hinterland. Young people, young men in particular, began to challenge patriarchal authority directly. Fei and Chang found that some of the modern educated young men of Yuts'un, Yunnan, resisted arranged betrothals and extravagant marriage expenses. The youth Osgood studied in Kao Yao, Yunnan, were not quite so bold, but even they found the temerity to refuse to accept betrothals arranged with physically disabled individuals.[112] Even among the peasantry, patriarchy was not what it once had been.

Vast numbers of peasant families felt their way of life profoundly threatened. The agrarian crisis destroyed their capacity to secure their family's livelihood through traditional means—if at all. But it was not material security alone that was endangered. When peasant families made desperate adjustments to the new structural imperatives, they implicitly questioned relationships of gender and generation. The moral security of peasant family life was in jeopardy, and that, as we have seen, was a patriarchal family morality. Peasant families in twentieth-century presocialist China experienced a realization crisis because the overwhelming majority of them wished to realize traditional patriarchal relationships and virtues but were denied the means to do so. Nor could they turn to patriarchy's former institutional supports to assist their efforts to restore the failing family system. The once united patriarchs of China were challenged and divided.

IMPLICATIONS OF THE FAMILY CRISIS

Family crisis was embedded in the agrarian and political crises that precipitated a revolutionary situation in twentieth-century

111. Witke, "Transformation of Attitudes," pp. 20–21.
112. Fei and Chang, *Earthbound China*, p. 259, and Osgood, *Village Life in Old China*, p. 279.

China. It could not have been otherwise in a society fundamentally structured by its patriarchal family system. When Confucian patriarchy forfeited political and cultural hegemony in China, elite and peasant culture bifurcated, causing the two social classes to experience family crisis in substantially different ways. The diverse ways in which they did so had important implications for the revolutionary process that lay ahead. The two-pronged family crisis structured the motivations of participants in a manner that provided revolutionaries with a complex set of challenges and opportunities.

The collapse of the Confucian state enabled elite youth to level a direct ideological attack at Confucian patriarchy. Feminism served as a radical incubator for the generation that soon supplied the leaders and cadres of China's revolutionary parties. Family reform programs designed to limit parental authority and diminish inequality between the sexes attracted many to the ranks of the two parties that contested for state power in China.

Peasants, on the other hand, experienced a brutal realization crisis in their traditional family economy. The material and ideological foundations of peasant patriarchy had been irrevocably impaired, but there is no reason to believe this led very many peasants to desire an alternative family system. More likely, what the majority of them desired, above all, was to return to the remembered conditions of family and community life. The remembered past[113] of independent, self-sufficient, family farming, of an unbroken male lineage to transmit the same farm and the same knowledge of farming, the same ancestral home to the sons of each succeeding generation—this likely was the structure of the most powerful motivations peasant patriarchs brought to the revolutionary situation. The degree to which this remembered past was real or imagined matters only slightly. Memories shape lived experience in directions that meet the needs of those doing the remembering. In those rare historical moments when masses become willing to define their needs in revolutionary terms, restorationist motives can transform the latent radicalism of their idealized past into a mighty revolutionary current. Eric Wolf has observed that "it is the very attempt of the middle and free

---

113. The concept comes from Frank Hearn, "Remembrance and Critique."

peasant to remain traditional which makes *him* revolutionary."[114]

If peasant patriarchs possessed weighty motives propelling them backward toward revolution, the situation of peasant women was rather more complex. Certainly the ancestral past offered them no comparable nourishment for radical idealization. Their objective stake in family reform seems overwhelmingly obvious. But rarely is the structure of subjective experience determined by objective calculation of long-range advantages. Most of the time, immediate opportunities and hazards are more compelling. As we have seen, the peasant family crisis presented peasant women with hazards that were extreme.

The threat to peasant patriarchy provided few benefits to peasant women. Instead, they suffered its most painful burdens. They bore the children that crisis conditions led them to miscarry, abort, and murder. They reared the children that the crisis caused to be sold, pawned, or starved. Females themselves were more often the children killed, sold, pawned or starved. Women bore the brunt of the worsening conditions—women were the last to eat the withering millet, the first to eat bark. Crisis conditions caused their workloads to expand and their compensations to dissipate. Women became more vulnerable than usual to male violence and sexual abuse. However limited were their rights under traditional patriarchal rule, the precrisis family must have appeared to many to represent a life of comparative security and respect. Because most Chinese peasant women lacked sources for alternative visions of life's possibilities in their experience with the present or the remembered past, it should not prove surprising if many of them would be more attracted to a secure form of patriarchy than to an uncertain, abstract notion of family reform. In this sense, peasant women, too, may have edged backward toward revolution, but toward one less directly in their own interests than in those of peasant men.

The dual family crisis was a crucial aspect of the revolutionary situation in twentieth-century China. It made family issues of profound concern to all who would participate in the revolutionary process, but it did so in contradictory ways. Forging a family policy capable of balancing the reformist goals of elite youth with the restorationist ones of the peasantry, while attending to

---

114. Eric Wolf, "On Peasant Rebellions," p. 270 (my emphasis).

antagonistic sexual and generational interests, would become one of the more urgent and delicate tasks the contending parties would confront.

The Chinese patriarchal family system in the presocialist period was not merely in transition;[115] it was in crisis. Its material and ideological foundations were faltering. Signs of family distress were everywhere. People were being politically mobilized by competing visions of resolving the crisis. The chance to restore Confucian patriarchy had long passed. Now, instead, there was an opportunity to reconstruct Chinese family and social life on the basis of radically different principles of gender, generation, and social integration. This was a rare opportunity to foment a family revolution.

---

115. This is the way Chinese family change generally has been portrayed. See, for example, Levy, *Family Revolution*, and William J. Goode, *World Revolution and Family Patterns*.

婦

4 People's War and the New Democratic Patriarchy

In 1932 the Kuomintang minister of foreign affairs, Dr. Wellington Koo, explained why communism was fated to fail in China:

> Communism considers society as being formed of individuals grouped according to their social functions, but not according to their personal sentiments or affections. This idea is alien to the Chinese, who regard family duties as being of great importance. Communism tends to destroy the family by the relaxation of the conjugal bonds, by entrusting the State with the care and education of children and by the abolition of private property. But tradition and the respect for ancestors are important Chinese social characteristics. It is the family which for the Chinese is at the bottom of social structure.[1]

Dr. Koo was correct, of course. The Chinese endowed family duties with the highest significance and the family system formed the foundation of Chinese social structure. But history was about to provide an ironic demonstration that the Chinese Communists were better able to appreciate and benefit from this than were the members of his own party. Far from abolishing the family, the Communist revolution in China rescued peasant family life from the precipice of destruction. It resolved the realization crisis of the peasant family through revolutionary policies and practices

---

This chapter originally appeared in *Journal of Comparative Family Studies* 13, no. 3 (fall 1982):255–76.
    1. Quoted in Victor A. Yakhontoff, *The Chinese Soviets*, p. 13.

that established the material and ideological basis for a new family system. The Chinese Communist Party (CCP) named this the "new democratic family," but this chapter and the next demonstrate why a more accurate identification is the "new democratic patriarchy." These two chapters assess the effect on peasant families of an array of CCP revolutionary-period policies, both direct and indirect, as well as the effect the peasant family had on CCP revolutionary strategy and tactics. They indicate that reconstruction of the peasant family system did not compete with broader Communist revolutionary goals. Nor was it an incidental by-product of the revolution. Instead, the reconstitution of the patriarchal peasant family economy was integral to the development of several of the most distinctive features and accomplishments of the successful revolutionary strategy known as People's War. In short, there was a family revolution at the center of the social revolution that brought the CCP to state power in China.

This chapter begins by reviewing the historical context in which the CCP attempted to develop a viable strategy for rural revolution and by discussing the essential features of that strategy, People's War. I then offer a feminist interpretation of the People's War policies of land reform, mutual aid, and military defense to illustrate their contribution to the establishment of the new democratic patriarchy. Revolutionary theory of the CCP regarded this arena as the transformation of the "base" of society—the pivotal realm of class struggle that established the context in which other, presumably subordinate forms of struggle could occur. But in a society dominated by a family mode of production, family relationships are simultaneously base and superstructure. Thus, changes in family structure were themselves integral to the process of transforming the social relations of production. Because the theoretical-political framework of the CCP did not treat family relationships explicitly in this manner, the party remained oblivious to the active role it played in constructing a new patriarchal family system in rural China. Chapter 5 explores revolutionary family policy as it was conceptualized and practiced by the CCP—a sphere of ideological struggle over gender and generational contradictions thought to be superstructural and nonantagonistic. An afterword to chapters 4 and 5 on the implicit rural family policy of the Kuomintang will indicate the price Dr. Koo's colleagues paid for their comparative inability to address the sources of peasant family distress.

ORIGINS AND DEVELOPMENT OF PEOPLE'S WAR

When in 1927 Mao Tse-tung and Chu Teh led remnant bands of their defeated forces from urban uprisings to the Chingkangshan Mountains of rural Kiangsi, they unwittingly inaugurated a world-historic epoch of People's War. For the next quarter-century the CCP was to devise a successful route to state power in near total isolation from urban centers or industrial proletariat. Instead, the prime carriers of socialist revolution in China were to be the impoverished victims of the crisis in the peasant family economy. The nature and terms of the alliance the CCP forged with the peasantry had profound implications for family and social transformation during and after the CCP's "long march to power." So integral is this alliance to a proper understanding of most everything distinctively Maoist that it is easy to forget it was originally a product of brute necessity, not of foresight.

From the wisdom of hindsight we can see that the orthodox Marxist-Leninist, urban-based strategy that the Chinese Communists pursued during the mid-1920s was a costly detour from the Chinese revolutionary course. But this was not apparent in those years of the first united front with the KMT (1924–1927). Then, under the guidance of the Comintern, the nascent CCP relinquished a fatal portion of its autonomy and devoted its major energies to mobilizing mass support for the KMT-led national bourgeois revolution.[2] The urban, industrial proletariat was the primary target of this mobilization, but fortunately for the later tasks of the CCP, it did not devote its exclusive attention to that small class. Under the rubric of the KMT alliance, the CCP dominated the leadership of the Peasant Movement of the mid-1920s. In peasant associations established in the Southeastern and South-Central provinces of China, the CCP gained its first

2. There were times, however, when the Comintern did promote a policy of organizing peasants. See Karl A. Wittfogel, "The Legend of 'Maoism,'" pp. 7–8, and Roy Hofheinz, Jr., *The Broken Wave,* pp. 7–8.

direct experience with the problems and potential of peasant organizing. There the party first encountered effects of the crisis in the peasant family economy, which it made preliminary attempts to address through its initial agrarian and family reform measures.[3]

However, this early experiment in devising a rural program was a subsidiary Chinese Communist venture during the period of the first united front. And even this subordinated interest was initiated by force of circumstance. The alliance with the KMT depended in good measure upon the CCP's ability to mobilize mass support for the national unification expeditions, but by 1924 the KMT—especially its leftist factions—had established leadership over urban workers in Kwangtung. Hence the CCP was encouraged to seek supporters among other sectors. Peasants were the only plausible alternative.[4] But they did not gain the center stage of Communist revolutionary strategy until the decimation of the CCP's urban forces by Chiang Kai-shek's counterrevolutionary massacres of 1927. Even then it took several disastrous years before the realization that the Communist movement in China had become a rural one received official recognition, via the unification of the party's central committee with the peasant forces of "the real power faction" in the rural Soviets.[5]

Many have commented upon the significance for the Communist revolution in China of this forced "heresy in act"—the severance of a Marxist-Leninist party from the urban proletariat.[6]

---

3. Hofheinz, *Broken Wave*, pp. 154 and 255, claims that in the first few months of the existence of Peng P'ai's peasant association arbitration department more than one-third of the cases handled involved family conflicts—marriage and divorce problems, lineage disputes, and so forth. See Elisabeth Croll, *Feminism and Socialism in China*, pp. 126–27, for an account of the activities and lessons of these early efforts to organize rural women.

4. This is not to suggest that none among the early Chinese Communists independently recognized the revolutionary potential of the peasantry. P'eng P'ai, organizer of the Haifeng Soviet (1927–1928), has earned ironic recognition as the first "Maoist" precisely because of the rarity of such vision in the early period (Hofheinz, *Broken Wave*, pp. 8, 10, 234).

5. Benjamin I. Schwartz, *Chinese Communism and the Rise of Mao*. Mao Tse-tung did not attain full leadership of the CCP until the Tsunyi conference, held in 1935 during the Long March.

6. See, for example, ibid., and Harold R. Isaacs, *The Tragedy of the Chinese Revolution*. But for a view that disputes the originality of Maoism, see Wittfogel, "Legend of 'Maoism.' "

Likewise, feminists have noted that the CCP lost its accountability to urban-based feminism when it was forced to abandon the cities. Further, the Kuomintang's brutal repression of militant activists in the women's movement, in rural as well as urban areas, caused the Communists to enter the period of rural revolution with a woefully inadequate complement of female cadres.[7] What was to prove most important for the fate of Chinese patriarchy was that the turn to the countryside shifted the decisive terrain for waging family revolution. Thereby the peasant family realization crisis and its complex legacy of restorationist motivations usurped the central revolutionary position, once held by the anti-Confucian crisis of the urban elite.

Banished from China's urban centers, the CCP spent more than two decades forging an alliance with the peasantry, which succeeded in defeating both the Japanese and the KMT. The successful process was People's War, a struggle that combined social revolution with a war for national sovereignty. Attempting to transform military weakness into strength, strategic necessity into virtue, the military objective of People's War is to conquer the cities from the countryside. Strategically this requires the establishment of rural base areas from which a protracted struggle of guerrilla warfare can be waged.

The three major forces of a People's War—peasants, party, and army—become interdependent. The party and army provide the coordinated leadership and protection the peasants require in their resistance to local and foreign enemies, while they depend upon peasant support for their very survival. Because all three share a stake in achieving economic self-sufficiency in the base areas, measures to insure the security of agricultural production, including direct participation by military and political personnel, must be at the heart of wartime economic policy. A viable program for rural development is integral to military success. In fact, a defining characteristic of People's War is the indivisibility of economic policy from military, political, and social goals. Mao Tsetung articulated this during the anti-Japanese war:

---

7. For discussion of the repression of the women's movement, see Croll, *Feminism and Socialism*, pp. 149–52. Analyses of the implications for feminism of the Communist urban defeat also appear in Suzette Leith, "Chinese Women in the Early Communist Movement"; Delia Davin, "Women in the Liberated Areas"; and Kay Johnson, "Feminism and Socialist Revolution in China."

> War is not only a military and political contest, but also an economic contest. In order to defeat the Japanese aggressors . . . we must apply ourselves to economic work . . . we must achieve greater results than ever before.[8]

Clearly the success of such a strategy depends upon active support by the rural population and the elimination of sharp distinctions between "the people"[9] and their political and military allies. A massive effort of political mobilization aims to create a militarized peasantry and a populist military. As Mao explained in "On Protracted War":

> A national revolutionary war as great as ours cannot be won without extensive and thoroughgoing political mobilization. . . . The mobilization of the common people throughout the country will create a vast sea in which to drown the enemy, create the conditions that will make up for our inferiority in arms and other things, and create the prerequisites for overcoming every difficulty in the war. . . . To wish for victory and yet neglect political mobilization is like wishing to "go south by driving the chariot north," and the result would inevitably be to forfeit victory."[10]

The distinctive Maoist response to this task was the development of the "mass line," a leadership principle summed up by Mao in the slogan, "From the masses, to the masses." The role of leadership was first to articulate the experience, needs, and goals of the masses, then to generate grassroots discussion and decision making so that policies could be implemented with widespread support.[11] Through sustained, intimate contact, cadres were to fuse their consciousness, concerns, and aspirations with those of the people they led. In this way the Chinese peasants' interest in resolving the crisis in their family economy was to be married

---

8. Mao Tse-tung, "Production Is Also Possible in the Guerrilla Zones," p. 200.

9. While the peasantry was the major class designated by this term, interclass alliances were essential to successful People's War. Consequently, precise criteria establishing membership in "the people" varied according to strategic considerations.

10. Mao Tse-tung, "On Protracted War," p. 154.

11. Mao Tse-tung summarized the mass line this way: "Sum up the views of the masses, take the results back to the masses so that the masses can give them their firm support and so work out sound ideas for leading the work on hand" ("On Methods of Leadership," quoted in Mark Selden, *The Yenan Way in Revolutionary China*, p. 274).

to the CCP's desire to attain national power and construct a socialist society. Together party and peasants were to forge a response to family and national crises that made mass-line politics the logo of Chinese communism and the reconstruction of patriarchy its hidden core.

While People's War was the broad historical process and the mass line the political technique through which the CCP achieved state power, the specific strategy of the decisive period of their victory was *new democracy*. Formally elaborated by Mao in 1940, "On New Democracy" was his attempt to defend theoretically the party's entry into a second united front with the KMT during the war of resistance against the Japanese invaders (1937–1945) and the moderation in Communist social and economic programs that ensued. In his essay, Mao explained the need for a two-stage struggle for socialism in China. Because Chinese society was "colonial," "semicolonial," and "semifeudal" rather than capitalist, the task of the first revolution was to defeat imperialism and feudalism in order to transform China into an independent, democratic nation. Mao conceded that this stage of the Chinese revolution had originated with the bourgeois-democratic world revolution, but he argued that the victory of the Bolshevik revolution in Russia transformed its nature into part of the proletarian-socialist world revolution. Therefore the goal of this stage of the Chinese revolution was "no longer democracy in general, but democracy of the Chinese type . . . namely, New Democracy."[12]

As new democratic society was to be a necessary, but transitional station on the trail to socialism, the revolutionary strategy was to construct a transitional economy and culture. Class alliances and protection for capitalist production were still necessary at this stage. The party's efforts to extend and protect private ownership of land by the peasants under Sun Yat-sen's principle of "land-to-the-tiller" were the essence of new democratic revolutionary policy, and they established the social basis of peasant support for the CCP.[13] New democratic culture was also a rev-

---

12. Mao Tse-tung, "On New Democracy." p. 342.

13. According to Suzanne Pepper, the CCP deliberately employed the Sun Yat-sen principle in an effort to win greater legitimacy among broad sectors of the Chinese populace in preparation for civil war (*Civil War in China*, p. 219). Her book includes a fine detailed discussion of the role of the land-to-the-tiller program in attracting peasant support for the CCP.

olutionary hybrid, "the ideological reflection of the new politics and the new economy which it sets out to serve." Mao argued the need to develop a new national culture before a socialist one could be built. He urged Communist cadres to study the development of the "splendid old culture" of Chinese feudal society in order to "reject its feudal dross and assimilate its democratic essence."[14] This, he maintained, was the precondition for developing a new democratic culture that would belong to and serve the broad toiling masses of China.

Although Mao explicated the new democratic strategy during a period of relative Communist social moderation, it was not a reformist program. The new democratic stage of the Chinese revolution was the period of its most violent class warfare. It was completed in 1953, when land reform and the marriage reform campaigns terminated. New democracy was the period of the Chinese family revolution.[15]

REBUILDING THE BASIS
FOR PEASANT PATRIARCHY

The ironic rescue of peasant family life by the Communist revolution is a process readily obscured and misunderstood. Neither fortuitous nor determined, it was the result of a family revolution the CCP and the peasantry conducted in the midst of People's War. The new democratic stage of the Chinese revolution reconstructed the material and moral foundations of peasant family life. The rural reconstruction policies of People's War salvaged and reorganized the peasant family economy. Land reform was the cornerstone and cooperative labor and military policies the crucial complements in this indirect, yet definitive arena of Communist family transformation.

Direct measures to reform family life, which will be analyzed in the next chapter, proceeded under the aegis of the party's

---

14. Mao, "On New Democracy," pp. 370, 381.

15. In customary CCP parlance the concept "new democracy" is used to designate a period lasting until approximately 1957, or the beginning of the Great Leap Forward. The National Women's Federation, for example, dropped the "new democratic" part of its name at that time. I focus on 1953, however, as the year that marks a key transition between the new democratic and the patriarchal-socialist agricultural and family systems in the PRC.

official ideological commitment to build the "new democratic family." The goals of this transitional family transformation were to destroy the remains of Confucian patriarchy and to establish a family system based upon free choice, monogamous, heterosexual marriage, with equal rights for the sexes. The party presumed that such marriages were universally desirable and the basis for stable, harmonious family life.

[margin note: New Democratic Family]

But the de facto family policy of the revolution was to create the new democratic patriarchy. I choose this term to take full advantage of its ironies. The new democratic patriarchy was a patriarchal system whose gender and generational relationships were reformed substantially at the same time that patriarchy was made more democratically available to masses of peasant men. It established a new moral economy in rural China, but one that still was family based. A radical redistribution of patriarchy was its revolutionary essence.

Far from distracting the Chinese Communists from more urgent tasks, their resolution of the peasant family crisis was the central social process of rural revolution. The crisis in the peasant family economy in the base areas provided the CCP with its most significant opportunity to mobilize masses around issues of immediate and urgent interest. The severity and nature of the crisis presented the party its greatest strategic challenge. In seizing the opportunity and addressing the challenge, the CCP forged the successful relationship with the peasantry that was a precondition to its victory and to the success of the second, socialist stage of rural revolution that quickly followed. The remainder of this chapter examines the reconstruction of the material basis for peasant patriarchy through an analysis of the familial implications of the major land reform, cooperativization, and military policies of the Chinese revolution.

Land Reform · Land reform was at the center of the comprehensive rural reconstruction program the CCP devised in response to the agrarian crisis.[16] Its essence was a self-conscious attempt to

---

16. The term "land reform" is somewhat ambiguous. The Chinese Communists typically employ it to refer specifically to the revolutionary confiscation and redistribution of land, particularly during the period 1946–1953. I am using it here, however, as a more general category to denote the entire range of Communist land policies prior to agricultural collectivization. "Land revolution" will refer specifically to the radical seizure and distribution of land.

rebuild the traditional peasant family economy. Measures the CCP took to solve the immediate economic needs of its Red Army and peasant supporters were measures to resolve the peasant family crisis by placing that family economy on a more secure and stable footing. The specific priorities and policies of land reform shifted as the military, political, and geographical conditions confronting the CCP changed and as the party gained experience in rural revolution. An analysis of the evolution of Communist land policy suggests a process in which the CCP learned first to accommodate to and then to exploit the restorationist family motives of its peasant collaborators.

Soon after their retreat from the cities, the Chinese Communists began to construct a land policy. In December 1928, the Hunan-Kiangsi border Soviet drafted the first land law of the Kiangsi Soviet period (1927–1934). The 1928 law required the confiscation of all land. The Soviet government was to become the sole legitimate landowner. Although the confiscated land would be redistributed among poor peasants, they would not receive private ownership rights.[17] This was the most radical land policy ever promulgated by the CCP and is important as evidence of the sort of policy the party quickly learned to eschew.

The moderating effects of the Communists' experience with rural revolution were soon evident. The basic agrarian law of the Kiangsi Soviet period, the Land Law of the Chinese Soviet Republic of December 1931, remained radical in its promotion of class struggle. It required the confiscation of land as well as liquid and fixed assets of "feudal" landlords, warlords, temples, and other large private landowners. However, this time private ownership of land was not abolished. On the contrary, the chief objective of the redistribution process was to make private land-ownership more widely available to poor and middle peasants. The law directed local Soviets to respond to variations in local conditions by selecting a principle of redistribution that would work to the greatest benefit of these groups. They could opt to distribute land according to the number of family members or the amount of labor power in each peasant household.[18]

17. Chao Kuo-chün, *Agrarian Policy of the Chinese Communist Party, 1921–1959*, p. 22.
18. Ibid., pp. 232–34.

The peasants had already taught the CCP the need to avoid alienating the owner-cultivator class among them. Confiscating land from middle peasants had led to sabotage and counter-revolutionary action on their part. Experience gained in the Soviet period taught the party the need to form an alliance with the middle peasants. Their compliance, if not active support, would be crucial to a successful strategy. Moreover, peasants who received land certificates made greater efforts to increase production.[19] As Mao soon learned, the middle peasant economy—a small family farming economy—was the most viable basis for People's War available to the party:

> The agrarian policy in the soviet area at the current stage of revolution is to continue the traditional form of the small farm unit as a consequence of the agrarian conditions found in the soviet area.[20]

Both these factors led the CCP to base its rural policy on the resurrection of the independent family farm.[21] The profound implications of the land law were not lost on the poor peasant masses. Victor Yakhontoff, a prophetic analyst of the Soviet period, pointed out an amusing consonance in the translation into Chinese of the word, "Soviet." The pronunciation of the Chinese ideograms for Soviet is *soo-wei-ai*, which, he claims, sounds quite similar to

19. Information and interpretations in this paragraph are based on Philip C. C. Huang, "Mao Tse-tung and the Middle Peasants, 1925–1928"; Sao-er Ong, "Agrarian Reform in Communist China to 1952"; and Kuo-t'ao Chang, *The Rise of the Chinese Communist Party, 1929–1938*.

20. Quoted in Ilpyong J. Kim, "Mass Mobilization Policies and Techniques Developed in the Period of the Chinese Soviet Republic," p. 83.

21. We lack reliable data on the number of peasants who achieved owner-cultivator status through the land revolution of the Kiangsi period. However, a careful, inductive reading of Mao's report on changes in class status in Hsinkuo County is highly suggestive. According to Mao, before the revolution in Hsinkuo, landlords and rich peasants constituting 6% of the population owned 70% of the land. Middle peasants, by definition the subsistence owner-cultivator class, owned somewhat less land (15%) than their proportion of the population (20%). Mao tells us that land and other goods were distributed to the poor peasants and farm laborers and that, on the whole, middle peasants also increased their landholdings. He does not say what proportion of rural families achieved the capacity for independent family farming in this manner. However, if he is correct that owner-cultivators subsisted on a smaller percentage of land than their percentage of the population, the redistribution of 70% of the county's land should have made independent family farming feasible for the majority of poor peasants in Hsinkuo. Hsinkuo was a model county; it is likely, therefore, that less egalitarian effects were achieved in most other localities. Data from Mao's report are recorded in Chao Kuo-chün, *Agrarian Policy*, p. 30.

she-wei-you, (*shih wo yu*), which means "this is mine."[22] It is easy to see how land revolution in the Kiangsi period would have given many poor peasants good and happy reason to confuse the terms.

The Kiangsi period of the Communist revolution came to a disastrous end in 1934 with the success of the KMT's fifth encirclement and extermination campaign. Not until the survivors of the Red Army's phenomenal Long March united with a small Communist outpost in a desolate area of Northwest China was the CCP again able to establish a base area secure enough for implementing social policies. Efforts to redistribute land were renewed immediately. However, the party soon entered the united front with the KMT against the Japanese invaders. The demands of Japanese military conflict and the terms of the alliance with the KMT caused the party to moderate its agrarian policy further still. During the war of resistance (1937–1945), the CCP abandoned land revolution, but its commitment to land reform continued and matured during these formative years of the new democratic strategy. Now the party turned to methods for the redistribution of land and wealth to the impoverished peasantry that were less direct than those inspiring peasants to forcibly confiscate landlord property. The major means employed were laws that reformed land rent, interest rates, and tax policies.

The principle of "double reduction," which was announced in Ten Great Policies of the CCP in August 1937, bore striking resemblance to the Kuomintang land law of 1930, which had never been implemented.[23] It placed a ceiling of 37.5 percent of the main crop on legitimate land rents in the Communist areas that had not conducted land revolution. The law revealed Communist sensitivity to the nuances of traditional landlord abuses by protecting tenant farmers against advance rental collection, rent deposits, or compulsory labor. Moreover, the party tried to provide peasants with disaster insurance by further reducing or precluding landlord rent collections in the event of unavoidable crop failures. Likewise usury was controlled by imposing ceilings on interest rates and legislating debt relief for the impoverished. On the other hand, in some regions the party tried actively to

---

22. Yakhontoff, *Chinese Soviets*, p. 86.
23. The information on "double reduction" that follows appears in Chao Kuo-chün, *Agrarian Policy*, pp. 38ff.

restore traditional land rights of peasants, such as long-term or permanent tenancy contracts as well as festival gleaning rights.[24] Thus "double reduction" implemented the new democratic strategy of appealing to restorationist sentiment by extracting from traditional practices their democratic essence.

Agricultural tax policies went through a variety of adjustments during the anti-Japanese war, but the principle underlying all of them was consistent. The CCP sought to collect from rural households the amount of revenue it needed at the time according to its estimates of the people's capacity to pay. When revenues from confiscated properties and other sources were sufficient to meet administrative and military needs, no taxes were collected from the peasants. When military pressures precipitated fiscal crisis, peasants were sometimes taxed beyond their capacities. In most cases, the tax was a steeply progressive one that attempted to protect peasant subsistence requirements.[25]

Concern for peasant interests was at the heart of the wartime economic reforms introduced by the Communists because peasants alone could provide the resources crucial to Communist victory. Mao understood land reform in precisely this manner:

> Once the Agrarian system is reformed, even in such an elementary way as by the reduction of rent and interest, the peasants' enthusiasm for production will grow.[26]

Although rent, interest, and tax relief was not the same thing as land revolution, it sought the same economic objective. Each of these measures attempted to support a small family farm economy to enable it, in return, to provide the productive resources needed for People's War. The Shen-Kan-Ning border region agricultural program was explicit on this point:

> In the economy of the Border Region, a small peasant economy still occupies an important position. Hence, the development of agriculture must be regarded as a central chain in economic construction and carried out according to a definite policy.[27]

---

24. Ralph Thaxton, "Tenants in Revolution," pp. 347–48.
25. For details and discussion of the Communists' wartime policies, see Carl E. Dorris, "People's War in North China," pp. 180–82; Linda Ann Grove, "Rural Society in Revolution," p. 225; and Selden, *Yenan Way*, pp. 181–87.
26. Mao Tse-tung, *On Coalition Government*, pp. 80–81.
27. Quoted in Chao, *Agrarian Policy*, p. 41.

Communist sources make the plausible claim that during the war their agrarian reform program in the base areas succeeded in establishing a trend toward the equalization of landownership and increasing the ranks of the rural middle classes.[28] Together this implied a growth in the extent of independent family farming.

Promoting the health of the peasant family economy was one of those causes in which peasant and party fortunes were interdependent. Economic self-sufficiency of the base areas was a crucial wartime objective, and the agrarian reform measures of

---

28. Once again, we lack comprehensive data on the proportion of peasants in Communist areas who achieved independent family farming status as a result of wartime land-reform measures. The extent and success of efforts at implementation varied considerably in the different base areas, largely in accordance with enormous differences in their degree of security and military activity. In some areas, the ravages of war were so extreme that the agrarian economy collapsed entirely. Power changed hands between Communist and collaborationist governments so frequently in certain regions of intense guerrilla warfare that land reform became highly dangerous politics. Peasants in such regions were rightfully wary to accept the benefits of double reduction, let alone to assume activist roles in demanding them, when Japanese and puppet forces were likely to overturn these and retaliate at a moment's notice. For a detailed discussion of one area that was devastated economically, see Grove, "Rural Society." Local control repeatedly changed hands, for example, in the Central Hopeh district of Chin-Ch'a-Chi border region (Dorris, "People's War," pp. 40–42). For other examples, see Ralph Thaxton, "When Peasants Took Power"; Selden, Yenan Way; and Isabel Crook and David Crook, Revolution in a Chinese Village.

In the more secure rear areas of the Shen-Kan-Ning border region, however, and even in certain of the base areas behind Japanese lines, wartime agrarian reform succeeded in promoting the small-farm economy. Whenever possible, the reforms were used to create a more equal distribution of land than pertained in the pre-Communist period. In twenty-four villages of Pei-Yueh in the Shensi-Chahar-Hopeh border region, for example, the reforms enabled poor and middle peasants to purchase 85% of the land sold by landlords and rich peasants during the first five years of the war. There the prewar situation of land accumulation by landlords and rich peasants was reversed, and the result was the growth of a new class of middle peasants from the ranks of the poor peasantry. A survey conducted in thirty-two villages in the consolidated district of Pei-yeng found that there were only 1,746 poor peasants remaining in 1941, where there had been 2,478 in 1937. The family economy of middle peasants also prospered as their landholdings increased by 20% (Dorris, "People's War," pp. 191–93). Similarly, in Shen-Kan-Ning an investigation of a "typical village" showed a wartime rise in the number of rich and middle peasant households from 68% to 88% and a corresponding decline in the proportion of poor peasants and farm laborer households from 32% to 12% (data collected by Israel Epstein and reported in Chao, Agrarian Policy, p. 63). Similar claims were made for the Shansi-Suiyuan liberated area, where 1,993 out of 3,378 poor peasant households achieved rich or middle peasant status between 1940 and 1944, while 100 of 1,961 middle peasant households joined rich peasant ranks (data collected by Mu Hsin and reported in Chao, Agrarian Policy, p. 63).

the period largely succeeded in achieving it. Production declined in many border localities with the onset of war, reaching a nadir during the heavy military and economic blockade years of 1940–1941. However, the Great Production Drive waged in 1944 accomplished a major upsurge in production that placed Communist forces in better circumstances to do battle with the KMT in the civil war years that lay immediately ahead.[29]

After the defeat of the Japanese and the official demise of the united front with the KMT, the CCP had less reason to suppress the poor peasants' rising clamor for land. CCP land policy drifted gradually but irrevocably back toward land revolution. During the civil war, there was considerable vacillation in the party's policy toward rich peasants and in the extremity of class warfare it officially encouraged or condoned, but mobilizing poor peasants to forcibly confiscate and redistribute landlord holdings was once again the basic agrarian program. The land law of September-October 1947 was a key document endorsing land revolution, and its implementation was largely completed in the Old Liberated Areas and in the newly-captured Northeast by March 1949.[30] This was the revolutionary tide that carried the party to national power. It overturned the rural order by eliminating landlords as a class, destroying the sources of power of the traditional rural elite, and radically equalizing the distribution of land and wealth. Land revolution was the key source of peasant support for the CCP, and thereby of Communist victory over the Kuomintang.[31]

Almost immediately after its triumphant return to China's cities, the CCP set out to complete the land revolution nationwide. The party recruited and trained thousands of educated youth to serve as cadres in work teams it dispersed throughout the re-

29. For economic success in Chin-Ch'a-Chi, see Dorris, "People's War", p. 210. Crook and Crook offer data on Ten Mile Inn (*Revolution in a Chinese Village*, p. 96). Grove depicts the success of the Communists in rescuing the weaving industry of the Gaoyang district ("Rural Society," pp. 251, 268).

30. Ralph Montée, "Agrarian Problems and Policies in China," p. 254, and Selden, *Yenan Way*, p. 6.

31. Chalmers Johnson's claim in *Peasant Nationalism and Communist Power* that nationalism was the major basis of peasant support for the CCP has been refuted rather persuasively. Among the more thorough critiques of this thesis are Donald G. Gillin, "Peasant Nationalism in the History of Chinese Communism," and Selden, *Yenan Way*. Pepper provides a detailed comparative analysis of the sources of support for the CCP and the KMT during that period (*Civil War*).

maining areas of rural China. From 1950–1953, the cadres unleashed the forces that completed the new democratic stage of
the Chinese revolution. The two basic documents that underwrote
the national land revolution were the Common Program of September 1949 and the Agrarian Reform Law of June 1950. Both
made explicit that economic development was the ultimate objective of agrarian reform. The Agrarian Reform Law reveals the
self-consciousness with which the party had learned to promote
private landholding among peasants to that end:

> The land ownership system of feudal exploitation by the landlord
> class shall be abolished and the system of peasant land ownership
> shall be introduced in order to set free the rural productive forces,
> develop agricultural production and thus pave the way for New
> China's industrialization.[32]

By now the CCP had accumulated vast experience with rural
revolution. It had become sophisticated organizationally and in
its development of mass line politics. The party exhibited this
sophistication impressively in its approach to land revolution.
It granted local cadres flexibility to adopt methods and timetables
appropriate to local conditions, but it directed a nationwide process
that followed a similar pattern everywhere.

Cadres were instructed first to recruit local activists, to organize
a peasant association, to raise consciousness for land revolution,
and to win peasant support. Then they were to mobilize the
peasants to assign all the village families into social classes, whose
membership criteria the CCP had by then defined in elaborate
and painstaking detail. Next came the "speak bitterness" sessions
that have been immortalized by William Hinton in *Fanshen*, where
the peasants identified the major local agents of their misery
and wrath. These became the primary "struggle targets" of the
ensuing, often violent, drive to seize landlord and counterrevolutionary property and to eliminate the landlords as a class.[33]

---

32. *Agrarian Reform Law of the People's Republic of China and Other Relevant
Documents*, art. 1, p. 1.

33. For data suggesting the extent of violence practiced during land revolution,
see Vivienne Shue, *Peasant China in Transition*, p. 80, n. 45. For first-hand accounts,
see William Hinton, *Fanshen*; Crook and Crook, *Revolution in a Chinese Village*;
Yuan-tsung Chen, *The Dragon's Village*; and Jack Belden, *China Shakes the World*.
Ting Ling, *The Sun Shines Over the Sangkan River*, is a gripping fictionalized
account of land reform.

Redistributing the "struggle fruits" was the next task of the peasant associations, which in the process established themselves as new organs of rural power. Demonstrating lessons learned in earlier periods, the Communists issued peasants title deeds to their land that guaranteed inheritance rights to legitimate heirs. Finally, the entire process of land revolution had to be evaluated by outside investigation teams, which typically discovered so many "deviations" from "correct" policy that the village was required to repeat most of the steps.

The party took care to conduct land revolution effectively because crucial economic and political objectives were riding on it. Economically, the party hoped that land reform would improve the livelihood of the peasants and provide the basis for increased agricultural productivity. Establishing a small-farm economy was the party's now time-tested means for accomplishing these goals. Thus, the immediate economic objective of land reform was to elevate the majority of poor peasants and farm laborers to the status of middle peasants.[34] Politically, land revolution was the process whereby the party sought to consolidate its leadership of the nation by securing peasant support and eliminating competing holders and seekers of power in the countryside.

Land revolution succeeded in attaining both these objectives. One of the major structural transformations it accomplished was the elevation of most poor peasants to middle peasant status. After agrarian reform the majority of Chinese peasants belonged to the new middle peasant class.[35] But no agrarian reformers in

---

34. Mao Tse-tung, "The Chinese Revolution and the Chinese Communist Party," cited in Ong, "Agrarian Reform," p. 25.

35. A survey of selected areas in the "early liberated" districts conducted by the party in 1950 reported that middle peasants comprised 60 to 70% of farm households in the Northeastern provinces and between 80 and 90% of farm households in villages surveyed in Hopei, Shansi, and Chahar (Ong, "Agrarian Reform," p. 41). In the Central South region (a "later liberated" area), Shue estimates that 40% of the cultivated land was confiscated and redistributed to 60% of the population; in Hunan and Hupei, the consequence was, on average, the addition of between one and two acres of land to a peasant family's holdings (*Peasant China*, p. 90). Montée's estimation of the aggregate effect of land revolution throughout China is that poor peasant families increased their landholdings on average from 4.03 to 10.86 *mou*, while landless farm families received an average of 9.63 *mou*. Montée records middle peasants holding an average of 8.09 *mou* per family prior to land revolution ("Agrarian Problems," p. 267). If his figures are accurate, new middle-peasant status had indeed become the rural norm by 1953, and a levelized small family farm economy was the new agrarian order.

China, least of all the Communists, ever imagined that a small private farm economy, even a nonexploitative one, could produce prosperity for the masses or an adequate surplus for industrial development. Stabilizing the small farm economy was an interim post on the trail to collectivization. Immediately the new government began to impose new taxes to appropriate resources for development purposes. In many areas of China peasants were soon finding it as difficult to accumulate grain stores as before land reform. Analysts of agricultural development in China agree that, overall, peasants did not experience a noticeable increase in real income due to land revolution. As Vivienne Shue aptly summarized, "Land reform made a relatively few people poorer, and a great many people somewhat better off. But it made no one rich."[36]

The fact that peasants realized limited income benefits due to land reform magnifies the significance of the political results the party achieved. The CCP cemented its relationship with the peasantry, because "the government was determined on a land policy which most peasants could agree was, in principle, morally right, and . . . in carrying it out the government tried, if it did not always succeed, to act with unusual scrupulousness, [and this] helped to create a reservoir of good will among villagers."[37] Even an explicitly anti-Communist evaluation of land reform, commissioned by the United States Air Force in the heat of Korean War hostilities, was forced to conclude that "no other movement in modern China has been as influential as the agrarian reform movement in mobilizing and organizing the peasants."[38] Land revolution was as much a political as an economic upheaval because the CCP had used it methodically "to *emasculate* the traditional village elite, the entire old rural power structure."[39] The party ensured its authority and eliminated the basis for the rise of future competitors for economic and political power by creating a vast class of small, private farming families dependent upon its structural and political support.

---

36. Shue, *Peasant China*, p. 90. Compatible evaluations appear in C. K. Yang, *Chinese Communist Society*; Paul Chao, "The Marxist Doctrine and the Recent Development of the Chinese Family in Communist China"; and Montée, "Agrarian Problems."

37. Vivienne Bland Shue, "Transforming China's Peasant Villages," p. 125.

38. Ong, "Agrarian Reform," p. 39.

39. Shue, *Peasant China*, p. 41 (my emphasis).

The Family Implications of Land Reform • Although changes in geographic, political, and military conditions led the CCP to modify its tactics—and experience to refine them—there was an underlying integrity to the implicit family policy of land reform in all its guises. True to its proclaimed new democratic spirit, the party sought to rescue peasant family life by simultaneously restoring and transforming its traditional material foundations. CCP land reform policy temporarily reestablished the viability of independent family farming while making it available to the poorest of Chinese peasants. The party's appreciation of family sentiment was evident throughout the revolutionary period. It scrupulously tried to avoid making demands that would confront peasants with direct conflicts between loyalty to the family and loyalty to the revolution. Indeed, land reform policy demonstrated the CCP's ability to turn familial sentiment and loyalties to its own advantage. Because that sentiment was so profoundly patriarchal, concessions to patriarchal morality came to facilitate and shape CCP mass-line politics.

The family restorationist aspects of land reform can be grasped most readily by viewing the way many policies and practices salvaged and buttressed the peasant family household under the authority of its patriarchal head as the basic unit of production. The family household was the effective unit for the implementation of all Communist agrarian policy. In the few instances when official party policy dictated othewise, the hegemony of family production and patriarchal morality asserted itself, and official policy was largely ignored.

The determination of a person's class status was the momentous occasion in land reform, because it established one's access to material rewards and political rights or vulnerability to revolutionary justice. It is of overarching significance, therefore, that class status was assigned to families rather than individuals. The party did recognize that the Chinese marriage system could create ambiguity in a woman's class position, and so it attempted to take length of marriage into account when women married into families with class status significantly different from that of their natal kin.[40] However, the unambiguous bias of the classification guidelines was to maintain the solidarity of the family unit.

40. Delia Davin, *Woman-Work*, p. 27.

By submerging a woman's political identity in that of her patriarchal family, the party structurally denied that a history of sex oppression constituted legitimate grounds for material compensation. This, as we shall see, assured that women's newly granted rights to land would remain largely formal. Classifying women by family membership also caused direct interference with the women's associations established by the party. For example, in Ten Mile Inn, a village in the Old Liberated Areas, every single one of the "old middle peasant" committee members of the local women's association was disenfranchised for belonging to a "feudal tail" family when the party conducted a Feudal Tails Campaign that defined exploiting classes more broadly than during the first round of land revolution. The consequence was that the "women's association became a formal structure with very little driving force."[41] Moreover, women classified as members of the exploiting classes suffered special vulnerabilities during class warfare. They might be raped by militant poor peasants who regarded them as legitimate "struggle fruits" or preferred this classically patriarchal means of disgracing the victims' families. By the time the CCP conducted the national land revolution, it tried to discourage such sexual expressions of class violence,[42] but Mao's early Hunan report had condoned it openly. Defending the role of terror in the revolution, Mao denied that rape was "going too far":

> People swarm into the houses of local tyrants and evil gentry who are against the peasant association, slaughter their pigs and consume their grain. They even loll for a minute or two on the ivory-inlaid beds belonging to the young ladies in the households of the local tyrants and evil gentry. . . . [But] the peasants are clear-sighted. Who is bad and who is not, who is the worst and who is not quite so vicious, who deserves severe punishment and who deserves to be let off lightly—the peasants keep clear accounts, and very seldom has the punishment exceeded the crime.[43]

---

41. Crook and Crook, *Revolution in Chinese Village*, p. 135.

42. Yuan-tsung Chen's, *Dragon's Village*, illustrates this concern. When the beautiful young daughter of a village landlord is raped during land reform, the party cadres worry that the rapist is a poor peasant engaged in a crime of class violence. They attempt to comfort the girl's *family* and condemn the deed. The story has a happy ending when the villain turns out to be a counterrevolutionary.

43. Mao Tse-tung, "Report on an Investigation of the Peasant Movement in Hunan," pp. 29–30. Apparently at that time Mao considered rape an appropriate punishment for the crime of being born a landlord's daughter.

When the time came for a peasant association to redistribute its village's land, the effects of family-based class assignment were apparent immediately. The principle of "land-to-the-tiller" translated into "land-to-the-families-of-tillers." Land, houses, and wealth were confiscated from families. Peasant families sometimes played a vanguard role in the "speak bitterness" and "settle accounts" meetings. The "struggle fruits" these plaintiffs reaped were then distributed not to individuals but to family households. The economic unity of the peasant family made it irresistible to redistribute land in this way. The particulars of the party's distribution practices make its concern to resurrect the self-supporting patriarchal family unit patently clear. The basic principle was to distribute land to families according to the number of workers and dependents contained in each household. As Weng Kuan-tan, land commissioner for provinces in the Old Liberated Areas, explained to Edgar Snow, the primary purpose of the land laws "was to provide for every person sufficient land to guarantee him and his family a decent livelihood—which was claimed to be the most 'urgent demand' of the peasantry."[44] Thus craftsmen and peddlers were to receive land only when this was necessary to support themselves and their families adequately. Households consisting of only one or two ablebodied members received small extra allotments so that they could become self-supporting.[45]

"Land-to-the-tiller" often meant something deeper than simply distributing land to farmers. In many cases the Communists tried quite literally to restore to tenants and farm laborers the actual plots of land they had worked for landlords. This was a policy that worked to the mutual advantage of traditional peasant sentiment and CCP economic concerns. Peasants were more likely to improve their fields if they knew them well and believed they would continue to own them after land reform. The party went further in attempting to restore elements of traditional farming communities. In the national land revolution period, unemployed

44. Edgar Snow, *Red Star Over China*, p. 224. Because the gender of pronouns in spoken Chinese is ambiguous, the use of masculine pronouns in this quotation may reflect a bias or an interpretation of Edgar Snow's.

45. Information in this paragraph comes from Shue, *Peasant China*, p. 61; Chao, *Agrarian Policy*, p. 28; and Thaxton, "When Peasants Took Power," pp. 601–726.

migrants to urban areas were given permission to return to their native villages to claim a share of land to farm. The new regime rounded up elderly vagrants and, whenever possible, reunited them with the families it located in their natal villages. Villages often retained land to distribute to families who had left during the crisis and might wish to return, even when their present whereabouts were unknown. Hired hands and servants who lived outside their native villages also had the right to return and receive their proper share of the "struggle fruits."[46]

Although many of these policies directly served the new government's interest in protecting agricultural production and curbing the growth of cities, they were implemented with self-conscious sensitivity to traditional family values. Long years of collaboration with the peasantry had taught the party the wisdom of this course. Thus the CCP occasionally chose to honor traditional sentiment that interfered with efficient production. There was, for example, only one kind of land that cadres were forbidden to confiscate from landlords—the grave mounds marking the burial sites of ancestors.[47] Later party propaganda even pointed to ancestral honor as a benefit of land reform. In *New Earth*, party publicist Jack Chen tells the story of Lao Wong, a poor peasant who was exploited, abused, and then murdered by landlords and the KMT armies. Lao Wong's family suffered for decades, but he is vindicated in the end when his sons receive their share of land and property: "Lao Wong could rest in peace. Historic justice had been done."[48]

Redistributing land to the families of tillers also gave Communist agrarian reformers an opportunity to address the problem of excessive land fragmentation. Full resolution of the problem awaited collectivization, but in this pivotal new democratic phase, reformers often attempted to consolidate the holdings of family members so that much of their land would be in the same area.[49]

---

46. Most of the information in this paragraph comes from Shue, *Peasant China*, pp. 65–66. For treatment of the elderly, see Deborah Davis-Friedmann, *Long Life*, pp. 281ff.
47. Shue, *Peasant China*, p. 48.
48. Jack Chen, *New Earth*, p. 195.
49. Ong, "Agrarian Reform," p. 11. The Communists could reconcile this goal with their effort to have peasants work their traditional plots by building a family's new farm around its traditional core strips of land.

The implicit effect was to solidify the peasant family as an integrated productive unit. It seems likely this also facilitated the capacity of peasant patriarchs to coordinate and supervise the labor of their women and children.

Land reform promised women equal rights to land, but the centrality of the family economy and the dominance of patriarchal values effectively prevented most women from realizing any direct benefits of this sort. Land was instead distributed to the head-of-the-household, typically a male, and so decisions over allocating land to women became largely a matter of determining which family had rights to which women. Divorced and widowed women who headed households were almost the only women who received land.[50] Land for wives was calculated into the portion distributed to their husbands' families. It became quite a thorny matter, therefore, to allocate the shares of young, unmarried women. Sometimes their shares went to their fathers. Frequently, when these women were betrothed and over age seventeen, their land was allotted to their future in-laws. Some villages avoided the problem altogether by refusing to allot any land for young, unmarried women. And, in some villages, unmarried men received additional land allotments in anticipation of the day that they would receive wives.[51]

The peasants who received land were issued title deeds to underscore the legitimacy of their new ownership rights. Here once again, women's rights were circumvented. Title deeds were made out to households,[52] and households, of course, were overwhelmingly headed by men. The party recognized the contradiction between this practice and its professed commitment to equal land rights for women. A resolution passed by the central committee in 1948 instructed land reform cadres to issue title deeds to women, even when their land was included in their families' allotments. Whenever this policy was implemented, it had profound symbolic significance. As Mariam Frenier has sug-

50. Shue, "Transforming Villages," p. 86. Shue claims that "single women" also received land shares, but it is unclear to me whom she means to include in this category.
51. Kay Johnson, "Feminism and Socialist Revolution," pp. 155–56, and Davin, *Woman-Work*, p. 116.
52. Shue, "Transforming Villages," p. 65.

gested, public acquisition of land could mean a woman assumed a name and a public identity. In 1938, Hsu Kuang, head of the propaganda department of the Hopei Women's Association for National Salvation, explained:

> To emphasize the fact that women had economic equality with the men we gave each woman a land certificate in her own name or wrote her name alongside her husband's on one certificate. Before, women had always been referred to by others as "so-and-so's wife or so-and-so's mother." Now for the first time in their lives many women heard their own names spoken in public.[53]

Unfortunately, but predictably, the resolution on title deeds was rarely implemented.[54]

The tax policies that accompanied land reform also supported the patriarchal family-based economy. According to Vivienne Shue, the new government used its tax policy to encourage a widespread peasant vision of the future that land reform would enable them to *fa chia chih fu* (set up a household and make one's fortune.)[55] Thus, tax relief was granted to the families of refugees who had fled their villages due to famine and other disasters. These families were allowed several years in which to claim their missing relatives as dependents when computing the family tax. Most importantly, the government made the family household the basic taxable unit. This was significant for what it forswore. Shue reports that earlier Chinese regimes had often allowed clans, hamlets, or villages to serve as the units of tax collection, and that in 1930 the CCP itself had experimented with assessing taxes by hamlet. Insisting upon individual household responsibility, therefore, was an important intermediate technique in the construction of new forms of collective responsibility. On the other hand, the government never considered assessing individuals for agricultural taxes because this was a tax on pro-

---

53. Mariam Darce Frenier, "Women and the Chinese Communist Land Reform, 1946–1952," p. 23.

54. Davin, "Women in Liberated Areas," pp. 82, 96. Frenier, "Women," takes the CCP at its word on the resolution and interprets this as a great gain for women, but Davin and Kay Johnson, "Feminism and Socialist Revolution," and, by implication, most descriptions of land reform, argue otherwise.

55. Shue, *Peasant China*, p. 99.

duction, and in the new democratic era, "the basic agricultural production unit was indisputably the farming household."[56]

The party applied its mass-line politics to the delicate matter of determining each family's fair tax, and again found patriarchal sentiment a useful ally. A farming household's tax rate was supposed to represent its total agricultural income divided by the number of its household members who relied for their support chiefly on agricultural production. To arrive at this figure, hamlets held a general meeting to engage in "self report, public discussion, and democratic determination of yield." Only heads of households participated in these important new collective deliberations![57]

Land reform gave the CCP ample opportunity to appreciate the depth of patriarchal family morality among the peasant villages, and the party's mass-line politics led cadres repeatedly to capitulate to its demands.[58] One effective means of mobilizing male peasants was to appeal to their desire to marry. Thus a local peasant association badgered a reluctant man to participate in the rent reduction drive of the united front period: "If you reduce rent, I guarantee that you will have enough to have a wedding. If you still refuse, you had better forget the ceremony and go fuck youself!" This man rushed home and pressured his strong-willed father to join the rent reduction drive.[59]

The educated urbanized youth who served as work team cadres were taught explicitly to assimilate their values and behaviors to those of the poor peasants. They quickly discovered that misogyny was a constitutive basis of the rural social universe. *The Dragon's Village*, Yuan-tsung Chen's fictionalized account of her own experience in a desolate village in Gansu, provides poignant examples of the process. Ling-ling, the young female land reform cadre/narrator, learned this aspect of mass-line work the painful

---

56. Ibid., p. 108.
57. Ibid., p. 131.
58. For an astute analysis of the antifeminist effects of the seemingly democratic aspects of Maoist forms of political decentralization, see Kay Johnson, "Feminism and Socialist Revolution," p. 175.
59. Quoted in Yung-fa Chen, "The Making of a Revolution," pp. 277–78. Chen interprets this as evidence that the CCP used material gain as a major appeal to mobilize peasants for class struggle, but, once again, the integration of material and moral benefits under patriarchy is striking.

way. When she and her male teammates arrived in the village and met with the local peasant leaders—all males—the men talked past her. If she asked a question, the village leaders replied to her comrades. Before long Ling-ling found her teammate adapting comfortably to this norm. He imitated the peasants by refusing to look at her when conversing in public: "When they talked to a woman, they looked straight ahead as if they were talking to some other man in the same room." Cadres were disciplined severely for breaches of local sexual norms. When the party discovered a romance between two young cadres working in a nearby village, it separated them after subjecting them to a humiliating cadre criticism session where they were educated soundly: "You know the peasants abhor the idea of young people falling in love and choosing their own marriage partners. To their minds, free choice in love is the same as adultery. If they find out what you've done, they'll distrust all of us." When Ling-ling left the meeting she made a vow to "avoid all scandal involving 'men and women relations.' "[60]

Land reform provoked not a few peasant men to rather bald expression of their patriarchal yearnings. Many regarded the women of the wealthier classes as appropriate "struggle fruits." Peasant bachelors in Ten Mile Inn went so far as to urge "that the wives of their former exploiters should be divorced so that they themselves might marry them." In this case, party cadres took care to make explicit that the purpose of the "new democratic family" policy was "to consolidate family life, not to break it up."[61] However, there were instances when extremes of patriarchal "justice" were tolerated, and even encouraged by the party. For example, the pre-Communist family crisis had motivated many poor women to leave their husbands and marry other men to keep from starving. Ralph Thaxton reports that after the Eighth Route Army liberated areas in the Yellow River region, many of the former husbands appealed to the Communists to "liberate" and return their former wives to them. The CCP was extremely sympathetic to these men. It endeavored to persuade the women to return to their original husbands, arguing that families should

---

60. Yuan-tsung Chen, *Dragon's Village*, pp. 75, 138, 163.
61. Crook and Crook, *Revolution in a Chinese Village*, p. 166.

suffer poverty together. The cadres relented in this persuasion only when a woman "steadfastly refused." And then they attempted to procure compensation from the second husbands for the deserted men: "The party requested these indemnity payments [!] partly as an expression of sympathy and partly as compensation for the harm done to the material well-being of the males who lost the services of their wives."[62]

In sum, the implicit family policy of Communist land reform was to establish the economic basis for the new democratic patriarchy. Land reform was the radical core of the new democratic stage of the Chinese revolution. It radically equalized the distribution of patriarchal authority in rural China. The traditionally dominant class of rural patriarchs was indeed "emasculated," when land, the economic base of their power, was forcibly confiscated and redistributed to the vast majority of impoverished peasant men. The latter, the major beneficiaries of land reform, found independent family farming—that most deeply desired but historically elusive goal of the peasantry—within their reach at last. Thereby, the traditional basis of peasant patriarchy and family security was restored, or first made accessible, to many of the victims of China's agrarian crisis.

But land reform did not simply restore patriarchy to the peasantry. By democratizing the distribution of its economic basis, land reform began also to transform the contents of patriarchal privilege. Instead of replacing one class of big patriarchs with another, land reform made small-scale patriarchy the new rural family order. Lineal power was undermined when corporate landholdings were appropriated, and patriarchal ritual life was democratized as well. No family retained or achieved the capacity to stage elaborate Confucian ceremonies or festivities. Nor could the new class of rural patriarchs afford its own retinue of concubines or servants. On the other hand, peasant families now had the means to avoid killing the infants, selling or betrothing the young daughters that landlessness had led them to discard.

---

62. Thaxton, "When Peasants Took Power," p. 200. Yung-fa Chen reports that a friend who spent a year in Hsinyang in the late 1950s also heard stories of men who had appealed to the Communists to retrieve their former wives for them (personal communication).

Moreover, Communist land reform policies leveled a more explicit challenge to patriarchal prerogatives. Women's new de jure rights to land, although easily circumvented, coupled with women's public participation in the process of land redistribution, materially enhanced their status within the newly democratized patriarchal order.

New Democratic Cooperative Policy ▪ Land reform was the core process in the Communists' new democratic revolution, but it did not operate alone. To grasp its revolutionary significance fully, one must view it in context of the entire rural reconstruction program of the CCP. While the economic strategy underlying land reform was to resuscitate the peasant family economy in order to support family subsistence as well as People's War, the CCP never imagined that land revolution was itself adequate to this task. Agrarian resources were so minimal, even when more fairly distributed, that they had to be stretched to their productive limits. This pressing need to share productive resources, combined with the ultimate socialist objectives of the revolution, motivated the party to encourage cooperative forms of production and consumption. Simultaneous with all phases of land reform, the CCP organized Mutual Aid Teams (MATs) and various cooperatives to meet these needs.

The principles and practices guiding the formation of MATs and cooperatives exhibited the most dialectical aspect of new democratic strategy. On the one hand, they provided crucial support to the traditionalist implications of land reform. Mutual aid and co-op policies buttressed the family household as the basic unit of production, reinforced the major features of the traditional sexual division of labor, and deferred to patriarchal mores in the process. On the other hand, they deepened the transformative implications of land reform because they further weakened the traditional bases of lineage power, created new roles for women that made inroads in the traditional division of labor, and, most importantly, laid the foundation for the collectivization of agriculture that eventually would replace the peasant family mode of production.

MATs were small, informal, and nominally voluntary groups of peasant households organized to exchange labor and to share work implements and beasts of burden. The MAT was the simplest, most basic form of producer cooperative encouraged by the CCP. More formal cooperative ventures based on purchased membership shares grew out of and supplemented the MAT program. Co-ops to organize trade, transport, and credit for the rural economy accompanied and supported the growth of the mutual aid movement.

The organization of mutual aid teams went hand in glove with land reform in all periods of rural revolution. Mutual aid movements always coincided with the major mass mobilization and production campaigns of the revolution. A major drive to organize MATs accompanied the 1933 Land Investigation Movement of the Kiangsi Soviet period.[63] The mutual aid program was central to the economic strategy of the war of resistance. It played a particularly crucial role in the Great Production Drive, which began in Shen-Kan-Ning in 1943 and spread to the other anti-Japanese bases in 1943–1944.[64] The mutual aid movement expanded during the land revolution of the war of liberation period, when, as Hinton has noted, "mutual aid was not only relatively easy to initiate, it was absolutely necessary if the peasants were to produce at all."[65] By the time land revolution became a national phenomenon in 1950, mutual aid had become "the basis of the government's entire development program."[66]

The historical development of CCP cooperative policy suggests that the peasants taught the party the same lesson about the centrality of the family economy they had had to learn in formulating land reform strategy. During the Kiangsi Soviet period, the party attempted to organize cooperatives from above that were based on government share-capital and were mainly managed by government and party officials. However, this approach to cooperative development failed because, as Selden suggests, "the peasants viewed the cooperatives not as their own but merely as agencies of government."[67] The party learned instead to base its cooperative ventures on the peasants' traditional forms

---

63. Ilpyong J. Kim, *The Politics of Chinese Communism*, pp. 142ff.
64. Selden, *Yenan Way*, p. 246, and Dorris, "People's War," p. 210. Dorris dates the Great Production Drive in Shen-Kan-Ning as 1942, but Selden is probably a more reliable source for the Shen-Kan-Ning region.
65. Hinton, *Fanshen*, p. 212.
66. Shue, "Transforming China's Villages," p. 189. See Montée, "Agrarian Problems," p. 304, for aggregate data concerning the 1950–1953 period.
67. Selden, *Yenan Way*, p. 238.

of mutual aid. A variety of mutual aid arrangements was historically practiced by Chinese peasants. Some involved cooperative labor on large-scale projects of mutual interest, such as reclamation or irrigation enterprises. Another form consisted of landless farmers banding into work groups, which were hired collectively. The most prevalent form, however—and the one that proved to be the most amenable to socialist development—was the voluntary, informal, seasonal arrangement to exchange labor and resources made between several households, typically united by bonds of kinship, friendship, and/or community.[68]

Far from trying to challenge the private family interests that underlay this third variety of mutual aid, the CCP learned to make these the center of its cooperative program. According to Ralph Thaxton, co-ops failed at first in the base region of the Yellow River precisely because the household economy had not yet been sufficiently strengthened to support cooperative ventures; experiences like these taught the party that "the crucial criteria for the development of the cooperative movement proved to be the preservation of the peasant family and its customary rights to private ownership and profit."[69] A Communist cadre who surveyed the relative success of various mutual aid arrangements in rural Shantung during the anti-Japanese war also reached that conclusion:

> No matter what kind of mutual aid arrangement we use, we cannot interfere with family household production, private profit, and voluntary joint self-help. If we depart from this principle, there is no way to realize mutual aid. Therefore, the best form is the third kind [family-centered, voluntary, self-help]. . . . As to the first form, collective production, it is not suitable to this stage. If we pursue it, we not only cannot actively develop each small productive unit, but, on the contrary, we most likely will reduce the will of the peasants to produce.[70]

---

68. Descriptions of traditional forms of mutual aid are available in Shue, *Peasant China*, pp. 149–53; Thaxton, "When Peasants Took Power," pp. 282–89; and Selden, *Yenan Way*, p. 243.

69. Thaxton, "When Peasants Took Power," pp. 203, 285; Dorris, "People's War"; Selden, *Yenan Way*; and Shue, *Peasant China*; all agree that the most successful MATs and cooperatives were those that built on traditional forms, particularly the private family unit.

70. Quoted in Thaxton, "When Peasants Took Power," p. 286.

Investigations like these probably underlay the subsequent self-conscious efforts by Communist governments to revert to small-scale, family-based, mutual labor forms. The Chin-Ch'ai-Chi border government, for example, designed a new set of mutual aid models in 1943 that tried to insure the return of profits from the harvest to individual households.[71] Small teams of three to five households, frequently formed around kinship groups, became a widespread and acceptable pattern during national land revolution in the early 1950s.[72]

Each peasant household retained full rights of ownership to its land while belonging to a MAT. Landlord and rich peasant families, however, were barred from membership. Although the Communists fully planned to integrate women into the agricultural labor force, their new democratic policy was to gain mass peasant compliance with organized cooperatives through concessions to patriarchal morality. Consequently, in areas where women's traditional role in agricultural production was limited, women initially were denied membership in the teams. When they were admitted, generally they were organized in segregated teams to avoid provoking villagers' suspicions about women and men relating outside the approved familial context. Moreover, MATs systematically discriminated against women when they awarded work points. Separate standards were devised so that a woman might earn a flat rate of three to five points on a task for which the standard male rate was ten points. Occasionally cadres protested, but "the simple assumption made by many that no women's work could be of any great value"[73] was so entrenched that peasant patriarchs successfully evaded compliance with the equal-pay-for-equal-work ideal. Once again, the Communists chose not to press the point.[74]

The work of the MATs typically was organized around the traditional familial division of labor. A man with more land to cultivate than his team members might contribute supplementary labor by his son to balance accounts. The team members' wives

---

71. Dorris, "People's War," p. 211.
72. Shue, *Peasant China*, p. 153.
73. Ibid., p. 168.
74. Information in this paragraph comes primarily from Davin, *Woman-Work*, p. 147, and Shue, *Peasant China*, pp. 155–68.

might take turns preparing meals for the team to free the remaining wives for cooperative spinning or weaving tasks. Economic planning at the household level was fostered. The party encouraged families to hold family councils, in which the male head-of-the-household was the chairman of meetings to plan the family's division of labor and work schedule and to discuss the quality and quantity of each member's work.[75]

Finally, mutual aid gave peasants direct support for family needs. MAT members in Hou Shan Ku, a model mutual aid experiment in the Yellow River region, were allowed to attend the birth, marriage, and funeral ceremonies of their relatives and friends without losing work points. The model teams also provided "social crisis insurance" to families by offering grain loans, household repair work, and additional labor to families in need.[76] Moreover, the party actively exploited familial idioms in advertising such benefits. Its promotional literature on agricultural cooperation might praise a team leader because "he takes care of the whole team like a father." And peasants were enticed to work together "as a brotherly collective."[77]

In all these ways the cooperative movement reinforced the tendency of land reform to rescue the traditional family economy, the economic basis for peasant patriarchy. But, at the same time, the cooperative movement was the embryonic form of the collectivization of the rural Chinese economy, which was to replace the private family economy with startling speed. The cooperative movement provided structural support to the transformative goals of the new democratic strategy. Women and youth achieved new roles and recognition within the family economy. Lineage power was undermined while the stability of the family economy became dependent upon the CCP.

The exigencies of People's War made female labor contributions crucial to Communist success. The cooperative movement was particularly significant in supporting these vital new roles for women. Mutual Aid Teams and co-ops were often the first women's groups organized in the liberated areas. Likewise, from the

75. Information in this paragraph is based on Chao Kuo-chün, *Agrarian Policy*, pp. 50–51, 144, and Dorris, "People's War," pp. 213ff.

76. Thaxton, "When Peasants Took Power," p. 134–36.

77. Jack Chen, *New Earth*, pp. 76, 127.

earliest days of CCP rural strategy, MATs appeared first and more frequently in localities forced to rely primarily on women for production. Mutual aid was frequently coordinated with land reform to enable women in labor-short villages to play the leading role in both. In areas where the traditional sexual division of labor barred women from agricultural work, cooperative labor first made their participation possible. Similarly, cooperative economic organization enabled women to enter new roles in marketing in areas where this had once been an exclusive male province.[78]

More frequently, however, women's cooperatives were organized to revive traditional handicraft production. In general these co-ops organized women around traditional female handicraft skills such as spinning and weaving. The revival of handicraft production had contradictory effects on the family economy and its sexual division of labor. When women were organized into spinning and weaving cooperatives they had the opportunity to emerge from the ccnfines of direct familial and patriarchal supervision of their labor and to form nonfamilial social bonds with other women. Moreover, the fact that they were remunerated for their work, even when patriarchal norms were so entrenched that compensation went directly into the hands of the head of the household, meant that women's productive contribution to the family economy received explicit recognition.

There were also instances when the revival of handicraft manufacture strengthened home production under the direct supervision of the family patriarch. A good example of this is the Gaoyang district of Hopeh, which had a long history as a weaving center.[79] By the early-twentieth century, textile production had become highly commercialized, organized into factories, and so central to the economy of the region that industrial weaving outstripped farming as the primary productive activity of local men. At the time the Communists achieved a secure foothold

---

78. For the Kiangsi Soviet, see Kathy Walker, "The Party and Peasant Women"; for the liberated areas, see Davin, *Woman-Work*, pp. 147–48. Grove discusses women in Gaoyang entering agriculture and marketing for the first time ("Rural Society," p. 264).

79. The account that follows is based on Grove, "Rural Society," but the interpretation is my own.

in Gaoyang in 1937 the weaving industry was in severe economic crisis. Land reform was by itself inadequate to rescue the local economy because the area was too land short to support its population. The Communists directed their major economic reconstruction efforts to restoring the weaving industry and making it a viable, less exploitative enterprise. Most of the local looms had been sold for scrap metal during World War II. Hence the Communists became involved in producing and distributing looms to rural households. They developed low-interest loan programs to enable poor families to purchase looms. This had the effect of restoring weaving to household production in a region that had already experienced an early form of capitalist industrialization. By distributing looms to poor families, the Communists were once again returning the means of production to the hands of peasant patriarchs. In Gaoyang, this quite literally restored weaving to male hands, this time as masters of their own family economy. However, the cooperative movement introduced a simultaneous countertendency to the restoration of peasant patriarchy among Gaoyang weavers. Many of the women of the weaver households were organized into spinning cooperatives which gathered women together outside private household production and paid them for their work.

Despite the contradictory tendencies of the restoration of home industry, contributions to the family economy by women were made more evident by the expanded productive roles, the remuneration, and the opportunities for social interchange the cooperative movement introduced. Not surprisingly this translated into improved status, self-confidence, and a larger voice in family affairs. Thus, while peasant patriarchs chaired the "family councils" that planned household production, women and young people were encouraged to voice their criticisms freely.[80] When the peasant women Jack Chen interviewed explained the benefits of the cooperative movement, they focused on this point: "And we've a full say, too, in everything that concerns our homes. Home life is happier."[81]

The cooperative movement made a lateral attack on the eco-

80. Chao, *Agrarian Policy*, p. 144.
81. Jack Chen, *New Earth*, p. 147.

nomic power of traditional rural elites, thereby undermining the power of patrilineages and making the stability of peasant families dependent upon the CCP regime. Land revolution put an end to private corporate economic holdings, which had been the material basis of lineage power. This made the collective resources of MATs and cooperatives an economic force to be reckoned with in the rural social structure. And landlords and rich peasants could not join. It is true and noteworthy that a good many of these cooperative ventures formed around male lineage links.[82] But it is also important that male lineage links were not the official basis of the new forms of economic and social association. This created space for people to develop significant nonkinship relationships, a space crucial for women's capacity to challenge their traditional restrictions.

As lineage power weakened and the cooperative movement grew, the vitality of the private family economy came to rest on an elaborate system of Communist supports. In fact, one method the party used to encourage peasant families to join the MATs and co-ops was to offer their members preferential treatment in requests for grain loans.[83] The party established co-ops for supply and marketing as well as credit co-ops. These cooperative ventures began to replace and democratize the availability of economic services traditionally provided by lineages and rural elites. Families needing help in repairing their houses, marrying or burying their members, expanding their cultivated acreage, or eating before the harvest turned increasingly to the CCP and the cooperative organizations it actively fostered.

Communist Military Policy • Economic policy was not the only arena in which Communist measures served to construct a new democratic patriarchal family system. Because People's War thoroughly integrated economic, social, and military activities, Communist military policy and practices complemented economic efforts that rescued and reformed the traditional peasant family system.

---

82. See Norma Diamond, "Collectivization, Kinship and the Status of Women in Rural China," for a superb discussion of the significance of this aspect of the collectivization process.

83. Shue, *Peasant China*, p. 197.

The popularity of the Communist Red Army has become legendary. In no small measure the Red Army won the affection of its peasant supporters through the respect and assistance it rendered to traditional family life. The military strategy of People's War, however, had implications for patriarchy that were particularly contradictory. Its dependence upon the active support of base area populations created important new roles and recognition for women. Yet the army was itself a male bastion and peasant men were its mass base. This placed crucial limits on the extent to which People's War challenged patriarchal prerogatives. Thus a variety of Red Army practices contributed to the emergence of the new democratic patriarchy.

As with land reform and co-ops, Communist military strategists quickly learned the need for a sympathetic approach to the material and spiritual needs of the traditional peasant family. Military failures of the Peasant Movement period of the 1920s taught the party to provide protection and preferential treatment for soldiers' dependents. Direct experiences with the day-to-day concerns of peasants taught the party the centrality of family issues. The arbitration department of the peasant association P'eng P'ai established in Haifeng in the 1920s found that almost one-third of the cases it handled during its first few months of existence involved family conflicts, such as marriage difficulties, divorce requests, and lineage disputes.[84] During the period of the Kiangsi Soviet, as the CCP formed its Red Army, it translated the Peasant Movement lessons into military policies that made protection of family life a cornerstone of People's War strategy. Both the recruitment and maintenance practices of the Red Army provide evidence that this is the case.

The Chinese Communists drew upon family ties and familial sentiment to recruit soldiers for its regular forces and to mobilize the rural populace for guerrilla activities and war support labor. Indigenous self-defense forces that peasants created to resist Japanese depredations commonly used such slogans as "Protect our homes, don't protect the country."[85] The Communists enlisted this parochial sentiment in the service of socialist and nationalist

---

84. Hofheinz, *Broken Wave*, p. 154.
85. Quoted in Grove, "Rural Society," p. 293, n. 9.

ends. Communist resistance propaganda underscored the relationship between familial and nationalistic concerns, and did so in a manner designed to appeal to the most conservative of peasant men. For example, in 1938 Shansi peasants were recruited to Communist resistance through such appeals as the following:

> Comrades! Japan has invaded our Shansi, killing large numbers of our people, burned thousands of our houses, raped our women in countless numbers, robbed us of our food and wealth, trampled on the graves of our ancestors, forced our wives and children to flee, destroyed our famous places. . . . Everybody! Rise up and join a guerrilla self-defense unit! . . . Defend our anti-Japanese patriotic people's government! . . . Act in unison with Army and people to overthrow Japanese imperialism![86]

The Communists built guerrilla institutions around family and local bonds. The army worked through local government and mass organizations in its enlistment drives. Members of women's groups were mobilized to encourage their husbands and sons to join the Red Army. Women were also the subject of explicit party appeals to pressure their husbands to abandon the White Army.[87] Their male kin were likely to be responsive because they knew the Red Army would reward their participation with close attention to the security of their families. In 1941, when the Army evaluated the contribution which its attention to family security had made to recruitment efforts, it found good cause for self-congratulation:

> Only with good dependents' work are we able continually to expand and consolidate the army and to obtain a dependable source for the continual growth of the resistance force. Dependents' work in various counties has gradually been realized and is widely in practice. In mass military mobilization meetings there is often a great wave of volunteers for the army and one may see fathers sending sons, wives encouraging husbands, and brothers joining

---

86. Quoted in Jean Chesneaux, *Peasant Revolts in China, 1840–1949*, p. 122.
87. For example: "In particular in the villages of Hunan there are many families of soldiers of the White Army. The women must be organized to write or to speak with their husbands and to induce them not to serve with the warlords against the Red Army and to persuade them to support the Soviet Government" (quoted in M. J. Meijer, *Marriage Law and Policy in the Chinese People's Republic*, p. 40).

the army together. The implementation of dependents' work has actually been quite effective and its importance is deeply apparent.[88]

The army found familial sentiment an equally effective motivation for participation in war support work. Once their sons, husbands, and brothers had enlisted in the army, civilians were ever more likely to participate willingly in war service activities integral to guerrilla warfare. As Thaxton has pointed out, the people who bore stretchers or tended pack animals and the women who volunteered their caves as makeshift medical centers for the Red Army were the fathers, mothers, grandmothers, and wives of young men risking their lives at the front. Thus, "the protection and preservation of their family was the principle social motivation for participating in war service duties."[89] Enlistment in Communist armies and participation in war service was generally voluntary, but whenever the army was forced to resort to conscription, it was careful to take account of the labor needs of peasant families. So thorough were the Communists in their efforts to reward peasant support for the Red Army that they even forced local gentry to humble themselves by visiting the homes of poor soldiers to comfort their family members.[90] Policies like these made even the coercive demands of the Red Army widely acceptable among the peasantry.

A second way in which Red Army recruitment took advantage of aspirations generated by family crisis was by providing a surrogate home for male social outcasts and drifters. The vast majority of Red Army soldiers were young and unmarried. Many had been propertyless victims of broken peasant families.[91] According to Edgar Snow, a fair number were "divorced," in the sense that they had willfully left their wives and families behind them. Snow suspected that the wish to divorce had been one reason why many of these soldiers had joined the army.[92] Belden, too, noted the relationship between family trouble and enlistment: "As a matter of fact, unhappy marriages, I found, were one of the big reasons why both men and women joined not only the

Red Army Recruitment

---

88. Quoted in Dorris, "People's War," p. 230.
89. Thaxton, "When Peasants Took Power," p. 390.
90. Gillin, "Peasant Nationalism," p. 285.
91. Thaxton, "When Peasants Took Power," pp. 224–25.
92. Edgar Snow, *Red Star Over China*, p. 259.

army, but the whole revolution."[93] In this sense, the army may have appealed to more "modern" family motives generated by patriarchy's decline. The complex intermingling of traditional and "modern" familial motives for enlistment is suggested in Snow's description of the circumstances that led a 24-year-old squad commander, whom he interviewed in 1936, to join the Eighth Route Army:

> He had been in the Red Army since 1931. In that year his father and mother were killed by a Nanking bomber, which also destroyed his house, in Kiangsi. When he got home from the fields and found both his parents dead he had at once thrown down his hoe, bidden his wife good-by, and enlisted with the Communists. One of his brothers, a Red partisan, had been killed in Kiangsi in 1935.[94]

The Red Army earned its popularity most directly through the manner in which it conducted itself and treated its peasant constituency. Here especially traditional family values received their due. The army became famous for its discipline. Its rules and regulations were carefully designed to avoid traditional military abuses or unnecessary disruption to the peasant family economy. They demanded scrupulous respect for persons and property, and spelled out the terms of this respect in minute detail:

1. Replace all doors when you leave a house.
2. Return and roll up the straw matting on which you sleep.
3. Be courteous and polite to the people and help them when you can.
4. Return all borrowed articles.
5. Replace all damaged articles.
6. Be honest in all transactions with the peasants.
7. Pay for all articles purchased.
8. Be sanitary, and, especially, establish latrines a safe distance from people's houses.[95]

The rank and file was taught not to violate local customs or superstitions. The Red Army's reputation was immeasurably

---

93. Belden, *China Shakes the World*, p. 353.
94. Edgar Snow, *Red Star Over China*, p. 84.
95. Quoted in ibid., p. 173.

enhanced because the rank and file and the officers seldom violated local women. This rather extraordinary record for a patriarchal army resulted from active learning and serious effort on the Red Army's part. Plagued from the outset by anti-Communist propaganda depicting Red orgies and plans to communalize women,[96] the Red Army took exceptional care to discover and correct sexual abuses within its ranks. For example, an autobiography by Chang Kuo-t'ao, a founder of the CCP and head of the Oyüwan Soviet during the Kiangsi period, reports on a party congress held in Oyüwan in 1931, where peasants were invited to criticize the army. Two major grievances were incidents in which food had been seized from people who were not tyrants and women had been raped. According to Chang, the congress experienced its most difficult moment when peasants directly attacked Hsu Chi-sheng, commander of the Eleventh Division of the Fourth Red Army for womanizing with a personal retinue of common-law wives. The congress took immediate steps to remedy these problems. It instituted a strict code of discipline in which convicted rapists were to be severely punished, even put to death. It inaugurated an educational campaign to encourage legal marriage between women and men. And it decided to establish "lovers' chambers" to accommodate husbands and wives in the army and government.[97] By the time Edgar Snow did his investigative reporting on the activities of the Red Army in the Northwest base areas of the anti-Japanese resistance war, Communist efforts to impose strict sexual discipline seem to have been quite effective. Snow reported that most Red Army men were virgins and that they treated peasant women with respect. He claimed that officers did not have concubines or mistresses. Soldiers who got women

---

96. Historically, ideas like these have encouraged undisciplined male converts to communism to commit sexual abuses. This was a serious problem in the immediate postrevolutionary years in the Soviet Union (Kent H. Geiger, *The Family in Soviet Russia*). The Chinese Communists encountered similar difficulties during the Kiangsi Soviet period (Hu Chi-hsi, "The Sexual Revolution in the Kiangsi Soviet").

97. Kuo-t'ao Chang, *Rise of the CCP*, pp. 24–30. According to Chang, the "lovers' chambers" were also available to "those who were truly in love with each other," a reflection, perhaps, of the lingering influence of May Fourth sentiment. Although the data are silent on this matter, one suspects that no such amenities were available to the unmarried during the ensuing periods in the more conservative Northwest.

pregnant were expected to marry them, but such incidents were rare, and he found no evidence of promiscuity. Instead, Snow concluded that despite anti-Communist propaganda, "the truth seemed to be that a revolutionary army anywhere was always in danger of becoming too puritanical, rather than the contrary."[98]

The army endeavored to become self-sufficient economically so that it would not overburden the minimal resources of the rural economy. In 1938 the army experimented with having units do their own farming, animal raising, and shoemaking. By the time of the 1943 production drive, all military units and party cadres were extensively involved in production. Many of these went to heroic lengths to support themselves under conditions of extreme natural adversity and material deprivation.[99] And there was great symbolic value to the fact that the highest-ranking leaders labored to supply some of their own provisions. Commander-in-chief Chu Teh grew cabbages, and Mao raised enough tobacco to supply smokes at party headquarters.[100]

Economic self-sufficiency was an ideal the Red Army approximated far better than almost any other army in the history of China or elsewhere,[101] but it was never possible to achieve fully. Nor could the army always depend entirely upon the voluntary contributions of the rural populace. When war pressure was most intense, the army was forced to require labor service from the peasantry. Because peasant labor capacity was already severely strained, mandatory war service threatened the family economy, and thereby jeopardized peasant support for the Communists. But the Communists thoroughly understood this danger and devised elaborate egalitarian systems to minimize peasant losses from participation in war service. They took care to consider the labor needs and the mores of the traditional family economy. The army took the peasant family as the unit for assigning and computing labor service days, and protected family interests while members labored for the military. For example, the army facilitated profitable trade ventures for peasants engaged in war transportation services. It considered the age, health, and strength

98. Edgar Snow, *Red Star Over China*, p. 259.

99. For an outstanding example, see the discussion of the model 359th Brigade in Selden, *Yenan Way*, pp. 251–52.

100. Theodore H. White and Annalee Jacoby, *Thunder Out of China*, p. 228.

101. Data on this are available in Selden, *Yenan Way*, p. 253.

of family members before assigning labor. The scheduling of war service obligations was coordinated with production seasons. Even when the labor of women, the elderly, or the weak was pooled to augment its contribution, the army converted work points earned in this manner into family scores for war service duties.[102] Thereby, once again, Communist policy gave implicit support to traditional patriarchal norms in an instance where new roles for women had the potential to threaten them.

The Red Army went much farther in promoting traditional family interests than simply minimizing peasant losses. It gave active and direct support to the families of its soldiers. The army's "dependents' work" succeeded in recruiting enlistees precisely because it methodically looked after family interests. Probably the most important program in this regard was the substitute cultivation of land for soldiers' dependents.[103] Village government, mass organizations, and available troops assumed the responsibility of maintaining the family economy for soldiers at the front. They plowed and harvested the fields, carried water from the wells, and gathered fuel for the hearths of soldiers' families. This is yet another way in which family and military interests were harmonized. Economic production, family morale, and military loyalty were promoted at once.[104]

Red Army families received many other forms of assistance and privilege. Their agricultural taxes were reduced or exempted. Families of revolutionary martyrs were allowed to include their martyred dead as part of their households when computing taxes. Dependent families were granted the use of specific public lands for production, and they sometimes received preferential treatment during land distribution. Their youth were offered free schooling. So sensitive were the Communists to the familial basis of peasant support that they even instructed local government officials to help families write letters to their sons, husbands, brothers, and fathers at the front.[105]

---

102. Thaxton, "When Peasants Took Power," pp. 384ff.
103. Some data on this policy are available in Selden, *Yenan Way*, p. 137.
104. Crook and Crook, *Revolution in a Chinese Village*, p. 76.
105. The privileges awarded Red Army families are documented in Shue, "Transforming China's Villages," pp. 149–50; Dorris, "People's War," p. 230; Kuo-t'ao Chang, *Rise of the CCP*, p. 348; Selden, *Yenan Way*, p. 137; Meijer, *Marriage Law and Policy*, p. 40; and Kim, *Politics of Chinese Communism*, p. 170.

Although soldiers' dependents received preferential treatment, the Red Army did not restrict its services to military families. The border government sponsored massive famine relief efforts in which military personnel played crucial roles. For example, in 1939 when a massive flood damaged 70 villages, over 10,000 homes, and more than 147,000 *mou* of land in the Pei-yueh district of the Chin-Ch'a-Chi border region, the government initiated a massive reclamation project. The military actively participated, recovering 110,000 *mou* of flooded land, plowing 180,000 *mou* of additional land, and digging 160 new wells.[106] These direct rescue efforts to families in crisis were characteristic of Red Army assignments. Thaxton claims that the 129th Division of the Eighth Route Army "took helping peasants recover from subsistence agricultural disasters as their main task."[107] They combatted floods, droughts, and locusts, as well as joining in regular farming tasks. Military assistance to production was not confined to disaster relief. At harvest times, the Eighth Route Army was joined by party and government personnel to help the peasants reap full yields. And, of course, the military had central responsibility for penetrating, first, the Japanese and, later, the KMT economic blockades, which were strangling the village supply routes.[108] By the time the peasant economy began to recover from the ravages of the worst war years, peasant families had indelible evidence that their resurrection was in considerable part attributable to the deeds of the Red Army.

But, as with land reform and cooperatives, when peasants joined the Red Army or labored for it their family relationships were reformed by the very processes that saved them. Because People's War strategy necessitated the active mobilization of the entire population of the base area, it dramatically expanded women's traditional social world. If military and economic activities are integrated in People's War, nowhere are they so indistinguishable as in the roles of women. The regular forces of the Red Army remained a male preserve. Although women occa-

---

106. Dorris, "People's War," pp. 201–202.
107. Thaxton, "When Peasants Took Power," p. 355.
108. Dorris, "People's War," p. 204, and Thaxton, "When Peasants Took Power," pp. 355ff.

sionally participated in local defense forces, these too were entirely dominated by men. Instead, peasant women were called upon to make a military contribution that was overwhelmingly economic. In home industry, cooperatives, and factories they produced the cloth, uniforms, shoes, quilts, drugs, vegetable oil, soap, leather, and other supplies upon which the survival of the armies depended. When a village's farm labor force was depleted by military service, women were mobilized to farm the fields. And the party persevered in this mobilization even in the face of resistance of family members, who considered female social labor to be indecent or who resented the loss of direct family control over and benefit from women's labor.[109] Here the needs of military success conflicted with patriarchal norms, and the Communists did battle with the latter.

Moreover, People's War did enable some women to perform services that challenged the familial parameters of their traditional social universe even more radically than by expanding their productive roles. During the Kiangsi Soviet period thousands of women joined the Women Guards to contribute to local defense, and there even were female militia units scattered throughout the conservative Northwest. A women's aid corps performed rescue missions, nursed the wounded, gathered intelligence, carried messages, and shared in the sabotage and repair activities, crucial complements of guerrilla warfare.[110] And the Red Army did make room for exceptional women to participate in direct combat. K'ang K'o-ch'ing, who joined the Communists in the Chingkangshan Mountains as a teenager and married Chu Teh soon after, is perhaps the most famous woman warrior of the revolution. In early 1932 she was detachment commander of the Women's Volunteers—a band of 200 peasant women, some of whom received training at the Red Military Academy in Juichin. Known as the Girl Commander because she was one of only two women ever to command regular Red troops, K'ang once led troops in battle. She was one of approximately fifty women who participated in the Long March. Although their numbers

109. Kay Johnson, "Feminism and Socialist Revolution," p. 72.
110. Davin, *Woman-Work*, pp. 31, 44–45, and Kuo-t'ao Chang, *Rise of the CCP*, p. 351.

were few, women were enrolled in Kang-ta, North Shensi Public School, and Yenan University, each of which included military education in its curriculum.[111] The symbolic significance of women warriors was augmented by party propaganda and official revolutionary histories, which publicized the feats of heroic women out of all proportion to their actual numbers.

Given the social conditions of the rural base areas, it is remarkable that women managed to participate in war service as extensively and heroically as they did. The social experience and recognition they received in the process had to have dramatic implications for their capacity to assert their newly attained rights within their families and local communites. It would be ahistorical and ethnocentric to minimize the transformation in the status of women that occurred in the midst of People's War. But to understand the process whereby the family crisis was resolved in a manner that produced among the Chinese peasantry a family system that—though new and far more democratic—was still a patriarchal one, we must focus our attention on the impressive challenges People's War directed at male domination *and* on the limitations of those challenges.

The limitations were profound. As Delia Davin has noted, most of the services women were called upon to contribute were extensions of their traditional domestic responsibilities.[112] Instead of doing laundry, sewing, cooking, shoemaking, nursing, and the like exclusively for their families, women now were asked to mother and wife the military and society as a whole. Expediency limited the extent to which women were allowed to participate in military activities. K'ang K'o-ch'ing, though personally exceptional and advantaged as the wife of Chu Teh, led troops in battle only once, because of a surprise attack. Despite her military expertise, ambitions, and prestige, she was consistently relegated to "more appropriate" women's service, such as setting up nurseries and schools and doing propaganda. When the All-China Democratic Women's Federation was formed in 1949, K'ang was

111. Jane Price, "Women and Leadership in the Chinese Communist Movement, 1921–1945." A biographical sketch of K'ang K'o-ch'in appears in Nym Wales, *Red Dust*, pp. 214ff.

112. Davin, *Woman-Work*, p. 23.

made chair of its child welfare department. Li Fa-ku, another woman warrior, disguised herself as a man, rose through the ranks of the PLA and earned its highest award as a "distinguished serviceman." But when she was hospitalized for battle wounds and her sex was discovered, she was transferred to a post in the public health section of the army.[113] Jane Price has pointed out that "of all aspects of the Chinese Communist leadership structure, the military was by far the most inaccessible to women and impervious to feminist concerns."[114] In part this was because most ranking Communist commanders received their training during the 1920s at highly professional military schools of the KMT or the Soviet Union. Neither these schools nor the most prestigious Chinese Communist military leadership training institutions were open to women. Thus women were excluded formally from revolutionary activities the more avant-garde among them deeply desired to perform.[115]

There were certain espionage assignments women alone could carry out, but the social consequences in patriarchal society were profound. Ting Ling's story, "When I Was in Sha Chuan [Cloud Village]," poignantly illustrates this dilemma. It tells the story of Ching-Ching, a beautiful, strong-willed teenage girl who had been raped and kidnapped by the Japanese. Contacted behind the Japanese lines by the Red Army, Ching-Ching took advantage of her position as a Japanese "devil-officer's wife" to perform sensitive espionage work for the Communists. Having escaped after she was stricken with venereal disease, Ching-Ching returned to her native village. While the homecoming for a male resistance fighter would be an occasion of honor and acclaim, Ching-Ching encountered a mixed welcome. Many of the politicized youth admired her sacrifice and courage, but the predominant sentiment

---

113. Janet Weitzner Salaff and Judith Merkel, "Women and Revolution," p. 164.

114. Price, "Women and Leadership," p. 22.

115. Kuo-t'ao Chang mentions in passing that during the Long March his troops found the women of Szechwan exceptionally eager to participate in revolutionary activity. According to Chang the women successfully demanded an independent regiment and "swarmed to apply for membership when the regiment was set up." More than 1,000 women were accepted after careful screening. However, the work assignment was predictable: "The regiment did a lot in taking care of the wounded and the sick in the Army" (*Rise of the CCP*, p. 351).

of the villagers was that she was a "broken shoe" and a disgrace to her family and community: "Some say that she has slept with at least a hundred men, some that she has even been the wife of Japanese officer. This disgraceful woman really should not be allowed to come back."[116] Although this is a fictional episode, there is good reason to believe it recorded faithfully the painful conditions of resistance work for heroic women.

The most dramatic challenge the process of People's War leveled at patriarchy was not in the realm of relationships between the sexes. Instead, relations between the generations, and especially relationships among men, were the most radically transformed. The rise in the status and responsibilities of youth, particularly male youth, was stupendous. Edgar Snow found that the average age of the rank and file of the Red Army was nineteen. Most of these had joined the Young Vanguards when they were adolescents or had enlisted in the army at age fifteen or sixteen. The average age of officers in the Northwest border regions was twenty-four. In addition, the regular troops were accompanied and tended by "little red devils," young boys attached to regular army units.[117] The Red Army offered hundreds of thousands of young peasant men and boys the opportunity to participate in a vast fraternity where they could develop relationships with one another that transcended kinship and village lines. Its radically egalitarian structure gave young men access to social authority and recognition without regard to family status. By excluding women, the Red Army made this military fraternity the basis for a new form of generalized male authority in China.[118]

It is true that war support work significantly expanded opportunities for women to relate to one another outside strict familial confines. However, so enormous is the contrast in the relative expansion of extrakinship solidarity People's War created for men compared with women that the gap in social power

---

116. Ting Ling, "When I Was in Sha Chuan," p. 259. The story has been translated into English, and it is discussed by Yi-tsi Feuerwerker.

117. Edgar Snow, *Red Star Over China*, pp. 258–59.

118. Feminist scholars are just beginning to study the relationship between fraternal organizations and patriarchal authority. For a fine analysis of this relationship in early modern Europe, see Mary Ann Clawson, "Early Modern Fraternalism and the Patriarchal Family."

between men and women may have widened despite the absolute gains women made. This was to have inestimable significance for the structure of CCP leadership and the future nature of Chinese Communist society. The revolutionary process of protracted guerrilla warfare resulted in a predominance of military men in the ranks of highest leadership. In 1945, for example, one-fourth of the central committee members were Red Army generals and 398 had risen through military careers.[119] The military fraternity of People's War helped to create a new political culture dominated by new democratic patriarchs.

CONCLUSION

By 1953 the revolutionary collaboration between the peasantry and the CCP had succeeded in resolving the family realization crisis. Almost all peasant families could reasonably hope to maintain and reproduce themselves. They could rear the infants born to them, arrange marriages for their sons and daughters, and bury their dead with honor. Families had been reunited; prospects for intergenerational geographic stability were better than they had been in decades. To many it seemed time to "set up a household and make one's fortune." Communism had played its ironic role as savior of peasant family life.

But People's War was a revolution, not a restoration. It had created the basis for a new family system—the new democratic patriarchy. Land revolution overthrew the former class of patriarchs and redistributed their resources to place small-scale independent family farming within reach of almost every peasant family. Land revolution radically equalized access to the means of patriarchal authority and thereby limited its scope. This patriarchal family economy rested upon different grounds than in the prerevolutionary past. It had been constructed and defended by a military fraternity that dramatically enhanced the status of young men. The crucial supportive role women played in People's War improved their circumstances within and outside the family economy, but did not challenge the structural sources of patriarchal authority itself. Each peasant household had been linked effectively

---

119. James Pinckney Harrison, *The Long March to Power*, p. 358.

to CCP-sponsored cooperatives and economic structures. The new democratic patriarchy depended upon, and could be held accountable to, a new politicized civic order.

The People's War programs discussed here contributed to a family revolution in the Chinese countryside, which, as we will see, was completed by a direct family reform program. The Communists had mobilized people to participate in revolutionary processes that reorganized the family economy on new principles of gender, generation, and social integration. No distraction from the fundamental tasks of People's War, this family revolution greatly facilitated their realization.

First, the peasant family had served as the basic unit of People's War, and its rescue as the Communists' pivotal economic strategy. Self-sufficiency of the base areas, the precondition for Communist victory, was achieved through measures that established the new democratic family economy.

Second, family revolution provided the CCP an arena for developing its broader new democratic strategy. Here the party learned how to tap the partially radical potential embedded in the peasants' restorationist motives. Rebuilding the basis for family life was the key to developing a transitional economy and culture in rural China. The CCP successfully assimilated what it considered the "democratic essence" of the peasants' "feudal" past when it learned to base its revolutionary strategy on the principle of "land to the families of patriarchal tillers."

Finally, the mass line itself was shaped profoundly by the family revolution. Mass-line politics were most characteristic of the major drives to rescue and reorganize the small family farm economy. Mutual aid and producer cooperatives were most urgent in villages forced to rely primarily on untrained, and frequently debilitated, female labor, because disproportionate numbers of men were away at the front. Women's participation in production could be achieved only through face-to-face efforts to teach them new productive skills and to overcome patriarchal resistance to their new extrafamilial roles. On the other hand, the party's conscious concessions to patriarchal sentiment served as convenient currency for legitimating the Communist revolution in many, especially male, peasant eyes.

Contrary to Wellington Koo's prediction, the Communists succeeded in China partly because they *saved* peasant family life. The Chinese Communists directly appealed to family sentiment to establish a new moral economy, but one still based on family, still patriarchal. Communist appeals to the material self-interest of the peasantry, accurately identified by analysts of China's rural revolution as the key to peasant cooperation,[120] were moral appeals as well. Many peasants found reason to believe family loyalty was compatible with support for the CCP, as this excerpt from a Communist "social history" suggests:

> As Cheng spoke Kuan Ying Pao was thinking, "This Party takes care of us even better than our mother." From this time on, Kuan Ying Pao considered the Communist Party the mother for all of the poor in the world, and the Party and his own small family became one and the same.[121]

The new democratic patriarchal revolution prepared the ground for the second, socialist stage of the Chinese revolution, which lay ahead, by granting Chinese patriarchs a new, more democratic basis for their unity.

---

120. This is one of the major arguments of Shue, *Peasant China*. Peter Schran makes a similar point about economic strategy during the war of resistance (*Guerrilla Economy*).

121. Thaxton, "When Peasants Took Power," p. 502. I have placed the term "social history" in quotation marks because of the ambiguous, frequently fictional, nature of the sources upon which Thaxton draws.

5 The Limitations of Family Reform and the Successful Family Revolution

While People's War constructed a new patriarchal family economy behind the back of Chinese Communist revolutionary theory, the party actively applied its Marxist methodology to developing an explicit program of family reform. Heir to the May Fourth critique of Confucian patriarchy, the Chinese Communist Party (CCP) made the liberation of women and youth the official objectives of family reform policy. As Marxists, the Chinese Communists considered family transformation superstructural and, therefore, secondary to the class struggle. Yet Chinese Communists also developed a distinctive variety of Marxism commonly referred to as Maoism. Maoism accepted the base-superstructure model of social change and the democratic centralist organizational form advanced by the Marxism of the Third International. However, Maoists also promoted a voluntarist approach to cultural politics that sanctioned direct ideological struggles in the superstructural arena.[1] During the rural revolution, the CCP placed family reform at the center of the cultural struggles it waged to construct the transitional culture of new democratic society.

---

1. Until the mid-1970s, voluntarism and ideological struggles were such prominent features of Chinese Communist society that Maoism was practically synonymous with Chinese Marxism. However, this has changed since Mao's death. With the fall of the Gang of Four and the official demotion of Mao, the present regime has attempted to isolate Maoism as a leftist tendency (now considered "incorrect") within Chinese communism.

An explicit program of family reform was integral to the Chinese revolutionary process. CCP family policy followed closely behind land reform, to which it was always subordinated. During land reform, as we have seen, the party consciously combined restorative and transformative measures to construct a mode of production accurately theorized as transitional to socialism. Family policy, however, was conceived by the party as exclusively transformative without restorative aims. The party regarded its frequent resort to traditionalist appeals and its capitulation to popular resistance in this realm as mere practical concessions rather than as integral to its family policy.

This chapter reveals the fallacy in this view. By examining the development and implementation of Chinese Communist family policy, I demonstrate that it possessed an integrity hidden from the party itself. CCP family reform policy and practice was the organic complement to the party's economic and military strategy. The party achieved success greater than its family theory allowed it to recognize in completing the family revolution that established the new democratic patriarchy in rural China.

THE DEVELOPMENT OF NEW
DEMOCRATIC FAMILY POLICY

The Soviet Period ▪ The commitment to family reform and women's liberation embedded in the Marxist tradition and the May Fourth heritage of the Chinese Communists was both fortified and modified by their experience in the Peasant Movement of the 1920s. With family conflicts dominating the attention of the arbitration departments of the newly established peasant unions,[2] women's movement activists learned quickly that family reform had considerable appeal to peasant women. Wherever activists established separate women's sections of the peasant unions, they attracted members who were particularly interested in divorce. Indeed, Suzette Leith points out that peasant women, in contrast with the proletarian women the CCP mobilized during the 1920s, seemed to experience their oppression primarily in gender terms.[3] However, this early experience with rural family

---

2. Roy Hofheinz, Jr., *The Broken Wave*, p. 154.
3. Suzette Leith, "Chinese Women in the Early Communist Movement," pp. 61–63.

reform also taught revolutionaries the divisiveness of these issues. According to Ts'ai Teng-li, a party leader in the Hailufeng peasant women's union, "some men hated the organization because it defended the rights of women and took care of the divorce problem."[4] Similarly, organizers in Hunan and Shenyang found that women's associations had to grant divorces to sustain support from their members, but as soon as they did so, they jeopardized their relationship with the superordinate, male-dominated peasant unions. Most peasant men were opposed to divorce because, as an activist explained to Anna Louise Strong, "It is hard for a peasant to get a wife, . . . and he's often paid much for his present unwilling one."[5]

The CCP emerged from the Peasant Movement period with a dawning awareness that rural family policy would have to tread a high wire between the politics of sex and class. For instrumental reasons alone, family reform was a necessary means for mobilizing peasant women, but it also threatened the class unity central to the party's vision of rural revolution. The party immediately applied this awareness in the Soviet base areas as it began to wage a People's War. The Kiangsi Soviet period served as an experimental fieldwork site for family reform, just as it did for land reform. These two policy programs became interdependent in the Communists' struggle to overturn the rural social order. An historical look at Kiangsi family policy reveals that it experienced the same moderating effects of rural revolution we observed when analyzing land reform.

Initial Kiangsi family policy was the most overtly radical the CCP ever promoted. The provisional marriage relations discussed by the Central Executive Committee of the Soviet Republic in January 1931 made *absolute* freedom of marriage and divorce a basic principle and proposed measures to guarantee women the special protection their situation required, because its authors believed that "under feudal domination, marriage is a barbaric and inhuman institution. The oppression and suffering borne by the women is far greater than that of men."[6] Yet even in this radical moment, when official party policy santioned the efforts

4. Quoted in ibid., p. 61.
5. Ibid.
6. Quoted in Elisabeth Croll, *Feminism and Socialism in China*, p. 194.

of feminist cadres to rescue peasant women from oppressive marriages, Mao Tse-tung took care to disassociate the Communists from an antimarital stance. In a 1930 decree he tried to reassure peasants that free marriage was less a threat than a promise: "Let those men who do not have wives be free to find themselves wives as rapidly as possible and let those women who do not have husbands be free to find themselves husbands as rapidly as possible."[7] Despite the seeming egalitarianism of Mao's proclamation, its actual intended beneficiaries were peasant men. The decree was directed at the 30 percent of poor peasant and artisan men, the 90 percent of the lumpen proletariat, and the 99 percent of the hired farm hands in Kiangsi whom Mao estimated to be bachelors. A marriage epidemic among these classes followed Mao's decree and served as evidence supporting his frequent claim that one of the crucial practical benefits the revolution brought to the exploited classes was the chance to find a wife.[8]

The free marriage platform, in both its guises, generated confusion about Communist morality, which resulted in various forms of resistance, abuses, and excesses on the part of peasants and cadres. Peasant men who dominated a mass meeting in one district succeeded in limiting conditions for divorce. Far more extreme were the peasants who demanded the death penalty for women attempting to exercise their new right to free marriage. Some peasant women presumed they had been granted the right to murder their oppressive husbands, while others joined their male kin in resolutely opposing the very idea of free marriage. Cadres, for their part, also obstructed free marriage. Local cadres were especially likely to defy the policy by denying divorces to women. Others translated freedoms into obligations, forcing widows into remarriages and women into sexual relationships in order to "combat feudalism." Zealous cadres radically extended the party's tendency to instrumentalize women's liberation when they used women as sexual inducements to recruit men into the Red Army.[9]

---

7. Quoted in Hu Chi-hsi, "The Sexual Revolution in the Kiangsi Soviet," p. 479.

8. Ibid., p. 480.

9. Information in this paragraph comes from Croll, *Feminism and Socialism*, pp. 194–95; Delia Davin, *Woman-Work*, p. 29; Kathy Lemons Walker, "The Party and Peasant Women," pp. 74–75; and Hu, "Sexual Revolution," pp. 483–84.

The free marriage doctrine and its abuses left the CCP vulnerable to rumors about free love and the communalization of women that long have been the stock-in-trade of anti-Communist propagandists. As early as 1927, the foreign press tried to discredit the Communists by claiming that the women's association in Hankow had staged a "naked body procession" of women carefully selected for their "snow-white bodies and perfect breasts."[10] In 1931, a KMT newspaper claimed the Red Army rebellion against Mao at Fu-t'ien had been caused by units opposed to sexual liberty and land reform in the Kiangsi Soviet.[11] Likewise, anti-Communists spread rumors that the one hundred women who joined the women's comfort team in the Oyüwan Soviet to launder, nurse, and care for soldiers were prostitutes.[12]

The Chinese Communists took immediate steps to combat this image. As we saw in chapter 4, the party imposed a strict sexual code on its soldiers and cadres. Encouraged, perhaps, by the puritanism of Stalinist morality in the Soviet Union, the CCP attempted to identify itself publicly with a moral code stricter that that of the local peasantry. Mao, for example, claimed that before the Communists came to the Changgang district of Kiangsi, 50 percent of the women had conducted secret love affairs, but Communist presence and policies had succeeded in reducing the figure to 10 percent.[13] The base-superstructure model and the general underdevelopment of Marxist theory on the dynamics of family transformation led the Communists to assume that family reform would be an automatic by-product of the revolution. This made it logical to retreat from radical family policies whenever popular resistance threatened class unity. Throughout the Kiangsi period the party moderated its assault on patriarchal authority.

The first discernible shift in this direction appeared soon after the provisional marriage policy and was codified in the formal marriage regulations promulgated at the end of 1931. A conference of CCP women's committees held that year still underscored the effectiveness of family reform in mobilizing women: "The implementation of freedom of marriage led the young women in

10. Quoted in Harold R. Isaacs, *The Tragedy of the Chinese Revolution*, p. 149.
11. Hu, "Sexual Revolution," p. 477.
12. Kuo-t'ao Chang, *The Rise of the Chinese Communist Party, 1929–1938*, p. 200.
13. Davin, *Woman-Work*, p. 30.

the villages to join the struggle against the feudal forces of the local bullies and the gentry landlords."[14] However, when the Northern Kiangsi central committee reviewed its early experience with these efforts, it saw the need to draw a new distinction between "freedom" and "absolute freedom" of marriage:

> In practice we must start from the premise that both parties, husband and wife, serve the cause of the revolution. Therefore, we must not only refrain from imposing limitations on the freedom of marriage, since this would be contrary to Bolshevist principles, but we must resolutely oppose the idea of absolute freedom of marriage as it creates chaotic conditions in society and antagonizes the peasants and the Red Army. We must make it clear that the Central Committee never maintained absolute freedom of divorce either, because that would be an anarchistic practice.[15]

This new distinction was incorporated in Article 2 of the Provisional Constitution of 1931, which now suggested that long-term material changes were necessary preconditions to free marriage and the liberation of women:

> The purpose of the Soviet Government is to guarantee the fundamental liberation of women. Freedom of marriage is recognized and measures for the protection of women will obtain the material basis to enable them to cast off the bonds of the family by gradual stages, and to participate in economic, political, and cultural life.[16]

Nonetheless, the marriage regulations of December 1931 retained a comparatively radical cast.[17] They repeated the Communists' intent to abolish China's "feudal" marriage system and expressly prohibited such patriarchal practices as arranged marriage, purchase and sale contracts, polygamy, and the foster daughter-in-law. The regulations contained the most radical divorce policy ever devised by the CCP. Divorce was available for the asking by just one of the married pair. Moreover, the child-custody and property-settlement principles of the regulations can be read as

---

14. Quoted in M. J. Meijer, *Marriage Law and Policy in the Chinese People's Republic*, p. 40.

15. "Plan for Work Among the Women," quoted in ibid., p. 39.

16. Quoted in ibid., p. 41.

17. An English translation of the 1931 law appears as appendix 1 in Meijer, *Marriage Law and Policy*, pp. 281–82.

an affirmative action program for women. Women were granted the right to choose whether or not they wished custody of their children. If a woman chose custody, the father was nevertheless responsible for two-thirds of the cost of living of the children. Otherwise, the man bore the entire financial responsibility. Regardless who caused or initiated the divorce, the man was responsible for his former wife's financial support until she married again.

Data are scarce on the extent or success of efforts to implement the 1931 regulations in the Soviets. Lifelong party women's movement leader Teng Ying-chao later claimed that this was a major focus of Kiangsi woman-work.[18] Principal demands advocated by the women who attended a Congress of Women Workers and Peasant Women in Ningdu County indicate considerable interest in defending new rights against male resistance: "Oppose confiscating the land, grains, or property of a woman after divorce," "Oppose not letting women study and learn to read," "Oppose husbands who refuse to let women work in the fields."[19] The party's own survey of implementation efforts, undertaken in 1932, found the record uneven. On the negative side, there was continuing obstruction of the law by government officials, the persistence of foster daughter-in-law marriages, and widows prevented from receiving their land or forced into precipitous remarriages. But, the party also claimed success in reducing wife abuse and adultery and facilitating more stable marital relationships.[20]

The fact that the party passed a new, somewhat-revised marriage law in April 1934[21] suggests the 1931 regulations had been more than formal proclamations. Although the spirit of the two marriage laws was similar, the new one moved to further subordinate the goal of liberating women to that of class struggle. Its most significant innovation was the divorce restriction it placed on the wives of soldiers. Army wives, even from "feudal" marriages, now needed consent from their husbands to obtain divorce. This restriction could be waived only if a woman had not heard

---

18. Croll, *Feminism and Socialism*, p. 195.
19. Quoted in Walker, "The Party and Peasant Women," p. 73.
20. Ibid., p. 75.
21. An English translation of the 1934 law appears as appendix 2 in Meijer, *Marriage Law and Policy*, pp. 283–84.

from her husband for two years or more, depending upon the feasibility of communication in the area. The fact that the CCP felt the need to institute this special military privilege after less than three years experience implementing the earlier legislation, and just when the Soviets were on the brink of annihilation, indicates that divorce had been popularly sought by women and had been a disturbing prospect to army men.[22] The 1934 law also retreated from the affirmative-action posture of the 1931 regulations by reducing male responsibility for alimony and child support. In short, the shift in Kiangsi family policy mirrored that of land reform. The Chinese Communists backed down on policies that threatened to deprive male peasants of their two most valuable possessions—land and women.

When the CCP curtailed its socialist policies in the land revolution, this was a temporary, strategic maneuver. The party's complementary retreat from the feminist vision of family reform had more permanent consequences. Conflict between CCP feminists and the party hierarchy emerged early in the Soviet period. A party evaluation of its women's movement in 1931 criticized the "left errors" of young female activists who focused too zealously on the question of free marriage, thereby obscuring the class basis of women's oppression.[23] The party leadership regarded the preoccupation of women's movement cadres with the "single" problem of family reform as fostering "the emergence of a contradiction between the sexes which could obstruct the land reform."[24] In a report to the executive committee, published at the March 1934 Congress of Soviets, Mao Tse-tung reminded the errant feminists that free marriage was a superstructural issue. Mao claimed that

> the disappearance of the feudal marriage system was dependent on the wider program to institute a new social, political, and economic system. Only when, after the overthrow of the dictatorship of the landlords and the capitalists, the toiling masses of men and women—in particular the women—have acquired political

22. Two counties in northeast Kiangsi reported 4,274 divorces registered in the brief period from 6 March to 27 June 1932 (Walker, "The Party and Peasant Women," p. 75).

23. Ibid., p. 59.

24. Quoted in Croll, *Feminism and Socialism*, p. 196.

freedom in the first place, and economic freedom in the second, can freedom of marriage obtain its final guarantee.[25]

While few feminists would quarrel with Mao's belief that full personal freedom for women is inseparable from economic and political freedom, debate continues over the nature of the causal relationships among these liberties. If this was a matter for internal party debate during the Soviet period, no notice of it appears in Western sources. The public record simply suggests a waning of feminist influence over family policy formation that would soon receive dramatic confirmation in Yenan.

Sino-Japanese War • When the survivors of the Long March joined indigenous partisan forces and proceeded to establish Communist base areas in the Northwest, they encountered family conditions even more restrictive and oppressive than they had dealt with in the South-Central Soviet bases. Although resistance to family reform would likely be greater than in the South, family issues had the same potential for mobilizing women and youth for revolution.[26] Moreover, among the stream of urban intellectuals and artists who poured into Yenan to contribute their talents to the Communist resistance were some of the most gifted and strongest feminist women in China. Ting Ling, the most famous of these, led the feminists in calling for an all-out attack on the patriarchal marriage system and publicly criticizing the party's inadequate attention to women's rights.[27]

But the Communists soon entered the united front period, when moderation was the by-word on all the social programs of the revolution. The anti-Japanese alliance with the KMT that initiated the general retreat from radical social policy and the Stalinist repudiation of Bolshevik family policy in the U.S.S.R.

---

25. Ibid.

26. Mark Selden claims youth joined the revolution in Shen-Kan-Ning to escape their families (*The Yenan Way in Revolutionary China,* p. 91). Mariam Darce Frenier says women in Chin-Chi-Ch'a joined the land reform movement to obtain divorces ("Women and the Chinese Communist Land Reform, 1946–1952," p. 28).

27. In 1942 Ting Ling published her criticism as "Thoughts on March 8," in *Liberation Daily,* the party newspaper in Yenan. A translation appears in Gregor Benton, "The Yenan Literacy Opposition." For a brief biographical sketch of Ting Ling, see the discussion by Yi-tsi Feuerwerker that follows her translation of Ting Ling, "When I was in Sha Chuan (Cloud Village)," pp. 270–79.

provided antifeminists in the CCP with an opportunity for backlash against feminism and family reform. Ting Ling was criticized publicly and forced to repudiate her "divisive" feminist demands. Feminists were told that full sex equality had already been achieved and that a continued emphasis on "narrow" feminist concerns was dated and destructive.[28]

This was the period when Mao Tse-tung formulated the theory of new democracy—the transitional economy and culture Chinese Communists must build to prepare their nation for socialism. As we have seen, the party's decision to moderate its land reform policy was part of a carefully theorized strategy of rural revolution. The new democratic economy in China was to be, in fact, transitional between "feudalism" and socialism. Therefore, some scholars have interpreted the social moderation of the early new democratic period as radicalism in disguise.[29] The meaning of the party's new democratic family policy, however, is more complex. The absence of an equivalent theoretical understanding of the dynamics of family transformation made the transitional nature of the new democratic family rather ambiguous. Except for Engels' vague, utopian, and extremely patient notion that under socialism, "the family" would wither away, the CCP lacked a conception of what sort of family system would replace the new democratic one. The party based its decision to moderate its family policy on the assumption that family change is superstructural. This encouraged the Communists to instrumentalize and misunderstand their own family politics. The CCP believed it was merely temporizing on family transformation in this period, granting concessions to patriarchal authority in the interest of compelling military and political priorities. It failed to recognize the profound shift its family policy underwent during the Sino-Japanese War, a shift that complemented and deepened its People's War strategy.

As concessions to the Kuomintang (KMT) the CCP abandoned its attack on the "feudal marriage system" and pledged itself to introduce a marriage system that respected the principles of democracy, the actual conditions in the border regions, and "the

---

28. The attack on Ting Ling was part of a general attack on dissent among party intellectuals in the Yenan Forum on Art and Literature (Merle Goldman, *Literary Dissent in Communist China*). An interview with Ting Ling appears in Gunther Stein, *The Challenge of Red China*, pp. 251–59.

29. Selden, *Yenan Way*, and Carl E. Dorris, "People's War in North China."

spirit of the legislation under the section 'Family' of the Civil Law of the Republic of China.''[30] Rather than trying to destroy the oppressive patriarchal system, the Communists limited their efforts to constraining its most abusive practices. Although at first the marriage law remained on the books, the party undertook no special drive to promote or enforce it.[31] Instead, the Communist border governments began to adopt an active profamily stance, reflected in an official shift in party slogans. In 1943 Ts'ai Chang proclaimed, ''Our slogans are no longer 'free choice marriage' and 'equality of the sexes,' but rather 'save the children,' 'a flourishing family,' and 'nurture health and prosperity.'''[32]

Marriage regulations in the border areas reflected the policy change. In 1941, for example, when the Chin-Ch'a-Chi government defined ''the basic spirit'' of its marriage regulations, it claimed new, democratic family life had already been achieved:

> The new democratic society of the Border Area has grown from the old, semicolonial, semifeudal society and therefore the women have also been liberated from the double oppression they suffered from the old society and the old family. This is one of the things brought about by the social system of the Border Area. Our Marriage Regulations are thoroughly permeated by the spirit of a new democratic, dignified family system.[33]

Divorce policy continued to retreat from the early radicalism. There were no more references to ''freedom of divorce.'' The regulations introduced lists of specific grounds for divorce, indicating thereby that divorce was an act requiring justification. One of the grounds was portentous. By listing collaboration with the enemy as cause for divorce, the party gave its first formal indication that it would view marriage as a political as well as a personal state.

As with land reform, in revising its family policy, the CCP began to accommodate, exploit, and then reform the traditional values and restorationist motives of the peasantry. The marriage regulations discouraged a casual attitude towards de facto marriage and sought to accord new respect to the marriage act itself. The

---

30. Meijer, *Marriage Law and Policy*, p. 55.
31. Kay Johnson, ''Feminism and Socialist Revolution in China,'' p. 68.
32. Quoted in Davin, *Woman-Work*, p. 37.
33. Quoted in Meijer, *Marriage Law and Policy*, p. 58.

Chin-Ch'a-Chi regulations even required a public ceremony for marriage, not the "ostentatious, expensive, feudal, and superstitious" variety, of course, but one that was "simple, serious, dignified, and above all educational."[34] The policy reflected the party's new sensitivity to the demands of local moral standards, as a 1943 document on marriage registration explained:

> If no public ceremony is held and no registration has taken place, there is no valid marriage and such conduct must be punished by the hsien [county] as corruption of morals, for such marriages easily corrupt the relations between men and women and may furnish our enemies and saboteurs with the excuse to spread rumors. This is the reason why they must be denied validity.[35]

The Chin-Chi-Lu-Yu border regulations went so far in this direction that they even protected betrothal contracts![36]

As with land reform, the Communists allowed peasant patriarchal mores to shape its mass work style. Urban women students who served as cadres adapted their costume and habits to suit peasant standards: "We students changed in the course of our work among village women. We discarded our city dress and put on peasant clothes. We became very close to the local people and many of the elderly women 'adopted' us as 'daughters.' "[37] Male cadres, on the other hand, were not allowed to mobilize women because this would be a gross violation of village morality. The party's extreme shortage of female cadres was therefore a serious limitation on its capacity to organize women. Women's associations were taught to promote family reforms via traditionalist appeals. Antifootbinding work was to proceed where possible, not in order to liberate women, but because bound feet were "harmful to both health and production."[38] Wife beating should be discouraged by reminding peasant men that it was so difficult for a poor man to find a wife that he should not risk driving the one he had to divorce him.[39] When children's

34. Quoted in ibid., p. 59.
35. Quoted in ibid., p. 60.
36. The revised marriage regulations of Chin-Chi-Lu-Yu are translated in ibid., appendix 6.
37. Quoted in Croll, *Feminism and Socialism,* p. 200.
38. Quoted in Davin, *Woman-Work,* p. 36.
39. William Hinton, *Fanshen,* p. 159.

associations were set up, the sexes were segregated and the girls' group called a needlework society, "indicating a need to use domestic skills as a pretext for organizational activities lest the work provoke peasants' suspicions."[40] The party soon was so comfortable with this approach that it even employed it with cadres. During the 1942 rectification drive, the party portrayed itself as a "Confucian patriarch." Rectification class members "began to view the party as a benevolent father who aimed to cure his child through rectification." One such cadre explained, "I feel proud to confess in front of the party. It is as if I admitted my mistakes before my own father."[41]

The war of resistance witnessed a marked decline in official support for an activist, feminist approach to family reform. The party advised women workers to focus on practical problems, such as wife beating, and to do so with tolerance and sensitivity. Efforts to mediate family conflicts should replace struggle against offending parties. Toleration of patriarchal abuses like footbinding and wife beating was better than to antagonize peasant supporters of the Red Army.[42] Some struggle against peasant patriarchs did occur. In Anlo, Huainan, for example, Liu Yü-lan was the first local woman to become active in the woman's association. Her enraged husband and father-in-law stopped her from attending meetings because "the purpose of organizing women is to give women a better chance to meet men. It is the first step toward 'common property and common wives.' " In this case, the women's association staged a "struggle meeting" where it forced the two men to apologize and detained them for the night.[43]

But often when women cadres took an activist approach to family reform, they were rebuked by the party leadership. For example, in the West Hopeh region of the Chin-Ch'a-Chi base area, a particularly militant women's movement developed. Cadres with feminist sympathies there exhibited acute sensitivity to the special sufferings of female victims of family crisis. When a major flood devastated part of the region in 1939, the women's association worked feverishly to halt the customary forms of peasant recourse.

40. Yung-fa Chen, "The Making of a Revolution," p. 329.
41. Ibid., pp. 551–52.
42. Kay Johnson, "Feminism and Socialist Revolution," p. 74, and Yung-fa Chen, "The Making of a Revolution," pp. 330–31.
43. Yung-fa Chen, "The Making of a Revolution," p. 331.

It assisted 275 families near Fuping, whose parents tried to sell their daughters in response to economic disaster. It introduced a day-care center in Wanhsien to free mothers to participate in the millet harvest. And it directly intervened in thirty Laiyuan cases where young girls were being forced into precipitous marriages. But these efforts received criticism rather than praise from Ts'ai Ch'ang, director of the CCP women's movement, for placing feminist goals above Communist wartime priorities.[44]

As Japanese military pressure mounted and the United Front disintegrated, CCP woman-work directives instructed cadres to devote their full energies to mobilizing women for production. In fact, women's associations were asked to hold fewer meetings and to minimize the mobilization of women for political and social reforms so that women would have more time to contribute to production. There were feminists who opposed this retrenchment, but they were persuaded to acknowledge that fanning sexual antagonisms would undermine the success of the war effort upon which women's liberation depended. They capitulated, going from home to home persuading frustrated young women to reason patiently with oppressive husbands and mothers-in-law.[45]

Although the reaction against family reform that dominated official family policy in the Japanese period was only temporary, it was also of consequence. The more moderate policy was not simply a product of the united front, of Japanese military pressure, or of Soviet influence. It represented a fundamental shift in family policy, which was emerging even before the Sino-Japanese War. We have already seen that the CCP had moved away from radical family reform during the Kiangsi period. The political and military aspects of the anti-Japanese period furnished legitimation for the policy change. The new, profamily stance of the Chinese Communists reflected cumulative experience with rural revolution, during which the party learned to shape its socialist objectives to accommodate the restorationist ones of the peasantry. Feminist goals for family transformation were especially

---

44. Dorris, "People's War," pp. 135–37.
45. This paragraph is based on Davin, *Woman-Work*, p. 36; Kay Johnson, "Feminism and Socialist Revolution," pp. 68, 70; Dorris, "People's War," p. 136; and Croll, *Feminism and Socialism*, p. 214.

expendable because the Communists never had possessed a clear conception of a socialist family system. For the majority of peasant men as well as the masses of peasant women, the right to family security was a more precious goal than the freedom to divorce. The new respect accorded these peasant priorities by CCP family policy during the war of resistance was more than temporary wartime expedience. All future CCP family policy—no matter how radical—would incorporate this sensitivity.

A related consequence of the caution of the resistance period also endured. The Chinese Communists acknowledged explicitly that China's rural families differed markedly from the Western capitalist conjugal family, and would continue to do so for the foreseeable future. A retrospective analysis of the wartime women's movement recognized that the "big family" of the village was the basic unit in the rural economy and in the resistance struggle. It called for the reform and consolidation of this family system.[46] Reforming and consolidating the peasant family economy was the formula for family and social transformation that underlay the future of rural economic development in China.

A third lasting feature of family policy during the war of resistance was the greater attention the CCP began to pay to the content of family relationships. Family policy was no longer restricted simply to regulating marriage and divorce procedures. Most of the border area regulations stated that grounds for divorce exist "when the sentiments and wills of the parties fundamentally do not harmonize and there is no way of continuing to live together."[47] The introduction of considerations of affection and compatibility into marital decisions reflected a lingering influence of the party's May Fourth heritage. However, there was also a less benign dimension to this new public interest in the quality of family life. The CCP began to intervene more directly in the personal lives of its cadres, most notably by assuming the authority to approve their selection of marriage partners.[48] The party soon was defining marital compatibility in the political terms of social class as it adopted a new, portentous role as "public patriarch."

---

46. Davin, *Woman-Work*, p. 37.
47. Quoted in Meijer, *Marriage Law and Policy*, p. 63.
48. Hua Chang-ming, "Révolutionnaires au Foyer: Les Femmes à Yan'an, 1935–1946," *Revue des Echanges Franco-Chinoise*, no. 2 (November-December 1979), p. 89.

Finally, the Yenan period had long-term implications for the relationship between feminism and Chinese socialism. To be sure, feminism had long been labeled bourgeois and divisive by Chinese revolutionaries. However, in both the early urban and the Soviet periods, women's rights activists had enjoyed greater autonomy and scope for their activities than they received during the Sino-Japanese War. Organizational and ideological subordination of the Chinese women's movement to the Communist Party was both dramatized and intensified in the years of anti-imperialist struggle. Although feminist issues would recapture official party favor shortly, they would do so in the context of their unambiguous subordination to the class struggle.

Civil War and Land Revolution ▪ There was a slow beginning to the period that was to conclude with the most intensive campaign for family reform in the history of Chinese communism and the completion of the new democratic patriarchal family revolution. Chinese victory over the Japanese did not bring as rapid a shift in family policy as it did in land reform. The Chinese Communists were still at war, and they retained their fear that radical family reform would offend peasant sensibilities, disrupt peasant unity, and thus threaten production and the military effort. The return to a more activist and feminist approach to family policy was gradual. A 1948 central committee directive on woman-work marked the official shift in policy by criticizing the efforts of the previous period. It blamed an exclusive preoccupation with mobilizing women for production for the inadequate progress of women's liberation. Shifting to a more Maoist stance on cultural change, the central committee warned that while participation in production was still the basic strategy of the women's movement, by itself this would not liberate women. The central committee called, therefore, for intensive ideological education on sexual equality and for government orders outlawing practices such as footbinding, infanticide, purchase marriage, and the taking of child brides. The directive gave official support to limited confrontational struggles against "backward elements" who "constantly oppress women." And it demanded immediate revision of sections of the marriage regulations, in certain of the liberated areas, that violated the principles of sexual equality and free marriage. Although this was a decidedly feminist revision of family reform policy, the directive took care to reaffirm the party's contention that family reform represented an ideological struggle *amongst* the peasants whose primary purpose was "to increase the harmony and unity of the family."[49]

The shift to a more activist approach to family reform was encouraged by the return to land revolution in the liberated areas. The history of land reform and family reform in rural China were thoroughly intertwined. Although the party never allowed superstructural struggles for family reform to jeopardize the success of land revolution, the two policies had important aims in common. Patriarchal authority buttressed the rural class structure as well as the power of men over women. Land reform and family reform were complementary efforts to eliminate the sources of authority for traditional rural elites. When the Communists attacked such practices as concubinage, widow chastity, and purchase marriage, they were attacking lineal power and large-scale patriarchs most of all. By curtailing that aspect of elite privilege whose source was property rights in women, the Communists, perhaps inadvertently, were fostering a redistributive effect to match that of land reform. The cult of widow chastity and the practice of concubinage reduced the supply of potential wives available to rural men. The superior purchasing power of wealthier families removed many peasant families from competition for wives. Ideological struggles to delegitimize such practices should be seen as constructing a new family morality that would complement the new family economy of the new democratic patriarchy.

Family reform and land reform also were compatible ways to mobilize women for participation in broader economic and social activities. An activist approach to family reform gave support to the efforts of local women's associations to combat patriarchal brutality, which, in turn, liberated many women for public service. The most famous example of such a militantly aroused women's association is probably "Gold Flower's Story," as recorded by Jack Belden.[50] Gold Flower was a victim of socially thwarted love and an arranged and brutal marriage. Beaten daily and on the verge of starvation, she was liberated from her living hell when

---

49. The directive is translated in Davin, *Woman-Work*, appendix 2.
50. Jack Belden, *China Shakes the World*, chap. 42.

the Eighth Route Army came to her village and established a local women's association. Gold Flower's husband had left her to serve his family while he migrated to Tientsin seeking work as a merchant. Thus the women first turned their attention to Gold Flower's tyrannical father-in-law. When he refused to listen to reason, the members of the women's association bound and imprisoned him, then subjected him to a struggle session where he was forced to admit and recant his crimes under the jeering, threatening attacks of the members. Later Gold Flower seduced her husband back to the village, where she outwitted him so that he, too, was subjected to the organized fury of the women's association. Gold Flower's gratitude to the Communists was boundless, and "the exhortations of the Communist party to increase farm production fell on her ears like a clarion call."[51] She devoted passionate energies to mobilizing women to work in the fields. In another village, the women's association successfully employed a Lysistrata strategy when women were excluded from the first village elections. Members of the women's association refused to sleep with their husbands until a new election was called, and in that election a woman was elected deputy head.[52] Thus the renewed activism of family reform also contributed to a new family morality by challenging the rigidity of the public-domestic division of labor. The new democratic morality released women for participation in the public work force, which was crucial to People's War and soon would underlie rural development strategies in socialist China.

The CCP was partially accurate in its claim that land reform was integral to family reform. Not only did land distribution restore family security but also it made divorce economically conceivable for some women. Hence the oft-quoted response of many Long Bow women, "When I get my share I'll separate from my husband. Then he won't oppress me anymore."[53] Of course, men succeeded in thwarting most women who attempted to realize such plans. The legal committee of the CCP reported that women were not allowed to take any property with them in 61 percent of the divorce cases settled in the liberated areas of Northern China between September and December 1949. In

---

51. Ibid., p. 294.
52. Croll, *Feminism and Socialism*, p. 220.
53. Hinton, *Fanshen*, p. 397.

another 20 percent of the settlements, women were allowed movable property, but no land.[54] Still, the fact that women had official rights to land enhanced their capacity to struggle against familial oppression.

The most dramatic shift in official family policy came after the end of the civil war. With the military phase of the revolution behind, the CCP turned its energies to accelerating the social revolution. Two of its earliest and most significant pieces of legislation, the marriage law and the land law, were passed in the spring of 1950 to guide the completion of the new democratic stage of the revolution. During 1950–1953, the party gave its official support to a series of direct campaigns to implement the marriage law. These campaigns generally were timed to coincide with the completion of land reform in a given locale. It is not surprising, therefore, that the greatest national campaign took place in the spring of 1953, when land reform had been largely completed. By 1953 the new democratic patriarchal revolution was over; since then the CCP has not initiated a major campaign to transform the family.[55]

The marriage law of 1 May 1950 codified the CCP's revolutionary experience with family change and set out self-consciously to destroy the "feudal" family and to construct a "new democratic family" system throughout the nation. Ch'en Shao-yü, chairman of the Legal Committee of the Government Administrative Council, made this purpose of the law explicit:

> By means of the law, which is a weapon that combines education with coercion, we shall hasten the collapse and the death of the old feudal marriage system and protect the growth and development of the new democratic marriage system for the benefit of the establishment of a new family system and the development of a new society, especially with a view to the stimulation of productive forces in the widest sense of the word. This is the meaning of the draft of the new Marriage Law of the Chinese People's Republic.[56]

---

54. Meijer, *Marriage Law and Policy*, p. 234.

55. In 1980, however, a new marriage law was passed in the context of the adoption of a stringent population control policy. I discuss the significance of these measures in the epilog to this book.

56. Quoted in Meijer, *Marriage Law and Policy*, p. 78. An English translation of the 1950 marriage law appears as appendix 8 of Meijer.

Although the law was similar to its predecessors, it also furthered the revisionist trends of the Yenan period. First, the marriage law continued the move away from divorce principles that favored women. Women still were to receive preference in child custody decisions and to be protected during their pregnancies against undesired divorce proceedings, but the law no longer favored them in property settlements. Second, the law retreated further from the early Kiangsi principle of absolute freedom of divorce. While it still promised divorce in cases of genuine mutual consent, the Communists now required mediation efforts to effect a reconciliation when only one party requested a divorce. This new divorce policy extended two Yenan family policy developments. The party sought to identify itself with a profamily stance by emphasizing its interest in marital stability, and it gave notice of the state's expanding involvement in matters of personal life. The CCP had traveled far from its orginal view that marriage and divorce should be private concerns.

Finally, the marriage law codified the CCP's evolving emphasis on the family as the basic unit of socialist development. Explicit doctrines of a new family morality were spelled out in new chapters that defined proper relationships between spouses and between parents and children. Chapter 3, "Rights and Duties of Husband and Wife," defined spouses as companions who were "in duty bound to love, respect, assist, and look after each other, to live in harmony, to engage in productive work, to care for the children and to strive jointly for the welfare of the family and for the building of the new society." Chapter 4, "Relations Between Parents and Children," was even more original in calling for genuine reciprocity in parent-child relationships. Not only were parents responsible for rearing their children, but the children, in turn, were given the "duty to support and to assist their parents."[57] Neither parents nor children were allowed to maltreat or desert each other. This ethical precept, a model of new democratic morality because it reformed Confucianist values to socialist ends, carried significant implications for social welfare in a nation of scarcity.

Implementation of the 1950 marriage law had a brief and stormy history. Between 1950 and 1953 the party placed the

---

57. Quoted in ibid., pp. 300–301.

emphasis of its family policy on dissolving "feudal" marriages. For this reason, peasants often referred to the policy as the "divorce law." M. J. Meijer estimates that the courts granted an average of 800,000 divorces per year in this period—a rate of approximately 1.3 per 1,000 population, which is extraordinarily high for China or any agrarian society.[58] As one would predict, the overwhelming majority of divorce plaintiffs were women. That is why peasants also called the bill the "women's law." But many women who tried to take advantage of "their law" encountered fierce, at times lethal, resistance from husbands, in-laws, and cadres. Family members kept young wives home from public meetings to prevent their being mobilized for divorce. Husbands regarded divorce as a "special way of losing both their land and their wives."[59] Cadres sympathetic to the men handed down decisions that denied divorce to women, at times ordering them to be more enslaved to their marital homes than they had been before they petitioned for release.[60] In a shocking number of cases women were murdered or driven to suicide when they attempted to gain their freedom. A 1953 government report estimated that in the three years that the law had been in effect 70,000 to 80,000 women per year had died in this way.[61]

To counter the massive resistance to family reform, the government dispatched investigation teams with public fanfare, flags, and drums to evaluate local campaigns. The teams found the efforts to be quite uneven. The 1952 national report, which collated their findings, divided the areas of the country into three categories—those where family reform efforts had been satisfactory ("still in the minority"), mediocre ("the majority"), or downright bad. The teams' analyses of the failures of local efforts to apply

---

58. Ibid., p. 114.

59. Ibid., p. 125.

60. A particularly brutal case is reported by Meijer. A woman in Hupeh who requested divorce was ordered restricted to her home. She was not allowed to leave the premises without the permission of her husband or mother-in-law, not even to excrete. In fact, the prescribed punishment for disobeying the restriction was to drink three cups of excrement (*Marriage Law and Policy*, p. 125).

61. M. H. van der Valk, *Conservatism in Modern Chinese Family Law*, p. 1, n. 2. Meijer claims that the CCP blamed the women's deaths on the "feudal" system, but his own view is that mismanagement of the cases by cadres and courts, plus the "inherent defects of the Communist system" were the major culprits (*Marriage Law and Policy*, p. 128).

the marriage law formed the backdrop for the General Directive of 1 February 1953, which initiated the last and most thorough implementation campaign by the PRC. This directive, and the guidelines that followed, modified the government's reform priorities. Marriage reform activists now were instructed to stress positive rather than negative goals of the law. They were to try to make people aware that the law aimed at equality because that was a secure basis for family harmony. The marriage law was to become a symbol for the attainment of happy marriages.[62] On the eve of the campaign the Women's Federation published a discussion of the marriage law which proclaimed that the goal of the campaign was an increase in the number of free marriages and harmonious and mutually helpful familes.[63]

To minimize the disruptive effects of the marriage law, cadres were directed to switch once again from confrontational to educational work methods. Instead of holding public struggle sessions against tyrannical husbands and in-laws, cadres were instructed to organize each category of family membership to meet in separate groups, where individuals could discuss their particular problems and receive group support for their efforts to reform. Once again, the party criticized overly feminist activists for fostering the widespread view that this was a women's law by stressing its relationship to women's rights. Now their goal should be to minimize antagonisms between husbands and wives. They should redouble their efforts to mediate troubled marriages and grant divorces only in cases of "completely feudal" marriages. The primary target of the new campaign was the obstructionist attitudes of cadres rather than those of "feudal" parents, husbands, or in-laws.[64]

Although the government moderated its approach, it also intensified its family reform efforts in the spring of 1953. Applying experience gained in land reform, the Communists selected pilot villages, factories, and neighborhoods for experimental campaigns so that future problems could be anticipated and work methods refined. The nationwide mobilization was not launched until

---

62. Meijer, *Marriage Law and Policy*, pp. 127–31.
63. The document is translated in Elisabeth Croll, ed., *The Women's Movement in China*, p. 34.
64. This paragraph is based on Croll, *Feminism and Socialism*, pp. 236–37; Meijer, *Marriage Law and Policy*, p. 131; and Davin, *Woman-Work*, p. 88.

cadres received more training than in previous marriage law campaigns. Then public fanfare beckoned people to mobilization meetings held in schools, factories, and streets. Small group techniques were used to maximize mass participation. People were encouraged to confess publicly errors of "feudal" thought. Models of family harmony were held up for emulation. Meetings closed with new democratic rituals—the declaring of public oaths and the signing of pacts of "happy democratic marriage relationships" and patriotism.[65]

Despite the campaign's emphasis on domestic harmony, it sparked a sudden and final rise in the number of Chinese divorces—evidence, it would seem, of the greater depth and scope of the mobilization. Yet, Western scholars disagree about the degree of commitment the CCP gave to the 1953 implementation campaign and about its effectiveness. Most who have written about Chinese family reform portray this campaign as thorough and militant. Meijer considers its scope "fantastic."[66] Most feminist interpretations of the Chinese revolution rely on such accounts, which explains the general impression that a serious reaction against feminist family reform occurred after 1953.[67] And certainly the family reform efforts of the 1950–1953 period are one source of a pervasive Western belief that Chinese communism set out to destroy family life in order to establish a totalitarian system of government.[68]

However, Kay Johnson's "Feminism and Socialist Revolution in China" suggests the mobilization has been overrated considerably. Johnson argues that the extensive public fanfare and national media coverage devoted to the 1953 implementation campaign have misled many to exaggerate the depth of CCP

65. This paragraph is based on Croll, *Feminism and Socialism*, p. 236, and Meijer, *Marriage Law and Policy*, p. 129.

66. Meijer, *Marriage Law and Policy*. See also C. K. Yang, *The Chinese Family in Communist Revolution*; Sheila Rowbotham, *Women, Resistance, and Revolution*; and Croll, *The Women's Movement*.

67. See, for example, Batya Weinbaum, *The Curious Courtship of Women's Liberation and Socialism*.

68. See, for example, Marion J. Levy, Jr., "Aspects of the Analysis of Family Structure," p. 18; M. F. Nimkoff, *Comparative Family Systems*, pp. 364–65; Neil Smelser, "Classical Theories of Change and the Family Structure," p. 28; and Peter Laslett, "The Family and the Collectivity," p. 439. Even Meijer, the legal scholar whose generally judicious account of marriage law in the PRC is the most complete source on this subject, concludes that the ultimate purpose of the 1950 marriage law was to abolish the family (*Marriage Law and Policy*, p. 27).

commitment to family reform. She argues persuasively that the party gave stronger support to other movements of the period that faced mass resistance than it did to the marriage campaign, which "was taken up with uncharacteristic organizational neglect."[69] Johnson concludes that family reform was never a top priority of the Communist regime.

Kay Johnson's work provides an important corrective to prevailing interpretations of CCP family policy, one which can help make sense of the abrupt end to direct marriage law implementation campaigns after 1953. This signified neither the realization of full sexual equality nor the betrayal of earlier policy. Communist family policy, as we have seen, always exhibited a delicate compromise between feminist and restorationist tendencies, and veered between economistic and volunteerist strategies. The exceptional activism of the 1950–1953 period was the plausible complement to the land revolution. Together land reform and family reform reconstructed Chinese family morality and economy. Although, as Johnson suggests, the abandonment of activist family reform after 1953 did represent the victory of one leadership faction over another, it also bore an organic relationship to the history of revolutionary family policy.

It is equally important, however, not to minimize the radicalism of early PRC family policy. The fact that the CCP subordinated activist drives on the marriage law to other economic and political priorities should not lead us to conclude it was not serious about family reform. There is probably not one comparable historical example of a national government responding to a family crisis by initiating family transformation on such a vast scale. Even by the party's own critical evaluation of the 1953 campaign, the overwhelming majority of Chinese people received marriage law education in this period.[70] Meijer is correct, I believe, in his view that the 1 May 1950 law "was intended to cause such fundamental changes in the existing family that it may be safely said to have aimed at a family revolution."[71]

Direct campaigns to implement the marriage law came to an end in 1953 mainly because the fundamental goals of family policy of the new democracy had been achieved. These always

---

69. Kay Johnson, "Feminism and Socialist Revolution," p. 137.
70. Meijer, *Marriage Law and Policy*, p. 132.
71. Ibid., p. 15.

had subordinated women's liberation to the priorities of the class struggle. Now with land reform completed and the period of new democracy drawing to a close, socialist economic development, which was about to accelerate, could proceed with the new democratic patriarchal family system securely in place. The second, and socialist, stage of Mao Tse-tung's two-stage revolution, the collectivization of agriculture, could begin to create the patriarchal socialist family system that continues to dominate rural China. That stage of family transformation would require far less direct intervention precisely because of the effectiveness of China's new democratic family revolution.

THE INTEGRITY OF NEW DEMOCRATIC FAMILY POLICY

New democratic family policy succeeded because of its organic relationship to the Chinese revolutionary process. The policy emerged through two decades of collaboration between the CCP and China's peasantry. Its most important features spanned the history of rural strategy, and were, in turn, refined by that history. From the earliest days of its existence the CCP took a public stand against the patriarchal oppression of women, but believing family reform to be "superstructural," the Communists were free to vacillate between economistic and more activist methods to promote women's liberation. When the party adopted activist family reform strategies, it was attempting to alter the superstructure directly, in accordance with the current stage of production relations and the class struggle. New democratic family reform aimed to establish a family appropriate to new democratic society—a family system compatible with the small-scale private farm economy. When the Communists launched their major efforts on this behalf, which followed closely on the heels of national land revolution, they believed they were conducting an ideological struggle. The party failed to recognize that family reform, like land reform, simultaneously revised both the base and the superstructure of Chinese society, because the changes in gender and generational relationships they produced transformed, as well, the social relations of production and the mechanisms of social integration.

Although CCP theory mistakenly treated family relationships as secondary, party practice always recognized the indivisibility of Chinese family and economy. The gap between theory and practice caused the Communists both to instrumentalize and to misunderstand the rhythms of their own support for family reform. Within the ranks of the revolutionary party, there always had been activists who worked tirelessly to liberate women from the myriad miseries of their social and familial subordination. At times such women developed strong local organizations, whose commitment to women took precedence over party priorities. But, as we have seen, the party consistently criticized the development of independent feminist tendencies because instrumental considerations dominated its interest in family reform. A report of the party Bureau for Central and South China, written in 1951, accurately represented a CCP attitude towards family reform that had been dominant throughout the history of rural revolution:

> The experience of the last few years shows that the mere carrying out of social reform of a general and fundamental character is not sufficient to mobilize the masses of the women. They are only willing to participate in political struggle and productive labor, when their special and immediate interests are at stake.[72]

The Communists' inadequate theoretical formulation made the party's efforts to explain the vagaries of its family reform efforts degenerate into tortuous apologetics and rationalizations—claims that sex equality had been achieved, Talmudic distinctions between "freedom" and "absolute freedom," or, more reasonably, acknowledgements that mass resistance threatened regime priorities. In this way, the party trivialized its own rather remarkable family policy, obscuring thereby the role patriarchal peasant forces played in the revolution and the integrity and irony of the Communists' collaboration with them. Together peasants and party had forged a policy that restored and transformed patriarchal family life in rural China. Viewed from a feminist perspective, Communist family reform had severe limitations; but for the masses of aspiring patriarchs, the family revolution was an impressive success.

---

72. Quoted in ibid., p. 122.

The most striking aspect of CCP family policy that emerged from the peasant-party alliance was the attempt actively to promote harmonious, stable marriages and family life. Although much of the revolutionary process, and particularly the activist family reform campaigns, exacerbated familial conflict in the short-run, the long-range goal of new democratic family policy was to resolve the family crisis by placing peasant family life on a more secure economic and social footing than it ever had enjoyed. At no time in CCP history was family life itself officially attacked. Rather, the Communists consistently identified themselves with marital stability. We have seen that as early as the Kiangsi period Mao took credit for stabilizing marital relationships and for offering marriage prospects to the formerly hopeless bachelors. There were many instances when party, government, and women's organizations played active roles as matchmakers and family counselors.[73] And the mediation process introduced by the 1950 marriage law gave local and official forces an opportunity actively to save troubled marriages. Helen Snow maintains that CCP prestige among the masses was partly a consequence of the successful marriages of its leaders.[74] Even during the most militant phase of the 1953 campaign to implement the marriage law, the party propagandists urged cadres to emphasize that reform would benefit all family members by creating greater harmony between the sexes and generations. The propaganda outline issued by the National Committee for Thorough Implementation of the Marriage Law claimed that traditional goals of secure, harmonious, intergenerational family life had eluded most people in the past because of economic adversity and the coercive, patriarchal basis of the traditional family. Kay Johnson interprets this document as an attempt by the party to couch the 1953 campaign in popular terms, and she suggests that the success of the revolution created "conditions favorable to the strengthening and reestablishment of feudal bonds."[75] Her sensitive analysis of the ironies of mass-

---

73. Hu Chi-hsi, "Sexual Revolution," p. 484; Hofheinz, *Broken Wave*, p. 154; Leith, "Chinese Women," p. 61; and Helen Foster Snow, *Women in Modern China*, p. 13.

74. Helen Foster Snow, *Women in Modern China*, p. 233.

75. Kay Johnson, "Feminism and Socialist Revolution," p. 241. Johnson uses the document as an illustration of the way Maoist mass-line politics could turn conservative when implemented, in this case by providing a logic to moderate the goals of feminists in accordance with mass sentiment.

line politics and of the traditionalist cast of Maoist family reform is a needed remedy to prevailing interpretations. However, it is important not to exaggerate the reestablishment of "feudal" bonds. The compromise between feminist and restorationist principles that defined the integral core of new democratic family policy made *selective* traditional familial goals more realizable, but precisely because the very character of Chinese family and society had been transformed by the process.

The Chinese Communists' interest in fostering harmonious family life was not purely altruistic, but an attempt to place family stability in the service of the revolution. Contrary to the view of many social analysts that communism in China, as elsewhere, regarded the family primarily as a competing system of loyalty whose influence over its members had to be diminished,[76] rural revolutionary experience early taught the CCP that family loyalties could be turned to its advantage. Hence the respect and favor the party accorded peasant family interests and values when designing its economic and military policies, as well as its direct appeals to family loyalties in recruiting peasants to war service. Whenever possible, the Communists avoided presenting peasants a direct conflict of interest between their families and the revolution. The educational principles of the Chin-Ch'a-Chi border government, for example, explicitly charged the education department to balance family and social demands in order to maintain family harmony. Schedules should be organized to synchronize with the requirements of family production. Family reading units and study groups were established as well.[77] Family reform efforts were soft-pedaled whenever they appeared threatening to social priorities. On the other hand, family reform sometimes was promoted as a means of increasing productive efficiency. In 1951, for example, the investigation teams evaluating the success of marriage law campaigns claimed that production fared best in areas with a high percentage of successfully reformed marriages.[78]

76. Compare C. K. Yang, *Family in Revolution;* Meijer, *Marriage Law and Policy;* and Rose L. Coser and Lewis A. Coser, "The Principle of Legitimacy and Its Patterned Infringement in Social Revolutions."

77. Dorris, "People's War," p. 129, and Chao Kuo-chün, *Agrarian Policy of the Chinese Communist Party, 1921–1959,* pp. 68–69.

78. Kay Johnson, "Feminism and Socialist Revolution," pp. 195–96. See Janet Salaff, "Youth, Family and Political Control in Communist China," for a detailed discussion of the marriage rankings.

While the CCP made exceptional efforts to balance the demands of the peasants' patriarchal moral economy with those of the revolution, it is undeniable that it also gradually introduced state regulation into the affairs of personal life. This happened first within cadre ranks as the party intervened in the selection of mates and introduced political and class definitions of marital compatibility. By the time of the 1953 marriage campaign, the population as a whole was encouraged to regard registering a marriage as a prosocial act and an indication of support for the CCP regime. When Ch'en Shao-yu explained the purposes behind the obligation to register a marriage, he maintained that citizens and state shared an interest in sustaining successful marriages:

> The only duty of the People's Government is to serve the people. It has no other interests but those of the people and it does not interfere in matters in which the people do not want it to interfere. Therefore the People's Government cannot keep aloof from that great event of marriage in the life of a man and a woman, which also affects the health of the whole people, and happiness of the family, the health of the whole nation and the reconstruction of the State. And not only can the Government not keep aloof, it must show greater concern in these matters than even the marrying parties themselves and their relatives do, and it has to assume an even more serious responsibility.[79]

Few Confucian emperors were more solicitous in this regard than the public patriarchs of the new democratic state.

Another notable feature of the Communists' family policy was their advocacy of a puritanical code of sexual morality—understanding puritanical to mean, in its full historic sense, support for conjugal sexuality. The Chinese Communists of the revolutionary period were not Victorians, but they consistently demanded that sexuality be confined to marriage and never allowed to interfere with a person's broader social responsibilities. Throughout the revolutionary period, enemies portrayed the Communists as sexually licentious.[80] But, as we have seen, the

---

79. Quoted in Meijer, *Marriage Law and Policy*, p. 179.

80. Evidence and examples of such charges are abundant. See, for example, Davin, *Woman-Work*, pp. 30, 62; Hofheinz, *Broken Wave*, p. 266; Isabel Crook and David Crook, *Revolution in a Chinese Village*, p. 107; Thaxton, "When Peasants Took Power," p. 600; Isaacs, *Tragedy of Chinese Revolution*, pp. 149, 226; Kuo-t'ao

CCP response to such charges was to identify itself publicly with a sexual code even stricter than that of prevailing contemporary standards.[81] Even the comparatively libertarian Kiangsi policy was converted quickly to this approach. A woman-work directive of the period set a goal of raising political and cultural levels among the population in order "to prevent morally loose behavior," and in patriarchal fashion, it called upon cadres to pay particular attention to the wives of Red Army personnel.[82] The minimum marriage age for men was set at twenty, and this over the objections of two-thirds of the soldiers of the Second Division of the Red Army who attended a debate on the problems of marriage.[83] The Red Army earned a well-deserved reputation for exemplary sexual restraint, in no small part because of the seriousness with which this was demanded by the party. Army regulations treated violation of women as a criminal offense, and the army engaged in conscious efforts to absorb the sexual energies of its soldiers.[84]

The sexual puritanism of the CCP must have had a variety of motives. Not only was the party battling against anti-Communist propagandists, but some of its own interests were served by a restrictive sexual code. In part this can be seen as a prowoman policy. The party perceived that under prevailing social conditions, women, the victims of a double standard, would be further exploited rather than emancipated by free love morality. In fact, peasant women tended to be more conservative than the party on this issue. All too frequently, women's associations faltered because "respectable" peasant women refused to participate in organizations that welcomed "broken shoes" as members.

Chang, *Rise of the Chinese Communist Party*, p. 200; and Hu Chi-hsi, "Sexual Revolution," pp. 477, 489.

81. However, recently suggestions have appeared that the top male leadership of the party engaged in transgressions and manipulations of the sexual code, such as assigning men to distant posts in order to seduce their wives, or sending their own wives to Moscow and replacing them with younger ones, or sexually harrassing women by promising them advancement in exchange for sex. See Hua Chang-ming, "Révolutionnaires au Foyer."

82. Meijer, *Marriage Law and Policy*, p. 40.

83. Hu Chi-hsi, "Sexual Revolution," p. 487.

84. Agnes Smedley, *Battle Hymn of China*, p. 180, and Hua Chang-ming, "Révolutionnaires au Foyer," p. 101. There are indications, however, of a double standard for the officers and the soldiers.

Women, of course, were not the only peasants concerned about sexual "virtue." Male proprietors worried about the purity of their womenfolk, and the party was willing to exploit this anxiety.[85] Hence, the stringent sexual code of the CCP also reflected its attempt to appeal to traditional, patriarchal peasant values.

But in sexual morality, as in family reform generally, the CCP demonstrated its extraordinary capacity to bend restorationist ideals to transformative purposes. The CCP was not simply resurrecting a code that had dissipated. Nor was it implementing a new moral code derived exclusively from either the demands of peasant women or the ideology of the Soviet Union. While responding to influences and pressures from all these sources, the CCP was shaping them into a new, distinctively Chinese Communist sexual code. This new democratic morality linked sexuality not with procreation, but with felicitous marital relationships and, thereby, with the construction of socialism. In the marriage law, impotence was legitimate grounds for divorce and a restriction against marrying in the first place, but sterility was not. The party reasoned that sexual relations were crucial to conjugal love, which, in turn, was essential to the harmonious family life the party considered crucial to the construction of socialism. Fertility, however, is a different matter:

> There are also people who, because the wife does not bring children into the world, think this is a reason for a divorce. This is unreasonable. The birth of children is the result of marriage between a man and a woman and is not a necessary condition for love between husband and wife, nor does the fact that there are no children mean that one cannot have marital life. This is not at all the same as having a physical defect and not being able to have sexual intercourse.[86]

Compared with the traditional extreme double standard of Confucianism and its overwhelmingly instrumental emphasis

---

85. This paragraph is based on Meijer, *Marriage Law and Policy*, p. 98; Dorris, "People's War," pp. 132ff; Crook and Crook, *Revolution in a Chinese Village*, p. 112; Davin, *Woman-Work*, p. 62; Kay Johnson, "Feminism and Socialist Revolution," pp. 87ff; Yung-fa Chen, "Making of a Revolution," p. 331; and Yuan-tsung Chen, *The Dragon's Village*.

86. Translated in Meijer, *Marriage Law and Policy*, p. 219. Such an ideology is highly compatible with current antinatalist policies in the PRC, but this does not explain its emergence in the pronatalist 1950s.

on marriage as route to the male progeny essential for perpetuating the male lineage, this Chinese Communist moral standard is revolutionary indeed. Less revolutionary, but equally innovative, was the CCP's attempt to mandate conjugal bliss as the single acceptable Communist lifestyle. While pre-Communist China did not offer a multitude of acceptable lifestyle options to its peasantry, economic diversity and cultural and religious practices combined to yield "deviant" patterns of family life that were socially validated in particular instances and localities. We have discussed the most intriguing of these—the non-marrying sisters of rural Kwangtung. After liberation, the Communist government eliminated the sisterhoods and forcibly returned the members to their natal families.[87] Lacking evidence, one can only speculate about their underlying political motivations. The Kwangtung sisterhoods violated Confucian morality. By eliminating them, therefore, the Communists once again paid respect to traditional patriarchal values. One piece of marriage law propaganda suggests this interpretation by using a cartoon of one of the sisterhoods as an example of the miserable choices that confronted women in prerevolutionary China.[88] By implication, the government viewed its action as liberating women from their undesired fate. However, the Communists imposed this generosity even on resistant beneficiaries. Perhaps the regime perceived any sort of lifestyle diversity as threatening to the labor and political discipline it was about to demand from the population. Equally likely, it experienced the form and membership of the sisterhoods as undesirable. Women who chose independently and collectively to resist patriarchal authority to live exclusively with other women violated the Chinese Communists' view of the proper relationship between the sexes and between communism and the women's movement. Had the CCP been the enemy of private family life its opponents made out, the marriage resistance movement would have been a natural ally. Instead, the party was so committed to sustaining private conjugal family life that it found the protosocialist, protofeminist communities of sisters less tolerable

87. Marjorie Topley, "Marriage Resistance in Rural Kwangtung," p. 85. According to Topley, only those women without kin who might take them in were allowed to remain in the halls. Remnants of the sisterhoods survive in Hong Kong, however, See Andrea Sankar, "Spinster Sisterhoods."

88. Davin, *Woman-Work*, p. 87.

than patriarchal "feudal remnants," such as purchase brides, dowry, ancestor worship, or wife beating. During the decades of its rural revolution, the CCP moved from promoting a universal right to marry to practically requiring marriage as a political obligation.

The basic coherence of new democratic family policy was that it complemented land revolution in completing the patriarchal revolution in rural China. The family reforms the Communists pursued with greatest vigor and success were those that curtailed rights to property in women. These were the privileges that had sustained an elite class of patriarchs. Concubines, servants, chaste widows, tiny feet—long the particular luxuries of more affluent lineages—were among the earliest casualties of Communist family reform. The liberating consequences for women were both inherent and intended. However, the CCP never confronted the root structures of small-scale patriarchal authority—the household mode of production and patrilocal marriage. On the contrary, it encouraged married daughters to waive their rights to parental property on the explicit grounds that "in China social conditions are such that the son is living with his parents and that such a household forms one economic unit."[89] Similarly, the Communists retreated or compromised most readily on family reforms that were unacceptable to poor, and particularly male, peasants— parentally arranged marriage, a woman's right to divorce, even wife beating. These structures and practices were not merely ideological remnants of China's "feudal" past. Rather, during its collaboration with the peasantry, the CCP actively reconstructed the faltering family economy and redistributed amongst the peasants the means of access to patrilocal marriages. In short, the Communist attack on the elite patriarchy of the few was integral to its success in making democratic patriarchy available to the many.

THE NEW RURAL FAMILY ORDER

By 1953 collaboration of the peasantry and the CCP had succeeded in resolving the family realization crisis through the new dem-

89. "Manual of People's University," quoted in Meijer, *Marriage Law and Policy*, p. 257. Davin confirms that patrilocality was not challenged in this period (*Woman-Work*, p. 113).

ocratic patriarchal family policy, whose complex processes of innovation and compromise we have just scrutinized. Family security and integrity had been placed within the means of the overwhelming majority of Chinese peasants. It seems likely that more peasants than ever could reasonably expect to marry, rear children, and live to see their children marry and produce heirs in turn. We have seen that the party actively supported such traditional aspirations in its family reform propaganda. But we have seen also that the revolutionary collaboration of the party and the peasantry went beyond restoration to create a new family system. The new democratic patriarchy was a historically unique family system. Just as Mao Tse-tung claimed, it differed both from the traditional Chinese peasant family and the "modern" capitalist conjugal one. At the end of the period of new democracy, when Mao was responding once again to Western propaganda about communism's assault on the family, he explained:

> It is true that the Chinese people have broken the feudal patriarchal system. It must be known that this patriarchal system has long since ceased to exist in capitalist society and that this is a sign of capitalist progress. However, we have gone a step further and established a democratic and united family which in general is rare in capitalist society. Only in the future, in those places where the socialist revolution has been carried out and the capitalist system of exploitation of man by man has been eliminated will it be possible to establish such families universally.[90]

Whatever the comparative merits of the new democratic patriarchy, it was indeed a new family system. It combined elements from both the traditional "feudal" Chinese peasant family and from the Western "bourgeois" conjugal family and introduced features foreign to both. The economic basis of the new democratic patriarchy was a private household unit of production, one that differed not only from the Western consumption and income-pooling family unit but also from the economy of the pre-Communist Chinese peasant family. Although still a private, family farm economy, it was effectively linked to and dependent upon larger, nonkinship-defined cooperative forms and state economic

---

90. Quoted in Meijer, *Marriage Law and Policy*, p. 268.

structures.[91] The family values of the new democratic patriarchy likewise borrowed and differed from both "bourgeois" and "feudal" ones. Several of the most pertinent ideological differences were indicated in the preceding discussion of the marriage law and sexual morality. In effect, the Chinese Communists were attempting to establish a new *li*. Their propaganda portrayed an ideal marriage as a free union of equal partners who made a lifelong commitment to one another on the basis of compatible class background and ideological unity. New democratic divorce was an instrument to end "feudal" oppression and to stimulate the productive forces necessary to the construction of socialism. Not a private route to individual fulfillment as in the West, divorce should be granted only when the proper basis for ideological unity was lacking or when marital conflict was severe enough to threaten production or collective life.[92] The legislated norms of new democratic marriage were a careful, self-conscious blend of traditional peasant virtues and socialist ideals: "the apogee of the development of the ideas of morality, mercy, filial piety, and benevolence that have always been practiced by the working people of China."[93]

Although the gap between ideals and reality pertained in China as elsewhere, there is good reason to accept Mao's claim that new democracy was no mirror image of Western bourgeois forms. To paraphrase Mao, the new democratic stage of the family revolution in China was no longer democratic family life in general, but a democratic family of the Chinese type, a new and special type, namely, new democratic patriarchy.[94] Contrary to the widespread belief that the Communist revolution in China simply accelerated processes of family change functional to modern industrial society and already under way, the Chinese revolution facilitated and depended upon a genuine *family revolution*. Far from merely hastening prerevolutionary processes of family

---

91. This is not intended to contradict Norma Diamond's claim in "Collectivization, Kinship and the Status of Women in Rural China" that kinship often underlay the collectivization structure. I am stressing instead the fact that kinship was no longer the idiom or rationale for cooperative relationships, nor was it necessarily or uniformly coextensive with the cooperative structure.

92. Meijer, *Marriage Law and Policy*, p. 225.

93. Chen Shou-yu, quoted in ibid., p. 262.

94. Here I am paraphrasing Mao, "On New Democracy."

change, the Communist revolution arrested many of them and initiated important new ones. In this way, the revolution succeeded in resolving the pre-Communist family crisis by establishing a family system radically different from the Western nuclear family.

The new democratic patriarchy was a family system based on new principles of gender, generation, and social integration. The gender distinctions of Confucian patriarchy had been ameliorated dramatically with women gaining legitimated access to the public sphere of Chinese society. But family production based on a division of labor by sex and age remained central to rural life. Patriarchal authority, while radically redistributed, still was rooted in rights to land and women secured through patrilocal marriage and household production. The radical redistribution of patriarchal privilege made monogamy the new marital ideal as well as practice, and it dramatically curtailed practices such as female infanticide, footbinding, child brides and foster daughters-in-law. The decline of the latter two marriage forms were indications, as well, of new generational roles in the Chinese peasant family. Family revolution increased enormously the familial value and influence of the young. Now youth were consulted, at the least, before their marriages were arranged, and few chose to be or receive a child bride. Furthermore, access to land enhanced a young couple's ability to establish their own patriarchal household in a comparatively short period after their marriage. This diminished the significance of a mother-in-law's stake in rearing a daughter-in-law of her own. Finally, the new small-scale patriarchy depended for its support on resources and institutions controlled by a new class of "public patriarchs"—the Chinese Communist Party.

Land reform generally has been considered the essence of the Chinese Communists' class revolution and family reform the essence of their attempt to liberate women. Commonly the former is judged a resounding success; the latter is thought to have been of lower priority, with more limited achievements. Certainly when the programs are distinguished in this manner, these judgments are appropriate. Land reform did much to overturn the rural class structure. Family reform, if evaluated in terms of official goals or those of Western feminism, was more disappointing. It did not achieve sexual equality, nor even put an end to patriarchy. Those who accept a base-superstructure model of social change attribute much of the disparity to inadequacies of the land revolution. Because the CCP was unable, or unwilling, to distribute land equally to women, its family reform program faltered. However, these chapters have suggested there was a different, far more coherent relationship between Communist economic and family policy. Land reform and family reform were complementary means of redistributing and reforming patriarchal authority. From this perspective, even the apparent limitations of Communist family reform contributed to the success of the patriarchal family revolution.

The Chinese Communists never intended to wage a feminist revolution; nor did they possess a theory of family transformation adequate to the task. Believing patriarchy derivative of "feudal" social structure, regarding gender oppression as a nonantagonistic contradiction, the CCP did not seek to eliminate patriarchs as a class,[95] but merely to eliminate a particular class of patriarchs. This they accomplished with dramatic success, thereby indirectly satisfying the demand of the majority of their peasant constituents that a new, more democratic form of patriarchal family life be made accessible to all. This unarticulated family revolution was the central medium of class struggle in the new democratic stage of China's revolution. Through its success, the CCP established the transitional moral economy it had sought—one that would respond to its impending program of agricultural collectivization. The successful family revolution provided Chinese patriarchs a new, more democratic basis for their unity—one that future Chinese feminists would find intensely difficult to challenge.

---

95. To do so would require eliminating men as a class, that is, the transcendence of gender as a basic social organizing principle.

AFTERWORD TO CHAPTERS 4 and 5
Kuomintang Family Policy

Chinese Communist family policy was an important source of peasant support for People's War. While the policy appealed to the peasantry on its own merits, its attractiveness was enhanced considerably when compared to the existing or imagined alternatives. Thus, the Chinese Communist Party (CCP) had few allies more effective than the family policy of the Kuomintang (KMT), its major competitor for state power in China. One of the ironies of this history is that the KMT, the party that most staunchly defended traditional Confucian familial values, did its utmost to speed their demise, while the CCP, the party vilified as a threat to Chinese families, proved to be their savior. Detailed analyses of Kuomintang economic and military policies lie outside the scope of this study, but I wish briefly to suggest how these exacerbated the realization crisis in the peasant family economy while offering no effective alternatives or remedies to its victims.

Initially a revolutionary party, the Kuomintang, as we saw in chapter 3, first supported family reforms similar to those the Communists advocated. These never were seriously implemented in rural areas, however, not only for lack of party effort, but because they were incompatible with the prevailing social and economic order.[96] To the limited extent that peasants even learned about the KMT marriage reforms, it seems likely they would have regarded them as alien and threatening to their entire way of life. And the KMT was no more successful with its New Life Movement, the reactionary family ideology it tried to promote after consolidating a modicum of national power and purging the Communists in 1928. Far more significant, however, than the ineffective reformist or reactionary varieties of KMT official family policies were the effects on the peasant family economy

---

96. For example, the civil code promised equal inheritance protection to women. However, if implemented, such a policy would have thoroughly disrupted peasant marriage and land-tenure arrangements. Consequently, it was not implemented. Cf. Hsiao-tung Fei and Chih-i Chang, *Earthbound China*, pp. 112–13.

of the party's agrarian and military policies. These were cata-strophic and, thus, a major source of peasant hostility to the Nationalists and dependence upon the CCP.

The KMT was as aware as the Communists of China's agrarian crisis. The "Three People's Principles" of the party's founder, Dr. Sun Yat-sen, gave a strong rural flavor to the party's early ideology. Moreover, the Nationalist regime enjoyed the support of many scholars and advisers who were dedicated to the cause of agrarian reform. Consequently, the KMT government initiated a number of experimental agrarian reform programs, and it went so far as to pass a land law in 1930 that called for a 25 percent reduction in rent. But, with the exception of a rare few local successes, KMT efforts at rural reform were paltry, late, and ineffective.[97]

A rent reduction campaign in Chekiang is illustrative. In 1927 party and government figures were agreed on the need to reduce land rents, but in 1928 Chekiang landlords protested the campaign by refusing to pay their land taxes. The provincial government capitulated immediately and abolished the campaign. Local party figures who criticized the government's response were silenced summarily. The government arrested the editor of the local party paper and suspended its publication. The party's mediation efforts led to a formal resumption of rent reform, but left responsibility for its implementation in the hands of the provincial government. The campaign died a quiet death.[98]

A similar fate met Chiang K'ai-shek's proposals to set a max-imum limit on landholding by imposing increased taxes on land-holdings that exceeded the limit, or to establish special land-purchase options for village cooperatives, or to extend rural credit.[99] The KMT was unable to relieve the peasants' burdens. Corruption and administrative deficiencies contributed significantly to the

---

97. Among the notable successes were certain of the tenant land-purchase projects of the 1940s and aspects of the Mass Education Movement in Ting Hsien. For the former, see Ralph Montée, "Agrarian Problems and Policies in China," p. 222; for the latter, see Sidney D. Gamble, *Ting Hsien*, and Carl E. Dorris, "People's War in North China," p. 127. Only in 1949, on the verge of defeat, did the KMT attempt belatedly to win popular support and additional U.S. aid by initiating national land reform. It was far too late. For data, see Montée, "Agrarian Problems," p. 233.

98. Noel R. Miner, "Agrarian Reform in Nationalist China."

99. James C. Thomson, Jr., *While China Faced West*, pp. 200–201.

failure, but it is unlikely that more honest and efficient personnel could have done much better. The root of China's agrarian problem, and the key to peasant distress, was the land problem. As Harold Isaacs suggested, "No hunger was greater than the land hunger, and in district after district the peasants reached out to satisfy their craving."[100] But this was the appetite the KMT could not assuage. An urban-based party, its inadequate base of rural support was the peasants' economic adversaries, the large land-owners. The KMT headed a central government that was far too weak to impose land reform on resistant local authorities. These problems were compounded when military reverses forced the government deep into the Chinese interior. There they became inescapably dependent upon local elites, whose interests were diametrically opposed to agrarian reform.

But the KMT did not merely fail to resolve the agrarian crisis. Its economic policies exhibited striking disregard for the familial basis of the peasant economy. For example, the KMT depended upon conscript labor for public works, such as road building and dike construction, but its conscription policies failed to consider family labor needs.[101] The tax policies of the KMT were as regressive as those of the Communists were progressive. In 1928 the Nanking government ceded all claims to the land tax to the provincial authorities. While landlords gained an enormous un-taxed source of accumulation, Nanking lost a major source of revenue and was forced to rely on salt and customs taxes, which placed a disproportionate tax burden on the poor. Instead of adjusting taxes to accommodate the subsistence needs of peasant families, tax quotas were assigned to provincial authorities who, in time-honored fashion, made sure they fell inordinately on the shoulders of the poor and middle peasantry.[102] Masses of peasant families were left destitute. Instead of stemming the traditional patriarchal responses to impoverishment, some government tax collectors encouraged them. Edgar Snow reported a conversation with an old peasant father in Northern Shensi, who had been urged to sell his daughter to pay his taxes: "Some of us here

---

100. Harold R. Isaacs, *The Tragedy of the Chinese Revolution*, p. 224.
101. Chen Han-seng, *Landlord and Peasant in China*, p. 78.
102. Montée, "Agrarian Problems," pp. 173ff., and Theodore White and Annalee Jacoby, *Thunder Out of China*, p. 69.

had to do that. Those who had no cattle and no daughters went to jail in Pao An, and plenty died from the cold." Another farmer summarized local experience with the KMT: "Taxing us to death, stealing our sons, burning and killing."[103] Corruption was so rampant in KMT famine relief agencies that it worsened the human toll of natural disasters. Officials hoarded and speculated in grain, then they purchased land from starving peasants to reap speculative profits from land as well.[104] Such deeds were adequate evidence of the disregard of KMT economic policies for the peasant moral economy, but the Nationalists occasionally underscored them by bulldozing peasant homes, graveyards, and temples that stood in the path of modern roads or reconstruction projects.[105]

By all accounts the most graphic contrast between the implicit family policy of the Communists and the KMT was in their respective military practices. Abuses of the White Army were as legendary and as valuable to Red Army recruitment as were Red Army virtues. Military conscription policies, like civilian ones, displayed total contempt for the most basic survival needs and sentiments of peasant families and communities. Families and villages were mercilessly depleted of ablebodied laborers. Because wealthier families could purchase substitutes, obtain student deferments, or bribe the recruiting officials, the poor and middle peasant families most dependent upon their male kin were the ones obliged to sacrifice them."[106] Fei and Chang observed at the time, "The draft scores a direct hit on the family unit."[107] Recruitment officers were callously indifferent to the extremity of sacrifice they inflicted. Graham Peck met a poor peasant couple who depended on wages their only son earned from coal mining. After they unexpectedly had a late-in-life boy, their older son was drafted because only one son per family

---

103. Quoted in Edgar Snow, *Red Star Over China*, pp. 243, 313.

104. For some shocking tales about corruption related to Honan famine relief, see White and Jacoby, *Thunder Out of China*. Famine casualty data is available in Edgar Snow, *Red Star Over China*, p. 216, and Lucien Bianco, *Origins of the Chinese Revolution, 1915–1949*, p. 157.

105. Ralph Thaxton, "Tenants in Revolution," p. 344.

106. See, for example, Fei and Chang, *Earthbound China*, p. 270; Myers, *The Chinese Peasant Economy*, pp. 281–82; Bianco, *Origins*, p. 155; and Hsiao-tung Fei, *China's Gentry*, p. 141.

107. Fei and Chang, *Earthbound China*, p. 271.

could be exempted legally. When the mother's desperate appeal was dismissed by local authorities, she went home and beat her new baby to death.[108] Village labor supplies were depleted and communities disrupted as the poor migrated in droves, attempting to save their families by escaping conscription.[109]

Family survival depended upon avoiding conscription, because unlike the Red Army, the KMT offered no assistance to families jeopardized by the "enlistment" of their men. While the Red Army heaped special protection, privileges, and honors on the families of its enlistees "so that the soldiers may kill the enemy without being disturbed by worries about their domestic life,"[110] White Army families received neither allowances nor aid. Whereas the Communists helped families and soldiers to write letters to each other, White Army families frequently lost all contact with their conscripted relative because they were illiterate and could not afford the fees of a scribe.[111] According to former Communist leader, Chang Kuo-t'ao, one of the clearest ways to determine whether an area in the Oyüwan Soviet had been attacked by White or Red troops was to see which buildings were left standing. Whites would destroy ancestral halls, temples, and even people's houses. The Reds would destroy fortresses, but "in deference to the clannish affection of the peasants" they usually left the ancestral halls alone, knocked down only the idols in the temples, and never destroyed the people's houses.[112]

Instead of aiding peasant families, the White Army often ravaged them. The military requisitioned scarce grain supplies from peasant villages. Red Army men often fought in their own localities, but KMT armies were imported from outside and generally lacked sympathy for the local population.[113] The discipline and propriety of the Red Army was in sharp contrast to the rampant violation of property, sexuality, and life committed by undisciplined soldiers and officers in KMT forces. Plunder, rape, and

108. Graham Peck, *Two Kinds of Time*, pp. 266–67.

109. Fei and Chang, *Earthbound China*, p. 270.

110. Ch'en Shao-yu, quoted in Meijer, *Marriage Law and Policy*, p. 240.

111. Bianco, *Origins*, p. 156.

112. Kuo-t'ao Chang, *The Rise of the Chinese Communist Party, 1929–1938*, pp. 220–21.

113. Gamble, *Ting Hsien*, p. 116, and Jack Belden, *China Shakes the World*, p. 334.

assault were endemic White Army abuses.[114] Rape of "their womenfolk" excited some of the fiercest hostility of local men. Jack Belden met landlords lost to the KMT cause for this reason. One such landlord hated the Communist Eighth Route Army for dividing his land. However, when the KMT wrested temporary control of his village, the local KMT commander forced the landlord's daughter, the best-looking girl in the village, to sleep with him. The landlord came to prefer the Communists as the lesser of evils.[115]

KMT military decisions often ignored human consequences. During the Fifth Encirclement campaign against the Communists in Kiangsi, for example, the KMT systematically annihilated and removed entire populations near the Communist borders so that those areas would be unable to support Communist forces. KMT officers then took thousands of children as prisoners and sold them into factories, prostitution, and slavery.[116] Perhaps the most infamous example of cold-blooded military strategy occurred in 1938 when Nationalist forces diverted the Yellow River from the North to the South of Shantung in an unsuccessful attempt to halt the advancing Japanese. Millions of Chinese were displaced and killed by the ensuing floods.[117] When nationalism was represented by deeds such as these, it was a masterful understatement to note that "the conflict of loyalty to the nation and to their own families is very great among the Chinese peasants."[118]

Civilians were not the only victims of KMT military exactions and abuse. Contemporary observers were nearly unanimous in the view that the KMT soldier was one of the world's most brutalized military men. Soldiers were kidnapped, chained, and driven into service in press-gangs. Discipline was arbitrary and

---

114. Compare Donald G. Gillin, "Peasant Nationalism in the History of Chinese Communism," p. 281; Crook and Crook, *Revolution in a Chinese Village*, p. 31; Belden, *China Shakes the World*, p. 334; and White and Jacoby, *Thunder Out of China*.

115. Belden, *China Shakes the World*, p. 334. See also, Edgar Snow, *Red Star Over China*, p. 302.

116. Edgar Snow, *Red Star Over China*, p. 301.

117. For antiseptic discussions of this, see James Pinckney Harrison, *The Long March to Power*, p. 277, and Ping-ti Ho, *Studies on the Population of China, 1368–1953*, p. 234; for morally outraged reports, see White and Jacoby, *Thunder Out of China*, p. 60, and Peck, *Two Kinds of Time*, pp. 333–34.

118. Fei and Chang, *Earthbound China*, p. 271. Such understatement was probably a conscious attempt to influence KMT policy makers.

brutal; punishment included beating, ear cropping, and killing. Recruits rarely received their pittance-level wages, they enjoyed no furloughs, and provisions were so inadequate—due as much to corruption as to shortages—that millions died of starvation and disease. More soldiers died in the recruitment and training processes than at the front. But even at the front, soldiers died of starvation. More than half of the KMT's soldiers were starving when General Albert Wedemeyer arrived in 1944. Little wonder that the KMT had to kidnap and truss recruits and that desertion and defection rates were enormous.[119]

KMT military "family policy" cost the Nationalists an enormous military price. A Sian newspaper gave three reasons for the failure of KMT conscription: money played a decisive role in the selection of recruits; inducted men were treated miserably; and soldiers' families were neglected.[120] Although Japanese military behavior was unspeakably brutal, there were instances when peasants welcomed the Japanese forces—as liberation from the plunder and raping of the KMT troops.[121] But the greatest beneficiary of KMT implicit family policy was the Red Army. Particularly in border areas where military control shifted between Communist and Nationalist forces, the contrast encouraged peasant receptivity to the Red Army. Under military policies of the KMT, peasants realized that "no family is secure,"[122] whereas they came to greet the Red Army with comparative enthusiasm and sentiments similar to these of an old peasant woman in Shansi:

---

119. This paragraph is based on White and Jacoby, *Thunder Out of China*; Peck, *Two Kinds of Time*; Edgar Snow, *Red Star Over China*; and Belden, *China Shakes the World*.

120. Suzanne Pepper, *Civil War in China*, p. 167.

121. White and Jacoby, *Thunder Out of China*, pp. 143–44, quote a poignant report by a Chinese journalist: Japanese troops entered a village peacefully, and they were welcomed by villagers weary of the KMT. The Japanese took the village without gunfire; then they implemented their policy—kill all, burn all. Pepper also reports on an area under KMT control; here villagers remembered the Japanese occupation with comparative nostalgia (*Civil War*, p. 169).

122. Edgar Snow, *Red Star Over China*, p. 313. For example, a journalist in the Northeast reported that during the Japanese occupation local people did not know there were two kinds of Chinese troops. However, they learned quickly after the defeat of the Japanese, when they preferred the Communists. Although the journalist was cynical about the Reds, his mother had been impressed by the Communist soldiers billeted with the family; they had respected her wishes, had not bothered her granddaughter, and stole nothing from the family (Pepper, *Civil War*, p. 204).

You are the Southern Army, the Eighth Route Army . . . the good army that doesn't harm people or do evil things. . . . You are the Red Army![123]

---

123. Quoted in Gillin, "Peasant Nationalism," p. 281.

6 Development and Constraints of Patriarchal-Socialism

Patriarchy achieved its developmental limits as a revolutionary force in China during the 1950s. Building upon the terms of its new democratic patriarchal alliance with the peasantry, the Communist regime elicited peasant collaboration in constructing a patriarchal-socialist rural order. This further democratization of patriarchal family life facilitated the success of agricultural collectivization in the People's Republic of China (PRC). However, in the waning years of the first decade of the Communists' rule, the contradictions of their atheoretical family revolution emerged. Chinese patriarchy reached the limits of its capacity to serve as a revolutionary force and became, instead, the constraining context in which strategies for socialist development were destined to proceed. Its constraints were all the more limiting because of the hidden nature of the prior patriarchal revolution and the inadequacy of the theoretical resources the Marxist regime could apply to an analysis of the difficulties its policies encountered. This chapter examines the major socialist process of rural transformation in the PRC and the principles and contradictions of the patriarchal-socialist rural order that prevailed in China from the mid-1950s until the death of Mao Tse-tung. It also looks briefly at contrasts between rural and urban family policy during that period. An epilog extends this analysis of the dialectics of patriarchy and socialism to the Four Modernizations program in contemporary China.

AGRICULTURAL COLLECTIVIZATION

When land reform was completed in 1953, most Chinese imagined the road to rural socialism would be slowly traveled. Indeed, by early 1955, only one out of ten peasant households was participating in team farming, despite a 1951 Chinese Communist Party (CCP) directive mandating membership in Mutual Aid Teams (MATs) for peasant households.[1] But, in July of that year, Mao Tse-tung suddenly prevailed over the gradualist approach towards collectivization supported by the majority of Chinese Communist leaders and unleashed the famous "high tide of socialism" that stormed over the countryside during the months that followed. Agricultural cooperatives were formed at a dramatic rate, and they converted rapidly from semisocialist form to full-fledged socialist collectives—the Advanced Production Cooperatives (APCs). By May 1956, 91.2 percent of Chinese peasant households belonged to cooperatives, and 61.8 percent of the households were in APCs.[2] By 1957, the socialization of rural production had been completed.

Throughout the 1960s and 1970s, PRC propaganda promoted the view, which many Western scholars and activists accepted, that collectivization destroyed the material basis of rural patriarchal power. Other, less sympathetic, scholars have viewed collectivization as a betrayal of the Chinese peasants, who thereby lost their rights to private ownership of their farms quite as precipitously as they had gained them. Both views are erroneous. Peasant patriarchs did not vigorously resist the socialization of their farms. They allowed the "high tide" to proceed without major disruption to agricultural production, which even sustained modest growth during the period.[3] A close look at the collectivization process and its consequences resolves the paradox. It suggests that collectivization did not betray the fundamental terms of the new democratic patriarchal revolution but, instead, extended its basic principles and policies.[4] Peasant patriarchy was not destroyed; it was further democratized and secured.

---

1. Ramon H. Myers, *The Chinese Economy*, p. 215.
2. Vivienne Shue, *Peasant China in Transition*, pp. 286–87.
3. Myers, *Chinese Economy*, p. 227.
4. For a different argument against the view that peasants were betrayed by agricultural collectivization, see Shue, *Peasant China*, pp. 332–33.

In collectivizing agriculture, the Chinese Communists followed the precedent of the People's War and based the cooperatives on the patriarchal family unit. Peasant households were the membership units of the agricultural collectives, as they had been when they participated in the MATs. The government's collectivizing strategy took care to tie the prosperity of the poor- and middle-peasant family economy to the success of the APCs.[5] Adopting measures that regulated the sale and supply of grain, the regime severely restricted opportunities for private profit and made peasant family security and prosperity contingent upon cooperation. The Three Fix policy of 1955 established per-household standards of grain consumption at the provincial level. Peasant households were placed in three categories according to their ability to meet standard consumption requirements and to pay taxes—grain-surplus, self-sufficient, and grain-short. Authorities computed a normal annual yield for each household, giving assurance the figure would remain fixed for three years. Quotas on mandatory sale of grain to the government and limits on the amount of grain each household could purchase were established in accordance with these calculations. This elaborate system encouraged families of unequal wealth to join together as APCs. In 1956 the APC became the unit of grain sale and supply by totaling the Three Fix figures of its member households. This allowed the poorer member families to raise the limits on their consumption, while grain-surplus households who linked with them hoped to reduce their mandatory sale quotas.

The People's Bank of China facilitated the cooperative movement by channeling loans to peasants through the supply and marketing cooperatives, rather than to individuals. These cooperatives extended loans to poor households to enable them to join production cooperatives, to meet financial obligations to their work teams, or to meet temporary family expenses—weddings, funerals, house repairs, and the like.

As in the People's War period, party propaganda promoted cooperation through direct appeals to family prosperity and happiness. For example, these themes dominate the text of *New Earth*, an in-house account of collectivization in Chekiang Province

---

5. The following account of the CCP's collectivization policies relies primarily upon Shue, *Peasant China*, especially pp. 263ff.

by Jack Chen, a prominent publicist for the PRC. Chen claims the benefits of the cooperatives were well explained and quickly demonstrated to the peasants. One advantage was a sharp reduction in family fights, which Chen has the peasants attribute to their newfound economic security: "All this [material benefit] makes a big difference. We used to have plenty of family quarrels in the old days. Worries got on our nerves. But we're not naturally that way. Now we've not had a tiff for five years."[6] Another advantage was a poor male peasant's enhanced capacity to afford a bride. Chen portrays a smiling bridegroom bringing his bride and her trousseau home in a wheelbarrow as "one of the most charming pictures" in the district.[7] Whatever allowances are necessary for such propagandistic accounts, Chen is correct: collectivization placed a security floor beneath poor peasant families. Thus, as Vivienne Shue suggests, by the mid-1950s, joining an APC "was often probably the best move a peasant head of household could make for himself and his family."[8]

Peasant patriarchs who made this decision did not forfeit much family authority in the process. Within the agricultural collective structure, a surprising number of the basic elements of a patriarchal family economy were preserved. Peasant families retained ownership rights to their houses, private garden plots, small livestock, and tools. This allowed a crucial portion of subsistence production to remain a family function. Moreover, some of the work of collective production was delegated to families who earned work points as a unit "for jobs in which the family remained the most effective or most relevant delineation of workers."[9]

Economic interdependence of family members was reinforced, too, by the accounting methods that collectives employed for computing work points, rations, taxes, and loans. The peasant household was the basic accounting unit, and whatever income a family earned was paid to its patriarchal head. Although collectives employed a wide variety of work-point allocation systems, all of these discriminated effectively against female labor. When individual laborers were awarded a set number of points for a

6. Jack Chen, *New Earth*, p. 122.
7. Ibid., p. 182.
8. Shue, *Peasant China*, p. 278.
9. Ibid., p. 304.

full day's labor, female labor was overwhelmingly undervalued. In 1956, women earned an average of four to six points per day, compared with ten for men. Where piecework point systems applied, women were barred from the higher-paying tasks on the basis of physical limitations, inexperience, or simple prejudice. Or, the jobs assigned to women were automatically underrated.[10] Moreover, the collectives did not release peasant women from, nor remunerate them for, the arduous burdens of domestic labor and child care. In fact, prior to the Great Leap Forward (GLF), even officers of the national Women's Federation spoke against establishing canteens and sewing groups to relieve rural women of housework burdens, as "not feasible and therefore mistaken and harmful."[11] As a result, women were able to contribute considerably fewer days and hours to collective production than their male relatives.

Although collectivization dramatically increased women's contribution to what was recognized as social production, women earned only 25 percent of the work points awarded by all co-operatives in 1956.[12] But the family economy—buttressed by the household-based, work-point accounting system—kept many peasant women from experiencing the undervaluation of their labor as unjust. As one former sent-down youth learned, peasant women felt "that when you add up the income of the husband and the wife you get the same total amount of money that you would get if things were done more equally."[13] Thus a peasant family's hand-to-mouth ratio remained the crucial factor in its prosperity. And, as Elisabeth Croll points out, in a society where

10. For examples and data on the undervaluation of rural women's labor, see Elisabeth Croll, "Women in Rural Development," pp. 28–31; Marina Thorborg, "Chinese Employment Policy in 1949–78," pp. 542–54; and Norma Diamond, "Collectivization, Kinship, and the Status of Women in Rural China," p. 338.

11. Teng Ying-chao, quoted in Delia Davin, *Woman-Work*, p. 128. Thorborg, however, claims canteens and nurseries were set up during a big push in 1956 to mobilize women for agricultural labor. The entire campaign was poorly handled, and women suffered badly from inadequate services and the excessive nature of dual work demands. The results were reflected in increased miscarriages and infant mortality. "Chinese Employment Policy," pp. 555–62.

12. Davin, *Woman-Work*, p. 148, and Croll, "Women in Rural Development," p. 17. Croll reports a six-fold rise in female contribution to social production between 1955 and the "high tide" of 1956.

13. From interview with an emigré conducted by Richard Madsen, 2 August 1975, Hong Kong.

hiring labor is precluded, recruiting women through marriage and controlling their reproduction are the only means available to expand a family's labor supply and to regulate its consumption demands.[14]

Agricultural collectivization was expected to increase rural productivity not only through economies of scale but through more efficient and extensive use of labor power. Female labor was regarded widely as China's great, untapped, rural resource, and the impetus to mine it received support from orthodox Marxist expectations that women would be liberated in the process. One dimension of the vision was realized. Productivity expanded largely through more extensive use of family labor power than had been possible under the independent family farming system. Men and women devoted a greater number of days and hours to field work in the collectives than they had in the precollective period. In many areas this increase was achieved largely by imposing a double work burden on peasant women. However, there was an uneven demand for labor in the countryside. Labor surpluses, particularly in single-cropping areas, often interfered with the drive to mobilize women for agricultural work.[15]

Where the demand for labor allowed the mobilization of women to proceed, the regime exercised concern to avoid undue threats to patriarchal sensibilities. Activists stressed the benefits to family prosperity peasants would derive if they allowed their women to work in the fields. Peasants with traditional beliefs about pollution—that menstruating women would harm the crops—were reassured by measures barring women from agricultural labor during their menses, this on the "scientific" ground of protection of health. Official investigation teams even published reports appreciative of local communities that excluded pregnant, lactating, and menstruating women from agricultural work.[16] Likewise, peasant concern that women who labored in public were subject to immoral temptations was allayed when cadres organized separate female work teams for work conducted away

14. Croll, "Women in Rural Development," p. 46.
15. Davin, *Woman-Work*, p. 137, and Myers, *Chinese Economy*, p. 230.
16. Diamond, "Collectivization, Kinship, and Women," pp. 385–87. Of course, as Thorborg's discussion of the overwork of women makes clear, the party had good reason to be concerned about the health of pregnant women. See fn. 11, above.

from direct familial supervision. Even when the government conducted ideological campaigns to combat peasant resistance to female agricultural labor, it attempted to reassure the public that families had little to fear. National female labor model Teng Yü-lan, for example, was portrayed as a young woman who had learned to work the land to assist her poor parents who had no sons; despite her heroic productive accomplishments, she was an excellent needlewoman.[17] The collectivization of agriculture succeeded in expanding the contribution of female labor and in modifying the specific contents of the traditional sexual division of labor, but it leveled no fundamental challenge to the traditional view that female labor was naturally different from and subordinate to that of men.

On the contrary, the period of collectivization was marked by a conservative profamily ideological context. The Five Goods campaign of the mid-1950s encouraged devotion to, and respect for, the role of "socialist housewife." Chinese housewives were encouraged to improve their attention to domestic thrift, hygiene, and child care, to support their husband's labor, and to participate in neighborhood services. This campaign symbolized the regime's recognition that the economy was as yet not capable of absorbing the full expansion of the female labor force, which its own ideology had affirmed. The government viewed the Five Goods campaign as a compensatory means by which housewives—the scorned step-sisters of classical Marxist doctrine—could "link up closely the household work with the work of constructing a socialist society."[18]

Yet the links between this housewife ideology and socialism were not always easy to perceive. During collectivization, China's major magazine for women was dominated by articles on love, marriage, children, and the domestic domain. It initiated a campaign of dress reform for women under the slogan "Let's Be Pretty," which fostered fashions in feminine self-decoration that had been neither feasible nor encouraged during the austere revolutionary years.[19]

---

17. Davin, *Woman-Work*, p. 135.

18. An official of the Women's Federation, quoted in Elisabeth Croll, *Feminism and Socialism in China*, p. 257. Davin also discusses the Five Goods campaign (*Woman-Work*, p. 152).

19. Davin, *Woman-Work*, pp. 108–109.

The period of collectivization also witnessed ideological efforts to restore filial piety. In 1955 the Ministry of Education promulgated rules of conduct for students. Rule 14 enjoined them: "Respect and love your parents. Love and protect your brothers and sisters. Do what you can to help your parents."[20] According to David Raddock, such efforts were a response to what the regime perceived as excesses of youthful rebellion, which had been triggered by the antipatriarchal aspects of class struggle during the early 1950s. At that time revolutionary youth had been encouraged "to draw a clear line" between themselves and their counter-revolutionary parents. But, from the regime's point of view, cooperation with this policy had gone too far when working-class youth denounced their parents and turned to the state for economic support. Adolescent rebelliousness spread to the schools, where some students attacked their teachers for holding bourgeois attitudes.[21] That the Chinese Communists would initiate an official drive to restore filiality as part of a general effort to legitimate authority should not surprise readers of this book.

Patriarchal-socialism received its most fundamental support from the lineal basis of the collectivization process. As Norma Diamond's pathbreaking analysis first revealed, the Chinese Communists relied on the links of male lineage to socialize the rural sector.[22] Producers' cooperatives were formed around existing hamlets, neighborhoods, and villages, where, due to prerevolutionary lineage structure and patrilocal marriage, most households were densely linked through male relatives. With former gentry landlords and rich peasant leaders eliminated or barred from initial membership, the APCs gave use rights in common over village lands, equipment, livestock, and resources to the egalitarian remnants of the former patrilineages. Moreover, as Shue has shown, collectivization was presented to poor peasants as an avenue for them to seize control over the remaining wealth in the villages.[23] Once again the patriarchal family served as the medium of rural class struggle.

20. Quoted in Jean Chesneaux, *China*, p. 79.
21. David Raddock, "Youth in the PRC." Paper read at annual meeting of the Association for Asian Studies, April 1976, New York City.
22. Diamond, "Collectivization, Kinship, and Women."
23. Shue, *Peasant China*, p. 285.

Relying on "natural" relationships and communities in this way greatly facilitated the cooperative movement, while assuring the preservation of its patriarchal foundation. In single-lineage villages, production teams often came to be referred to by the lineage surname. After 1955, women who divorced their husbands were not allowed to take their hypothetical share of land with them out of the cooperative. Thus, as Diamond suggested, collectivization strengthened networks of cooperating male kinsmen, who soon assumed political leadership roles that complemented their newly won collective economic power.[24] Through collectivization the Chinese Communists achieved the last major successful redistribution of village wealth and security—the further democratization of patriarchy, which transformed it into its socialist stage. The Chinese Communists and the peasants once again had collaborated in a process that strengthened patriarchal family security and promoted socialist development. That process made the two more interdependent than the Maoist regime was ever able to acknowledge.

THE GREAT LEAP FORWARD

Agricultural collectivization had scarcely been completed when Chinese Communist development policy took one of those dramatic turns that have come to be identified as the Maoist approach to socialist development. In 1958 the government of the PRC launched the Great Leap Forward (GLF), a monumental effort to make a quantum jump towards socialism. At its core, GLF strategy aimed to substitute China's massive human resources for capital investment. Repudiating the Soviet-inspired extreme emphasis on industrial development in China's first Five Year Plan, PRC leaders now sought to make the economy "walk on two legs." In the rural sector recently formed APCs were to merge into People's Communes of from 10,000 to 20,000 households, where the productive advantages of collective organization were expected to multiply.

24. Diamond, "Collectivization, Kinship, and Women," p. 380. William L. Parish and Martin F. Whyte make a similar point in *Village and Family in Contemporary China*, pp. 304ff. See also M. J. Meijer, *Marriage Law and Policy in the Chinese People's Republic*, p. 264.

Ensuing events showed little respect for the strategists' script. The GLF violated the unarticulated terms of the new democratic patriarchal pact between China's peasants and the CCP, and it foundered, in part, on this violation. The most radical aspects of the GLF posed a severe threat to the patriarchal family economy. Within a short, tumultuous time span, peasant resistance to these policies joined the catastrophic natural and international circumstances that forced the party to capitulate. The ensuing patriarchal-socialist rural accommodation has not subsequently been jeopardized.

Many GLF policies challenged important aspects of patriarchal authority that the formation of the APCs had just secured. The GLF ventured far beyond acceptable contemporary family values in its challenges to the sexual division of labor. If China's untapped human resources were the key to GLF strategy for accelerating productivity, female labor was its most important target. The government initiated a massive effort to mobilize women to participate fully in agricultural labor. Not that the basic fact of a sexual division of labor was ever in jeopardy. The policy of the GLF was to substitute women for men. Women would do field work to free men to develop rural industry and technology. Even during this radical drive the party tried to preserve gender distinctions at work. Women workers were granted certain privileges that were believed to match their physiological needs, such as exclusion from wet field work during the four periods of menstruation, pregnancy, postpartum, and lactation.[25]

This time, however, such patriarchal concessions were to prove insufficient. Women were propelled too suddenly and on a stupendous scale into labor traditionally considered unfitting. Phyllis Andors claims the government's goal was to involve 300 million women in production. There are estimates that one-third of this number was added to the rural labor force in the 1958–1960 period. In 1958 women made up 50 percent of the agricultural labor force, and considerably more than this in areas where men were heavily involved in industrial work. The National Conference

---

25. Phyllis Andors, "Social Revolution and Women's Emancipation," p. 34; Thorborg, "Chinese Employment Policy," pp. 568–80; and Croll, *Feminism and Socialism*, p. 263.

on Women and Work estimated that 90 percent of rural women participated in agricultural work during the GLF.[26]

This massive female influx in the collective labor sector meant that many more women were entitled to work points. Even more striking, GLF dependence on female labor was accompanied by policies that raised women's daily work-point earnings over those of the pre-Leap period. While women's average daily work points had been between four and six (compared with ten for men) in 1956, by 1960 women earned an average of seven to eight points (while those of men had not changed). And the GLF went so far as to promote direct payment of income to individual workers.[27] This placed peasant patriarchs in a contradictory situation. On the one hand, the entire family benefited from added income earned by women. But the sharp rise in work-point earnings also cheapened the basic value of the work point, because the total work points earned rose faster than the distributable income of the collectives. The new democratic patriarchs were soon to make clear that they preferred to limit women's participation in the collective sphere.

Hostility to the GLF was provoked most seriously by policies with the most radical antipatriarchal implications—efforts to eliminate family production and to socialize domestic work. During the GLF, private family plots were abolished and rural free markets closed down. Family grave mounds were leveled in the interest of productivity. Producers were expected to shift to a higher level of collective accounting—the production brigade, or even the People's Commune. In some communes there were even efforts to have families turn their entire income and stock of tools over to the collective.[28] Moreover, this effort to leap over scarcity to socialism included a direct reversal of the earlier stance of the Women's Federation against the socialization of housework. Now there was rapid, chaotic establishment of collective dining-halls, nurseries, kindergartens, sewing centers, food-processing

---

26. This paragraph is based on Croll, *Feminism and Socialism*, pp. 263, 279; Andors, "Social Revolution," p. 36; and Thorborg, "Chinese Employment Policy," p. 582. Here Thorborg estimates that 80-95% of women participated in agricultural production in 1958–1959, which lends credibility to the government's claim.

27. Croll, "Women in Rural Development," p. 29.

28. Chesneaux, *China*, pp. 102–103.

centers, and old-age homes—all with the explicit goal of removing the contradiction between household and social production. There were estimates that 4,980,000 nurseries and kindergartens and more then 3,600,000 dining-halls were set up in rural areas by 1959.[29] Thus patterns of family consumption were threatened, and with them a sphere of domestic autonomy.

The central objective of these measures was to enhance rural productivity. Collective dining-halls, for example, were meant not only to achieve economies of scale but also to contribute to the establishment of time and work discipline, by regularizing meal hours and work time.[30] Nevertheless, such measures were promoted with an antipatriarchal ideological campaign. The GLF witnessed the brief, rather uncoordinated revival of a politicization of questions of gender and generation. Leveling of graves took place, for example, in the context of an attack on superstition.[31] Measures to abolish family production and to limit family consumption functions were introduced with explicit antipatriarchal justifications. The press ran articles explaining that family production was the basis of feudal patriarchal authority, and it invoked as support for this view Lenin's pronouncement that "paternalism is a product of a small-producer economy."[32] The campaign renewed public commitment to the liberation of women through their participation in social production, and it cited Engels as its authority: "Participation in social labor by all women is a prerequisite to their emancipation. To attain that aim, it will be necessary to eliminate the family as an economic unit of the society."[33] The government also sponsored direct ideological challenges to the conventional sexual division of labor. There were campaigns to organize "bumper-crop maidens" and "women red-flag holders" to spearhead female use of advanced farming methods. And the GLF hosted the return of comparatively utopian family reform ideals—isolated nuclear family life was to disappear while commitment to community was to supplant family com-

---

29. Croll, *Feminism and Socialism*, p. 268.
30. Davin, *Woman-Work*, p. 128.
31. Chesneaux, *China*, p. 103.
32. Croll, *Feminism and Socialism*, p. 275.
33. Ibid., p. 276.

mitments.[34] As a result, the period of the GLF led many Western observers to believe what they long had suspected—Chinese communism was destined to abolish the family.

There was little cause for such alarm. As Phyllis Andors has argued, the antipatriarchal aspects of GLF policies were inadequately developed or planned for by the regime, which failed to appreciate the extent of the social programs, rural infrastructure, and political transformation that would have been necessary to accomplish GLF goals.[35] The instrumental attempt of the Maoists to enlist feminist ideals to serve plans for further socializing and expanding productivity was destined, therefore, to fail. As we have seen, analytical failure long preceded the GLF. Chinese Communist policy makers never had understood the significance of the new democratic patriarchy. Peasants, however, were less confused. They responded with active and successful resistance to the GLF, and, most of all, to its feminist policies.

Peasant men resisted government efforts to achieve the mass entry of women into agricultural production and to encourage equal pay systems. They particularly resented policies that led women to neglect their traditional domestic duties. Jean Chesneaux claims that many rural women, on the other hand, greeted the introduction of collective dining-halls with the extravagant symbolic gesture of hoisting their pots out of the windows.[36] However, there were also many women who opposed GLF policies. The majority were women over forty, the most victimized generation of women in modern Chinese history. Repeatedly they drew the short straw in the oppression-liberation cycle. Now, just when most had achieved the status of mother-in-law and grandmother—which in presocialist China would have guaranteed them respite and increased domestic authority—they were expected to assume added domestic burdens and diminished familial authority to liberate their daughters and daughters-in-law for collective labor. Opposition to public dining-halls and nurseries was widespread among the peasantry, many of whom genuinely

34. Janet Salaff, "Youth, Family and Political Control in Communist China," p. 211, and Andors, "Social Revolution," p. 38.

35. Andors, "Social Revolution."

36. Chesneaux, *China*, pp. 103–104.

feared their "small families" would disappear in communes, which were depicted by the regime as "big families."[37]

The GLF was an unmitigated failure. To the extreme misfortune of its advocates, its implementation coincided with catastrophic climatic and diplomatic events—severe droughts and floods coupled with the withdrawal of Soviet aid. Nonetheless, it is generally agreed that GLF policies and peasant resistance to them deserve much of the credit for the economic disaster that ensued. Terrible harvests in the years 1959–1961 brought the PRC the first, and only, threat of a widespread famine in its history.[38] The state was forced to capitulate. Communes were subdivided into units one-half to one-third smaller than they had been during the GLF. Collective-management and income-sharing units were also decentralized, at first back to the level of the brigade, and ultimately, in 1962, to the level of the production team. The unpopular canteens, nurseries, and public old-age homes were abandoned; private family plots and a free market sector were restored. Most of these accommodations were codified in the "Sixty Articles"—the "Working Regulations for People's Communes"—which are still in force. Once again, peasant profit norms were guaranteed on a familial rather than individual basis.[39] This allowed many of the women who had been mobilized during the GLF to return to the homes China's peasant patriarchs had defended successfully against the breach in their alliance with the CCP.

One can interpret the GLF experience, as Phyllis Andors has done, as evidence that the fate of socialism and the liberation of women were far more intertwined in China than the regime appreciated.[40] Or one can focus, as I do here, on the other side of the coin: China's Communist regime was equally unaware that Chinese socialism had its roots in a patriarchal revolution. The point at which Chinese patriarchy became a constraint instead of an aid to further collectivization of the rural sector was the GLF.

37. Croll, *Feminism and Socialism*, p. 278. See also Andors, "Social Revolution," p. 38, and Thorborg, "Chinese Employment Policy," p. 547.

38. Myers, *Chinese Economy*, pp. 216, 234.

39. Parish and Whyte, *Village and Family*, p. 34, and Chesneaux, *China*, p. 106. For a discussion of the old-age homes see Deborah Davis-Friedmann, *Long Life*, p. 265.

40. Andors, "Social Revolution."

PATRIARCHAL-SOCIALISM IN
THE RURAL PEOPLE'S REPUBLIC OF CHINA

During the 1960s the Communist regime and the peasantry established a modus operandi regarding the rural familial order. Although the ensuing years brought dramatic shifts in national political direction, periodic ideological campaigns for family reform and gradual economic development, the basic outlines of the accommodation survived until after the death of Mao Tse-tung. William L. Parish and Martin King Whyte, in *Village and Family in Contemporary China*, describe and analyze, in terms not readily surpassed, the principles and practices of this family system. They explain the pattern of continuity and change in the rural family as an indirect effect of the structural changes in economic and political organization introduced by the Chinese Communists. The rich data and cogent structural interpretations Parish and Whyte present can be incorporated into an historical analysis of Chinese patriarchy that assigns it a more dynamic role. The rural Chinese family system they describe can best be characterized as patriarchal-socialism, which represents the socialization of most, but not all, productive activities in the context of sustained, but reformed, patriarchal authority over women, marriage, and the domestic economy.

Although the rural economy had been collectivized in the 1950s, the peasantry managed to secure important elements of the patriarchal family economy within the collective order—elements that survive, and have even been strengthened in post-Mao China. Instead of being reduced to a mere income-sharing unit, the peasant family retained significant productive activities. The restoration of small private garden plots and rural free markets in the early 1960s enabled families to generate from 10 to 25 percent of their income from private labor—raising pigs, growing crops, and engaging in small handicraft production.[41] Thus, many peasant families still have the opportunity to train and supervise the labor of their members. This allows household heads to pass on skills to the young and to oversee the work habits and public behavior of subordinates. Even when family labor is integrated

---

41. Parish and Whyte, *Village and Family*, p. 119.

into the work teams, the supervision of new laborers rests generally in patrilineal hands—an uncle, brother-in-law, or older cousin.[42]

Preservation of patriarchal authority within the collective order rests on even stronger structural supports. The continuation of a patrilocal marriage system in which women marry outside their natal villages is one of the most important of these. It was never seriously challenged by the government. Rural China has experienced major changes in its traditional system of arranged marriages, as we have seen. Parents did not recapture the absolute authority they once exercised over the marital destinies of their young. The family revolution brought the younger generation an important voice in the selection of mates. The typical pattern of mate selection in the rural PRC involves a joint venture and compromise between the generations. In the majority of instances, parents, at times with the assistance of a professional matchmaker, negotiate a match for their children, who then have the opportunity to veto a choice they find unacceptable. In the other typical pattern, the young make use of their new, but limited, opportunities to meet members of the opposite sex in order to find fiancés. Respective parents then have an opportunity to approve or refuse the match. But "free marriage" almost never means that rural youth have independent control over their marital destinies, and courtship is still an unusual and constrained event.[43] Rural marriage remains a crucial family decision because so much of a family's fortune depends upon the timing and the criteria for selecting new members.

The essence of marriage in rural China continues to be an exchange of rights in women between two families. What has changed since 1949 is the value of those rights; the value has increased. The groom's family is concerned, above all, with the character, health, and temperament of a prospective bride. Is she a good worker? Will she fit into the family? The bride's family

42. Davis-Friedmann, *Long Life*, p. 211.
43. For detailed discussion of mate selection in rural areas, see Elisabeth Croll, *The Politics of Marriage in Contemporary China*; Salaff, "Youth, Family and Political Control"; and Parish and Whyte, *Village and Family*. For a vivid illustration of one rural betrothal and wedding, see "Little Brother's Wedding," in Michael B. Frolic, *Mao's People*, pp. 87–99.

gives greater attention to economic considerations.[44] They will be losing a laborer and wish both to ensure their daughter's welfare and to receive reasonable compensation. The economics of the marital transaction involve both bride-price and dowry, with considerable haggling among the negotiators. Frequently the bride's family uses the bride-price to help a son to marry.[45]

Families retain powerful leverage over the marital options of their children through their control of rural housing. Housing, the last important patrimony in rural China, is inherited through the male line. Housing sites are generally available through the collective, but the cost of new housing is high.[46] Sons wishing to marry, therefore, are dependent upon parental willingness to add a room to accommodate the new bride or to shoulder the cost of new construction.

As feminist sinologists have demonstrated, China's patrilocal marriage and patrilineal inheritance system have great significance in reproducing female subordination.[47] They encourage the traditional preference for sons who continue to provide the basic form of social security for aging rural parents. Ties between rural parents and their adult sons are consistently stronger than ties of rural parents with adult daughters. The preference for, and advantage of, male offspring translates, predictably enough, into significant advantages for sons over daughters. Families discrim-

---

44. Parish and Whyte, *Village and Family*, p. 178; and Salaff, "Youth, Family and Political Control," pp. 152–55.

45. Parish and Whyte claim there may even be an increase in bride-price under communism due to the increased value of female labor (*Village and Family*, p. 187). The story of "Little Brother's Wedding," in Frolic, *Mao's People*, lends support to this view. However, other sources provide contradictory evidence. Jack Potter's data from a village in Kwangtung suggest that the local bride-price is inadequate to cover the cost of the dowry ("Change and Continuity in the Chinese Family," public lecture, 23 October 1980, University of California, Berkeley). Croll suggests both bride-price and dowry are standard, with no clear predominance of one over the other (*Politics of Marriage*, pp. 113–16).

46. Parish and Whyte, *Village and Family*, p. 184. In the Kwangtung brigade Jack Potter studied, a new house cost approximately 4,000 *yuan* ("Change and Continuity"). Davis-Friedmann estimates that throughout the 1970s a new house cost 1,000-3,000 *yuan*, which was 2-6 times the average annual family income (*Long Life*, p. 150).

47. See, for example, Diamond, "Collectivization, Kinship, and Women," and Croll, *Politics of Marriage*. Parish and Whyte elaborate many of the intervening mechanisms in *Village and Family*.

inate against daughters where education is concerned. Daughters are less likely than sons to complete even a primary education, because they are called upon by their families to care for younger children or to work in the fields to boost the family income. Production teams continue this discrimination when selecting local candidates for specialized vocational training. Traditional prejudices receive rational support; peasants recognize that the skills of local daughters will be lost to the sponsoring community when the daughters marry.[48]

Service in village offices tends to run in families, and, predictably, brothers rather than sisters inherit such public responsibilities. Although the regime has advocated including women in political leadership positions, resistance is strong in rural areas. There are many sources of this opposition, but patrilocal marriage exacerbates the problem by severing women from the strong local ties crucial to community support. Similarly, patrilocal marriage thwarts the regime's intention to favor women in divorce settlements. Most divorced women move back to their native villages. Despite legal guarantees to protect the women's rights, their former in-laws have a decided upper hand in child-custody and property settlements. Generally the man's family gains custody of children or, when children are separated, only those the man's family agrees to relinquish (daughters more often than sons) may accompany the woman. Not only does the groom's family retain most of the couple's worldly goods, but the woman's family is expected to return the bride-price it received when the match was secured.[49]

If patrilocal marriage is the first major structural support for patriarchal authority in rural China, an entrenched sexual division of labor within and outside the family economy is the second. Although the Communist regime has succeeded in integrating women into rural production, it never leveled a challenge to a sexual division of labor. On the contrary, PRC policy makers follow the prejudice of the majority of the world, which regards

---

48. This paragraph is based on Davis-Friedmann, *Long Life*, p. 183; Salaff, "Youth, Family and Political Control," pp. 240–41; Parish and Whyte, *Village and Family*, p. 228; and Diamond, "Collectivization, Kinship, and Women."

49. This paragraph is based on Parish and Whyte, *Village and Family*, pp. 112, 195; Salaff, "Youth, Family and Political Control," p. 230; Martin King Whyte, "Revolutionary Social Change and Patrilocal Residence in China," p. 223; and Diamond, "Collectivization, Kinship, and Women."

such a division of labor as natural. As one policy statement issued in 1972 explicated:

> Physically some people are stronger while others are weak; some heavy manual farm jobs fit the stronger sex better. This is a division of labor based on physiological features of both sexes, and is appropriate. We can't impose the same framework on female and male commune members alike in disregard of the former's physiological features and physical power. In some kinds of work, women are less capable than men, but in others, they are better.[50]

Consequently, men generally are assigned work considered heavier, such as plowing, tractor driving, and irrigation work, while women weed, transplant, and harvest crops. However, the arbitrariness of such "natural" divisions results in regional variations in sex-assigned tasks.

Moreover, an important shift in the contents of the sexual division of labor has been developing over the past two decades. In many areas, men initially resisted female participation in agricultural labor. Increasingly, however, industry and agriculture are becoming the basic poles of the sexual division of labor, and women are being assigned primary responsibility for farming. This tendency was an official development strategy in the late 1950s. A news release stated:

> Women should shoulder agricultural production. Men's labor power is needed to open mines, expand machine-building industry, power plants, cement plants. These all call for new labor inputs. Generally speaking, these departments of industry employ mainly men laborers and provide only a few types of work that can be undertaken by women workers. Thus, up to a certain stage in development of socialist construction, agricultural production will have to be undertaken mainly by women. Of course with the process of agricultural production mechanized and electrified agricultural production will follow the pattern of industrial production. By that time women can completely shoulder the responsibility.[51]

The failure of the GLF postponed this strategy because retrenchment led to a decline in female labor force participation in the 1960s and early 1970s. However, the Cultural Revolution reaffirmed this strategy, urging peasants to emulate Ta-ch'ing, where

---

50. Quoted in Croll, "Women in Rural Development," p. 25.
51. Quoted in ibid., pp. 26–27.

such a division of labor was established.[52] Contemporary field studies indicate that, at least in Kwangtung, women now have become the mainstay of agricultural production.[53]

Women also continue to bear primary responsibility for most domestic labor and child care; even official efforts to promote male participation in housework are deeply equivocal:

> Domestic work should be shared by men and women. But some household chores, such as looking after children, sewing, and others, should generally be done by women. . . . After a certain phase of farm work is completed during very busy seasons or on rainy days or in winter, women should be given some time off to attend to some essential household chores.[54]

The economic consequences of the sexual division of labor are also familiar. Women receive considerably less income for their labor than do men. Even when women and men perform the same labor, they rarely receive equal pay. The inequity is justified by Chinese peasants on the grounds of differential physical strength and skill. Female tasks are routinely assigned lower rates of pay. Although the government has instituted periodic campaigns to combat such discriminatory pay systems, rural resistance to equal pay for women has repeatedly triumphed. Men argue successfully that their authority over the household legitimates disproportionate pay.[55] Rural men also monopolize available state jobs, which offer enormous advantages in pay and benefits over those in the collective sector.

Male authority in the rural economy is underscored by supervisory and payment procedures. Most production teams are headed by men.[56] The household accounting system records family work points against rations and loans. When the time comes to distribute the work team's earnings, whatever payment a family is due still is paid to the household head.[57]

---

52. Thorborg, "Chinese Employment Policy," p. 580.
53. This was true of the rural areas studied by Potter, "Change and Continuity," and Croll, *Politics of Marriage.*
54. Quoted in Croll, "Women in Rural Development," p. 34.
55. Ibid., p. 30.
56. Parish and Whyte, *Village and Family,* p. 101.
57. Croll claims that women receive individual remuneration for their work ("Women in Rural Development," p. 28). Most of the other sources, however, indicate otherwise. See, for example, Parish and Whyte, *Village and Family;* Thorborg, "Chinese Employment Policy"; and Potter, "Change and Continuity."

It is clear that peasants have successfully preserved important aspects of a patriarchal family economy in socialist China. The Communist regime has either tacitly supported or quietly accommodated its development policies to these patriarchal structures. In addition, PRC policies governing migration, employment, and social welfare indirectly have led peasants to realize several prerevolutionary patriarchal ideals. Tight restrictions on immigration to and employment in urban areas result in greater intergenerational patrilineal stability among village families than was achieved ever before. Parish and Whyte estimate, for example, that 90 percent of young rural men now remain in their native villages. Elisabeth Croll's respondents spontaneously contrasted current kin stability with the dispersal of kin caused by prerevolutionary crisis conditions. Three-generational family ties have been extended as well by the additional life expectancy of fifteen to twenty years produced by the regime's impressive achievements in reducing infant and adult mortality. Most important is the estimate that all citizens under the age of forty can reasonably expect to marry and to raise at least one child to maturity.[58]

The patrilineal stem family also has received reinforcement from the prevailing logic of a family economy and the regime's social welfare policies. When a man's family takes in a new bride, it adds a valuable source of income to the family budget. The new bride "releases" one of the family's older women from collective labor to provide child care and domestic labor, and to contribute to the private sector, a net gain to the household economy.[59] Furthermore, both the marriage law and social practice make the older generation dependent upon their patrilineal ties for care in old age. Indeed, until the late 1970s, the rural elderly could qualify for public assistance only if they lacked a son. Deborah Davis-Friedmann finds that this social norm has been instilled in the younger generation, which regards supporting aged parents as part of a life debt owed for care received as children.[60]

The stability of rural patriarchy in the PRC should not be understood as a mere survival of traditional familial ideals. Pa-

---

58. Parish and Whyte, *Village and Family*, p. 54; Croll, *Politics of Marriage*, p. 176; and Davis-Friedmann, *Long Life*, p. 71, n. 25; p. 262.

59. Croll, *Politics of Marriage*, p. 155.

60. Davis-Friedmann, *Long Life*, pp. 50, 173.

triarchal-socialism represents, instead, the last democratization of peasant patriarchy that is likely to occur within the basic framework of China's socialist order. Socialist criteria and processes underlie both the redistribution and reform of patriarchal privilege this family system entails.

First, the land revolution eliminated the basis for elite patriarchy and extended basic patriarchal rights to the masses. Then the collectivization of land and productive resources undermined the system of partible inheritance. Now the youngest son of a poor peasant could expect to remain in his village and find a wife. In fact, China's socialist order granted former "poor peasant" men marital advantages over their once-wealthier neighbors. Throughout the Maoist era the class labels assigned during land reform carried significant political implications, and these labels were inherited patrilineally. Not only were families of the former exploiting classes and "bad elements" stripped of most political rights but they also became the most vulnerable targets of the periodic ideological campaigns the government waged in the name of class struggle. This made it difficult for families with bad class labels to find wives for their sons. A girl's family was properly wary of consigning its daughter to an unstable future. Moreover the social status of the girl's family might be jeopardized by kinship ties to an "undesirable" family. "Poor peasant," on the other hand, became one of the more desirable patrilineal legacies a rural man could inherit. "Poor peasant" men enjoyed educational and material advantages that enabled their families to rise in the economic order. Moreover, their high political status made it easier and cheaper for their families to find wives for all of their sons. Now they could marry somewhat earlier than other men. The effect of patrilineal class status on female marital prospects was paradoxical. It combined with patrilocal marriage to make it possible for women from undesirable class backgrounds to escape their disreputable fate. Thus, despite an overall reduction in the incidence of hypergamous marriage in China, elements remained. Marriage became easier for the daughters than for the sons of stigmatized families.[61]

---

61. This paragraph is based on Parish and Whyte, *Village and Family*, pp. 99, 166, 179; Croll, *Politics of Marriage*, p. 97; and Salaff, "Youth, Family and Political Control," p. 282. "Little Brother's Wedding," in Frolic, *Mao's People*, shows how

Patriarchal-socialism also means that patriarchal power has been partially collectivized. Many decisions that once were made by families have become the prerogative of production teams and brigades: the choice of crops, the delegation of tasks, the allocation of resources for local welfare needs, and so forth. At the village and brigade level, power became a male responsibility that was shared more democratically than in traditional rural society. The old class structure was inverted—with the sons of former landlords and rich peasants losing ground in educational and political status to the politically favored sons. Yet the outcome was not a simple economic reversal between the two groups. Village leadership no longer bestowed the economic advantages of the past. In fact, the costs of village authority are high. Local leadership responsibilities take time away from more lucrative efforts in the family's private economy, and they subject incumbents to criticism and crossfire from above and below. Thus, Parish and Whyte find no support in their data for the view that traditional lineage politics continue as usual, or for the claim that a "new class" has emerged that controls village affairs.[62]

The ways in which socialism has reformed patriarchal privilege are equally significant. China's rural young gained considerable status and authority at the expense of their elders. The decline of patriarchy's cultural hegemony is reflected as well in the substantial rise of female status within and beyond the family. We have observed that the gains of youth are reflected in marital reforms. The prevailing rural compromise between the generations on marriage arrangements represents a noteworthy limitation of parental authority. Moreover, a minority of village youth now enjoys the opportunity to engage in courtship and to select their own spouses.[63]

---

the matchmaking parents of a "lower-middle peasant" prospective bride and a "middle peasant" groom took differences of political status into account during the fiscal negotiations of the matchmaking process.

62. Parish and Whyte, *Village and Family*, pp. 106–14. See "A Foot of Mud and a Pile of Shit," in Frolic, *Mao's People*, for an explanation by one work-team head of why he wished to step down after ten years of leadership.

63. Salaff, "Youth, Family and Political Control," and Croll, *Politics of Marriage*. Even "Little Brother's Wedding," which stresses the survival of traditional marital concerns and practices, includes reference to a peasant girl who refused to marry Little Brother for the heretical reason of her love for another (Frolic, *Mao's People*).

The substantial rise in the status of youth also undergirds the pattern of earlier household divisions that came to be practiced in China's countryside. Full joint-family households are exceedingly rare. The prevalent stem family system includes only one married son. In the new typical household life cycle, a family would marry out a daughter and bring in a wife for its eldest son. The new couple would move into a separate residence after the birth of two or three children or when the second son takes a bride.[64] Division of the household is less likely if there is only one son. Even then, the transfer of family headship from father to son occurs earlier than it did in the past. Sons in their thirties are able to challenge their fathers for family leadership. Likewise, public authority rests on younger shoulders than before. Most production-team leaders and brigade leaders are men in their early forties.[65] These are the men who have assumed the fullest rights and responsibilities of patriarchal-socialism at the village level.

Improvements in female family status, while profound, are as much generational as they are an indication of flagging male privilege. Young women have gained influence and respect largely at the expense of older women. This is reflected, first of all, in the later age of marriage. The legal marriage age was twenty years for men and eighteen for women, but the regime succeeded in establishing later norms in many areas—most villagers are in their early twenties when they marry. Because young women contribute so much to the family economy, their natal families are less eager than in the past to part with daughters. The delay expands a daughter's opportunity to influence the selection of her mate. Moreover, brides receive far better treatment than they once did in the patrilineal home. There has been a genuine decline in deferential behavior on their part. Far from serving new mothers-in-law, brides are apt to take their places in the collective sector. When the mother-in-law "retires" to the private

---

64. Potter, "Change and Continuity," and Croll, *Politics of Marriage*, p. 146.
65. Parish and Whyte, *Village and Family*, pp. 101, 135, and Davis-Friedmann, *Long Life*, p. 195. Richard Madsen suggests, however, that the advantage of youth may prove to be specific to the generation of men that came of age in the 1950s, many of whom have managed to retain the power they achieved after liberation (personal communication).

family, she performs the major share of domestic labor and provides child care for her daughter-in-law.[66]

Not all of a new bride's improved status has been bought at her mother-in-law's expense. Researchers find a general decline in the overt deferential behavior wives bestow on their husbands. Although the man is the clear head of the family, and a wife is expected to honor her husband's will, his authority over her is less absolute than in the past. Wife beating survives, but it seems to have diminished and to receive less community support. Terms of address between spouses have begun to reflect these reforms. Although traditional formal terms of address survive, many young couples supplement these with "my beloved."[67]

Female status has also improved in the public arena. Even in rural areas, there is some acceptance of female leadership. Mostly this is a response to governmental pressure; rural female cadres are typically consigned to female posts in the women's associations or as the perfunctory team "vice-head." But there are occasional exceptions.[68] And while new public collectivities, such as women's associations, are quite restricted in local power, access to them indirectly enhances a woman's leverage in the patrilineal community.

THE NEW PUBLIC ORDER

The democratization and socialization of patriarchal family life in rural China is embedded in a new public order. The term "patriarchal-socialism" suggests as well the authority structure of China's new political culture. Building on the military fraternity of the People's Liberation Army (PLA) during the revolutionary decades, the PRC made a new "public patriarchy," in which Communist party leaders assume the paternal role, integral to its civic society. The term "public patriarchy" is used here in a metaphorical sense to refer to an important aspect of authority under patriarchal-socialism rather than to designate yet a new sex-gender system. "Public patriarchy" introduces elements of

---

66. Parish and Whyte, *Village and Family*, p. 175, and Croll, *Politics of Marriage*, chap. 4.

67. Parish and Whyte, *Village and Family*, pp. 214–15.

68. Ibid., pp. 101, 239.

a state-centered sex-gender system into the patriarchal-socialist accommodation. These elements are far more pronounced and effective in urban China, but they are also part of the context in which revitalized rural patriarchal power is exercised and limited. There are two key dimensions to this "public patriarchy": the formal subordination of mass organizations to the CCP and state supervision over personal life.

Mass organizations, like the Women's Federation and the trade unions, which were created by the party partly to enhance the power of formerly subordinate social groups, operate in formal subordination to the CCP and exist only at its pleasure. Thus, in 1967 the Women's Federation was suspended entirely and its national magazine was shut down, when the class struggle priorities of the Cultural Revolution held sway over all other social antagonisms.[69] The federation was not reestablished at the local level until the early 1970s—and at the national level in 1978. The purpose of mass organizations, when they are called upon to function, is to mobilize their constituents to implement current governmental policies. They also serve an information transmission function, informing the "public patriarchs" of mass concerns and attitudes. However, they have no capacity to initiate policy or to mobilize their constituencies to struggle autonomously for group-defined interests.

At the local level, therefore, local cadres supervise the activities of the women's associations, and here the historical links between China's military fraternity and the new "public patriarchy" are discernible. During the 1950s and 1960s, the PLA was a major cadre recruitment source for rural government posts. The army provided men with literacy courses, political training, and an enhanced opportunity to join the CCP, all of which made returned soldiers desirable cadres from the regime's point of view. For example, in a rural county studied in the 1970s by Victor Nee, the local militia had been the major retirement ground for returned PLA soldiers. During the Cultural Revolution, the district PLA garrison placed militia commanders in control of the new revolutionary committees. According to Nee, strong camaraderie based upon a common history in the army and the militia forged

---

69. The trade unions, and even the Communist Youth League, were also suspended at that time.

these officials, who also had deep roots in the villages, into "a cohesive elite group of local men."[70] In such instances, local kin-based patriarchal power has been reinforced by new forms of exclusively male public authority.

Within the CCP (like most of the world's political institutions, a male-dominated body),[71] a patriarchal authority structure is deeply entrenched, and not only in the sense that strict discipline is imposed by a hierarchical command chain. The party also assumes many patriarchal supervisory roles over the personal lives of its members. It requires cadres to lead lives it considers to be politically and morally exemplary. Cadres are expected to practice far more of the government's official family policies than ordinary citizens. Even in the countryside, generally they are under strong pressure to delay their marriages until their late twenties, to refrain from traditional betrothal and dowry exchanges, to marry by simple public ceremony, to restrict their fertility, to set examples of good intrafamilial relationships, and to cremate their dead without ostentation.[72]

Furthermore, the party has a history of more direct intervention in the marital arrangements of its members. Each couple needs the approval of the CCP secretary of its work or school unit in order to register the marriage. This is generally a formality for all but party and army members. Youth League and party men in one area, for example, were required to receive their organization's approval before they could court or betroth a woman. They also were prohibited from marrying outside party or league ranks. Many local restrictions such as these, which were widespread during the 1950s, were later criticized as being elitist.

70. Victor Nee, "Post-Mao Changes in a South China Production Brigade," p. 39.

71. No recent figure on the national percentage of female party members is available. However, women were 19% of the 1,510 delegates to the 11th Party Congress in 1977 and 11.4% of the members of the central committee elected there. Only one of the twenty-eight politburo members was a woman, and she was an alternate. Martin King Whyte, "Sexual Inequality Under Socialism," p. 21; I am grateful to the author for permission to cite data from this unpublished paper.

72. See, for example, Salaff, "Youth, Family and Political Control"; Davis-Friedmann, *Long Life;* and Parish and Whyte, *Village and Family.* It is also true, however, that rural cadres prove adept at ignoring these pressures. For an example of cadre lip service to restrictions on bride-price and ceremonies, see "Little Brother's Wedding," in Frolic, *Mao's People.*

However, throughout the Maoist era, the party exercised control over the moral and marital standards of its own. Indeed, after the Cultural Revolution, party control over private life increased. The party fostered political criteria for mate selection—cadres were to seek mates with high political consciousness.

Several foreign visitors to China claim that members of the party and army "would lose their posts if they married anyone whose curriculum vitae didn't come up to their superiors' expectations."[73] Statements by party officials suggest that an unmarried, pregnant cadre might be encouraged to have an abortion rather than to proceed with a marriage deemed politically undesirable:

> If, in the case of an unmarried mother, marriage offers no way out, or because it is a bad match politically or otherwise, no one will insist upon the birth; the abortion is performed.[74]

Occasionally, to facilitate politically desirable marriages among its members, the party has assumed the patriarchal matchmaking function. Likewise it has introduced political considerations into many divorce proceedings. Divorce, in fact, is an area of personal life in which the state requires public bodies to intervene, generally in an effort to dissuade unhappy couples or individuals. However, divorces have been granted readily, and have been encouraged, when the party considered one spouse guilty of "political errors."[75]

The "public patriarchs" of the CCP also strictly enforce their view of socialist sexual morality. Always puritanical, the party's repressive stance toward sexuality intensified during the Cultural Revolution, when sexual desire itself seemed to be identified as antisocialist. Although the post-Mao regime has eased official mores somewhat, it maintains the CCP standard that heterosexual intercourse between husband and wife is the only legitimate form of sexual activity, and that in moderation. An official 1980

---

73. Claudie Broyelle et al., *China, A Second Look*, p. 32.

74. Vice-director of Women's and Children's Health Administration of Peking, quoted in Edgar Snow, *The Long Revolution*, p. 47.

75. The information in this paragraph is drawn from: Croll, *Politics of Marriage*, pp. 97–98; Salaff, "Youth, Family and Political Control," pp. 280–81; Broyelle et al., *A Second Look*, pp. 32ff.; Fox Butterfield, "Love and Sex in China"; Michael Weisskopf, "China Discovering Sex," *San Francisco Chronicle*, 13 November 1980; and "Easier Divorces in China Soon," *San Francisco Chronicle*, 17 October 1980.

sex manual, which updates a 1957 manual that had been suppressed since the Cultural Revolution, codifies contemporary CCP sexual mores. It condemns masturbation (meaning, in Chinese, "hand lewdness") as a practice that causes impotence and nervous disorder and interferes with work and study, the individual's "responsibility for country and the socialist system." The manual recommends nighttime as the best time for intercourse of married couples because it enables them to rest "to repair strength" for the next day's work; it suggests a frequency of sex once every one or two weeks as normal practice.[76] Moreover, the party actively discourages premarital sex and adultery. Throughout the Maoist era, contraceptives were not readily available to the unmarried, despite the fact that cadres were under pressure to delay their marriages until their late twenties. The party has imposed sanctions for moral "transgressions" by issuing marks on cadre dossiers, obstructing marriage certifications, and subjecting identified sinners to public criticism.[77] Women, whose transgressions are more easily identified, are the most vulnerable victims of such discipline.

Patriarchal-socialist political culture is far less developed at the village level, where, as we have seen, the CCP made use of, or accommodated itself to, many elements of traditional culture. However, ordinary rural Chinese are not entirely free from socialist supervision of their personal lives. On a basic level, the regime relies on marriage registration as a screening device to enforce minimal requirements of its family policy, such as a minimum age at marriage and a modicum of individual consent to the match. During the early 1950s, however, peasants, like cadres, were discouraged actively from intermarrying with "bad" classes and elements in order to prevent disruption of the class struggle.[78] This policy was later abandoned, but, as we have observed, political criteria for mate selection took hold as a basic element in the rural marital system. Political criteria affect other family relationships as well. Sons are under less pressure to obey or to support politically stigmatized parents. There is evidence that

76. Weisskopf, "China Discovering Sex." See also Butterfield, "Love and Sex," p. 46.
77. Salaff, "Youth, Family and Political Control," pp. 280–81; Broyelle et al., *A Second Look*, pp. 34–36; and Butterfield, "Love and Sex," p. 15.
78. Croll, *Politics of Marriage*, pp. 88–89.

many take advantage of this opportunity to remove themselves from such relationships. By the same token, rural sons seem to be less likely to support mothers who remarry as widows, or fathers who marry widows.[79] This is evidence, of course, that widow remarriage continues to arouse disrespect in China's villages, but it also reveals the unique blend of patriarchy and socialism that peasants have woven into village culture.

Formal party intervention in intrafamilial village relationships is minimal. Still, there is now cautious public interference with extremes of child abuse.[80] This represents a significant departure from traditional cultural prerogatives and might be regarded as one of the more benevolent aspects of the party's role as "public patriarch." Likewise, the regime has tolerated a good portion of traditional marital ceremonies and rituals among the peasantry, although it has played a more interventionist role in limiting traditional funerals and burial practices. Whereas during the new democratic phase of the revolution the Communists guaranteed a proper funeral to the destitute, by 1956 they reneged on this commitment and began to cremate wards of the state. After a brief retreat from this unpopular stance following the GLF, the party continued (in a more conciliatory vein) its efforts to simplify funerals and burials under the Socialist Education Movement and the Cultural Revolution. By the 1970s, some of the reforms had taken effect. While cremation remains unusual in rural areas, where respect for ancestors is still a spiritual value, peasants have moved to simplify and, in part, to secularize funeral practices.[81]

Population policy is the most significant arena in which the party has assumed the role of public patriarch. Contrary to popular understanding, the Chinese Communists never actively pursued a pronatalist policy, as the Soviet Union and other nations of Eastern Europe did in the post-World War II period. However, throughout the Maoist era, anti-Malthusianism figured prominently in, and at times constrained, the regime's approach to population control. Direct efforts to curb the growth of China's phenomenal population began in the mid-1950s, but they were

---

79. Davis-Friedmann, *Long Life*, pp. 140, 190–92.
80. Parish and Whyte, *Village and Family*, pp. 222, 227.
81. Davis-Friedmann, *Long Life*, pp. 225ff.

halted by the strong anti-Malthusianism and overconfidence of the GLF period. Population planning efforts resumed in the early 1960s; they were disrupted once again by the Cultural Revolution. They have intensified since the early 1970s, when the economic and social burdens of China's expanding population became inescapably evident. Only since Mao's death in 1976 has the regime begun an all-out campaign to limit births, the implications of which I discuss in the epilog.

The population programs of the 1950s and 1960s had scant success in reducing China's birth rate. However, the more thorough, sustained efforts of the 1970s appear to have achieved moderate success.[82] Birth control committees have been established at all levels of administration, with the direct participation and supervision of party members. In addition, population-control work has been assigned to local party and government organizations, to health clinics, and to mass organizations such as the revived women's associations. Propaganda and technical assistance teams have been dispatched to local areas, and inspection teams similar to those employed during land reform make periodic visits to targeted sites. Local birth control committees are charged with establishing local population-growth targets, based on national targets and coordinated with national and local economic development plans.

Implementation of the program subjects the Chinese to a massive education campaign conducted by the media, local study groups, educational institutions, and the traveling propaganda groups. Socialist ideology focusing on the virtues and economic rewards of planning has been combined with family-reform and feminist propaganda. The goals of late marriage and a small family (two or three children in rural areas, one or two in the cities) were integrated with the feminist values of the criticize-Confucius-and-Lin Piao campaign and the equal-pay-for-equal-work campaign of the mid-1970s. These included attacks on the

---

82. Demographic data for the PRC are extremely problematic. For thorough discussions of the significance and limitations of available data, see John S. Aird, "Fertility Decline and Birth Control in the People's Republic of China," and idem, *Population Policy and Demographic Prospects in the People's Republic of China.* The account of population policy that follows is based on these sources and on Leo A. Orleans, ed., *Chinese Approaches to Family Planning,* and Leo F. Goodstadt, "Official Targets, Data, and Policies for China's Population Growth."

preference for bearing sons, on exchange-of-women marriages, and on patrilocality as "feudalistic" practices that oppress women and inflate population increase.[83] However, the feminist advantages of birth control were generally presented in a careful manner, which demonstrated the regime's sensitivity to traditional familial values. One propaganda skit, for example, focused on a young couple breaking the news to grandmother of the birth of a second granddaughter.[84]

Whereas the population planning campaigns of earlier decades relied almost exclusively on ideological persuasion, during the 1970s the government began to impose material sanctions against "excess" family growth. At the very least, local areas were urged to remove such fertility incentives as the full-share rations and additions to the family garden plot awarded on the birth of each child. Contraception in various forms was made available free to married couples, and abortion and sterilization procedures were also offered without charge. In fact, incentives in the form of "nutrition fees" and released time from work were offered to women who agreed to abortion or sterilization.[85]

The comparative success of the 1970s population program in rural China is a product of both the greater determination applied by the regime and a shift in the balance of considerations that structure peasant reproductive decisions.[86] Having several children, at least one of which is male, still makes considerable sense in the rural patriarchal-socialist family economy. However, structural changes have also reduced the incentive to have as many sons as were desirable in the past. Sons provide less access to amassing family wealth than was possible under private land and property holding. Moreover, the value and status of daughters have increased. Steady increases in women's participation in the labor force add to the burdens of frequent childbearing for women. A married couple's interest in early household division is hand-

83. Goodstadt, "Official Targets," pp. 264–67, and Orleans, *Chinese Approaches*, pp. 23–24.

84. The skit is translated in Orleans, *Chinese Approaches*, pp. 65–78.

85. Parish and Whyte, *Village and Family*, p. 144.

86. Parish and Whyte downplay the significance of direct efforts by the regime and emphasize instead the structural context in which peasants calculate the material implications of childbearing (*Village and Family*). Aird, however, suggests that the regime's strategy has achieved a degree of success in recent years that cannot be explained by material explanations alone (*Population Policy*).

icapped as well by having many children. In short the increasingly determined goals of the state to reduce fertility have been seriously constrained in rural China by the patriarchal-socialist accommodation, but they can draw upon the effects of the rise in influence over reproduction decisions now enjoyed by the younger generation and by women. There now are instances when the interests of private and public "patriarchs" are at odds.

URBAN FAMILY CONTRASTS

The new democratic patriarchal revolution had been a rural transformation. When the Communists returned to the cities in 1949, they reunited with the population that had experienced the antipatriarchal family crisis of the early-twentieth century. This was a population predisposed to be far more responsive than were peasants to antipatriarchal family policies. Urban victory over the KMT was a rapid, decisive process based upon more conventional military methods than the rural strategy, which had depended upon mobilizing people through social and economic reforms. A high proportion of the major surviving urban patriarchs and their families left the mainland. Thus, the new regime was not constrained by the patriarchal accommodation that continued to guide its rural hand. It was possible, perhaps necessary, to develop somewhat contradictory family policies for urban areas and to implement family reform in an uneven pattern. The overpopulation of Chinese cities encouraged social policies that have intensified rural-urban family contrasts.

In urban areas, such traditional bases of patriarchal authority as the corporate family estate and lineage structures had been permanently eroded by the time the Communists assumed state power. Communist reconstruction policies removed further structural supports to patriarchal family authority and did not replace these with new ones equivalent to those it developed in rural areas. Private ownership of industry and most housing was eliminated in rapid stages. Urbanites rarely encounter opportunities to re-create their families as partial production units. Not organized into full collectives, urban workers are remunerated individually for their work. While this continues a class of dependent housewives, it also circumvents the household accounting system of the rural work teams. Urban areas also lack the geographic concentration of kin ties that has been an effective base of patriarchal culture in the countryside. In fact, the density of rural kinship is partly a function of restrictions on migration to urban areas, while urbanites have been pressured and even required to disperse.

For all these reasons, Communist family reforms have encountered weaker resistance and wider appeal in urban areas. Thus, when measured simply against its stated family goals, the Communist record appears more successful in the cities. There youth have gained enormously in family status, and this is reflected in an overall pattern of urban marital reform identified by Elisabeth Croll. Greater opportunities for youth to meet outside a familial context underlie the predominance of limited courtship over arranged betrothal in their matchmaking. Couples tend to initiate their matches and then turn to their parents for consent. If parental consent is not forthcoming, however, urban youth have more effective recourse to political associations and legal support in insisting on their rights. The urban pattern involves a later age at marriage—middle to late twenties—which also gives the parties greater control over their decisions. Political criteria tend to outweigh economic considerations when urbanites select their spouses, and they are more likely than villagers to accept simple wedding ceremonies. In fact, urban youth save their income to meet their own marital expenses.[87]

Beyond these enormous generational transformations, urban family reform includes noteworthy gender rearrangements. The most dramatic is the shift away from patrilineality toward bilateral kin relationships. The preference for patrilocal marriage has diminished in the cities. And there is reason to believe the traditional preference for having sons is declining as well. The urban elderly expect and receive support from all their children and are almost as likely to live with an adult daughter as with a son. Available housing and interpersonal relationships are now the primary determinants of such decisions.[88] All of this translates into greater improvement in the family status of urban women than rural women have attained. Urban daughters, unlike rural ones, are

---

87. Croll, *Politics of Marriage*, pp. 128, 160.
88. Davis-Friedmann, *Long Life*, p. 200.

likely to inherit a share of parental property. Urban husbands tend to participate somewhat more than their rural counterparts in domestic chores. And urban divorces tend to be far more egalitarian in custody and property settlements.[89]

Erosion of the patrilineal family has not led to a conjugal family system, as modernization theorists predicted. Rather, there are powerful supports for intergenerational shared households in urban China. The housing shortage is a strong inducement, but it is not the only one. There is considerable evidence of a widespread Communist policy to maintain the shared household as a basic family living unit. New urban housing construction in the mid-1970s, for example, built units for four or five people,[90] in the context of serious efforts to restrict urban population growth to one child per couple. And, although the vast majority of urban housing is publicly owned, much-coveted tenancy generally passes to the family's survivors. The regime has favored shared living through various exemptions to its migration restrictions. Old parents needing care have been allowed to migrate to the residence of an urban child or to send for a rural child to care for them in their urban residence. Generally the regime encourages its citizens to rely on shared households for social services to supplement its impressive, but inadequate public system. Migration restrictions have also been lifted, therefore, to allow a rural parent to migrate to provide child care for a two-worker urban family.[91] And, while individual wages circumvent a full household accounting system, the urban commodity rationing system is based on the family household. Basic grain allotments vary by sex, age, and work. Each household is issued a certificate that records the sex, age, and occupation of every family member and is the basis for determining the monthly grain ration for the household.[92]

Urban family life is significantly less patriarchal than in pre-revolutionary urban or contemporary rural China. However, systemic supports for male domination are as alive and familiar in urban China as in most modern cities. A sexual division of labor in which men dominate employment positions in the highly

89. Martin King Whyte, "Family Change in China," p. 157.
90. Davis-Friedmann, *Long Life*, p. 153.
91. Ibid., p. 154.
92. Dennis L. Chinn, "Basic Commodity Distribution in the PRC," p. 747.

238 • Patriarchal-Socialism

favored state sector is the most significant of these.[93] China's urban women are used quite consciously by the regime as a flexible, reserve army of labor. As late as 1972, Mao identified them as such: "China's women are a vast reserve of labor power. This reserve should be tapped in the struggle to build a great socialist society."[94] Women endure far higher rates of unemployment than men, and they are called upon to advance or retreat from the labor front in accordance with state demand.[95] Those women who are employed in the state sector are treated to preferential protective legislation, some of which, like the 56-day paid maternity leave, are clearly beneficial, but other features, like earlier retirement, work to women's ultimate economic and social disadvantage. "Privileges" such as these help to rationalize the double work burden women carry, with primary responsibility for domestic labor assumed to be both natural and fair. Female participation in the labor force is concentrated, then, in light industry, handicrafts, and services—all of which offer the lower wage scales and benefit systems of female work.[96]

Most of the features described above are nearly universal aspects of women's position in an urban, industrial work force. And they are complemented by equally familiar patterns of sexual subordination in education and political power.[97] However, the PRC also contributes a few unique policies which directly reinforce male family authority. Soon after capturing the cities, for example, the Communists set out to mobilize urban women through a

93. Whyte reports that in the urban sample of the Parish and Whyte study, women occupied 45% of the jobs in the state sector compared with their 59% share of the positions in the neighborhood collective enterprises, which have considerably lower status and material rewards ("Sexual Inequality," p. 17).

94. Quoted in Thorborg, "Chinese Employment Policy," p. 584.

95. Davin reprints a document calling on women to withdraw from the labor force during a period of labor surplus (*Woman-Work*, pp. 170–71).

96. Whyte calculates that the mean income of women in the Parish and Whyte urban sample is 77% that of men, which, he suggests, compares favorably with the male-female income gap in most of the major capitalist and socialist societies ("Sexual Inequality," pp. 18–21).

97. See fn. 71, above, for data on female membership in the CCP. National statistics for 1978 indicate that females constitute 45% of primary-school enrollment, 41% of secondary-school enrollment, and 24% of college enrollment. In the Parish and Whyte urban sample, however, 30% of the adults with some postsecondary education were female ("Sexual Inequality," pp. 14–15). Consult this source for additional data and a useful comparative analysis of sexual inequality in socialist and capitalist societies.

variety of organizational forms. One of the preferred forms was the dependents' organization designed to mobilize housewives of urban male workers according to the employment of their husbands. Initially the purpose of the organizations was to encourage these wives to nurture their husbands' capacity for productive labor by creating harmonious home environments. Soon dependents' organizations were encouraged to initiate small-handicraft or light-industrial shops outside the state sector.[98] Thus, women's formal contribution to production was organized through their subordinate familial position and designed to reproduce it. A similar, but indirect, effect results from aspects of urban housing allocation. Housing for state sector workers is often provided by their factories. Male dominance in this employment translates, therefore, into a dominant capacity to determine family residence. Finally, the revival in 1978 of a unique pre-Cultural Revolution employment policy called the *Ting-t'i* helps to sustain a modest patrilineal legacy in urban China. Each retiree from the state sector is allowed to pass on one of these coveted full-time jobs to one child. Theoretically a bilateral right, the sex-segmented labor force transforms the *Ting-t'i* characteristically into a valuable patrimony.[99]

Patriarchal family life has been constrained, but not eliminated, in China's cities. However, the decline of private patriarchy is offset by the disproportionate exposure of urban families to the "public patriarchy." Urban residence is a much coveted privilege, and the bureaucratic measures which the regime has constructed to restrain its growth—state allocation of urban jobs, housing, rations, and social services—subject the "privileged" to an extensive apparatus of social control. Therefore, urban youth are far more subject than their rural counterparts to processes of state socialization. Political campaigns are more readily and effectively transmitted to them and to their parents through public child care and social service institutions, the public educational system, state sector employment, and mass political organizations.

98. Davin, *Woman-Work*, pp. 60, 159.
99. Indeed, the female narrator of the oral history, "Chairman Mao's Letter to Li," refers to the policy as one in which sons could inherit fathers' jobs when their fathers retired (Frolic, *Mao's People*, p. 50). For a discussion of how the *Ting-t'i* affected the protests of sent-down youth in Shanghai in 1978, see Thomas B. Gold, "Back to the City," p. 763.

This is one reason the Cultural Revolution was primarily an urban phenomenon. Urban families have too few independent resources in the way of kin or local relationships and too little control over the future employment and housing prospects of their children to foster strong resistance to unwelcome directives. Urban families are more vulnerable, therefore, to state intervention into their family relationships. Political considerations more frequently influence urban decisions concerning marriage, divorce, and support for aging parents.[100] With the important exception of the sent-down youth program, discussed below, there is no clear evidence of serious conflict between urban families and the state. Yet, it is undeniable that regime-controlled terms of ideological discourse and policy directives exercise far greater impact on urban than rural families.[101]

In short, it is more credible to depict China's urban centers in a continuing process of prerevolutionary family change than is true of the rural sector. Even here, however, the Communist revolution introduced significant modifications and new directions to the earlier "evolutionary" processes that have been allowed to structure modern family life in nonrevolutionary societies. One distinctive outcome is far greater marital stability than is expected under modernization. In fact, there are indications that divorce is harder to obtain, even in urban China, than it had been in the prerevolutionary period.[102] And both the distinctive and familiar qualities of modern urban family change were achieved through more overtly politicized processes than occur in most nonrevolutionary contexts.

The Sent-Down Youth Program ▪ The sent-down youth program represents such an enormous departure from the terms of new democratic patriarchy and from the general popular acceptability

---

100. Croll, *Politics of Marriage*; Davis-Friedmann, *Long Life*, pp. 190–92; and Whyte, "Family Change." Whyte reports that rural respondents rarely mentioned political reasons for divorce, while 29% of the divorces in the Parish and Whyte urban sample were based on "political errors" ("Sexual Inequality," p. 30).

101. Whyte, "Family Change," provides an astute structural analysis of the role of the urban bureaucracy in fostering greater compliance in the cities with the official family policies of the regime. By treating that bureaucracy under the rubric of "public patriarchy" here, I intend to emphasize the historical and cultural dimensions of its authority structure.

102. Davin, *Woman-Work*, p. 102.

of PRC family policy that it merits close attention. The program, which developed slowly before the GLF, reached its full strength after the heat of the Cultural Revolution in 1968; it has involved a massive transfer, on a semipermanent basis, of urban youth to rural areas.[103] It was designed to reverse the tide of urbanization, to address motivational and employment problems of the growing ranks of educated urban youth without access to white-collar jobs, to recruit talented labor for rural areas, and to mitigate the social cleavage between mental and manual labor. Ten percent of China's urban population was transferred between 1968 and 1978. The program continues on a smaller scale in post-Mao China.

Although the government has administered the sent-down youth program with its characteristic sensitivity to the strength and significance of Chinese family sentiment, this policy directly undercuts private patriarchal authority over children and disrupts family life. Urban families have been forced to relinquish family autonomy and integrity, human resources for pooling income and family services, and to witness the downward mobility of their progeny. Moreover, the males among the transferred youth find their ability to form their own marriages and families severely handicapped in the rural setting. The men lack access to the prerequisites for rural marriage—housing, familial relationships and resources, and local status. Moreover, the youth have been reluctant to marry in the countryside because a rural marriage can jeopardize permanently any prospect of returning to the city.

The parents of urban youth have bitterly resisted the policy, urging children not to leave, sheltering those who escape from rural posts, and using their influence with officials to receive exemptions or special assignments for their kin. At first some young people, particularly women, regarded the transfer as liberatory, adventurous, and a means of realizing political idealism. However, as this wall poster, which appeared during a massive student protest against the program in 1978, suggests, most

103. Most of the information concerning the sent-down youth program in the following account is based on Thomas P. Bernstein, *Up to the Mountains and Down to the Villages.* For a vivid, personal account of the program by a former sent-down youth, see "Chairman Mao's Letter to Li" in Frolic, *Mao's People.* Additional information appears in Gold, "Back to the Cities."

youth have been as reluctant to separate from their urban families and culture as their parents have been to lose them:

> Under this oppressive policy, a tragic separation of flesh and blood took place in the home of every educated youth. There were so many heads of families with educated youth whose hearts were almost broken. Some who were not sick became sick. Worse, some died.[104]

The sent-down youth program is unusual, however, because the regime has considered it important enough to warrant direct conflict with family values. The government has gone to great lengths, therefore, to secure compliance. Many of the measures adopted were designed to take advantage of the very strength of family structure and sentiment on which the program infringes. Family members have been pressured to join study classes on the purposes and merits of the program. Factory and trade union organizations have set up special offices to organize small groups of family heads to launch a support campaign in their work places. The government has even manipulated family sentiment by threatening the job security of parents whose children refuse to comply. Program officials engage in extensive follow-up work with the parents of transferred youth, in order to influence the content of the letters they write to their children. One compromise in the revolutionary tradition of the PLA is to grant exemptions to youth whose families depend upon them for economic subsistence and to restrict the number of young people from each family who can be forced to leave home.

The unpopularity of the transfer program is not merely an urban problem. Receiving rural communities are rarely thrilled about the task of integrating inexperienced, alien, and disruptive young labor crews into their midsts. Here the Communists have taken particular care to respect rural concerns. They generally house the youth separately in a deliberate effort to avoid "disrupting the family life of the masses"[105] by imposing young strangers on their households. They have urged the youth to adapt to local norms. They have stressed the benefits of the program to rural communities. One advantage some peasants perceive is the arrival of young urban women as potential marriage

---

104. Quoted in Gold, "Back to the Cities," p. 758.
105. Bernstein, *Up to the Mountains*, p. 133.

partners for village men. Although many communities are suspicious of urban morals and competence, some villagers view the women as brides "sent by the state."[106] Patrilocality makes it possible for urban women to marry into rural communities, and they are cheaper than local brides because no father is present to demand a bride-price. Here the state is once again, however inadvertently, in the business of redistributing women to China's rural patriarchs.

It has been possible for China's "public patriarchs" to impose the unpopular, antipatriarchal family policy of the transfer program on its urban population because of the relative weakness of urban family autonomy and because they could appeal simultaneously to strong family ties and to the residue of antipatriarchal sentiment alive among urban youth. The party never sealed the same pact with urban patriarchs it had negotiated through decades of revolutionary collaboration with the peasantry. The Maoist regime could not, and would not, have persevered with an equivalently unpopular, antipatriarchal rural program.

THE CONSTRAINTS OF THE PATRIARCHAL-SOCIALIST ACCOMMODATION

Patriarchal-socialism represents a significant further transformation of the rural family system in the PRC. Unlike the new democratic patriarchy, however, this transformation was not achieved by a family revolution. Patriarchal-socialism emerged instead as a product of reforms that could be achieved within the limits of the new democratic patriarchal revolution. It was constructed upon a strong profamily platform that avoided direct assaults on local patriarchal prerogatives. It did not establish radically new principles of gender, generation, or social integration; it settled for gradual development of those introduced during the new democratic period. Patriarchal-socialism did not develop in response to a new family crisis, but made its gradual progress on the basis of new democracy's successful resolution of the prerevolutionary family crisis.

The patriarchal-socialist accommodation succeeded in restoring stability to the Chinese countryside. This stability proved to be

---

106. Ibid., p. 162.

a serious constraint upon the regime's capacity to implement further socialist development strategies for the rural sector. The experience of the GLF should be interpreted in this light. Its policies did include a utopian family movement, and the policies once again politicized basic questions of gender, generation, and social integration. However, these very aspects of the GLF violated the implicit pact on family and community life that bound the Communists and the peasantry. The GLF strategy attempted to forge socialist collectivities that transcended the boundaries of the newly constructed patriarchal-socialist family and community ties. But, the pre-Leap process of collectivization had fortified these relationships and granted greater autonomy to local communities than they had previously enjoyed. In fact, Parish and Whyte find that a paradoxical narrowing of rural social ties and economic interests resulted from the consolidation of land and resources and the wide dispersal of educational and social services that allow many needs to be met locally, where, one should add, they are conducted within the terms of local authority relationships. Curiously, even the gradual weakening of traditional patriarchal norms feeds this insular tendency. The decline of taboos on intravillage marriage lessens the need to maintain intervillage alliances.[107]

The new strength of the local democratized patriarchal community allowed the peasants to resist successfully revolutionary GLF measures that threatened the patriarchal-socialist accommodation. Thus, Chinese peasants have established constraints upon the Communists' capacity to develop the rural sector in a manner that would infringe upon the autonomy of the patriarchal moral economy, eliminate a private sector, or raise the level of socialist cooperation much beyond the new village authority structure. Lacking a theoretical analysis of processes of family transformation, or even a full awareness of its own historical family policy, the Chinese Communists are constrained as well in their capacity to comprehend these limits. Maoist leaders interpreted peasant resistance to GLF development policies as a two-line class struggle in which defense of peasant capitalism

107. Parish and Whyte, *Village and Family*, pp. 304ff.

was the major barrier to change.[108] The party failed to see that rural patriarchy had reached the end of its curious historical revolutionary role.[109] From then on it could act only as a resistance movement against further socialist development of the countryside. What is more, it had achieved sufficient power to resist effectively.

Patriarchal-socialism in the rural PRC also has had the capacity to resist direct efforts at family reform. The Maoists appreciated this, if their reticence on such issues serves as fair indication. During the 1960s and 1970s, they engaged in sporadic, but rather feeble, family reform campaigns under the aegis of the Socialist Education Movement, the Cultural Revolution, and the campaign to criticize Lin Piao and Confucius. Family reform was always presented as an ideological struggle, and always with great caution in the villages. With the exception of its population program during the 1970s, the program's rather uneven rural achievements prove the rule that none of the campaigns signified a fundamental shift in family policy.

Patriarchal-socialism has dramatically improved the circumstances of family and social life for most Chinese citizens. Particularly in the villages, the Communist regime's success in establishing conditions of basic economic and social security, advancing literacy and public health, and restoring hope constructed a wide margin of local tolerance for its periodic interventions and abuses. A share, albeit unequal, of most of the major benefits accrued to women as well as to men, to the elderly

---

108. Several Western scholars have reproduced these interpretations uncritically. Chesneaux, for example, identifies middle peasants as the base of resistance to the GLF. *China*, p. 103.

109. The post-Mao leadership has come closer to an awareness of the inhibiting effects of patriarchy. It has blamed patriarchy, which in orthodox Marxist fashion it identifies with feudalism, for many of the evils in contemporary Chinese society. For example, one recent CCP article attributed arbitrary, callous behavior on the part of cadres to "the shadow of patriarchy that long accompanied the small producers' economy." Quoted in Kwang-Ching Liu, "World View and Peasant Rebellion," pp. 317–18. Liu's fascinating article, which contains several other examples, makes clear that a major motive for such interpretations is the revisionist effort to downgrade the peasantry. Even so, the current regime is still treating patriarchy as a cultural residual. What it overlooks is the dynamic process through which patriarchy was reconstructed in rural China.

as well as to youth. Only an ahistorical feminist perspective could overlook the advances women made under patriarchal-socialism. But the patriarchal route to socialism also established an authority structure and a political culture that curtailed the possibility that a mass-based feminist movement would soon emerge in the PRC to question the profoundly unequal terms of the newly constructed order.

Viewing the dynamics of CCP family policy from the 1930s through 1976 in these terms suggests the need to modify a wide-spread conception of the Maoist legacy. According to that view, Maoist socialist development strategy, with its emphasis on class struggle and mass mobilization, should be traced from the anti-Japanese war period in Yenan through the Great Leap Forward to the Cultural Revolution and contrasted with intervening prag-matic, economistic periods.[110] From a feminist perspective, how-ever, Yenan was a contradictory seedbed, whose radical class politics and mass-line tactics were wedded to patriarchal recon-struction of the peasant family economy. The GLF built upon only one dimension of this legacy—material egalitarianism—while violating its patriarchal principles. Seemingly economistic development periods, on the other hand, return to more than simple material incentives. While eschewing active class struggle, they also restore to peasant family and village life important elements of a patriarchal moral economy and authority structure. The comparative popularity such periods enjoy among the peas-antry suggests that patriarchal motives may be more powerful than class interests in structuring Chinese peasant responses to socialist development. Peasants readily embraced the class struggle policies of land reform which simultaneously reconstructed their patriarchal family economy. They even cooperated with the class struggle implicit in collectivizing their new land so long as pa-triarchal family rights were respected and preserved. However, when class struggle threatened to collectivize domestic production and to bypass patriarchal authority over family economic and

---

110. For a coherent presentation of this analysis, see Mark Selden, "The Yenan Legacy."

reproductive decisions, many peasants resisted fiercely. They did so, I believe, because they interpreted such events as a betrayal of patriarchal-socialism, which reasonably enough had come to be their understanding of the parameters of the Maoist revolution.

7 Theoretical Legacy of the Chinese Family Revolution

Socialism long has promised to extinguish patriarchy, but patriarchy is alive and well in socialist China. Yet China has experienced a profound family revolution. This book has presented a feminist analysis of this seeming paradox. I will conclude by assessing the implications of my analysis for the theoretical discourses in family studies, feminist theory, and peasant studies discussed in the Introduction. It may be useful first to review the major elements of the historical relationship between patriarchy and socialist revolution in China.

THE CHINESE FAMILY REVOLUTION

Imperial China was a social formation which, even for an agrarian civilization, was characterized by an unusually explicit and hegemonic patriarchal mode of authority. Peasants generally aspired to achieve the same family structure and ideals as those of the Confucian elite—a family based on principles of gender and generational hierarchy expressed formally in a doctrine of filial piety supported by the full weight of social custom and legal authority. The mode of production in Confucian China was a patriarchal family economy in which the private family economy served as the basic social and economic unit. The patriarchal marriage and inheritance system had demographic and economic dynamics that played a role in the imperial dynastic cycle and, hence, contributed their share to the emergence of a revolutionary situation in postimperial China.

Because of the predominance of patriarchy and the family mode of production, China's revolutionary crisis was also a family crisis—a period when irreversible decline in the material and ideological foundations of a family system produced, as one symptom, the politicization of the family's relationships of gender, generation, and social integration. The collapse of the Confucian state in 1911 bifurcated the previously integrated elite and peasant cultures in China and unleashed a two-pronged family crisis. Elite families found themselves subjected to a sustained anti-patriarchal attack by urban-educated youth of the May Fourth generation. This patriarchal legitimation crisis produced Republican China's ephemeral (and male-led) version of radical feminism.

Peasant families, on the other hand, experienced a serious "realization crisis"—an ominous decline in their capacity to realize any form of family life at all. Familiar signs of family trouble reappeared in the new context of the patriarchal legitimation crisis among the elite. The collapse of the traditional structures that had integrated family and society both weakened peasant families and made them important to their members. Crisis conditions thrust greater economic responsibilities and opportunities upon the backs of peasant women, but conditions also made the abuses of the patriarchal family system less responsive to traditional social controls, and, it is likely, more brutal. Thus many peasants, including the women among them, were encouraged to long for a restoration of the traditional family economy. The family was the prism through which Chinese of elite and humble background experienced the political and agrarian crises of Republican China, and separate perspectives produced two contradictory forms of family values—feminism and restorationism. The Chinese Communist Party (CCP) was formed from the ranks of the urban youth radicalized by the patriarchal legitimation crisis, but was destined to depend for its mass base upon the peasantry. Hence a successful resolution of the peasant family crisis became a crucial task for the socialist revolution in China.

People's War, the Chinese Communists' successful route to state power, was, in large part, a response to the peasant family crisis. Through a costly process, the CCP and its peasant constituency learned to collaborate in activities that simultaneously reconstructed the patriarchal peasant family economy and defeated the Kuomintang and the Japanese. The victorious strategy was new democracy, the winning tactic was the mass line. These were developed in land reform, the cooperative movement, and military policy—in each sphere the CCP learned to take the peasant family household as the basic unit of policy and to make what it regarded as mere concessions to popular patriarchal mores.

Land reform, the center of the rural social revolution, progressed from more radical to more conservative measures. Instead of nationalizing land, the CCP organized peasants to seize and redistribute it among their families on an egalitarian basis. Through this stage of class struggle, the class of big patriarchs was eliminated, and the material basis of peasant patriarchy was radically redistributed. Similarly, the early cooperative measures of People's War took the peasant family as the membership unit and helped to resurrect the flagging family economy. This entailed notable shifts in the traditional sexual division of labor as the party sought to mobilize women for crucial productive activities. Here it occasionally drew upon its feminist heritage in formulating appeals, but always the Communists took care not to threaten unduly rural patriarchal sensibilities. Finally, Communist military policy took the peasant family as the basic unit for conscription, war service, and relief measures. Once again a mild feminism interlaced the predominantly traditionalist efforts to mobilize peasant women for support work. However, the People's Liberation Army (PLA) functioned virtually as a male fraternity, and this had significant consequences for sustaining male political authority in postrevolutionary China.

The result of People's War in China was ironic. Socialist revolution rescued the peasant family economy and placed it on a more secure and egalitarian foundation than it had ever enjoyed. Yet this was the result of a family revolution, not of a restoration. Together peasants and party had constructed the new democratic patriarchy in rural China. Patriarchy was democratized in two senses of the term. It was limited and reformed substantively, but, equally important, it was made more democratically available to masses of peasant men who had been denied its most meager trappings in the crisis period. New democratic strategy succeeded in resolving the peasant family crisis and in bringing the CCP to state power. The family crisis served as a major arena for the development of Mao's new democratic strategy. This strategy tapped the radical potential of peasant restorationist motives, or, as Mao put it, studied China's "splendid old culture" in order to "reject its feudal dross and assimilate its democratic essence."[1] The result was a new moral economy in the Chinese countryside, but one that remained patriarchal. This moral economy was to serve as a useful foundation for the collectivization process that lay ahead.

While People's War policies of the CCP laid the groundwork for the patriarchal revolution, the party also devised explicit family reforms that drew upon its feminist heritage. Marxism, the CCP's revolutionary theory, taught it to regard family reform as superstructural. The policy of the "new democratic family," as the CCP called it, sought to establish an egalitarian, monogamous system of free marriage and divorce. Feminists who have analyzed the implementation of new democratic family policy generally view it as a rather limited, inadequate program of family reform.[2] Although this is a fair appraisal of its feminist achievements, on a deeper level, one that was hidden from the CCP itself, new democratic family policy served as the organic complement to Communist economic and military strategy. Because it helped to foster the patriarchal family revolution, it should be judged successful in completing the construction of the new democratic patriarchy.

Chinese Communist family policy underwent the same developmental process as land reform—from a more radical to a more conservative stance—but with a crucial difference. Whereas the conservatism of new democratic economic policy was a strategic step in the implementation of a carefully theorized transition to socialism, this was not the case with family policy. The CCP had no parallel theory or vision of family and gender transformation to guide its strategic retreat on family reform. This made the shift to an active profamily stance more permanent and con-

---

1. Mao Tse-tung, "On New Democracy," p. 381.

2. For the most detailed and astute feminist critique of Maoism, see Kay Johnson, "Feminism and Socialist Revolution in China." Other useful feminist sources include Batya Weinbaum, "Women in Transition to Socialism"; Elisabeth Croll, *Feminism and Socialism in China;* and Delia Davin, *Woman-Work.*

sequential. Even the most radical family reform efforts in PRC history, the marriage law implementation campaigns of the early 1950s, occurred in this conservative framework. The reform measures that achieved the greatest success were those that complemented the economic reforms by curtailing the elite form of patriarchy and redistributing and limiting patriarchal privileges in rural China. These measures helped to redistribute women to peasant men. An attack on the elite patriarchy of the few was integral to democratizing the availability of a reformed patriarchy to the many. It was a means whereby the CCP and the peasantry succeeded in constructing a new family morality to match the new family economy of the new democratic patriarchy. Yet this family reform program never confronted the root patriarchal structures in China's rural family system. Instead of eliminating the patriarchal household unit of production or patrilocal marriage, the new democratic stage of the socialist revolution in China made these more accessible and viable.

The irony of Chinese communism's role as "savior" of the peasant family economy is underscored by its contrast with the destructive family policy of its rival for state power in China—the Kuomintang (KMT). After advocating a moderate family reform program in the 1920s, the KMT reverted to the neo-Confucianist New Life Movement in the 1930s. However, neither its reformist nor its restorationist measures had much effect in China's hinterland. The economic and military policies of the KMT, on the other hand, exacerbated the crisis in the peasant family economy. Under its regime, rural taxes multiplied without providing central authorities adequate revenues to maintain the rural infrastructure. Nor could the KMT solve China's land problem. Moreover, KMT military policy was as insensitive to peasant family needs as that of the CCP was solicitous. Peasants were pressed into service regardless of their families' labor needs, only to be treated brutally. All of this made the CCP appear to be the last hope for peasant family survival.

The new democratic patriarchy occupied a formative, but brief, moment on the stage of socialist transformation in China. Scarcely had land and marriage reform been completed when the PRC government launched an all-out effort to collectivize agricultural production, during which peasants lost their access to private land quite as suddenly as they had gained it. The potential for this process to free women from patriarchal control of their labor and resources was not realized. Rather, the collectivization process built upon and deepened the achievements of the new democratic patriarchal revolution. Cooperatives were formed around male lineage links in "natural" neighborhoods, hamlets, and villages. Families joined as units and earned work points, which were paid to their patriarchal heads. Collectivization represented a further democratization of patriarchal authority in the countryside. Through this stage of class struggle, the poorer rural patriarchs gained use rights in common over the remaining village wealth. This gave them greater access to marriage and family life. The new democratic patriarchy was thus transformed into a patriarchal-socialist family economy. Families retained small garden plots and control over sideline crafts and animal raising. Housing remained private and a patrilineal inheritance. Significant patriarchal authority over marriage was sustained.

The Great Leap Forward (GLF), however, violated the unarticulated terms of the patriarchal-socialist accommodation and faltered in part due to this error. GLF policies attempted to bypass the peasant family economy in both production and consumption patterns, and peasants actively resisted the antifamily implications of these efforts. Their resistance, combined with natural and diplomatic disasters, wreaked havoc on the nation's economy. The regime was forced to capitulate. By 1962 it had restored private garden plots and rural free markets, abandoned most collective dining and child-care facilities, and retreated generally to the pre-Leap patriarchal-socialist family economy that continues to dominate the rural areas of the PRC.

In short, the socialist revolution in China was a patriarchal revolution as well—a radical transformation in the rural patriarchal family mode of production. Confucian patriarchy was replaced first by new democratic patriarchy, and then by patriarchal-socialism. This revolution had mixed effects on women and on socialist development options, but the CCP was poorly placed to appreciate these effects. Guided by Marxist-Leninist theory, it had led the peasants in a revolution fought exclusively in the name of national and class struggle. Its theoretical corpus gave it few tools to analyze a transformation in patriarchal structures.

Yet the political acumen of the CCP had far exceeded its theoretical sophistication. During two decades of People's War it had developed a remarkable and successful family policy, but behind the back of its revolutionary theory. Not until the GLF did the party directly encounter major problems due to the gap between its family theory and practice. When Leap policies violated the unspoken terms of the patriarchal-socialist alliance, the latent contradictions between the two emerged. Whereas rural patriarchy once had served as a progressive impetus to socialist transformation, by 1958 it became instead a context of constraints in which rural socialist development was destined to proceed. The constraints were all the more limiting because of the atheoretical nature of the earlier policies.

THEORETICAL LEGACY OF
THE CHINESE FAMILY REVOLUTION

China's patriarchal revolution was atheoretical in conception. Yet that revolution provides a fruitful opportunity to rethink significant theoretical issues. This book presents an analysis of its development, with implications for discourses in peasant studies, family sociology, and feminist theory.

Peasant Patriarchy and Socialist Revolution • China's socialist revolution certainly can be read as a process in which peasants reached backward toward revolution. Chinese peasants fought, among other reasons, to restore their traditional moral economy, which had been a family economy. The family economy formed the basis for their spiritual and material sustenance. Edward Friedman is correct to say that "the authenticating mobilization of the rural revolution [was experienced] partially in terms of a response to a familial-religious crisis."[3] We have seen how during its protracted experience with People's War, the CCP tapped the restorationist impulses of the peasantry, modifying and being modified by them in a manner that resulted in a revolution. Thus James C. Scott is also correct to infer that "far from being a handicap, the 'obsolete' values of peasants and their local

3. Edward Friedman, *Backward Toward Revolution*, p. 159.

orientation may well be the source of their radical action."[4] It is also legitimate to associate certain distinctive features of Maoist society and development processes with its People's War heritage and the restorationist dimension of the revolution. Such an analysis helps to explain both the comparatively noncoercive course of collectivization and the propensity for mass-line politics.

However, this book's feminist analysis of the role played by the rural family system in the Chinese revolution suggests the need for a more balanced understanding of the progressive uses of the past and of the revolutionary capacity of the peasantry than has been suggested in most of the literature on this subject. The traditional moral economy of the Chinese peasantry was a patriarchal family economy. Hierarchical principles of gender and generation governed the structure of the traditional peasant family and community and framed the peasants' sense of justice. When peasants calculated their interests, as they did, in familial rather than individualist terms, they applied a patriarchal calculus which assured different costs, opportunities, and benefits to the sexes and generations.

Thus, as we have seen, Chinese women suffered the greatest deprivations of the family crisis. The CCP began with a feminist ideology, and its experience in the early Peasant Movement sensitized the party to female suffering and the potential of family reform to attract oppressed women to the Communist cause. But when the party moved to rural base areas, where it learned to ground its socialist strategy on a traditionalist foundation, it found that patriarchal mores were more sound as a bridge to community support. As the CCP mobilized men to join the army and the party, it cast most peasant women in an auxiliary revolutionary role. The subsequent new democratic strategy reconstructed the traditional family economy, and the resulting patriarchal community limited the gains from socialist revolution peasant women would enjoy.

Most contributors to the literature on the progressive aspects of the peasant past uncritically identify brotherhood and fraternity as vital peasant sentiments easily adaptable to socialist revolutionary ends. Scott characterizes the peasant utopia as a "society of brotherhood."[5] Friedman views the Chinese revolution as a

---

4. James C. Scott, "Hegemony and the Peasantry," p. 281.
5. Ibid., p. 285.

process in which "the bonds of brotherhood were extended."[6] Yet feminist scholars correctly stress the historical relationship between patriarchy and fraternity: fraternal bonds derive from a patriarchal order whose authority relationships they generally help to sustain.[7] In China, appeals to brotherly sentiment served to construct the military fraternity of the PLA. There young peasant men enjoyed relatively egalitarian relationships as well as the opportunity for heroism that allowed them to reenter their traditional families and communities with enhanced status and expectations. Then, in postrevolutionary China, members of this military fraternity enjoyed political and economic privileges and served as favored candidates for the highest positions in state authority.

China's socialist revolution, however, denied peasant women equivalent sororal opportunities. Women served the revolution from the confines of their relative isolation in traditional patriarchal families and communities. When the Communists sought to disturb this isolation by organizing women's associations, they proceeded cautiously and placed the women's organizations under the authority of the male-controlled peasant associations. This pattern was exaggerated in the PRC, where the National Women's Federation was to survive at the pleasure of the male-controlled socialist state. The new democratic patriarchy and patriarchal-socialism secured for most peasant women enormous gains over their status in pre-Communist family and community life, but as subordinate daughters rather than equal sisters of fraternal Communist men.[8] Both the gains and the continued subordination

---

6. Friedman, *Backward Toward Revolution*, p. 120. John Berger makes a similar observation: "The peasant ideal of equality recognizes a world of scarcity, and its promise is for mutual fraternal aid in struggling against this scarcity and a just sharing of what the work produces" ("Towards Understanding Peasant Experience," p. 350). Feminist sinologist Kay Johnson, however, does not share this uncritical appreciation of Chinese peasant fraternalism ("Feminism and Socialist Revolution").

7. For a fine analysis of the relationship between patriarchy and fraternalism in early modern Europe, see Mary Ann Clawson, "Early Modern Fraternalism and the Patriarchal Family." Batya Weinbaum offers an unusual Freudian interpretation of fraternalism, revolution, and antifeminism in *The Curious Courtship of Women's Liberation and Socialism*.

8. Weinbaum makes this inequity the basis for an analytic model she develops to compare gender and generational work and family roles. Men occupy roles of father and brother while women are cast as wives and daughters (*Curious Courtship*).

of Chinese women are integrally related to the restorationist dimension of protracted People's War. Thus one should neither overlook nor overdraw the progressive implications of restorationist consciousness adapted to revolutionary ends.

Nor is this a limitation only from a feminist perspective. Other central socialist objectives are proscribed by the fraternal legacy of such a socialist revolution. Alvin Gouldner suggested that both the egalitarianism and the authoritarianism of Cuban socialism derived from the experience of shared danger and struggle

[which were] characteristic of a military brotherhood, and that this brotherhood became the guerrillas' tacit paradigm of a good social order, which they subsequently sought to reproduce in society at large. It may be that it is precisely this use of the military brotherhood as societal paradigm that helps explain how egalitarianism can be associated with concentrated decision making at the top and with strict control over dissent.[9]

The same judgment should be applied to socialist China, while our understanding of this process can be deepened by identifying patriarchal authority as a pivotal element in the brotherly paradigm.

The Family and Social Change • This book's analysis of the Chinese peasants' backward road to revolution not only supports the internal critique which scholars have been developing of the family modernization thesis; it suggests they have not yet ventured far enough. One must discard a modernization framework to appreciate fully the dynamic, complex relationship between family transformation and macrosocial change.

Modernization theorists long have read the Chinese family revolution as one more case of a worldwide evolutionary process of family modernization.[10] According to this interpretation, the Chinese revolution simply accelerated processes of family change that were already under way. William Goode, for example, in

---

9. Alvin Gouldner, "The Two Marxisms," p. 445.

10. See, for example, William J. Goode, *World Revolution and Family Patterns*; Marion J. Levy, Jr., *The Family Revolution in Modern China*; and C. K. Yang, *Chinese Communist Society: The Family and the Village*. Despite his sophisticated understanding of Chinese family patterns, even Maurice Freedman accepted this interpretation ("The Family in China, Past and Present").

World Revolution and Family Patterns, introduced his chapter on China with the claim that "current changes in the family and other areas of Chinese social life were not initiated by the Communist regime. . . . These changes have been going on over the past half-century. Many merely represent an intensification of social pressures and alterations which began long ago."[11] Those traditional practices and values that survived the revolutionary cataclysm have been read as evidence of "cultural lag," slated for eventual demise. Yet a more complicated relationship between family and revolutionary change existed in China. While China's socialist revolution did accelerate certain prerevolutionary processes of family change, it also decelerated a few, reversed others, and initiated some new ones. For example, while socialism hastened the decline of corporate lineage estates, the collectives established a new basis for male kinship solidarities. Rather than aggravating prerevolutionary causes of family crisis, the revolution resolved the land problem, thereby establishing an unprecedented basis for peasant family security. Indeed, one surprising implication of this study is that modernization conducted under revolutionary socialist auspices can be less destructive of premodern family ties than has been the case with capitalist modernizing processes. Most of the traditional family values and practices which survived China's socialist revolution are not anachronisms; they were actively defended through a process that gave them new and sounder structural support.

The revisionist model of family change developed by Joan Scott and Louise Tilly, which emphasizes European peasant families' traditionalist response to modern social transformations, transcends many of the limitations of the family-modernization thesis and can be applied profitably to the Chinese case. According to their analysis, capitalist industrialization in Europe provoked peasant families to devise new strategies to meet traditional goals.[12] If we substitute socialist revolution and development for capitalist industrialization, we can see that Chinese peasant families, as they were confronted with rapidly changing circumstances, also devised new strategies to achieve many of the traditional goals

11. Goode, *World Revolution,* p. 270.
12. Joan Scott and Louise Tilly, "Woman's Work and the Family in Nineteenth-Century Europe," pp. 145–78.

of their family economy. One strategy was to enlist their sons in the PLA in exchange for Communist protection for their subsistence activities. A more active course was to participate as families in land revolution while resisting the distribution of land to women. Likewise, the Scott and Tilly model accurately indicates that these new experiences affect peasant family relationships and ultimately encourage peasants to modify traditional ideas. Thus the young Chinese men who filled the ranks of the PLA participated, however unwittingly, in a major shift in generational relationships in China. We have seen how their wartime gains were translated into earlier access to familial and political authority in postrevolutionary society. Similarly, the rise in the value of female labor stimulated by collectivization facilitated the cultural legitimation of marriage at a later age and a more active role for young peasant women and men in the selection of their mates. A "backward toward modernization" perspective far exceeds the analytic utility of the concept of "culture lag" in explaining the checkered pattern of change and continuity noticed repeatedly by observers of contemporary Chinese family life.[13]

However, even Tilly and Scott's model has a limited capacity to respond to the full complexity of China's family revolution. It remains rooted in a modernization framework, because it implicitly accepts the inevitability of the direction and nature of the social structural changes that shape the traditionalist strategies of peasant families. This leaves the peasant family in an exclusively reactive historical role. It is forced to adjust to an exogenous process of social change. Close analysis of a revolutionary situation such as China's enables one to discern a more dynamic relationship between the peasant family and social change. We have seen that the traditional Chinese peasant family economy did not merely resist or adapt itself to Communist-induced changes in social structure. Peasant family structure and consciousness actively helped to shape these changes. Family change in China was neither a "dependent" nor an "independent variable." Rather it was integral to and inseparable from the general causes, proc-

13. Among those who have emphasized the mixture of change and continuity in the Chinese family are Jack Potter, "Change and Continuity in the Chinese Family," public lecture, 23 October 1980, University of California, Berkeley; Ruth Sidel, *Families of Fengsheng;* and Maurice Freedman, "Family in China."

esses, and outcomes of socialist revolution. The dual family crisis helped to generate contradictory forms of consciousness and simultaneously to open and to limit possibilities for social change. Under such circumstances, neither a New Life Movement nor bourgeois or radical feminism offered much of relevance to a peasant constituency. Yet family issues were central to revolutionary mobilization, and the demands of family reconstruction helped to shape the character of new democratic strategy and the mass-line tactics of Maoism. Thus China's family revolution was a crucial aspect of the socialist revolutionary process; it helped to shape the terms of socialist victory and to establish limits on development strategy options.

The familial outcome of China's socialist revolution also indicates the dialectical relation between family and social change. The new democratic patriarchy and patriarchal-socialism are distinctive family systems which arose from the contradictions of the prerevolutionary family system and those of the processes of People's War. Neither represents the restoration of the pre-Communist peasant family system; nor did either establish a "modern nuclear" family system. And both can be characterized as "transitional" only in the broadest, and unenlightening sense that all family and social systems are transitional between one historical form and the next.

Perhaps the causal role which a family system can play in shaping macrostructural aspects of social change is less visible when the object of study is a modernizing society in the capitalist West. Ironically, there the terms of the alliance between family and social change have been far less favorable to the structure and values of the traditional peasant family economy than they proved to be in socialist China. This contradicts a widely held view that revolutionary regimes, unlike evolutionary ones, must compete with families for the loyalties of their members.[14] It is true, of course, that a certain degree of conflicted family loyalties is endemic to any major social cataclysm. It is also true that the Chinese revolution stimulated the divisive impact of class struggle

---

14. This view is based primarily on interpretations of the Russian case. See, for example, Kent H. Geiger, *The Family in Soviet Russia,* and Alex Inkeles, *Social Change in Soviet Russia.*

upon clan loyalties. However, if one distinguishes between kinship and family loyalties, the case for regime-family conflict diminishes considerably.[15] Although the Chinese revolution disrupted and transformed many kinship ties, one of its remarkable features was its capacity to transform peasant family loyalties into a substantial revolutionary asset. The counterrevolutionary KMT pitted peasant loyalty to the family against loyalty to the state, while the CCP, to its profit, found a way to harmonize many of the interests and loyalties of peasant families and the regime. This historical process later enabled peasant families to resist successfully regime policies which threatened their integrity. Family solidarity appears both to participants and observers to be more intact in socialist China than in the capitalist societies of the West.

Socialism, Women's Liberation, and Feminist Theory • Feminists commonly view each new socialist revolution as an opportunity to answer the question, "Does Socialism Liberate Women?" Although the present case analysis of the Chinese revolution can be read as one more reason for a negative response, it would be far more useful to reformulate the question in historical terms. It should be incontrovertibly clear by now that no society that calls itself socialist has succeeded in fully liberating women.[16] Nor has any society even succeeded in establishing full gender equality within the bounds of its particular social structure. The present study suggests several basic reasons for this failure.

Foremost are limits rooted deeply in the societies in which all socialist revolutions have occurred. As in China, these have been poor, primarily agrarian societies with deeply patriarchal family systems. If the Chinese case is a reliable indicator, revolutionary crises in such societies are likely to generate among the peasantry a restorationist consciousness, which can be harnessed to rev-

---

15. Martin K. Whyte, in his presentation on a panel on Chinese youth at the annual meeting of the Association for Asian Studies, April 1976, in New York City, directly rejected the idea that Chinese families were forced to compete with the state for the loyalty of their children.

16. Of course, it is also clear that none have realized other central socialist ideals, such as democracy or an end to alienated labor. This has inspired considerable debate over the proper labeling of societies that identify themselves as socialist.

olutionary ends. As we have seen, the desire to restore threatened patriarchal order may become intense (and not only among peasant men) in such circumstances.[17] There have been historical instances where this motivation was strong enough to jeopardize the political control of a revolutionary regime.[18]

Moreover, such societies provide a weak basis for the development of an autonomous feminist movement that is strong enough to play an independent role in the revolutionary process. While the crisis of Confucian patriarchy generated radical feminist ideas among its critics, these ideas could appeal to only the narrowest sector of the Chinese population, and they were rapidly subordinated to the goals of the contending revolutionary parties. Then China's protracted rural revolutionary process hastened feminism's demise. The development of a centralized single-party state in the PRC (as in most other socialist societies) consolidated the formal subordination of the women's movement to the administrative structures and political priorities of its male-dominated polity. As we have seen, even the subordinate Women's Federation was entirely suspended when it fell out of favor during the Cultural Revolution. When one adds to these internal structural considerations the formidable constraints on all varieties of social revolutionary transformation imposed on newly developing socialist societies by a world capitalist economic order and the military competition of the international system of nation-states, it appears remarkable that women in socialist societies have fared as well as they have. While capitalism has not liberated women, many capitalist societies have been able to provide richer soil for the growth of feminist consciousness and an independent feminist movement.

A second source of the failure of socialism to liberate women can be located in the inadequacy of socialist theory. Socialist revolutionaries have adapted Marxism to their purposes, and many feminists have argued correctly that Marxism is inherently limited in its capacity to theorize the sources of female subor-

17. The Islamic revolution in Iran appeared to contain considerable sentiment of this sort. See, for example, the newspaper stories cited in fn. 26 to the epilog of this book.

18. The most notable is the case of Moslem Central Asia, analyzed in Gregory J. Massell, *The Surrogate Proletariat.*

dination.[19] Regarding class struggle as the primary historical dynamic leads Marxists to relegate family and gender transformation to what most tend to regard as a secondary and ideological realm. Marxism lacks a conceptual framework for an analysis of a relatively autonomous sex-gender system. Thus it tends to ignore the social significance of historical varieties of patriarchy.

This study suggests, however, that a patriarchal family system deserves close attention in an analysis of revolutionary processes. Patriarchy is a useful concept to retain in feminist theoretical tool kits, but only if we take care to historicize our use of the term. It is necessary to periodize transformations that occur in patriarchal sex-gender systems. We have seen the significant distinctions in gender *and* economic relationships that pertained in China under three distinct patriarchal orders—Confucianism, the new democratic patriarchy, and patriarchal-socialism. Although each is characterized by identifiably different principles of gender, generation, and social integration, all three are clearly patriarchal. Under each of these sex-gender systems, authority of men over women is closely tied to the rights and responsibilities of social fatherhood which include strong elements of control over female productive and reproductive activity within a patrilocally established family economy. This study cannot resolve the feminist debate over whether or not patriarchy is the best term to employ as a description of systemic male authority in advanced capitalist societies. However, even under the most stringent definitions, a transformed patriarchy endures in the PRC.

If patriarchy remains a useful feminist concept, this need not imply that "the family" is bankrupt as a descriptive term.[20] Cer-

---

19. Several anthologies attempt to analyze the possible relationships between Marxism and feminism. See Annette Kuhn and Anne Marie Wolpe, eds., *Feminism and Materialism*, and Zillah Eisenstein, ed., *Capitalist Patriarchy and the Case for Socialist-Feminism*. One collection is organized directly around the question of the compatibility of Marxist and feminist analyses (Lydia Sargent, ed., *Women and Revolution*).

20. As discussed in chap. 1, several feminists have argued that "the family" is strictly an ideological concept and should be abandoned. See, for example, Rayna Rapp, "Household and Family," in Rapp et al., "Examining Family History"; Michele Barrett, *Women's Oppression Today*; and Heidi I. Hartmann, "The Family as the Locus of Gender, Class, and Political Struggle."

tainly, feminists are correct to criticize its reification at the hands of many family scholars. "The family" is neither natural, nor universal, but is an institution differentiated by relationships of gender, generation, and class. Restorationist and feminist consciousness in China had different meanings for different families, and individual family members could and did embrace opposing family ideologies and goals. Likewise China's family revolution brought different opportunities and burdens to family members of different sex and age. However, despite internal differentiation and historical variation, the Chinese family was and remains a real institution reducible neither to an ideology nor to the households within which people live. In China, as elsewhere, the family has so much subjective meaning to its members that it can and has functioned as a historical force that transcends the boundaries of gender or class interests and goals. In this sense, the family is somewhat analogous to "the state"—another ambiguous, highly variable structure which serves many legitimation functions, but is also not reducible to these. The formulation of "the family" as exclusively ideological presumes economic and political activities to be more "real" than the lived experience of their performers. If "the family" is merely ideological, then it must be viewed as the major perpetrator of false gender consciousness. Tempting as such an analysis of "the family" may be to feminists, I believe we must resist this facile and somewhat patronizing solution to a far more complicated theoretical and political dilemma.[21]

A historicized use of "patriarchy" and "family" can augment feminist understanding of the relative autonomy of a sex-gender system. There is no necessary contradiction between such a concept and developing a feminist historical materialism. The relative autonomy of sex-gender suggests that the structure of a society's gender relationships has an internal logic and character not reducible to that of its mode of production, nor even to its sexual

---

21. Conventional Marxist uses of the concept "false consciousness" depend upon a base-superstructure formulation of society. Raymond Williams discusses some of the problems with this formulation in his well-known essay, "Base and Superstructure in Marxist Cultural Theory." Williams situates "false consciousness" within Marxist treatments of ideology (*Marxism and Literature,* chap. 4).

division of labor.[22] As Zilla Eisenstein suggests in her discussion of the relationship between patriarchy and capitalism, "neither is the mere instrument of the other, yet they are completely intertwined."[23] Thus, in the Chinese revolution, we have seen the interdependence of patriarchy and socialism, how each system of relationships served as a medium for revolutionary transformation in the other. Neither class nor gender was primary in the Chinese revolution, nor was either superstructural. During the revolutionary process the two were inextricably related. At moments either class or gender relationships were more visible and politicized, but they were rarely easy to distinguish. The patriarchal peasant family served as the medium of class struggle, and class struggle was the medium of China's patriarchal family revolution.

Acknowledging the relative autonomy of sex-gender is not the same as adopting a "dual systems theory"[24] approach which segregates economy and gender, or production and reproduction, and applies Marxist and feminist analyses separately to these distinct social spheres. Rather, both relatively autonomous systems should be viewed as constitutive of the entire social order. Chinese patriarchy did not merely structure family and gender relationships; it helped to shape the economy, military, and state as well. Likewise, Chinese socialism has had profound effects on gender and family relationships. Most of the time the two systems operate via compatible processes that are difficult to distinguish. But there are moments when the separate principles or sets of interests of these systems become visible and the latent contradictions between them revealed. The Great Leap Forward was such a moment in patriarchal-socialist China, as patriarchal family

---

22. This formulation of the relative autonomy of sex-gender is similar to discussions within contemporary Marxism regarding the relative autonomy of the state. The latter are summarized by Theda Skocpol, who argues for a more radical position on the question of state autonomy (*States and Social Revolutions,* pp. 27–33). There are, however, certain ambiguities that result when the term "system" is applied to sex-gender. The term should not be understood to imply that there is an independent motor governing the transformation of sex into gender, or that a sex-gender system is precisely analagous to a class system.

23. Zillah Eisenstein, *The Radical Future of Liberal Feminism,* p. 20.

24. The term, which is discussed in chap. 1, above, comes primarily from Iris Young, "Socialist-Feminism and the Limits of Dual Systems Theory."

structure limited the options for socialist development strategy, and the more radical among Chinese socialist planners were forced to capitulate.

Socialism has not liberated women because a socialist mode of production has proven to be compatible with a patriarchal sex-gender system. We have seen that a patriarchal family economy and patriarchal consciousness can even serve to facilitate the construction of a socialist society. This appears to be particularly likely when a socialist revolution takes place in a society dominated by a peasant family economy. In such a setting socialism can reform and reconstruct a besieged patriarchal order so that it comes to rest on new and firmer joists. The reconstruction of peasant patriarchy restores family solidarity, and this may further inhibit prospects for the development of feminist consciousness. An unresolved family crisis, it appears, offers a social context conducive to the growth of feminist ideologies. The breakdown of traditional family solidarities encourages many to seek new ways of organizing their personal lives, and feminism suggests new principles to these ends. Perhaps this is part of the reason why feminism has found more hospitable environments in capitalist than in socialist societies. Capitalist development has tended to destroy traditional patriarchal family structures without reconstructing a stable family system. China's socialist revolution, in contrast, by successfully resolving the prerevolutionary family crisis, may have curtailed the future development of an indigenous feminist ideology and movement. This suggests the need for feminists to distinguish between a family revolution and a feminist revolution and to continue the attempt to develop theory adequate to the latter task.

Patriarchy and socialism coexist in China due to the success of a patriarchal family revolution. This suggests that socialist modernization, like capitalist modernization, is compatible with patriarchy, at least up to a very far point. Patriarchy may even be more compatible with socialist than with capitalist development processes, although a deeply male-supremacist sex-gender system is common to both forms of society. Socialism, like capitalism, transforms a traditional patriarchal order, but it also is structured by it. Eventually, contradictions emerge between patriarchy and socialist development. But socialist family politics cannot be theorized adequately within Marxism, and the contradictions cannot be resolved via socialist theory and practice alone.[25] Of course, the contradictions do not have to be resolved at all. They can fester beneath the surface of the social fabric, invisibly structuring political and social issues and taking their toll in the personal conflicts and strains borne by vast numbers of a society's citizens. Or they can emerge as the source of new political struggles whose consequences will help to determine how long patriarchy can continue to survive under socialism.

25. Once more there is a parallel development within capitalist societies, where contradictions—which cannot be resolved via liberal feminist theory and practice alone—emerge between a male supremacist sex-gender system and the capitalist social order. This is one of the central themes of Eisenstein's interesting study, *Radical Future*.

EPILOG   The Four Modernizations
and the Fate of
Patriarchal-Socialism

The death of Mao Tse-tung in 1976 and the ensuing fall of the
Gang of Four seemed to terminate the revolutionary era in China.
Rapidly the new regime began to propagate development policies
they dubbed the Four Modernizations. To many observers, these
policies appear to repudiate Maoism and destroy whatever was
distinctive in the Chinese model of socialist development. Among
the many rapid changes initiated by the new leadership in post-
Mao China was the first new marriage law in the history of the
People's Republic of China (PRC). These policies raise new questions about the fate of patriarchal-socialism in China and thus
about the utility of the analytic framework presented in this
book. Do events in contemporary China relegate the patriarchal
revolution to the status of a brief, historically anomalous detour
in an inexorable march to a modern conjugal family system?
Does the Four Modernizations program threaten to dismantle
patriarchy in China? The political situation is too uncertain and
the data too scarce for anything but informed speculation regarding
the future of socialism or patriarchy in the PRC.

   This epilog is not a comprehensive analysis of post-Mao China;
it simply tries to interpret key lines of Four Modernizations development strategy within the feminist historical-materialist
framework of this book. I suggest that new contradictions between
patriarchy and socialism may emerge, particularly in the area of
population policy. For the foreseeable future, however, these
contradictions are not likely to lead to a drastic restructuring of

Chinese family life or to provide a more promising basis for the liberation of Chinese women.

Although the Four Modernizations program represents a significant departure from the political ideology and most of the distinctive development policies of the era of the Cultural Revolution, the program is less an historic innovation than a sharp swing towards the right pole of the two basic development strategies that have contested for control in China since the 1950s.[1] After a period of successional instability and the trumpeting of grandiose plans to modernize Chinese society at breakneck speed, the new regime stabilized under the leadership of Teng Hsiao-ping, and modernization goals and policies were moderated. The policy that emerged aims at the balanced growth and modernization of four sectors—agriculture, industry, science and technology, and defense. It is clear, however, that this strategy depends most of all on plans for agricultural development. Agriculture, the weakest link in the Chinese economy, has barely managed to sustain growth rates commensurate with population growth during the past two decades.[2] Yet, it is the only base possible for economic development in China's overwhelmingly agrarian society.

The central goal of the Four Modernizations strategy, therefore, is to achieve a favorable ratio of agricultural productivity to population growth through policies that attack both sides of the production-population equation. One group of policies set the ambitious goal of increasing agricultural growth rates by 4-5 percent for each of the years from 1978 to 1985; another aimed to lower population growth to 1 percent per year by 1980 or 1981.[3] The widespread use of material incentives and sanctions is integral to both sets of policies, and the policies appear at first glance to be compatible.

1. For thoughtful analyses of rural policy under the Four Modernizations, which discuss continuities with Maoist rural development policies, see Victor Lippit, "The People's Communes and China's New Development Strategy," and Peter Nolan and Gordon White, "Distribution and Development in China."

2. It is estimated that both agricultural productivity and population have grown an average of 2-3% per year since the 1950s. See Nai-ruenn Chen, "Economic Modernization in Post-Mao China," p. 20. Chen argues that agriculture is the major bottleneck in the Chinese economy. Lippit agrees ("People's Communes").

3. Chen, "Economic Modernization," p. 201.

Further change in the lives of rural women seems to be the key to the success of both efforts. To raise agricultural productivity, China will have to expand its rural labor force, and women are the obvious source. Likewise, women must reduce their child-bearing if China's enormous population is to stop growing. Thus it would seem that women should be the primary target population of the Four Modernizations and that a feminist strategy could be effective in eliciting their cooperation with production and reproduction goals. The actual policies of the post-Mao era, however, have been less compatible and far less feminist than this logic would indicate. The contradictions in these policies suggest that the patriarchal-socialist order continues to exert constraints upon the development options of the state.

STIMULATING AGRICULTURAL PRODUCTIVITY

Because China's economy is land short and capital short, all PRC development strategies have attempted to substitute the under-utilized labor capacities of its ample population for these deficits. Labor shortages, especially during peak planting and harvesting seasons, continue to limit productivity in the agrarian sector.[4] After a brief euphoric fantasy that rapid mechanization would prove a panacea, post-Mao leadership returned to the sober recognition that manual labor will remain the base of Chinese agricultural production for a considerable period. Wang Keng-chin, vice-director of the Institute of Agricultural Economics in the Chinese Academy of Social Sciences, articulated this realization:

> Our country's agricultural production is currently still based on manual labor. From the national perspective, agricultural mech-anization and modernization are still only in their initial stages and in some areas have not even begun. The modernization of agriculture is not the work of a day and a night; it requires a process of gradual development. At present, in conditions of manual labor and backward means of production, in order to develop agricultural production we must still rely directly on the experience and labor capacity of the laborers.[5]

4. Bill Brugger, "Rural Policy," and Lippit, "People's Communes."
5. Quoted in Nolan and White, "Distribution and Development," p. 8.

At the present stage of development, rural mechanization will do more to expand rather than to contract the need for labor inputs.[6] Estimates of rural female labor participation rates during the 1970s vary, but they all report that childbearing and domestic labor responsibilities cause rural women to contribute significantly fewer years and days to the labor force than their male relatives.[7] The regime could adopt a range of measures that would facilitate participation in agricultural production by rural women. A more egalitarian method of allocating work points to women could help to make their participation in productive labor more valuable to their families than their domestic labor responsibilities. Expansion of rural social services would alleviate some of the formidable practical barriers to wider participation in the labor force by rural women, while renewed ideological campaigns could once more attack patriarchal resistance to female participation in the public domain. All of these measures would rely upon renewing feminist appeals in rural China. However, thus far little evidence exists that the regime is making serious efforts in this direction.

Perhaps this reticence is best explained by the general thrust of the Four Modernizations strategy to intensify the output of the present rural work force. The organizational reforms and material incentives of current rural policy designed to stimulate "peasant enthusiasm" are likely to calcify the structures that

6. Lippit argues that mechanization will have this effect ("People's Communes"). The implications of Thomas G. Rawski's detailed study, *Economic Growth and Employment in China,* are ambiguous on this point. Rawski demonstrates the success of the farming system in absorbing increased labor and machinery inputs simultaneously between 1957 and 1975. He seems to imply, however, that further agricultural mechanization would be likely to reduce the demand for labor.

7. Brugger calculates that in 1979 50% of the adult female population in China formed part of the rural labor force, which, he suggests, leaves some room for expansion ("Rural Policy," p. 145). Rawski, however, estimates that in both 1957 and 1975 "no fewer than 84% of rural females aged from sixteen to fifty years were regularly employed," which, he believes, brought female participation rates, "near their natural limit" (*Economic Growth,* p. 34). While Rawski's estimate may be the more realistic, one must question the concept of a "natural limit." Biological factors are less significant than social ones in explaining why women contribute fewer days and years than men to the collective work force. It is difficult, for example, to provide a sound biological explanation for an earlier retirement age for female laborers. Yet Rawski's calculations are based upon an uncritical acceptance of a retirement age of fifty for rural women, compared with fifty-five for rural men.

sustain rural patriarchy. They reinforce the private aspects of the patriarchal family economy and extend the social and economic domain of male kin and neighborhood-based work groups.

The post-Mao leadership has restored the public legitimacy of the private sector of household production. In its effort simultaneously to raise peasant income and increase national food supplies, the regime has reaffirmed the right of the peasant household to hold and to manage private plots. In some areas households even have been allowed to subcontract cultivation of the production team's collective lands.[8] The regime has granted peasant families loans and access to fodder lands in order to encourage private livestock raising and sideline production. The scope of rural market fairs has been allowed to expand. An explanation of such reforms given to Victor Nee by a brigade secretary in a South China commune demonstrates that building upon and invigorating family production is a deliberate policy: "Because of the strong tradition of individual household production, the closer we can approximate individual household production while still maintaining the collective system of ownership, the higher productivity we can expect to achieve."[9] There are indications the strategy has achieved short-run success, at least. Victor Lippit estimates that in 1979 sideline household productive activities contributed 30–40 *yuan* per year to peasant family income, which was 36-48 percent of the average income peasant families earned from the collective sector.[10]

A second major component of Four Modernizations rural policy involves restoration of the autonomy of production teams from incursions from above. Development policy during the period of the Cultural Revolution had revived the Great Leap Forward goal of a transition from the production team to a higher-level unit of ownership and accounting—the brigade, and ultimately the commune. Although this had been experienced by collectives

---

8. Victor Nee, "Post-Mao Changes in a South China Production Brigade," and Nolan and White, "Distribution and Development."

9. Quoted in Nee, "Post-Mao Changes," p. 33.

10. Lippit, "People's Communes," p. 29. Although Margery Wolf has not yet calculated her data on the profit derived from sideline activities, she estimates the figure will be higher than Nee's—close to 50%, and even more in some areas (personal communication).

more as a threat than as a widespread reality, where successful, the transition had the potential to undercut the authority of local "natural" solidarity groups, which, as we have seen, generally were based upon male kinship relationships. Current policy largely retreats from this goal. Peter Nolan and Gordon White detected a three-tiered policy concerning collective ownership level emerging in 1979–1980. A small minority of relatively affluent "advanced" areas were still being encouraged to move to higher forms of ownership. The vast majority of "average" areas, however, were urged to stabilize production-team ownership of the means of production and distribution. The third tier of "backward" areas was moving in precisely the opposite direction. Production teams were being allowed to subdivide into smaller work groups— occasionally as small as one or two households—that contracted for work on a collective piecework rate basis. These work groups assumed responsibility for a productivity quota on a fixed plot of land and were awarded bonuses or charged penalties when they exceeded or failed to meet their quota.[11]

Although the party did not intend the new policy to sanction the abolition of production teams, there is evidence that this is a frequent side effect of the subcontracting system. The small work groups, whose members are often from the same male lineage, have been able to attain a measure of permanent identity and even to assume many of the functions of the production teams.[12] Consequently collective production has been threatened. In the brigade studied by Victor Nee in 1980, for example, there had been a rash of team fissions since 1978. The number of production teams in the brigade increased from eleven to twenty-one in that period, the smallest of which consisted of seven households. By 1981 collective agriculture had nearly broken down

11. Nolan and White, "Distribution and Development," pp. 13–16. Margery Wolf reports that during her visit to Shensi in 1981, major portions of team land were being assigned on the basis of production quotas to individuals, female as well as male. However, because women were not allowed to plow, men, in fact, managed land assigned to women, and "of course all the work points went into the same family pot at the end of the year anyway, so you will not be surprised to hear that most of these strips were worked by family groups" (personal communication).

12. Brugger, "Rural Policy," p. 161, and Nolan and White, "Distribution and Development," p. 16.

with some teams reduced to a membership of only two house-holds.[13]

In short, a major effect of Four Modernizations effort to increase agricultural productivity has been a partial retreat from patriarchal-socialism to new democratic patriarchy in rural China. The scope of the peasant family economy has expanded, and the domain of local male kinship-based solidarity groups has been strength-ened. Little wonder then that the regime has proven reticent to undertake antipatriarchal campaigns that would facilitate wider participation by women in the collective rural labor force. While present trends continue, rural women will labor increasingly under the supervision and control of their patriarchal families.

POPULATION POLICY AND FAMILY REFORM

What about the second flank of Four Modernizations strategy—curbing population growth? Should feminists find greater cause for optimism there? At first glance, the goals of family limitation appear compatible with women's interests. The regime seemed to link population policy to a new program of family reform when, in September 1980, the National People's Congress adopted the first new marriage law in PRC history, an antinatalist document that includes many provisions with potential feminist implications. Closer scrutiny of the available evidence, however, suggests that Four Modernizations population policy is not likely to advance the prospects for Chinese feminism.

Successional instability in post-Mao China briefly interrupted the serious family planning campaigns of the early 1970s. Soon, however, Four Modernizations strategists elevated family planning to priority status. The official goal of present population policy is to establish a national norm of one child per family. Realism, however, leads the regime tacitly to work for a two-child norm in most rural areas. Efforts to achieve these goals are the most vigorous the Chinese Communists have ever applied. China's new constitution enshrines family planning as a civic respon-sibility. Family planning is also central to and, most likely, the chief motivating force behind the 1981 marriage law, which in-cludes the injunction, "Family planning shall be put into practice."

13. Nee, "Post-Mao Changes," pp. 33–34.

The law raises the legal marriage age to twenty-two for men and to twenty for women and explicitly makes reduced fertility a goal: "Late marriage and late births should be encouraged." Moreover, it links demographic issues to feminist issues by making family planning the duty of both husband and wife.[14]

A recurrent theme in the new marriage law is bilateral rights and responsibilities for both sexes. In most instances, this must be understood as an attempt to extend to women privileges and obligations that conventionally belong to men and their families. Thus the law reaffirms the principle of equal status between the sexes, and specifies that neither spouse may restrict or interfere with the other's right to "free participation in production, work, study, and in social activities."[15] Several articles assume the norm of extended family life, but attempt to shift the norm in a bilineal direction. One article, for example, enjoins couples about to marry to reach mutual agreement over whether to join the family of the husband or the wife. Other articles specify not only that both spouses retain the right to use their own family names but also that children may use the family name of either parent. Both paternal and maternal grandparents are made responsible for the support of orphaned grandchildren; grandchildren, in turn, are obligated to support any set of grandparents whose children are deceased. Daughters as well as sons are responsible for supporting aging parents, and elder sisters as well as elder brothers must support dependent siblings when parents are dead or indigent. Child-support and alimony regulations for divorcing couples are also bilateral. Whereas the provision against interfering with a spouse's public activities seems directed towards facilitating female labor force participation, almost all of the remaining egalitarian principles involve a challenge to patrilineality. Demographic, rather than feminist, concerns are likely the strongest motivation for these measures, which attempt to undermine the social and economic logic of son preference because the preference for sons raises the birth rate.

---

14. The marriage law was adopted by the third session of the Fifth National People's Congress on 10 September 1980, to take effect on 1 January 1981. For a translation, see U.S. Foreign Broadcast Information Service (FBIS), *Daily Report*, 19 September 1980, pp. L22–L26.

15. Ibid., p. L22.

It is possible to view China's new marriage law and population policy as a form of "feminism from above," because they strive to constrict the realm of private patriarchal control over women's productive and reproductive activities. One could find support for this interpretation in the fact that the post-Mao regime formally reconvened the National Women's Federation, which held its Fourth Congress in 1978, at last. But attention to the implementation of these efforts suggests that "above" is far more significant than "feminism" in Four Modernizations policy on women.

First, as Phyllis Andors has observed, the party made instrumental use of the Women's Federation Congress, which was dominated by the old-guard leadership and stressed women's supportive role in the construction of the Four Modernizations.[16] Second, the sex division of labor in the family-planning campaigns institutionalizes this subordinate role. Family-planning committees have been placed under the control of party committees, revolutionary committees, and production units, all of which are generally led by men. Women, however, implement the policy in their roles as women's organization cadres, barefoot doctors, or clinic personnel.[17]

Domination of the state over women's interests is most apparent in the regime's shift to a coercive population policy in the form of material incentives and sanctions. Whereas the material incentives of Four Modernizations rural-production policy generally expand the arena of private initiative, the exact opposite is the case with population policy. Here the state offers incentives to command compliance with its reproduction goals. Population targets and material incentives vary somewhat regionally and locally, but the broad features are similar. Urban residents face strong pressure to conform to the one-child norm. Married couples are pressured to take out "one-child certificates," which pledge their intention not to exceed the norm. They are rewarded for doing so by wage increases, preferential housing assignments, and special consideration for their child in education and job assignments. If a second child is born, these advantages are rescinded, and various sanctions are apt to be applied. Wages

---

16. Phyllis Andors, " 'The Four Modernizations' and Chinese Policy on Women," p. 46.
17. Ibid., p. 52.

may be docked, promotions deferred, maternity leave denied, and grain rations reduced.[18]

Population targets are more flexible in rural areas, but parallel measures for meeting them are applied. For restricting family size to one child, rural families are eligible for additional work points, increased grain rations, and special consideration in the allocation of private plots. The brigade Victor Nee studied offered direct inducements for agreeing to sterilization after the birth of one child—a sewing machine, 30 *yuan*, and 50 *jin* of rice. Couples who did not accept the bargain, however, experienced economic pressure to refrain from having a second child for at least five years. If the woman did not accept an intrauterine device, the birth of the first baby would not be registered, and thus no additional grain ration or free plot was distributed to the family.[19]

In essence these measures combat the economic utility of large families. They are accomplished more easily in the cities, where housing shortages are acute, jobs are scarce, public assistance for the elderly—albeit inadequate—is available, and families still face the threat of losing teenage children to the rural resettlement program.[20] However, in rural areas population policy runs counter to the logic of the patriarchal-socialist family economy. Collectivization eased the burden of additional dependents on individual families, while the family economy embedded within the collectives (and currently being strengthened by Four Modernizations rural policy) makes additional home-grown workers a welcome prospect. Even the antinatalist new marriage law confirms the centrality of children in the social welfare system, and rural areas, as we have seen, rarely provide viable alternatives. Peasant patriarchs, therefore, are beginning to confront a direct contradiction between their individual interests and the preferences and population policies of the state.

---

18. See, for example, U.S. Joint Publication Research Service (JPRS), "One-Child Family Becoming Norm in Beijing West District," *China Report: Political, Sociological and Military Affairs*, no. 192 (18 May 1981), pp. 40–49; idem, "Hainan Planned Parenthood Conference," *China Report*, no. 196 (12 June 1981), pp. 38–39; John S. Aird, "Fertility Decline and Birth Control in the People's Republic of China," p. 244; and Andors, "Four Modernizations," pp. 51–52.

19. Nee, "Post-Mao Changes," p. 36.

20. Post-Mao leadership has modified and contracted the sent-down youth program, but, contrary to the expectations of many, it has not been eliminated. For an interesting discussion of the politics of the program in 1980, see Thomas B. Gold, "Back to the City."

To resolve the contradiction, the regime will be hard pressed to avoid strong-arm methods, because it does not consider population control an expendable policy—unlike the situation with policies to improve women's lives. Not surprisingly, therefore, there is increasing evidence of cadres supplementing economic coercion with direct forms of social control. Birth quotas for local areas seem to be negotiated by national, regional, and local leaders. The local leadership, under political pressure to satisfy these limits, exerts intensive efforts to secure compliance. One frequently cited technique is to post charts that record the reproductive histories of local women and the planned reproduction schedule for the village or neighborhood. The schedule allocates "birth rights" to families on a priority basis under the banner "late, spaced, few." Priority in permission to give birth goes to childless married couples; second, to couples with one older child; and, third, to couples whose single child was born more recently. The charts publicize the number and ages of children in local families, each couple's chosen method of birth control, and the year, if any, in which they have been authorized to have a child.[21]

Cadres from the party and the mass organizations adopt various strategies to persuade local residents to cooperate with such plans. The cadres might visit each couple individually, meet with relatives who object to birth control, and hold mandatory study sessions on population policy. In some areas cadres have conducted meetings in which they urge participants to make collective decisions about allocating local births.[22] Local officials also seem to adopt more authoritarian methods to avoid exceeding local birth quotas. There are indications that involuntary abortions and sterilizations are being imposed on transgressing women and even, occasionally, on men. In the brigade Nee studied, for example, couples had to apply to the commune administration for permission to remove an intrauterine device. After the second birth in a family, one spouse was required to agree to sterilization or the couple had to contract to abort unauthorized pregnancies that might occur.[23] Other examples come directly from the Chinese media, which has publicized punishments meted out to couples

21. See, for example, JPRS, "Hainan Conference"; idem, "One-Child Family"; Aird, "Fertility Decline"; and Elisabeth Croll, "Women in Rural Development," pp. 43–44.

22. Croll, "Women in Rural Development," pp. 43–44.

23. Nee, "Post-Mao Changes," p. 36.

who have violated family-planning restrictions. One such case involved a couple in Kuei-chou who had a third child. As punishment the couple had their salaries reduced, the mother lost her position as deputy head of a county people's court, and the *father* was ordered to be sterilized.[24]

Coerciveness of current efforts to reduce population growth must be judged within the context of the urgency of China's population problem. Certainly this is an area in which the interests of society and those of individuals and families can be at odds. It is also likely that many Chinese women privately welcome the family-limitation campaign as public support for their own desire to limit their childbearing against the wishes of husband and in-laws. However, women of childbearing age typically bear the brunt of this conflict between regime and family goals. According to Margery Wolf, women in the countryside are still blamed if their two-pregnancy quota fails to produce a son. Then they are caught in the cross fire between public pressure to obey the family-limitation rules and private pressure to evade them.[25] Four Modernizations population policy is far less an advance for women than a shift of patriarchal power from private to public hands.

Family structure and gender relationships could shift dramatically if the one-child norm were to succeed in the countryside. A one-child family system could level a serious challenge to patrilineality by making parents as dependent upon their daughters as their sons. Were all families to have only one child, marriage would set up a competition between the couple's two sets of parents for the loyalty and support of their progeny. This could significantly raise the family status of daughters and dissolve the patrilocal marriage system. However, the preexisting patrilineal principle might bias the resolution of such conflicts in favor of the parents of sons. Thus it is conceivable that a rather arbitrary two-class system could emerge in rural China (composed of families with and those without sons). In either situation, the one-child family would shift an enormous social welfare responsibility from familial to public hands.

---

24. "Quarterly Chronicle and Documentation," *China Quarterly*, no. 83 (September 1980), p. 619.
25. Margery Wolf (personal communication).

Neither scenario is likely to materialize. Peasant patriarchs are not likely to accept, nor the regime to impose, the severe social dislocations of a one-child family system. A two-child norm seems feasible, and this would tend to weaken—but not destroy—the patrilineal base of rural family structure.

It seems reasonable to predict that the terms of patriarchal-socialism in China will continue to oscillate in the years ahead, but without a major overhaul of family structure or gender relationships. The contradictory aspects of Four Modernizations development strategy must be resolved in the context of the entrenched patriarchal base of the rural economy. Thus, feminist initiatives from above are likely to be tepid. The relative quiescence of the Chinese press on women's issues during the past few years lends support to this view. From a feminist perspective, perhaps this is just as well. Although it offers little to women, at least it avoids the identification of women's liberation with state coercion that could enable patriarchal resistance to assume, once again, the appearance of a progressive and democratic force.[26] Genuine progress towards the liberation of women—in China, as elsewhere—will depend most of all on antipatriarchal efforts by feminists on their own behalf. There are few signs of such activity in post-Mao China.

---

26. Current events in Iran suggest that such a popular equation can be extremely harmful to women. Because certain reforms concerned with women's rights were enacted during the regime of the popularly detested modernizing Shah Pahlavi, women's rights, modernization, and imperialism came to assume a negative identity among the mullahs and religious masses of Iran's Islamic revolution. The new regime has rescinded the shah's reforms and reaffirmed patriarchal order. There are indications that "modern" Iranian women have been subjected to sexual and physical brutality for offending the patriarchal mores of the Islamic revolution. See, for example, "New Iran Executions Defy Premier's Order," *San Francisco Chronicle* (12 March 1979); "Three Madams Executed in Iran," *San Francisco Chronicle* (14 July 1979); and "Khomeni Government Plans Trial for Shah and His Family," *San Francisco Chronicle* (7 March 1979). Underground pamphlets, such as one prepared by Etehad-e Meli-e Zanan, (National Unity of Women), which identifies itself as a democratic women's organization established in March 1979 "to fight for social democracy and equal rights for women," report torture and rape of imprisoned teenagers, gang rapes of opposition girls, public undressings and beatings of girls, and other brutal forms of patriarchal justice administered by revolutionary guards in Iran.

BIBLIOGRAPHY

Adorno, Theodore W.; Frenkel-Brunswik, Else; Levinson, Daniel J.; and Sanford, R. Nevitt. *The Authoritarian Personality*. New York: Harper & Brothers, 1950.

Agrarian Reform Law of the People's Republic of China and Other Relevant Documents. 4th ed. Peking: Foreign Languages Press, 1952.

Aird, John S. "Fertility Decline and Birth Control in the People's Republic of China." *Population and Development Review* 4, no. 2 (June 1978):225–53.

————. *Population Policy and Demographic Prospects in the People's Republic of China*. Washington, D.C.: National Institute of Health, Center for Population Research, 1972.

Alexander, Sally, and Taylor, Barbara. "In Defense of 'Patriarchy.' " *New Statesman*, 1 February 1980, p. 161.

Amin, Samir. *Unequal Development: An Essay on the Social Formations of Peripheral Capitalism*. New York: Monthly Review Press, 1976.

Anderson, Michael. *Family Structure in Nineteenth-Century Lancashire*. Cambridge: Cambridge University Press, 1972.

Anderson, Perry. *Lineages of the Absolutist State*. London: New Left Books, 1974.

Andors, Phyllis. " 'The Four Modernizations' and Chinese Policy on Women." *Bulletin of Concerned Asian Scholars* 13, no. 2 (April-June 1981):44–56.

————. "Politics of Chinese Development: The Case of Women, 1960–1966." *Signs* 2, no. 1 (Autumn 1976):89–119.

————. "Social Revolution and Women's Emancipation: China During the Great Leap Forward." *Bulletin of Concerned Asian Scholars* 7, no. 1 (January-March 1975):33–42.

Bane, Mary Jo. *Here to Stay: American Families in the Twentieth Century*. New York: Basic Books, 1976.

Barrett, Michele. *Women's Oppression Today: Problems in Marxist Feminist Analysis*. London: Verso, 1980.

Bástid-Bruguiere, Marianne. "Currents of Social Change." In *The Cambridge History of China: Late Ch'ing, 1800–1911*, edited by John K.

Fairbank and Kwang-Ching Liu. Vol. 11, pt. 2. Cambridge: Cambridge University Press, 1980.

Beahan, Charlotte. "Feminism and Nationalism in the Chinese Women's Press, 1902–1911." *Modern China* 1, no. 4 (October 1975):379–416.

Beauvoir, Simone de. *The Long March*. Cleveland: World Publishing Company, 1958.

Beechey, Veronica. "On Patriarchy." *Feminist Review* 1, no. 3 (1979):66–82.

Belden, Jack. *China Shakes the World*. New York: Monthly Review Press, 1970.

Bell, Lynda Schaefer. "Agricultural Laborers and Rural Revolution." In *Chinese Communists and Rural Society, 1927–1934*, by Philip C. C. Huang, Lynda Schaefer Bell, and Kathy Lemmons Walker. China Research Monographs, no. 13. Berkeley: Center for Chinese Studies, 1978.

Bell, Norman W., and Vogel, Ezra F. *A Modern Introduction to the Family*. New York: Free Press, 1961.

Benet, Sula. *The Village of Viriatino*. Garden City, N.Y.: Anchor Books, 1970.

Bengelsdorf, Carolee, and Hageman, Alice. "Emerging from Underdevelopment: Women and Work in Cuba." In *Capitalist Patriarchy and the Case for Socialist-Feminism*, edited by Zillah R. Eisenstein. New York: Monthly Review Press, 1979.

Benton, Gregor. "The Yenan Literacy Opposition." *New Left Review*, no. 92 (July-August 1975), pp. 93–106.

Berger, John. "Towards Understanding Peasant Experience." *Race and Class* 19, no. 4 (Spring 1978):345–59.

Berkin, Carol R., and Lovett, Clara M. *Women, War and Revolution*. New York: Holmes & Meier Publishers, 1980.

Bernstein, Thomas P. "Leadership and Mass Mobilization in the Soviet and Chinese Collectivization Campaigns of 1929–1930 and 1955–1956: A Comparison." *China Quarterly*, no. 31 (July-September 1967), pp. 1–47.

————. *Up to the Mountains and Down to the Villages: The Transfer of Youth from Urban to Rural China*. New Haven: Yale University Press, 1977.

Bianco, Lucien. *Origins of the Chinese Revolution, 1915–1949*. Stanford: Stanford University Press, 1971.

Bodde, Derk, and Morris, Clarence. *Law in Imperial China.* Cambridge: Harvard University Press, 1967.

Boserup, Ester. *Woman's Role in Economic Development.* London: George Allen & Unwin, 1970.

Breines, Wini; Cerullo, Margaret; and Stacey, Judith. "Social Biology, Family Studies and Anti-Feminist Backlash." *Feminist Studies* 4, no. 1 (February 1978):43–67.

Brinton, Crane. *French Revolutionary Legislation on Illegitimacy, 1789–1804.* Cambridge: Harvard University Press, 1936.

Broyelle, Claudie. *Women's Liberation in China.* Translated by Michele Cohen and Gary Herman. Atlantic Highlands, N.J.: Humanities Press, 1977.

Broyelle, Claudie; Broyelle, Jacques; and Tschirhart, Evelyne. *China, A Second Look.* Translated by Sarah Matthews. Atlantic Highlands, N.J.: Humanities Press, 1980.

Brugger, Bill. "Rural Policy." In *China Since the "Gang of Four,"* edited by Bill Brugger. New York: St. Martin's Press, 1980.

Buck, John Lossing. *Land Utilization in China.* 1937. Reprint. New York: Council on Economic and Cultural Affairs, 1956.

Buck, Pearl S. *Of Men and Women.* New York: John Day, 1941.

Burgess, Ernest W., and Locke, Harvey J. *The Family: From Institution to Companionship.* New York: American Book, 1953.

Butterfield, Fox. "Love and Sex in China." *New York Times Magazine,* 13 January 1980, p. 15.

Cameron, Meribeth E. *The Reform Movement in China, 1898–1912.* 1931. Reprint. New York: Octagon Books, 1963.

Carr, Edward H. *The October Revolution: Before and After.* New York: Vintage, 1969.

Casal, Lourdes. "Revolution and Conciencia: Women in Cuba." In *Women, War, and Revolution,* edited by Carol R. Berkin and Clara M. Lovett. New York: Holmes & Meier Publishers, 1980.

Caulfield, Mina. "Imperialism, the Family, and Cultures of Resistance." *Socialist Revolution,* no. 20 (October 1974), pp. 67–86.

Chai, Ch'u, and Chai, Winberg. *The Changing Society of China.* New York: New American Library, 1962.

Chang, Chung-li. *The Chinese Gentry: Studies on Their Role in Nineteenth-Century Chinese Society*. Seattle: University of Washington Press, 1955.

Chang, Kuo-t'ao. *The Rise of the Chinese Communist Party, 1929–1938*. Vol. 2. Lawrence: University Press of Kansas, 1972.

Chao Kuo-chün. *Agrarian Policy of the Chinese Communist Party, 1921–1959*. Bombay: Asia Publishing House, 1960.

Chao, Paul. "The Marxist Doctrine and the Recent Development of the Chinese Family in Communist China." *Journal of Asian and African Studies* 2 (1967):161–73.

Chen Han-seng. *Landlord and Peasant in China: A Study of the Agrarian Crisis in South China*. New York: International Publishers, 1936.

Chen, Jack. *New Earth: How the Peasants in One Chinese Country Solved the Problem of Poverty*. Peking: New World Press, 1957.

———. *A Year in Upper Felicity: Life in a Chinese Village during the Cultural Revolution*. New York: Macmillan Press, 1973.

Chen, Nai-ruenn. "Economic Modernization in Post-Mao China: Policies, Problems and Prospects." In *Chinese Economy Post-Mao*. Vol. 1. U.S. Congress, Joint Economic Committee, 95th Cong., 2d sess., November 1975.

Chen, Ta. *Emigrant Communities in South China: A Study of Overseas Migration and Its Influence on Standards of Living and Social Change*. New York: Institute of Pacific Relations, 1940.

Chen, Theodore Hsi-en, and Chen, Wen-hui C. "Changing Attitudes Toward Parents in Communist China." *Sociology and Social Research* 43, no. 3 (January–February 1959):175–82.

Chen, Yuan-tsung. *The Dragon's Village*. New York: Pantheon Books, 1980.

Chen, Yung-fa. "The Making of a Revolution: The Communist Movement in Eastern and Central China, 1937–1945." Ph.D. dissertation, Stanford University, 1980.

Chesneaux, Jean. *China: The People's Republic, 1949–1976*. Translated by Paul Auster and Lydia Davis. New York: Pantheon Books, 1979.

———. *Peasant Revolts in China, 1840–1949*. Translated by C. A. Curwan. New York: W. W. Norton & Co., 1973.

Ch'i, Hsi-sheng. *Warlord Politics in China, 1916–1928*. Stanford: Stanford University Press, 1976.

Chin, Ai-li S. "Family Relations in Modern Chinese Fiction." In *Family and Kinship in Chinese Society*, edited by Maurice Freedman. Stanford: Stanford University Press, 1970.

Chinn, Dennis L. "Basic Commodity Distribution in the People's Republic of China." *The China Quarterly* 84 (December 1980):744–54.

Chodorow, Nancy. *The Reproduction of Mothering: Psychoanalysis and the Sociology of Gender*. Berkeley and Los Angeles: University of California Press, 1978.

Christ, Carol. "Why Women Need the Goddess." *Heresies: A Feminist Publication on Art and Politics*, no. 5 (Spring 1978), pp. 8–13.

Ch'ü, T'ung-tsu. *Law and Society in Traditional China*. Paris: Mouton & Co., 1961.

Clawson, Mary Ann. "Early Modern Fraternalism and the Patriarchal Family." *Feminist Studies* 6, no. 2 (Summer 1980):368–91.

Clubb, O. Edmund. *Twentieth-Century China*. New York: Columbia University Press, 1964.

Cohen, Charlotte Bonnig. "Experiment in Freedom: Women of China." In *Sisterhood Is Powerful: An Anthology of Writings from the Women's Liberation Movement*, edited by Robin Morgan. New York: Vintage, 1970.

Cohen, Jerome Alan. "Chinese Mediation on the Eve of Modernization." *Journal of Asian and African Studies* 11, nos. 1–2 (January-April 1967):54–71.

Cohen, Myron L. "Developmental Process in the Chinese Domestic Group." In *Family and Kinship in Chinese Society*, edited by Maurice Freedman. Stanford: Stanford University Press, 1970.

———. *House United, House Divided: The Chinese Family in Taiwan*. New York: Columbia University Press, 1976.

Colegrave, Suki. "Chinese Women." *Spare Rib*, August 1976, pp. 44–47.

Collier, Jane; Rosaldo, Michelle Z.; and Yanagisako, Sylvia. "Is There a Family? New Anthropological Views." In *Rethinking the Family: Some Feminist Questions*, edited by Barrie Thorne with Marilyn Yalom. New York: Longman, 1982.

Coser, Lewis A. "Some Aspects of Soviet Family Policy." *American Journal of Sociology* 56 (1951):424–34.

Coser, Rose Laub, ed. *The Family: Its Structure and Functions.* New York: St. Martin's Press, 1964.

Coser, Rose L., and Coser, Lewis A. "The Principles of Legitimacy and Its Patterned Infringement in Social Revolutions." In *Cross-National Family Research,* edited by Marvin B. Sussman and Betty E. Cogswell. Leiden: E. J. Brill, 1972.

Couling, Samuel. *The Encyclopaedia Sinica.* London: Oxford University Press, 1917.

Croll, Elisabeth. *Feminism and Socialism in China.* London: Routledge & Kegan Paul, 1978.

———. "The Movement to Criticize Confucius and Lin Piao." *Signs* 2, no. 3 (Spring 1977):721–26.

———. *The Politics of Marriage in Contemporary China.* Cambridge: Cambridge University Press, 1981.

———. "Social Production and Female Status: Women in China." *Race and Class* 18 (Summer 1976):39–51.

———. "Women in Rural Development: The People's Republic of China." Mimeographed. Geneva: International Labour Office, 1979.

———. ed. *The Women's Movement in China: A Selection of Readings, 1949–1973.* Modern China Series, no. 6. London: Anglo-Chinese Educational Institute, 1974.

Crook, Isabel, and Crook, David. *The First Years of Yangyi Commune.* London: Routledge & Kegan Paul, 1966.

———. *Revolution in a Chinese Village: Ten Mile Inn.* London: Routledge & Kegan Paul, 1959.

Curtin, Katie. "Women and the Chinese Revolution." *International Socialist Review* 35, no. 3 (March 1974): 8–11, 25–40.

Davin, Delia. *Woman-Work: Women and the Party in Revolutionary China.* Oxford: Clarendon Press, 1976.

———. "Women in the Liberated Areas." In *Women in China: Studies in Social Change and Feminism,* edited by Marilyn B. Young. Michigan Papers in Chinese Studies, no. 15. Ann Arbor: Center for Chinese Studies, 1973.

Davis-Friedmann, Deborah. *Long Life: Aging and Old Age in the People's Republic of China.* Cambridge: Harvard University Press, forthcoming.

Diamond, Norma. "Collectivization, Kinship, and the Status of Women in Rural China." *Bulletin of Concerned Asian Scholars* 7, no. 1 (January-March 1975):25–32.

———. "The Status of Women in Taiwan: One Step Forward, Two Steps Back." In *Women in China: Studies in Social Change and Feminism*, edited by Marilyn B. Young. Michigan Papers in Chinese Studies, no. 15. Ann Arbor: Center for Chinese Studies, 1973.

Dorris, Carl E. "People's War in North China: Resistance in the Shansi-Chahar-Hopeh Border Region, 1938–1945." Ph.D. dissertation, University of California, Berkeley, 1975.

Duggett, Michael. "Marx on Peasants." *Journal of Peasant Studies* 2, no. 2 (January 1975):159–82.

Dunham, Vera S. "Sex: From Free Love to Puritanism." In *Soviet Society: A Book of Readings*, edited by Alex Inkeles and Kent Geiger. Boston: Houghton Mifflin Co., 1961.

Eastman, Lloyd E. *The Abortive Revolution. China Under Nationalist Rule, 1927–1937*. Cambridge: Harvard University Press, 1974.

Easton, Barbara. "Feminism and the Contemporary Family." *Socialist Review*, no. 39 (May-June 1978), pp. 11–36.

Eberhard, Wolfram. "Research on the Chinese Family." *Settlement and Social Change in Asia*. Hong Kong: Hong Kong University Press, 1967.

———. "Social Mobility and Stratification in China." In *Class, Status and Power*, edited by Reinhard Bendix and Seymour Martin Lipset. 2d ed. New York: Free Press, 1966.

———. "The Upper-Class Family in Traditional China." In *The Family in History*, edited by Charles E. Rosenberg. Philadelphia: University of Pennsylvania Press, 1975.

Eckstein, Alexander. "The Chinese Development Model." In *Chinese Economy Post-Mao*. Vol. 1. U.S. Congress, Joint Economic Committee, 95th Cong., 2d sess., November 1975.

Ehrenreich, Barbara, and English, Dierdre. *For Her Own Good: 150 Years of the Experts' Advice to Women*. New York: Doubleday, 1978.

Eisenstein, Zillah. *The Radical Future of Liberal Feminism*. New York: Longman, 1981.

———, ed. *Capitalist Patriarchy and the Case for Socialist Feminism*. New York: Monthly Review Press, 1979.

Engels, Friedrich. "Communist Credo." In *Birth of the Communist Manifesto*, edited by Dirk Struik. 1847. Reprint. New York: International Publishers, 1971.

———. *The Origin of the Family, Private Property and the State*. New York: International Publishers, 1972.

Epstein, Israel. *The People's War*. London: Victor Gollancz, 1939.

Esherick, Joseph W. *Reform and Revolution in China: The 1911 Revolution in Hunan and Hubei*. Berkeley and Los Angeles: University of California Press, 1976.

Fairbank, John King. *The United States and China*. 1948. Reprint 8th ed. Cambridge: Harvard University Press, 1972.

Farnsworth, Beatrice Brodsky. "Communist Feminism: Its Synthesis and Demise." In *Women, War, and Revolution*, edited by Carol A. Berkin and Clara M. Lovett. New York: Holmes & Meier Publishers, 1980.

Fee, Elizabeth. "The Sexual Politics of Victorian Social Anthropology." *Feminist Studies* 1, nos. 3–4 (Winter-Spring 1973):23–29.

Fei, Hsiao-tung. *China's Gentry: Essays in Rural-Urban Relations*. Edited by Robert Redfield and Mary Redfield. Chicago: University of Chicago Press, 1953.

———. *Peasant Life in China: A Field Study of Country Life in the Yangtze Valley*. London: Routledge & Kegan Paul, 1939.

Fei, Hsiao-tung, and Chang, Chih-i. *Earthbound China: A Study of Rural Economy in Yunnan*. Chicago: University of Chicago Press, 1945.

Feuerwerker, Albert. *The Chinese Economy, 1912–1949*. Michigan Papers in Chinese Studies, no. 1. Ann Arbor: Center for Chinese Studies, 1968.

———. *The Chinese Economy, 1870–1911*. Michigan Papers in Chinese Studies, no. 5. Ann Arbor: Center for Chinese Studies, 1968.

Feuerwerker, Yi-tsi. "Ting Ling's 'When I Was in Sha Chuan (Cloud Village),' " *Signs* 2, no. 1 (Autumn 1976):255–79.

Fitzgerald, C. P. *The Birth of Communist China*. Baltimore: Penguin Books, 1964.

Flandrin, Jean-Louis. *Families in Former Times: Kinship, Household, and Sexuality*. Translated by Richard Southern. Cambridge: Cambridge University Press, 1979.

Freedman, Maurice. *Chinese Lineage and Society: Fukien and Kwangtung.* New York: Humanities Press, 1966.

———. "The Family in China, Past and Present." In *Modern China,* edited by Albert Feuerwerker. Englewood Cliffs, N.J.: Prentice-Hall, 1964.

———. *Lineage Organization in Southeastern China.* London: The Athlone Press, 1958.

———, ed. *Family and Kinship in Chinese Society.* Stanford: Stanford University Press, 1970.

Frenier, Mariam Darce. "Women and the Chinese Communist Land Reform, 1946–1952." Mimeographed. Morris, Minn.: University of Minnesota, 1978.

Fried, Morton H. *Fabric of Chinese Society: A Study of Social Life in a Chinese County Seat.* New York: Octagon, 1969.

———. "Trends in Chinese Domestic Organization." In *Symposium on Economic and Social Problems of the Far East,* edited by E. F. Szczepanik. Hong Kong: Hong Kong University Press, 1962.

Friedman, Edward. *Backward Toward Revolution: The Chinese Revolutionary Party.* Berkeley and Los Angeles: University of California Press, 1974.

———. "Engels' Peasant War in Germany." *Journal of Peasant Studies* 3, no. 1 (October 1975):117–23.

———. "Power and Progress in Revolutionizing China." *Journal of Asian and African Studies* 1, no. 2 (April 1966), 118–28.

Frolic, B. Michael. *Mao's People: Sixteen Portraits of Life in Revolutionary China.* Cambridge: Harvard University Press, 1980.

Fung, Yu-lan. "The Philosophy at the Basis of Traditional Chinese Society." In *Ideological Differences and World Order,* edited by F. S. C. Northrup. New Haven: Yale University Press, 1963.

Furth, Charlotte. "The Transformations of Time: Intellectual Change in China from the Reform Movement to the May Fourth Movement." In *The Cambridge History of China: The Republic, 1912–1948,* edited by John K. Fairbank. Vol. 12, pt. 1. Cambridge: Cambridge University Press, forthcoming.

Gamble, Sidney D. *North China Villages: Social, Political, and Economic Activities Before 1933.* Berkeley and Los Angeles: University of California Press, 1963.

———. *Ting Hsien: A North China Rural Community.* 1954. Reprint. Stanford: Stanford University Press, 1968.

Geiger, Kent. "Changing Political Attitudes in a Totalitarian Society: A Case Study of the Role of the Family." In *A Modern Introduction to the Family,* edited by Norman W. Bell and Ezra F. Vogel. New York: Free Press, 1961.

———. *The Family in Soviet Russia.* Cambridge: Harvard University Press, 1968.

Genovese, Eugene. *Roll, Jordan, Roll: The World the Slaves Made.* New York: Pantheon, 1974.

Gillin, Donald G. "Peasant Nationalism in the History of Chinese Communism." *Journal of Asian Studies* 23, no. 2 (February 1964):269–89.

Gold, Thomas B. "Back to the City: The Return of Shanghai's Educated Youth." *China Quarterly* 84 (December 1980):755–70.

Goldman, Merle. *Literary Dissent in Communist China.* Cambridge: Harvard University Press, 1967.

Goode, William J. "Family and Mobility." In *Class, Status and Power,* edited by Reinhard Bendix and Seymour Martin Lipset. New York: Free Press, 1966.

———. *World Revolution and Family Patterns.* New York: Glencoe Free Press, 1963.

Goodstadt, Leo F. "Official Targets, Data, and Policies for China's Population Growth: An Assessment." *Population and Development Review* 4, no. 2 (June 1978):255–75.

Goody, Jack. *Production and Reproduction: A Comparative Study of the Domestic Domain.* Cambridge: Cambridge University Press, 1976.

Goody, Jack, and Tambiah, S. J. *Bridewealth and Dowry.* Cambridge: Cambridge University Press, 1973.

Gordon, Linda. "The Fourth Mountain." *Working Papers* 1, no. 3 (Fall 1973):27–39.

Gouldner, Alvin. *The Coming Crisis of Western Sociology.* New York: Basic Books, 1977.

———. "The Two Marxisms." *For Sociology: Renewal and Critique in Sociology Today.* New York: Basic Books, 1973.

Graham, Ruth. "Loaves and Liberty: Women in the French Revolution." In *Becoming Visible: Women in European History,* edited by Renate Bridenthal and Claudia Koonz. Boston: Houghton Mifflin Co., 1977.

Greene, Felix. "A Divorce Trial in China." Pamphlet. Boston: New England Free Press, n.d.

Greenfield, Sidney. "Industrialization and the Family in Social Theory." *American Journal of Sociology* 67 (1961–1962):312–22.

Grove, Linda Ann. "Rural Society in Revolution: The Gaoyang District, 1910–1947." Ph.D. dissertation, University of California, Berkeley, 1975.

Gutman, Herbert G. *The Black Family in Slavery and Freedom, 1750–1925.* New York: Pantheon, 1976.

Hamilton, Gary. "Patriarchy, Patrimonialism, and Structures of Orthodoxy: An Appreciative Revision of Max Weber." Paper read at American Council of Learned Societies-National Endowment for the Humanities Conference on Orthodoxy and Heterodoxy in Late Imperial China, 20–26 August 1981, Montecito, California.

Han Suyin. *The Crippled Tree.* New York: Bantam, 1972.

————. *A Mortal Flower.* New York: Bantam, 1972.

————. "Population Growth and Birth Control in China." *Eastern Horizon* 12, no. 5 (1973):8–16.

Hareven, Tamara. "Family Time and Historical Time." *Daedalus,* Spring 1977, pp. 57–70.

————. "Family Time and Industrial Time: Family and Work in a Planned Corporation Town, 1900–1924." *Journal of Urban History* 1 (1975):365–89.

————. "Modernization and Family History: Perspectives on Social Change." *Signs* 2, no. 1 (August 1976):190–206.

Hareven, Tamara, and Modell, John. "Urbanization and the Malleable Household: An Examination of Boarding and Lodging in American Families." *Journal of Marriage and the Family* 35 (August 1973):467–78.

Harris, Barbara J. "Recent Work on the History of the Family: A Review Article." *Feminist Studies* 3, nos. 3-4 (Spring-Summer 1976):150–78.

Harrison, James Pinckney. *The Long March to Power: A History of the Chinese Communist Party, 1921–1927.* New York: Praeger, 1972.

Hartmann, Heidi I. "The Family as the Locus of Gender, Class, and Political Struggle: The Example of Housework." *Signs* 6, no. 3 (Spring 1981):366–94.

———. "The Unhappy Marriage of Marxism and Feminism: Towards a More Progressive Union." In *Women and Revolution*, edited by Lydia Sargent. Boston: South End Press, 1981.

Hearn, Frank. *Domination, Legitimation, and Resistance: The Incorporation of the Nineteenth-Century English Working Class*. Westport, Conn.: Greenwood Press, 1978.

———. "Remembrance and Critique: The Uses of the Past for Discrediting the Present and Anticipating the Future." *Politics and Society* 5, no. 2 (1975):201–27.

Heitlinger, Alena. *Women and State Socialism: Sex Inequality in the Soviet Union and Czechoslovakia*. Montreal: McGill-Queen's University Press, 1979.

Hinton, William. *Fanshen: A Documentary of Revolution in a Chinese Village*. New York: Vintage, 1966.

Ho, Ping-ti. *Studies on the Population of China, 1368–1953*. Cambridge: Harvard University Press, 1959.

Hobsbawm, Eric J. "Peasants and Politics." *Journal of Peasant Studies* 1, no. 1 (October 1973):3–22.

Hofheinz, Roy, Jr. *The Broken Wave: The Chinese Communist Peasant Movement, 1922–1928*. Cambridge: Harvard University Press, 1977.

———. "The Ecology of Chinese Communist Success: Rural Influence Patterns, 1923–1945." In *Chinese Communist Politics in Action*, edited by A. Doak Barnett. Seattle: University of Washington Press, 1969.

Horkheimer, Max. "Authority and the Family." *Critical Theory*. Translated by Matthew J. O'Connell. New York: Herder & Herder, 1972.

Hsiao Ching, The. Translated by Mary Lelia Makra. New York: St. John's University Press, 1970.

Hsiao, Kung-chuan. *Rural China: Imperial Control in the Nineteenth Century*. Seattle: University of Washington Press, 1960.

Hsu, Francis L. K. *Under the Ancestors' Shadow: Chinese Culture and Personality*. New York: Columbia University Press, 1948.

Hu Chi-hsi. "The Sexual Revolution in the Kiangsi Soviet." *China Quarterly* 59 (July-September 1974):477–90.

Huang, Philip C. C. "Mao Tse-tung and the Middle Peasants, 1925–28." *Modern China* 1, no. 3 (July 1975):271–96.

Huang, Philip C. C.; Bell, Lynda Schaefer; and Walker, Kathy Lemmons. *Chinese Communists and Rural Society, 1927–1934*. China Research Monographs, no. 13. Berkeley: Center for Chinese Studies, 1978.

Inkeles, Alex. *Social Change in Soviet Russia*. Cambridge: Harvard University Press, 1968.

Isaacs, Harold R. *The Tragedy of the Chinese Revolution*. 1938. Reprint. Stanford: Stanford University Press, 1951.

Jancar, Barbara W. "Women's Lot in Communist Societies." *Problems of Communism*. November-December 1976, pp. 68–73.

Jing Su and Luo Lun. *Landlord and Labor in Late Imperial China: Case Studies from Shandong*. Translated and with an Introduction by Endymion Wilkinson. Cambridge: Harvard University Press, 1978.

Johnson, Chalmers. *Peasant Nationalism and Communist Power: The Emergence of Revolutionary China*. Stanford: Stanford University Press, 1962.

Johnson, Kay. "Feminism and Socialist Revolution in China: The Politics of Women's Rights and Family Reform." Ph.D. dissertation, University of Wisconsin, Madison, 1977.

———. "Women in China: Problems of Sex Inequality and Socioeconomic Change." In *Beyond Intellectual Sexism*, edited by Joan J. Roberts. New York: David McKay Co., 1976.

Karol, K. S. *China: The Other Communism*. New York: Hill & Wang, 1967.

Kenniston, Kenneth. *All Our Children: The American Family Under Pressure*. New York: Harcourt Brace Jovanovich, 1977.

Kerblay, Basile. "Chayanov and the Theory of Peasantry as a Specific Type of Economy." In *Peasants and Peasant Societies*, edited by Teodor Shanin. Harmondsworth, England: Penguin, 1971.

Kessen, William, ed. *Childhood in China*. New Haven: Yale University Press, 1975.

Kim, Ilpyong J. "Mass Mobilization Policies and Techniques Developed in the Period of the Chinese Soviet Republic." In *Chinese Communist Politics in Action*, edited by A. Doak Barnett. Seattle: University of Washington Press, 1969.

———. *The Politics of Chinese Communism: Kiangsi Under the Soviets*. Berkeley and Los Angeles: University of California Press, 1973.

Kingston, Maxine Hong. *The Woman Warrior: Memoirs of a Girlhood Among Ghosts*. New York: Alfred A. Knopf, 1976.

Kracke, E. A., Jr. "Family vs. Merit in Chinese Civil Service Examinations Under the Empire." *Harvard Journal of Asiatic Studies* 10 (1947):103–23.

Kristeva, Julia. *About Chinese Women*. London: Marion Boyars, 1977.

Kuhn, Annette, and Wolpe, Anne Marie. *Feminism and Materialism: Women and Modes of Production*. London: Routledge & Kegan Paul, 1978.

Kuhn, Philip A. "Local Self-Government Under the Republic: Problems of Control, Autonomy and Mobilization." In *Conflict and Control in Late Imperial China*, edited by Frederic Wakeman, Jr., and Carolyn Grant. Berkeley and Los Angeles: University of California Press, 1975.

Lang, Olga. *Chinese Family and Society*. New Haven: Yale University Press, 1946.

Lapidus, Gail W. "Changing Women's Roles in the U.S.S.R." In *Women in the World: A Comparative Study*, edited by Lynne B. Iglitzin and Ruth Ross. Santa Barbara, Calif.: Clio Books, 1976.

————. *Women in Soviet Society: Equality, Development, and Social Change*. Berkeley and Los Angeles: University of California Press, 1978.

Lasch, Christopher. *Haven in a Heartless World: The Family Besieged*. New York: Basic Books, 1977.

Laslett, Peter. "The Comparative History of Household and Family." In *The American Family in Social-Historical Perspective*, edited by Michael Gordon. New York: St. Martin's Press, 1973.

————. "The Family and the Collectivity." *Sociology and Social Research* 63, no. 3 (April 1979):432–42.

Laslett, Peter, and Wallis, Richard, eds. *Family and Household in Past Time*. Cambridge: Cambridge University Press, 1972.

Leader, Shelah. "Development and Women: A Case Study." Paper read at Conference on Women and Development, April 1976, Wellesley College. Mimeographed.

Lee, Sarel. "Subterranean Individualism: Contradictions of Politization." *Telos*, no. 33 (Fall 1977), pp. 5–25.

Leith, Suzette. "Chinese Women in the Early Communist Movement." In *Women in China: Studies in Social Change and Feminism*, edited by Marilyn B. Young. Michigan Papers in Chinese Studies, no. 15. Ann Arbor: Center for Chinese Studies, 1973.

Lévi-Strauss, Claude. "The Family." In *Family in Transition*, edited by Arlene S. Skolnick and Jerome H. Skolnick. Boston: Little, Brown, 1971.

Levy, Howard S. *Chinese Footbinding: The History of a Curious Erotic Custom*. New York: Walton Rawls, 1966.

Levy, Marion J. "Aspects of the Analysis of Family Structure." In *Aspects of the Analysis of Family Structure*, edited by Anley S. Coale. Princeton: Princeton University Press, 1965.

————. *The Family Revolution in Modern China*. 1949. Reprint. New York: Octagon, 1971.

Lewis, John Wilson, ed. *Peasant Rebellion and Communist Revolution in Asia*. Stanford: Stanford University Press, 1974.

Liang, Yen. *The House of the Golden Dragons*. London: Souvenir Press, 1961.

Lin, Yu-tang. *My Country and My People*. New York: Reynal and Hitchcock, 1937.

Lippit, Victor D. "The People's Commune and China's New Development Strategy." *Bulletin of Concerned Asian Scholars* 13, no. 2 (1981):19–30.

————. "The Transition to Socialism in China." Paper read at California Regional Seminar, Center for Chinese Studies, 6 December 1980, University of California, Berkeley. Mimeographed.

Litwak, Eugene. "Geographic Mobility and Extended Family Cohesion." *American Sociological Review* 25 (June 1960):385–94.

————. "Occupational Mobility and Extended Family Cohesion." *American Sociological Review* 25 (February 1960):9–21.

Liu, Hui-chen Wang. "An Analysis of Chinese Clan Rules: Confucian Theories in Action." In *Confucianism and Chinese Civilization*, edited by Arthur F. Wright. Stanford: Stanford University Press, 1975.

Liu, Kwang-Ching. "World View and Peasant Rebellion: Reflections on Post-Mao Historiography." *Journal of Asian Studies* 40, no. 2 (February 1981):295–326.

Macciocchi, Maria A. *Daily Life in Revolutionary China*. New York: Monthly Review Press, 1972.

McDonald, Angus W., Jr. *The Urban Origins of Rural Revolution: Elites and the Masses in Hunan*. Berkeley and Los Angeles: University of California Press, 1978.

McLaughlin, Virginia Yans. *Family and Community: Italian Immigrants in Buffalo, 1880–1930.* Ithaca: Cornell University Press, 1977.

———. "Patterns of Work and Family Organization: Buffalo's Italians." In *The Family in History,* edited by Theodore Rabb and Robert Rothberg. New York: Harper & Row, 1973.

Maloney, Joan M. "Women in the Chinese Communist Revolution: The Question of Political Equality." In *Women, War and Revolution,* edited by Carol R. Berkin and Clara M. Lovett. New York: Holmes and Meier Publishers, 1980.

Mandel, William M. *Soviet Women.* Garden City, N.Y.: Anchor Books, 1975.

Mao Tse-tung. *On Coalition Government.* Peking: Foreign Languages Press. 1960.

———. "On the Correct Handling of Contradictions Among the People." *Four Essays on Philosophy.* Peking: Foreign Languages Press, 1968.

———. "On New Democracy." *Selected Works of Mao Tse-tung.* Vol. 2. Peking: Foreign Languages Press, 1965.

———. "On Protracted War." *Selected Works of Mao Tse-tung.* Vol. 2. Peking: Foreign Languages Press, 1965.

———. "Production Is Also Possible in the Guerrilla Zones." *Selected Works of Mao Tse-tung.* Vol. 3. Peking: Foreign Languages Press, 1967.

———. "Report on an Investigation of the Peasant Movement in Hunan." *Selected Readings from the Works of Mao Tse-tung.* Peking: Foreign Languages Press, 1971.

———. "Talks at Cheng-tu: Against Blind Faith in Learning." In *Chairman Mao Talks to the People,* edited by Stuart Schram. New York: Pantheon, 1974.

Marcuse, Herbert. "A Study on Authority." *Studies in Critical Philosophy.* Boston: Beacon Press, 1973.

Massell, Gregory. "Family Law and Social Mobilization in Soviet Central Asia: Some Comparisons with Communist China." *Canadian Slavonic Papers* 17, nos. 2-3 (1975):374–402.

———. *The Surrogate Proletariat: Moslem Women and Revolutionary Strategies in Soviet Central Asia, 1919–1929.* Princeton: Princeton University Press, 1974.

Meijer, M. J. *Marriage Law and Policy in the Chinese People's Republic.* Hong Kong: Hong Kong University Press, 1971.

Meisner, Maurice. "Yenan Communism and the Rise of the Chinese People's Republic." In *Modern East Asia: Essays in Interpretation,* edited by James B. Crowley. New York: Harcourt, Brace & World, 1970.

Migdal, Joel S. *Peasants, Politics and Revolution: Pressures Toward Political and Social Change in the Third World.* Princeton: Princeton University Press, 1974.

Milton, David, and Milton, Nancy. *The Wind Will Not Subside: Years in Revolutionary China, 1964–1969.* New York: Pantheon Books, 1976.

Milton, Nancy. "Women and Revolution." *Socialist Revolution* 1, no. 6 (1970):135–51.

Miner, Noel R. "Agrarian Reform in Nationalist China: The Case of Rent Reduction in Chekiang, 1927–1937." In *China at the Crossroads,* edited by F. Gilbert Chan. Boulder, Colo.: Westview Press, 1980.

Mitchell, Juliet. "Women: The Longest Revolution." *New Left Review* 40 (1966):11–37.

Montée, Ralph. "Agrarian Problems and Policies in China: The Nationalist Era and the Early Communist Period of Reconstruction." Mimeographed. Berkeley: Center for Chinese Studies, n.d.

Moore, Barrington, Jr. *Injustice: The Social Bases of Obedience and Revolt.* White Plains, N.Y.: M. E. Sharpe, 1978.

———. *Social Origins of Dictatorship and Democracy: Lord and Peasant in the Making of the Modern World.* Boston: Beacon Press, 1969.

Murdock, George P. "The Universality of the Nuclear Family." In *A Modern Introduction to the Family,* edited by Norman W. Bell and Ezra F. Vogel. New York: Free Press of Glencoe, 1960.

Myers, Ramon H. *The Chinese Economy, Past and Present.* Belmont, Calif.: Wadsworth, 1980.

———. *The Chinese Peasant Economy: Agricultural Development in Hopei and Shantung, 1890–1949.* Cambridge: Harvard University Press, 1970.

———. "The Commercialization of Agriculture in Modern China." In *Economic Organization in Chinese Society,* edited by W. E. Willmott. Stanford: Stanford University Press, 1972.

————. "Socioeconomic Relations in Northern Chinese Villages During the Republican Period." Mimeographed. Stanford: Hoover Institution on War, Revolution, and Peace, n.d.

Myrdal, Jan. *Report from a Chinese Village*. New York: New American Library, 1965.

Myrdal, Jan, and Kessle, Gun. *China: The Revolution Continued*. New York: Pantheon, 1970.

Nee, Victor. "Post-Mao Changes in a South China Production Brigade." *Bulletin of Concerned Asian Scholars* 13, no. 2 (1981):32–43.

Nimkoff, M. F. *Comparative Family Systems*. Boston: Houghton Mifflin Co., 1965.

————. *Technology and the Changing Family*. New York: Houghton Mifflin Co., 1955.

Nolan, Peter, and White, Gordon. "Distribution and Development in China." *Bulletin of Concerned Asian Scholars* 13, no. 3 (July-September 1981):2–18.

Ogburn, William F. *Social Change*. New York: Viking Press, 1922.

O'Hara, Albert. *The Position of Women in Early China—According to the Lieh Nü Chuan, "The Biographies of Eminent Chinese Women."* Taipei: Mei Ya Publications, 1971.

Ong, Sao-er. "Agrarian Reform in Communist China to 1952." Mimeographed. Lackland Air Force Base, Texas: Air Force Personnel and Training Research Center, 1955.

Orleans, Leon A., ed. *Chinese Approaches to Family Planning*. White Plains, N.Y.: M. E. Sharpe, 1978.

Ortner, Sherry B. "The Virgin and the State." *Feminist Studies* 4, no. 3 (Fall 1978):19–35.

Osgood, Cornelius. *Village Life in Old China*. New York: Ronald Press, 1963.

Oxaal, Ivar; Barnett, Tony; and Booth, David, eds. *Beyond the Sociology of Development: Economy and Society in Latin America and Africa*. London: Routledge & Kegan Paul, 1975.

Pa Chin. *Family*. 1931. Reprint. Garden City, N. Y.: Doubleday, 1972.

Pang Yong-pil. "Peng Pai: From Landlord to Revolutionary." *Modern China* 1, no. 3 (July 1975):297–322.

Parish, William L. "Socialism and the Chinese Peasant Family." *Journal of Asian Studies* 34, no. 3 (May 1975): 613–30.

Parish, William L., and Whyte, Martin F. *Village and Family in Contemporary China*. Chicago: University of Chicago Press, 1978.

Parsons, Talcott. "The Kinship System of the Contemporary United States." *Essays in Sociological Theory*. Glencoe, Ill.: Free Press, 1954.

Parsons, Talcott, and Bales, Robert F. *Family, Socialization and Interaction Process*. Glencoe, Ill.: Free Press, 1955.

Peck, Graham. *Two Kinds of Time*. Boston: Houghton Mifflin Co., 1950.

Pepper, Suzanne. *Civil War in China: The Political Struggle, 1945–1949*. Berkeley and Los Angeles: University of California Press, 1978.

Perkins, Dwight H. *Agricultural Development in China, 1368–1968*. Chicago: Aldine Publishing Co., 1969.

———. "Introduction: The Persistence of the Past." *China's Modern Economy in Historical Perspective*. Stanford: Stanford University Press, 1975.

Popkin, Samuel. *The Rational Peasant: The Political Economy of Rural Society in Vietnam*. Berkeley and Los Angeles: University of California Press, 1979.

Potter, Jack. "Change and Continuity in the Chinese Family." Public lecture, 23 October 1980, Center for Chinese Studies, University of California, Berkeley.

———. "Land and Lineage in Traditional China." In *Family and Kinship in Chinese Society*, edited by Maurice Freedman. Stanford: Stanford University Press, 1970.

Price, Jane. "Women and Leadership in the Chinese Communist Movement, 1921–45." *Bulletin of Concerned Asian Scholars* 7, no. 1 (January–March 1975):19–24.

Pruitt, Ida. *A Daughter of Han: The Autobiography of a Chinese Working Woman*. New Haven: Yale University Press, 1945.

Raddock, David. "Growing Up in New China: A Twist in the Circle of Filial Piety." *History of Childhood Quarterly* 2, no. 2 (Fall 1974):201–20.

Rankin, Mary B. *Early Chinese Revolutionaries: Radical Intellectuals in Shanghai and Chekiang, 1902–11*. Cambridge: Harvard University Press, 1971.

Rapp, Rayna; Ross, Ellen; and Bridenthal, Renate. "Examining Family History." *Feminist Studies* 5, no. 1 (Spring 1979):174–200.

Rawski, Evelyn Sakakida. *Education and Popular Literacy in Ch'ing China*. Ann Arbor: University of Michigan Press, 1979.

Rawski, Thomas G. "China's Republican Economy, An Introduction." Paper read at California Regional Seminar, Center for Chinese Studies, 31 May 1980, University of California, Berkeley. Mimeographed.

————. *Economic Growth and Employment in China*. New York: Oxford University Press, 1979.

Record, Jane Cassels, and Record, Wilson. "Totalist and Pluralist Views of Women's Liberation: Some Reflections on the Chinese and American Settings." *Social Problems* 23, no. 4 (April 1976):402–14.

Rhodes, Robert I., ed. *Imperialism and Underdevelopment: A Reader*. New York: Monthly Review Press, 1970.

Riskin, Carl. "Surplus and Stagnation in Modern China." In *China's Modern Economy in Historical Perspective*, edited by Dwight H. Perkins. Stanford: Stanford University Press, 1975.

Rowbotham, Sheila. "The Trouble with 'Patriarchy.'" *New Statesman*, 21/28 December 1979, pp. 970–71.

————. *Woman's Consciousness, Man's World*. Baltimore: Penguin, 1973.

————. *Women, Resistance and Revolution*. New York: Vintage, 1974.

Rubin, Gayle. "The Traffic in Women: Notes on the 'Political Economy' of Sex." In *Toward an Anthropology of Women*, edited by Rayna R. Reiter. New York: Monthly Review, 1975.

Runck, Bette. "Families in Hard Times: A Legacy." In *Families Today*. Vol. 1. National Institute of Mental Health Science Monograph 1. Rockville, Md.: National Institute of Mental Health, n.d.

Sakai, Tadao. "Confucianism and Popular Educational Works." In *Self and Society in Ming Thought*, edited by William Theodore DeBary. New York: Columbia University Press, 1970.

Salaff, Janet. "The Emerging Conjugal Relationship in the People's Republic of China." *Journal of Marriage and Family* 35, no. 4 (November 1973): 704–17.

————. "Youth, Family and Political Control in Communist China." Ph.D. dissertation, University of California, Berkeley, 1972.

Salaff, Janet, and Sheridan, Mary, eds. *Lives: Chinese Working Women*. Bloomington: Indiana University Press, forthcoming.

Salaff, Janet Weitzner, and Merkel, Judith. "Women and Revolution: The Lessons of the Soviet Union and China." In *Women in China: Social Change and Feminism*, edited by Marilyn B. Young. Michigan Papers in Chinese Studies, no. 15. Ann Arbor: Center for Chinese Studies, 1973.

Sankar, Andrea. "Spinster Sisterhoods." In *Lives: Chinese Working Women*, edited by Janet Salaff and Mary Sheridan. Bloomington: Indiana University Press, forthcoming.

———. "Strategies for Aging Among Non-Marrying Domestic Servants in Hong Kong." Paper read at Association for Asian Studies, New York, April 1976.

Sargent, Lydia, ed. *Women and Revolution: A Discussion of the Unhappy Marriage of Marxism and Feminism*. Boston: South End Press, 1981.

Schlesinger, Rudolf. *The Family in the U.S.S.R.* London: Routledge & Kegan Paul, 1949.

Schran, Peter. *Guerrilla Economy: The Development of the Shensi-Kansu-Ninghsia Border Region, 1937–1945*. Albany: State University of New York Press, 1976.

Schurmann, Franz. *Ideology and Organization in Communist China*. Berkeley and Los Angeles: University of California Press, 1968.

Schwartz, Benjamin I. *Chinese Communism and the Rise of Mao*. New York: Harper & Row, 1951.

———. "The Legend of the 'Legend of Maoism.' " *China Quarterly*, no. 2 (April-June 1960), pp. 35-42.

Scott, Hilda. *Does Socialism Liberate Women? Experiences from Eastern Europe*. Boston: Beacon, 1974.

Scott, James C. "Hegemony and the Peasantry." *Politics and Society* 7, no. 3 (1977):267-96.

———. *The Moral Economy of the Peasantry: Rebellion and Subsistence in Southeast Asia*. New Haven: Yale University Press, 1976.

———. "Protest and Profanation: Agrarian Revolt and the Little Tradition." *Theory and Society* 4, no. 1 (1977):1-38; and 4, no. 2 (1977):210-42.

Scott, Joan, and Tilly, Louise. "Woman's Work and the Family in Nineteenth-Century Europe." In *The Family in History*, edited by Charles E. Rosenberg. Philadelphia: University of Pennsylvania Press, 1975.

Selden, Mark. "Report from a People's Commune." *Eastern Horizon* 12, no. 2 (1973):37-50.

————. "Revolution and Third World Development: People's War and the Transformation of Peasant Society." In *National Liberation and Revolution in the Third World,* edited by Norman Miller and Roderick Aya. New York: Free Press, 1971.

————. "The Yenan Legacy: The Mass Line." In *Chinese Communists: Politics in Action,* edited by A. Doak Barnett. Seattle: University of Washington Press, 1969.

————. *The Yenan Way in Revolutionary China.* Cambridge: Harvard University Press, 1971.

Shanin, Teodor. "The Nature and Logic of the Peasant Economy 1: A Generalization." *Journal of Peasant Studies* 1, no. 1 (October 1973):63–80.

————. "Peasantry as a Political Factor." In *Peasants and Peasant Society,* edited by Teodor Shanin. Harmondsworth, England: Penguin, 1971.

Shanin, Teodor, ed. *Peasants and Peasant Society.* Harmondsworth, England: Penguin, 1971.

Sheridan, Mary. "Young Women Leaders in China." *Signs* 2, no. 1 (Autumn 1976):59–88.

Shorter, Edward. *The Making of the Modern Family.* New York: Basic Books, 1975.

Shue, Vivienne. *Peasant China in Transition: The Dynamics of Development toward Socialism, 1949–1956.* Berkeley and Los Angeles: University of California Press, 1980.

Shue, Vivienne Bland. "Transforming China's Peasant Villages: Rural Political and Economic Organization, 1949–1956." Ph.D. dissertation, Harvard University, 1975.

Sidel, Ruth. *Families of Fengsheng: Urban Life in China.* Baltimore: Penguin Books, 1974.

————. *Women and Child Care in China.* Baltimore: Penguin Books, 1972.

Skinner, G. William. "Family Structure and Politics in Modern China." Edward H. Hume Memorial Lecture, 26 February 1975, Yale University. Mimeographed.

————. "Mobility Strategies in Late Imperial China: A Regional Systems Analysis." In *Regional Analysis, Vol. 1, Economic Systems,* edited by Carol A. Smith. New York: Academic Press, 1976.

————. "Regional Systems in Late Imperial China." Paper read at Social Science History Association, 21-23 October 1977, Ann Arbor, Michigan. Mimeographed.

Skocpol, Theda. "France, Russia, China: A Structural Analysis of Socialist Revolutions." *Comparative Studies in Society and History* 18, 2 (April 1976):175–210.

————. "Old Regime Legacies and Communist Revolutions in Russia and China." *Social Forces* 55, no. 2 (December 1976):284–315.

————. *States and Social Revolutions: A Comparative Analysis of France, Russia, and China.* Cambridge: Cambridge University Press, 1979.

Smedley, Agnes. *Battle Hymn of China.* New York: Knopf, 1943.

————. *Portraits of Chinese Women in Revolution,* edited by Jan MacKinnon and Steve MacKinnon. Old Westbury, N.Y.: The Feminist Press, 1976.

Smelser, Neil. "Classical Theories of Change and the Family Structure." Paper read at Seventh World Congress of Sociology, September 1970, Varna, Bulgaria. Mimeographed.

————. *Comparative Methods in the Social Sciences.* Englewood Cliffs, N.J.: Prentice-Hall, 1976.

————. *Social Change in the Industrial Revolution: An Application of Theory to the British Cotton Industry.* Chicago: University of Chicago Press, 1959.

Smith, Arthur H. *Village Life in China.* New York: Fleming H. Revell Co., 1899.

Snow, Edgar. *The Long Revolution.* New York: Random House, 1972.

————. *Red Star Over China.* 1938. Reprint. New York: Grove Press, 1968.

Snow, Helen Foster. *Women in Modern China.* The Hague: Mouton & Co., 1967.

Spence, Jonathan D. *The Death of Woman Wang.* Harmondsworth, England: Penguin, 1979.

Stacey, Judith. "When Patriarchy Kowtows: The Significance of the Chinese Family Revolution for Feminist Theory." *Feminist Studies* 2, no. 213 (1975):64–112.

Stack, Carol B. *All Our Kin: Strategies for Survival in a Black Community.* New York: Harper & Row, 1974.

Stein, Gunther. *The Challenge of Red China*. New York: McGraw-Hill, 1945.

Strong, Anna Louise. *The Rise of the People's Communes in China*. New York: Marzani & Munsell, 1960.

Sweeten, Alan Richard. "Women and Law in Rural China: Vignettes from 'Sectarian Cases' (Chiao-an) in Kiangsi, 1872–1878." *Ch'ing-shih wen-t'i* 3, no. 10 (November 1978):49–68.

Sweezy, Paul M. *The Theory of Capitalist Development*. 1942. Reprint. New York: Monthly Review Press, 1970.

Taeuber, Irene B. "The Families of Chinese Farmers." In *Family and Kinship in Chinese Society*, edited by Maurice Freedman. Stanford: Stanford University Press, 1970.

Talmon, Yonina. "The Family in a Revolutionary Movement—The Case of the Kibbutz in Israel." In *Comparative Family Systems*, edited by M. K. Nimkoff. Boston: Houghton Mifflin, 1965.

Tawney, R. H. *Land and Labour in China*. London: George Allen & Unwin, 1932.

Thaxton, Ralph. "Some Critical Comments on Peasant Revolts and Revolutionary Politics in China." *Journal of Asian Studies* 33, no. 2 (February 1974):279–88.

———. "Tenants in Revolution: The Tenacity of Traditional Morality." *Modern China* 1, no. 3 (July 1975):323–58.

———. "When Peasants Took Power: Toward a Theory of Peasant Revolution in China." Ph.D. dissertation, University of Wisconsin, Madison, 1975.

Thompson, E. P. *The Making of the English Working Class*. New York: Vintage Books, 1963.

———. *The Poverty of Theory and Other Essays*. London: Merlin Press, 1978.

Thomson, James C., Jr. *While China Faced West: American Reformers in Nationalist China, 1928–1937*. Cambridge: Harvard University Press, 1969.

Thorne, Barrie. "Feminist Rethinking of the Family: An Overview." In *Rethinking the Family: Some Feminist Questions*, edited by Barrie Thorne with Marilyn Yalom. New York: Longman, 1982.

Thorborg, Marina. "Chinese Employment Policy in 1949–1978, with Special Emphasis on Women in Rural Production." In *Chinese Economy*

Post-Mao. Vol. 1. U.S. Congress, Joint Economic Committee, 95th Cong., 2d sess., November 1975.

Thorner, Daniel. "Peasant Economy as a Category in Economic History." In *Peasants and Peasant Societies,* edited by Teodor Shanin. Harmondsworth, England: Penguin, 1971.

Tien, H. Yuan, ed. *Population Theory in China.* White Plains, N.Y.: M. E. Sharpe, 1980.

Tilly, Louise A., and Scott, Joan W. *Women, Work, and Family.* New York: Holt, Rinehart & Winston, 1978.

Timasheff, Nicolas S. "The Attempt to Abolish the Family in Russia." In *A Modern Introduction to the Family,* edited by Norman W. Bell and Ezra F. Vogel. New York: Free Press, 1961.

Ting Ling. *The Sun Shines Over the Sangkan River.* Peking: Foreign Languages Press, 1954.

Tipps, Dean C. "Modernization Theory and the Comparative Study of Societies: A Critical Perspective." *Comparative Studies in Society and History* 15, no. 2 (March 1973):199–226.

Topley, Marjorie. "Marriage Resistance in Rural Kwangtung." In *Women in Chinese Society,* edited by Margery Wolf and Roxanne Witke. Stanford: Stanford University Press, 1975.

Trotsky, Leon. *The Revolution Betrayed.* 1937. Reprint. Translated by Max Eastman. New York: Pathfinder Press, 1972.

Tsao Hsueh-chin. *The Dream of the Red Chamber.* With a continuation by Kao Ou. Translated by Chi-chen Wang. New York: Twayne Publishers, 1958.

U.S. Congress, Joint Economic Committee. *Chinese Economy Post-Mao.* Vol. 1. 95th Cong., 2d sess., November 1975.

U.S. Foreign Broadcast Information Service. "Marriage Law Adopted by Fifth National People's Congress." *Daily Report: People's Republic of China* 1, no. 184 (19 September 1980):L22–L26.

Van der Valk, M. H. *Conservatism in Modern Chinese Family Law.* Leiden: E. J. Brill, 1956.

Van Gulik, R. H. *Sexual Life in Ancient China.* Leiden: E. J. Brill, 1974.

Vincent, Clark E. "Familia Spongia; The Adaptive Function." *Journal of Marriage and the Family* 28 (1966):29–32.

Vogel, Ezra F. "A Preliminary View of Family and Mental Health in Urban Communist China." In *Mental Health Research in Asia and the Pacific,* edited by William Caudill and Tsung-yi Lin. Honolulu: East-West Center Press, 1969.

Wakeman, Frederic E., Jr. *History and Will: Philosophical Perspectives of Mao Tse-tung's Thought.* Berkeley and Los Angeles: University of California Press, 1973.

————. "Rebellion and Revolution: The Study of Popular Movements in Chinese History." *Journal of Asian Studies* 36, no. 2 (February 1977):201–37.

————. *Strangers at the Gate: Social Disorder in South China, 1839–1861.* Berkeley and Los Angeles: University of California Press, 1966.

Wales, Nym. *Red Dust: Autobiographies of Chinese Communists.* Stanford: Stanford University Press, 1952.

Walker, Kathy Lemmons. "The Party and Peasant Women." In *Chinese Communists and Rural Society, 1927–1934,* by Philip C. C. Huang, Lynda Schaefer Bell, and Kathy Lemmons Walker. China Research Monographs, no. 13. Berkeley: Center for Chinese Studies, 1978.

Wallerstein, Immanuel. *The Modern World System: Capitalist Agriculture and the Origins of the European World-Economy in the Sixteenth Century.* New York: Academic Press, 1974.

Watson, Andrew J. "A Revolution to Touch Men's Souls: The Family, Interpersonal Relations, and Daily Life." In *Authority, Participation, and Cultural Change in China,* edited by Stuart Schram. Cambridge: Cambridge University Press, 1973.

Webster, Paula. "Matriarchy: A Vision of Power." In *Toward an Anthropology of Women,* edited by Rayna Reiter. New York: Monthly Review Press, 1975.

Weinbaum, Batya. *The Curious Courtship of Women's Liberation and Socialism.* Boston: South End Press, 1978.

————. "Women in Transition to Socialism: Perspectives on the Chinese Case." *Review of Radical Political Economics* 8, no. 1 (Spring 1976):34–55.

Weins, Thomas B. Review of *The Chinese Peasant Economy: Agricultural Development in Hopei and Shantung, 1890–1949,* by Ramon H. Myers. *Modern Asian Studies* 9, pt. 2 (April 1975):279–88.

White, Theodore H., and Jacoby, Annalee. *Thunder Out of China.* New York: William Sloane Associates, 1946.

Whyte, Martin King. "Bureaucracy and Modernization in China: The Maoist Critique." *American Sociological Review* 38, no. 2 (April 1973):149–63.

———. "Equality and Stratification in China." *China Quarterly*, no. 64 (December 1975), pp. 684–711.

———. "The Family." In *China's Developmental Experience*, edited by Michael Oksenberg. New York: Praeger, 1973.

———. "Family Change in China." In *The Enduring Chinese Dimension: Proceedings of the Eighth Sino-American Conference*. Columbia: University of South Carolina, 1979.

———. "Revolutionary Social Change and Patrilocal Residence in China." *Ethnology* 28, no. 3 (July 1979):211–27.

———. "Sexual Inequality under Socialism: The Chinese Case in Perspective." Mimeographed. Ann Arbor: University of Michigan, n.d.

Wilkinson, H. P. *The Family in Classical China*. Shanghai: Kelly and Walsh, 1926.

Williams, Raymond. "Base and Superstructure in Marxist Cultural Theory." In *Problems in Materialism and Culture*. London: Verso, 1980.

———. *Marxism and Literature*. Oxford: Oxford University Press, 1977.

Witke, Roxanne Heater. "Mao Tse-tung, Women and Suicide." In *Women in China: Studies in Social Change and Feminism*, edited by Marilyn B. Young. Michigan Papers in Chinese Studies, no. 15. Ann Arbor: Center for Chinese Studies, 1973.

———. "Transformation of Attitudes Towards Women During the May Fourth Era of Modern China." Ph.D. dissertation, University of California, Berkeley, 1970.

Wittfogel, Karl A. "The Legend of 'Maoism.' " *China Quarterly* 1 (January-March 1960):72–86.

Wolf, Arthur. "The Women of Hai-shan: A Demographic Portrait." In *Women and Chinese Society*, edited by Margery Wolf and Roxanne Heater Witke. Stanford: Stanford University Press, 1975.

Wolf, Arthur P., and Chieh-shan Huang. *Marriage and Adoption in China, 1845–1945*. Stanford: Stanford University Press, 1980.

Wolf, Eric. "On Peasant Rebellions." In *Peasants and Peasant Societies*, edited by Teodor Shanin. Harmondsworth, England: Penguin, 1971.

———. *Peasants*. Englewood Cliffs, N.J.: Prentice-Hall, 1966.

———. *Peasant Wars of the Twentieth Century.* New York: Harper & Row, 1969.

Wolf, Margery. "Child Training and the Chinese Family." In *Family and Kinship in Chinese Society,* edited by Maurice Freedman. Stanford: Stanford University Press, 1970.

———. "Chinese Women: Old Skills in a New Context." In *Women, Culture and Society,* edited by Michelle J. Rosaldo and Louise Lamphere. Stanford: Stanford University Press, 1974.

———. *The House of Lim: A Study of a Chinese Farm Family.* New York: Appleton-Century-Crofts, 1968.

———. *Women and the Family in Rural Taiwan.* Stanford: Stanford University Press, 1972.

———. "Women and Suicide in China." In *Women and Chinese Society,* edited by Margery Wolf and Roxanne Witke. Stanford: Stanford University Press, 1975.

Wright, Mary Clabaugh. *The Last Stand of Chinese Conservatism.* Stanford: Stanford University Press, 1957.

Wrigley, E. A. "Reflections on the History of the Family." *Daedalus* 106 (Spring 1977):71–86.

Yakhontoff, Victor A. *The Chinese Soviets.* New York: Coward-McCann, 1934.

Yang, C. K. *Chinese Communist Society: The Family and the Village.* Contains *The Chinese Family and the Communist Revolution* and *A Chinese Village in Early Communist Transition.* Cambridge: Massachusetts Institute of Technology Press, 1959.

Yang, Martin. *A Chinese Village.* New York: Columbia University Press, 1945.

Young, Iris. "Socialist Feminism and the Limits of Dual Systems Theory." *Socialist Review,* nos. 50/51 (March-June 1980), pp. 169–88.

Young, Marilyn B., ed. *Women in China: Studies in Social Change and Feminism.* Michigan Papers in Chinese Studies, no. 15. Ann Arbor: Center for Chinese Studies, 1973.

Yu, Elena S. H. "Family Life and Overseas Remittances in Southeastern China." *Journal of Comparative Family Studies* 10, no. 3 (Autumn 1979):445–54.

Zagoria, Donald S. "Asian Tenancy Systems and Communist Mobilization of the Peasantry." In *Peasant Rebellion and Communist Revolution in Asia,* edited by John Wilson Lewis. Stanford: Stanford University Press, 1974.

INDEX

Abortion, 230, 234, 278

Adopted daughter-in-law marriages, 95, 164

Advanced Production Cooperatives (APCs), 204, 205; merged into People's Communes, 211. *See also* Cooperatives

Age: care of the elderly, 223, 236, 275; for marriage, 93, 226, 236, 275; and physical survival of landless peasant families, 88; of Red Army soldiers, 154; of victimized women during the Great Leap Forward, 215

Agrarian crisis, 59, 79–97; causes and sources of, 80–86; Chinese Communist response to, 86, 116–157; contributions of the Confucian family system to, 62–65, 68; controversies about, 83–86; effect on peasant marriage patterns, 92–95; familial values and rituals jeopardized by, 94–99; as a family crisis, 15, 86–97; females as the primary victims of, 89–90, 91, 96–97, 106; generation of new peasant families threatened by, 92–94; Kuomintang response to, 196–198; physical survival of peasant families endangered by, 88–90; reform vs. revolution in resolution of, 85–86; role in the origins of the Chinese revolution, 62–65, 79, 84, 86, 93, 97; size of peasant households diminished by, 90–92

Agrarian Reform Law, 123

Agricultural collectivization, 203, 204–211; effect on the new democratic peasant patriarchy, 204–211, 252–253; labor by women in, 206–209, 253; lineage system utilized in, 210–211, 253; private gardens and rural free markets in, 272; role of production teams in, 272–274

Agriculture: Communist tax policies for, 120, 131–132; cultural obstacles to the development of, 63; effect of

family size on, 22; family basis of, 16, 20–29, 136–137, 139 (*see also* Peasant family economy); labor for, 22–24, 135–142 *passim;* 270–274; and land reform, 116–135; mechanization vs. manual labor for, 270–271; and "nobody crops," 90; in presocialist China, 21–29; private garden plots and rural free markets in, 213, 253, 272; problems of "bumper crops" in, 85; relative to population growth, 269–270; role of women in, 23, 41, 101, 138, 139–140, 151, 175, 206–209, 212–215, 220–222, 270, 271; strategies to increase the productivity of, 86, 120, 124, 128–129, 208, 270–274. *See also* Labor; Farming

Alimony, 164, 165, 275

All-China Democratic Women's Federation, 115*n*, 152, 179, 207, 213; revival of, 276; subordinate to the Chinese Communist Party, 228, 256; suspension of, 228, 262

Anarchists, 73–74; feminism advocated by, 74–76

Ancestor worship, 63, 70, 97, 190; and continuity of lineage, 32; and land reform, 129

Anger, used by women, 46

Andors, Phyllis, x, 212, 215, 216, 276

Anti-Communist propaganda, 162, 187

Antifootbinding societies, 72–73, 103. *See also* Footbinding

Anti-Malthusianism, 232–233

Antipatriarchal family reforms, 3–4; during the Great Leap Forward, 213–216; in marital law, 3, 176–182; by May Fourth radicals and anarchists, 73–74; in urban areas, 235–236, 243

APCs. *See* Advanced Production Cooperatives

Authority, patriarchal, 37, 59, 78, 97; challenges to, 73, 101–103, 154; in the Chinese Communist Party, 229–230; effect of collectivization on, 206,

310 • **Index**

253; effect of family reform on, 174–175; effect of land reform on, 134, 155, 174; and the "public patriarchy," 227–231; relationship with fraternal organizations, 154, 250; structural supports in patriarchal-socialism, 217–218, 220–223, 227–231; in urban families, 235; violated by the Great Leap Forward, 212–216, 244, 246, 253. *See also* Confucian patriarchal order

Bachelorhood, 93, 161, 184
Belden, Jack, 96, 123*n*, 145–146, 200; and "Gold Flower's Story," 174–175
Bianco, Lucian, 79, 84*n*, 198*n*, 199*n*
Birth: control measures, 231, 233, 234, 277, 278; of daughters, 43–44; restrictive quotas for, 274, 276, 278–279
Bolshevik revolution, 114; family reform in, 3–5
Bride-price, 35, 219, 243
Brides: adopted daughters-in-law as, 95; and conflicts in traditional family life, 53–56; household economy augmented by, 223; in rural patriarchal-socialism, 218–219, 223, 226–227, 243; and transfer of urban youth to rural areas, 243. *See also* Wives
Brigades, 225, 226, 272, 273
Brutality, patriarchal, 40, 43
Buck, John L., 89*n*, 90, 91*n*
"Bumper-crop maidens," 214
Bumper crops, 85
Burial practices, 63, 95; and land reform, 129; and leveling of family grave mounds, 213, 214; in patriarchal-socialism, 232

Cambridge Group for the History of Population and Social Structure, 6
Cameron, Meribeth, 91
Cannibalism, 89, 91
Capitalism: and family change, 6–8, 258; and feminism, 266; liberation of women by, 262; male authority in, 263; relationship with patriarchy, 9
CCP. *See* Chinese Communist Party
Ceremonies, 139; effect of land reform on, 134; expenses for marriage, 33, 92, 94–95

Chang, Chih-i, 24, 88, 104, 195*n*, 199*n*, 200*n*; on KMT military conscription policies, 198; on marriage prospects for poor peasants, 93–94
Chang, Kuo-t'ao, 147, 153*n*, 162*n*, 199
Chao Kuo-chün, 117*n*, 119*n*, 128*n*, 139*n*
Chastity: Confucian value of, 40; and radical demands for marital reforms, 74; of widows, 34, 40, 57, 174
Chayanov, Alexander, 20
Chekiang: collectivization in, 205–206; rent reduction in, 196
Chen Han-seng, 71, 101
Chen, Jack, 129, 139*n*, 141, 206
Chen, Yuan-tsung, 127*n*, 132–133, 188*n*
Ch'en Shao-yü, 176
Chesneaux, Jean, 215, 216*n*
Chia: defined, 32; and family conflicts, 53
Chiang K'ai-shek, 77, 111; land reform proposals of, 196; wife of, 78
Children: abuse of, 232; custody after divorce, 163–164, 177, 220, 275; day-care centers for, 171, 214, 215, 253; education of vs. farm labor by, 102; and family planning, 274–275; as prisoners, 200; relationships with parents, 177, 210, 219–220, 223, 236; sale of, 58, 91, 200; urban factory labor by, 101. *See also* Daughters; Infanticide
Chin-Ch'a-Chi border region, 138, 150; education in, 185; marriage regulations in, 168–169
Chinese Communist Party (CCP): alliance with the Kuomintang, 76–77, 110–111, 114, 119, 122; approach to the agrarian and peasant family crises, 86, 116–157, 249–250, 251; attitudes on footbinding, 103, 169, 170, 173; collectivization policies of, 205–211; as a "Confucian patriarch," 170; cooperative policy of, 135–142; and the elimination of the family, 108, 214–215; and the emergence of feminism, 76, 79; establishment of, 76, 249; family reform policies of, 3–5, 116, 126–135, 158–198, 209–211, 246, 251–252; feminist influences on family policies of, 165–166, 167, 170–172, 173–174, 251, 255, 256–257; land reform by, 115–135, 250 (*see also* Land

White Army, 144; compared with the Red Army, 198–202

White, Gordon, 273

White, Theodore H., 89, 200*n*, 201*n*

Whyte, Martin King, 216*n*, 217, 219*n*, 220*n*, 222*n*, 223, 224*n*, 226*n*, 227*n*, 229*n*, 234*n*, 237*n*, 238*n*, 240*n*, 261*n*; on consolidation of land and resources, 244; on village leadership, 225

Widows, 38*n*, 91; chastity of, 34, 40, 57, 174; Confucian attitudes toward, 34; remarriage of, 34, 57–58, 232

Witke, Roxanne Heater, 71*n*, 72*n*, 73*n*, 74*n*, 76*n*

Wives: beating and abuse of, 40, 53, 169, 170, 174, 190, 227; of Communist army personnel, 147–148, 164–165; and conflicts in joint family households, 53–56; conjugal family of, 53–54; role in socialism, 209; sale of, 58, 91; suicide by, 43; traditional Chinese linguistic symbol for, 39; of urban male workers, 239. *See also* Brides; Husband/wife relationship; Women

Wolf, Arthur, 95

Wolf, Eric, 33, 57*n*, 105–106

Wolf, Margery, ix, 38, 39, 272*n*, 273*n*, 279; on joint families, 55; strategies of Confucian women analyzed by, 45–46; studies in modern Taiwan by, 49, 50*n*, 52*n*

Women: agricultural labor by, 23, 41, 101, 138, 139–140, 151, 175, 206–209, 212–215, 220–222, 270, 271; associations of, 127, 131, 159–160, 162, 169, 170, 174–175, 187, 227, 228, 233, 256; attitudes toward revolution, 106, 255; classified by family membership, 126–127; common term for, 39; and the Confucian marriage system, 34–35, 42, 47–48, 51–52, 54, 57–58, 71; in the Confucian peasant economy, 23, 41, 91, 100–101; in cooperatives, 139–140, 141, 206–208; discrimination against labor by, 206–208, 222; education of, 36, 69, 73, 152; effect of the Great Leap Forward on, 212–216; employment of, 71, 100–101, 222, 238; equal rights to land, 127, 130–131, 135, 176, 194;

improved family status of, 226–227, 236–237; interest in divorce, 159–160, 172, 178; military participation by, 151–154; mobilization for production by, 171, 173, 208, 212–214, 250; participation in mass struggle, 62, 150–154, 169; power of, 45–46, 50, 52; as the primary victims of the agrarian crisis, 89–90, 92, 96–97, 106; as revolutionary cadres, 77, 132–133, 169, 170–171; sale of, 44, 58, 91, 171, 197–198; sexual abuse of, 96–97, 127, 161; socioeconomic roles influenced by Chinese military policies, 150–155; subordinate status of, 4, 38–56, 219–223; wages earned by, 24*n*, 48, 101, 140, 207, 222; in urban areas, 235–243 *passim*; value in the peasant family, 61, 91. *See also* Brides; Daughters; Feminism; Wives

Women, liberation of: in Chinese Communist family reform policies, 158, 163, 164, 171, 173, 174–176, 178, 182, 189, 190, 255, 256–257; via economic productivity and labor, 208, 214, 215; limitations of Marxist theory on, 262–263; for peasant females, 206–209, 256–257; in rural patriarchal-socialism, 226–227, 256–257; via socialism, 1–5, 10, 158, 163, 164, 171, 173, 174–176, 178, 182, 189, 190, 216, 226–227, 255–257, 261–267, 269, 275, 280; subordinated to the class struggle, 164, 182, 228, 263

Women Guards, 151

"Women red-flag holders," 214

Women's Volunteers, 151

Wright, Mary C., 68–69

Yakhontoff, Victor, 118–119

Yang, Martin, 93, 100*n*

Yellow River region, 137, 139

Yenan, 166, 173, 246

Yenan University, 152

Yenan Way, 15

Yen-liao farm families, 25–26

Young, Iris, 10

Young Vanguards, 154

Youth: increased status of, 225–226, 236; patriarchal family structure criticized by, 73–74, 249; rebellion by, 210;

Designer: Marilyn Perry
Compositor: Kazuko D. Nishita &
U.C. Printing Department
Text: 10/12 Palatino
Display: Palatino
Printer: Maple-Vail Book Mfg. Group
Binder: Maple-Vail Book Mfg. Group